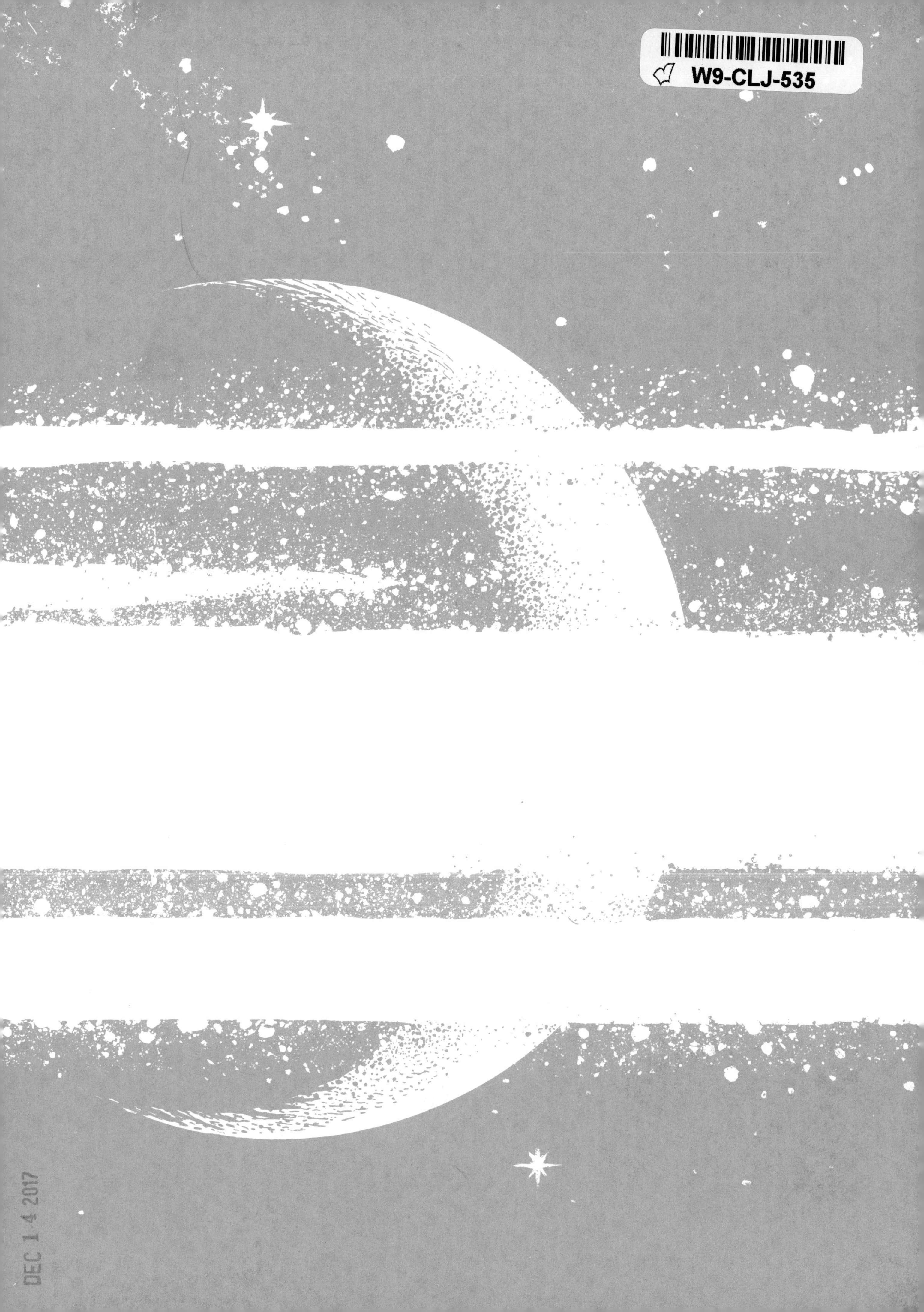

CHRISTIN   MÉZIÈRES

VALERIAN

THE COMPLETE COLLECTION VOLUME 3

9th CINEBOOK
The 9th Art Publisher

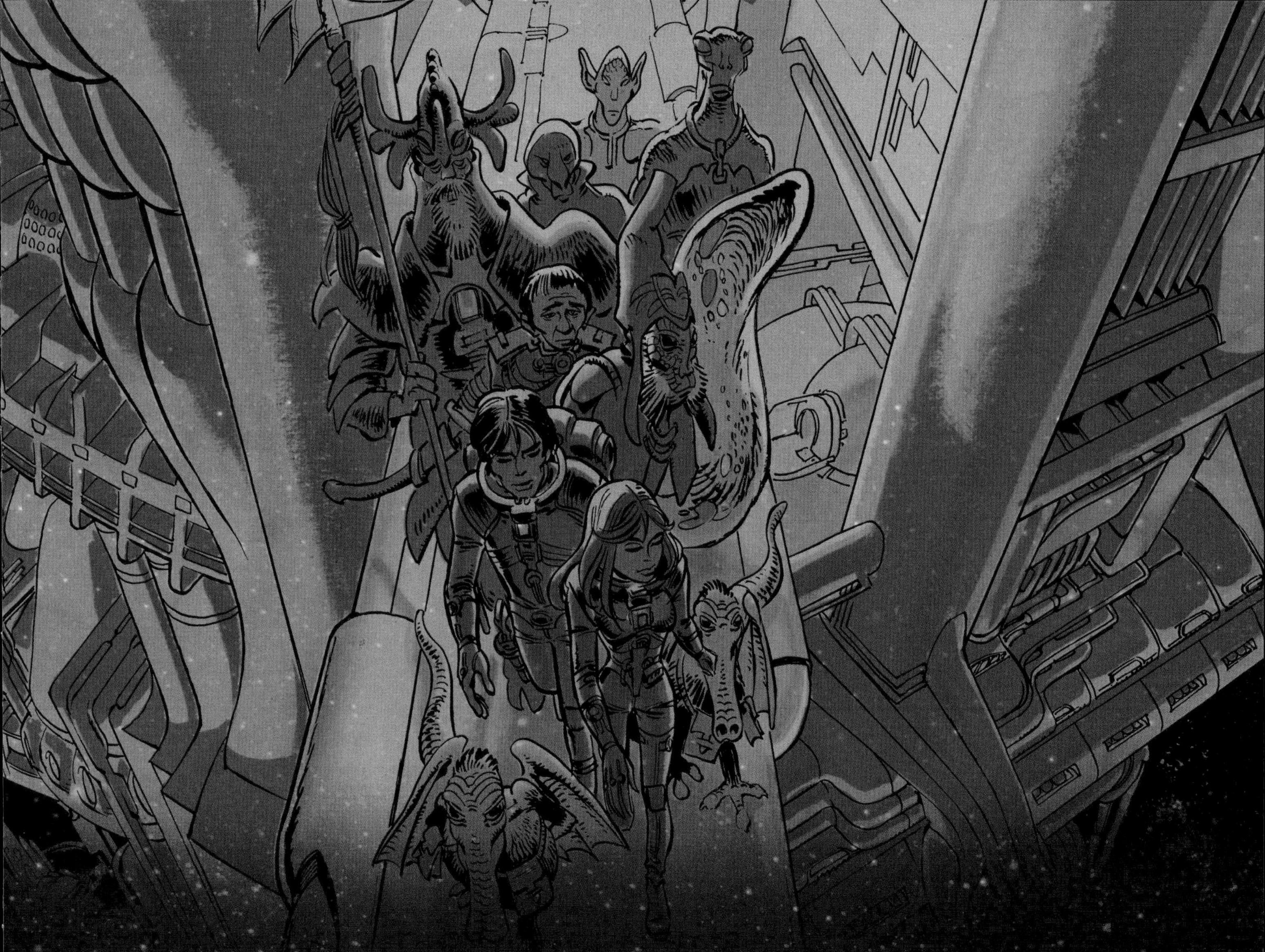

VALERIAN

THE COMPLETE COLLECTION VOLUME 3

SCRIPT PIERRE CHRISTIN ARTWORK JEAN-CLAUDE MÉZIÈRES

COLOURS ÉVELYNE TRANLÉ

CINEBOOK
The 9th Art Publisher

Original title: Valerian – L'Intégrale Volume 3
Original edition: © Dargaud Paris, 2016 by Christin, Mezières & Tranlé
www.dargaud.com
All rights reserved
English translation: © 2016 Cinebook Ltd
Translator: Jerome Saincantin
Lettering and text layout: Design Amorandi
This edition first published in Great Britain in 2017 by
Cinebook Ltd
56 Beech Avenue
Canterbury, Kent
CT4 7TA
www.cinebook.com
Second printing: June 2017
Printed in Spain by EGEDSA
A CIP catalogue record for this book
is available from the British Library
ISBN 978-1-84918-357-4

INTERVIEW LUC BESSON, JEAN-CLAUDE MÉZIÈRES AND PIERRE CHRISTIN (PART 3)

BY CHRISTOPHE QUILLIEN

WHY DID LUC BESSON CHOOSE TO ADAPT *AMBASSADOR OF THE SHADOWS*? WHY ARE THE ADVENTURES OF VALERIAN AND LAURELINE MORE EXCITING THAN AMERICAN SUPERHERO STORIES? IS VALERIAN'S VERY '70S HAIRDO FINALLY GOING TO GET UPDATED? IN AN EXCLUSIVE AND PREVIOUSLY UNPUBLISHED INTERVIEW CONDUCTED FOR THIS NEW COLLECTED EDITION OF *VALERIAN AND LAURELINE*, LUC BESSON, JEAN-CLAUDE MÉZIÈRES AND PIERRE CHRISTIN REVEAL HOW THE SERIES WAS ADAPTATED FOR THE BIG SCREEN.

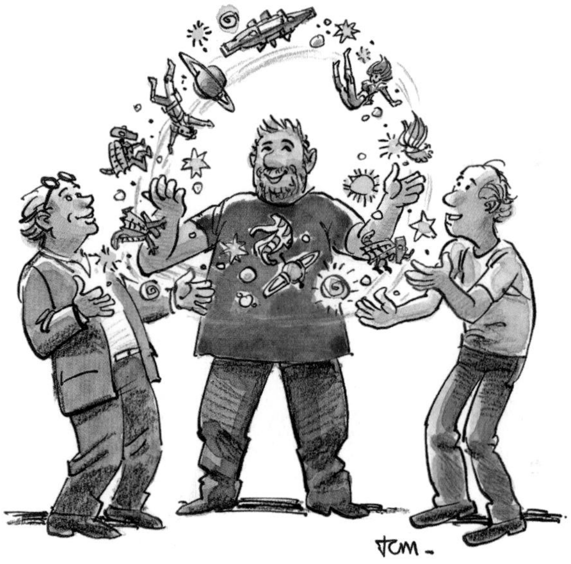

Jean-Claude Mézières, Luc Besson and Pierre Christin as seen by Mézières.

Why adapt *Ambassador of the Shadows*?

Luc Besson: Some volumes have more potential than others. There are Valerian and Laureline stories I absolutely love, but that I'd have a very hard time making into a two-hour film. *Ambassador of the Shadows* is interesting for a scriptwriter. It's structured like a police investigation, and that leaves room for suspense and mystery. Another interesting aspect lies in the relationship between Valerian and Laureline. The plot relies on the love between them. The two characters are looking for each other. They're not always together and each must save the other. It asks the question: Do you love the other to the point of risking everything to save them?

Is its narrative structure different from that of traditional science-fiction films?

Luc Besson: It has precious little in common with the films produced by Marvel, where a superhero is opposed to a supervillain who wants to destroy the world. And where the superhero always wins in the end... Those films are very well made, but they work in a very monolithic fashion. After five minutes you already know what's going to happen. Here it's the other way around. Each adventure of Valerian and Laureline is treated like a classic police investigation, with two super-agents whose mission is to solve a mystery.

© Feng Zhu

How will they figure it out? You'll have to wait until the end to know the answer!

Pierre Christin: I think that different approach to the story comes from the context in which *Valerian* was formed. When we created the series, we were heavily influenced by American science-fiction literature, which was experiencing a golden age. The structure of superhero stories was indeed set in stone: it featured the struggle of Good versus Evil, and Good had to win. I wanted nothing to do with that dichotomy, which dictates that you know how it'll end right from the start! *Valerian* remains undecided until the very end. It's a series that's deliberately ambiguous, through which the reader must make their own way if they want to find their own truth. You have to understand both what's going on - that's the 'police investigation' aspect - and what it means.

Luc Besson: *Valerian* is closer to real life in that regard.

Pierre Christin: *Ambassador of the Shadows* is also one of the titles that introduces the largest number of new creatures of all kinds. You'll find some in all volumes, but we really went crazy in this one! Flipping through the series nowadays, I sometimes feel that I occasionally went overboard. I'd just place an order for some creatures from Jean-Claude, the way you'd order a dish in a restaurant - I'll have one like this here, make up another like that there... I didn't realise the amount of work it all entailed!

Can any *bande dessinée* be adapted?

Luc Besson: Some series are wonderful and full of charm, but unfortunately wouldn't be suitable for cinema. No one's ever managed to translate all the poetry of *Gaston* (*Gomer Goof*), with Gaston Lagaffe's old car, Miss Jeanne and Mr De Mesmaeker. On the other hand, the animated films of *Asterix* were very

good, and Spielberg's *Tintin* is true to its paperbound model. For the adaptation of *Valerian*, I can count on the skills of a production designer and a costume designer who are incredibly gifted, and that's allowed us to go one step further than the original series. The first spacesuits drawn in the '70s are a bit dated - we ought to be able to do better... Same for the hero's hairdo - fashion has moved on since then, and that's a good thing! I hope the film will bring something more, add something to the *bande dessinée*. I aim to modernise it without betraying it.

Jean-Claude Mézières: I'm curious to see what new things Luc is going to propose compared with the tone of the book. I'm of the opinion that he must be entirely free to imagine his own *Valerian*. If all he did was follow the comic panel by panel, as if a storyboard, it would be completely uninteresting.

Luc Besson, are you trying to be faithful to the comic or, rather, trying to interpret it?

Luc Besson: I use the book as a starting point, and then I pull the string and unravel it. The advantage of cinema is that it can enrich the *bande dessinée*'s universe. That said, I still keep the angle and composition of some of the panels, because I find them extremely cinematic. As for the rest, an adaptation is like an opening through which I dive head-on. When I see the Shingouz while reading *Ambassador of the Shadows*, for example, I immediately feel that they must use an extreme form of politeness, worthy of an ambassador's. They're very diplomatic, and I have a great time watching them do their thing in the comic. So I start from a scene that's only a few panels long in the book, and I can stretch it over five minutes in the film.

Did the authors of *Valerian* ever dream of seeing its protagonist on the big screen one day?

Pierre Christin: I would have been miffed if I'd been told that *Valerian* was going to be adapted for an animated film - even though ten, fifteen years ago I'd have been happy with that. But today, with the advances of new technologies, I'm convinced that only a film with real actors can do the series justice.

Jean-Claude Mézières: I've always dreamed of an adaptation, although I didn't have anything specific in mind. In the '80s I did some experiments with paper cutouts, but it didn't go any further due to lack of budget. Today, cinema is taking up the baton... It's a dream come true!

Pierre Christin: It was actresses that were more likely to make me think about a potential adaptation. I'd see

one that I liked and think, *This one would make a great Laureline!* Then the years would go by, the actress would be too old for the role and a new face would replace her in my mind. But my contemplations of a movie never started from an actor that would have made a great Valerian. His face just never fired my imagination!

Luc Besson: When Julia Roberts started, I thought that she'd make a perfect Laureline. She had both the character's sassy side and the ideal voice.

Jean-Claude Mézières: Let's not kid ourselves, anyway. We'll get the usual disgruntled reactions, like 'Pah! Her acting's not exactly like Laureline in the book!'

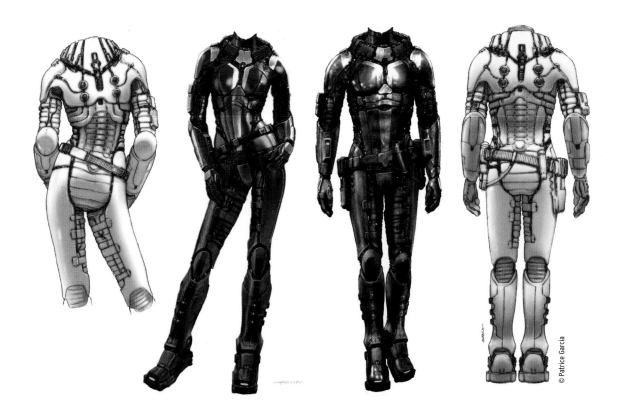

© Patrice Garcia

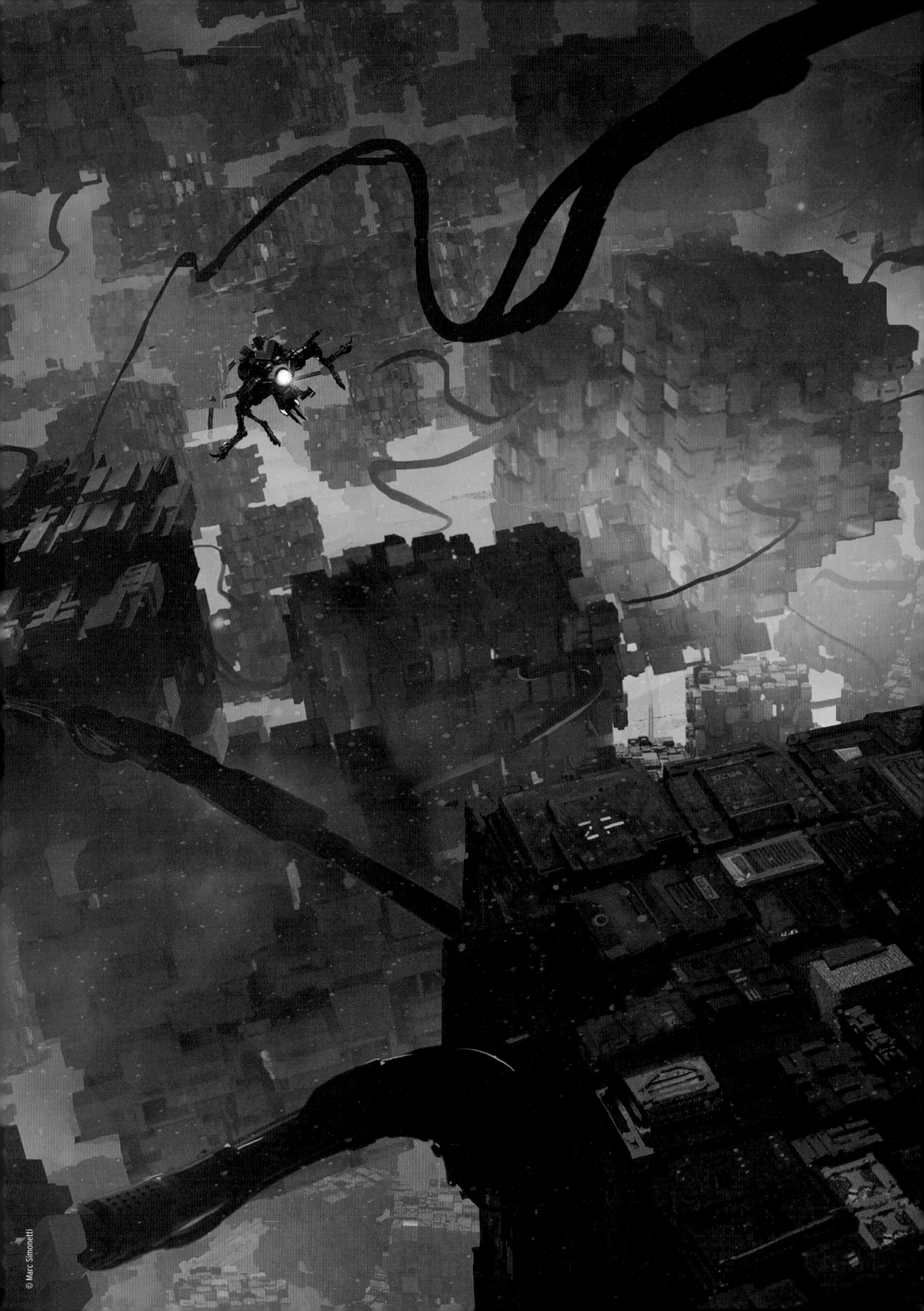

© Marc Simonetti

Are you worried about criticism from the fans, who are often averse on principle to an interpretation of their favourite universe?

Pierre Christin: I imagine the film will spawn its lot of critical analyses from specialists on the Internet and social media… That's not a new phenomenon. I remember the Wednesday night quiz at the Studio Parnasse cinema in Paris. The competitors were veritable founts of knowledge who knew the answers to ridiculous questions like 'What was the name of the third director of photography on such-and-such film that Otto Preminger never finished?' And you'd see ten hands shoot up in the air at the same time! The winner would get a free ticket for a showing the next week… That thirst for encyclopedic knowledge was there already. Today, with the Internet, it's grown to a much bigger size. I imagine the fans of *Valerian* won't pull their punches…

Luc Besson: Any time a comic-based film is made, the fans – who think of themselves as the guardians of the temple – speak up and denounce every little thing they see as problematic. But they can come. I belong to the fandom too! I've loved Valerian and Laureline since I was ten. I've earned my badge, same as them… With this film I'm trying to make something that I, as a fan of the series, would love. I'm not going to betray myself. Anyway, you'll always find at least three or four diehards who claim the film's a bust. It's got to make you smile… The question isn't even whether they like the adaptation or not. What bothers them is to have to share a series with a mainstream audience, when they're convinced it belongs to them. Such a reaction is sad. When you love a character or a universe, you should be happy to share them and recruit new fans.

Valerian and Laureline are much more in favour of negotiating and hearing out the other side than

of violence. Are these traits compatible with a blockbuster science-fiction film?

Luc Besson: I'm not worried, because there are no rules there. Just look at films such as *Inception*, *Interstellar* or *Gravity*. And *Avatar* is founded on the discovery of other people and on accepting the differences between cultures.

Pierre Christin: With *Valerian*, we've tried to offer an ethnographic approach to science fiction. If I had to choose one key word to describe the series, it would be 'otherness': in our books, everyone is different. At the time we started, it was a pioneering move. Sci-fi wasn't exactly soft-hearted, and aliens were never on the side of angels. The genre has evolved considerably since then, and involves increasing numbers of women. I've always conceived the series as a sort of *Darwin's Diary* – an undertaking of discovery of the Other. At each stage, Laureline and Valerian encounter some new creature. Most of them are, at first sight, rather repulsive beings. Then you realise that's not true at all; you discover we can understand them and there's no need to colonise them…

Luc Besson: What I like in the *Valerian* saga is how it constantly thumbs its nose at racism. We're not even capable of getting along today because of our differences in skin colour or religion. But in *Valerian*, there are five thousand alien species from every corner of space! They all look absolutely wild, with unbelievable numbers of legs and eyes… In Valerian and Laureline's world, there can be no racism. There are so many differences between any two creatures that everyone accepts all species as they are.

Can *Valerian* be considered a political series?
Pierre Christin: In the '60s, *bandes dessinées* rarely dealt with current events. *Valerian*, on the other hand, has always been concerned with our contemporary world. You can even see that the

tone has changed. The last volumes tend to have harder edges because the situation hasn't improved – far from it. When we started out, it was a time of optimism. Between the conquest of space and the civil rights movements, we were full of hope. Terrible events have taken place since, and the series has become darker. That evolution probably happened subconsciously – even if a science-fiction story takes place in the future, it's still the product of an environment that gives it a general tone. Still, optimism appears to have won out after all: the human race is still around in the 28th century, which is far from a given seen from today!

Luc Besson: It's still there, but no longer living on Earth... While *Valerian* is a political series, it's never about partisan, dogmatic or militant politics.

Which side does the movie lean towards: optimism or pessimism?

Luc Besson: A bit of both, because one doesn't go without the other. When painting, if you want to bring out the white, the advice is to contrast it with black. It's the same with *Ambassador of the Shadows*: the story offers some solid reasons to worry, but also to rejoice.

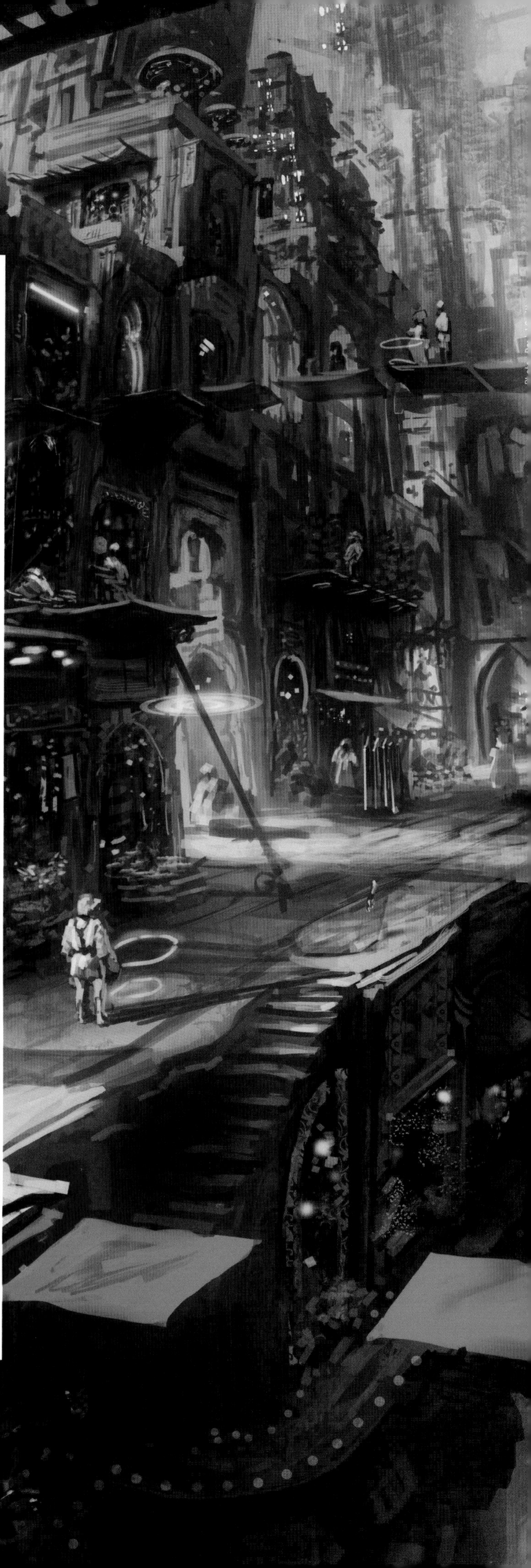

The illustrations accompanying this interview are studies made by the film's team, based on the work of Jean-Claude Mézières.

MÉZIÈRES, OR THE ART OF *BANDE DESSINÉE*

BY STAN BARETS

'WITH VALERIAN, I HAVE ALL THE ADVANTAGES OF A SERIES WITHOUT ANY OF THE INCONVENIENCES. THANKS TO CHRISTIN'S SCRIPTS AND SCIENCE FICTION'S SPATIO-TEMPORAL ASPECT, I CAN BREAK ALL THE MOULDS AND TELL WIDELY DIFFERENT STORIES EACH TIME.'
JEAN-CLAUDE MÉZIÈRES

He could have been an accountant like his father. Except that Jean-Claude Mézières caught a bad case of illustritis. 'My only joy is to draw what I've never drawn before,' he confesses. He doodled from an early age, then as a teenager he sent the first draft of a comic to Hergé. The master responded with 'Keep at it!', so Mézières persevered. He sold his first pieces to *Spirou*, *Coeurs Vaillants* or *Fripounet et Marisette*, but he was still looking for his style. 'Back then it was a Franquin/Morris/ *MAD* mix... I loved Jack Davis, Kurtzman, Elder, Wood and the others. With a helping of Jijé/Giraud on top.'

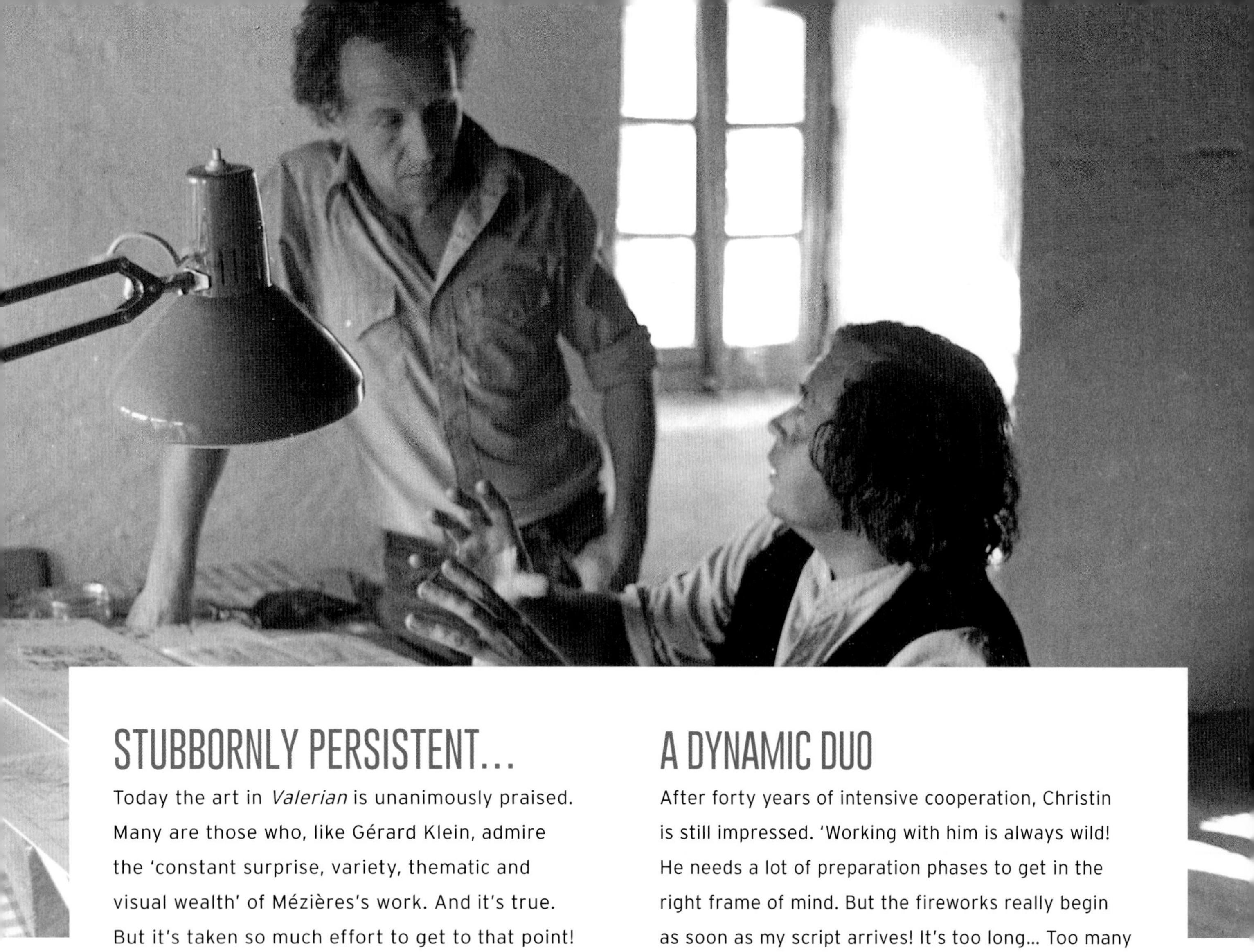

STUBBORNLY PERSISTENT...

Today the art in *Valerian* is unanimously praised. Many are those who, like Gérard Klein, admire the 'constant surprise, variety, thematic and visual wealth' of Mézières's work. And it's true. But it's taken so much effort to get to that point! Pierre Christin, who knows Mézières better than anyone, admits that 'it's always a difficult, painful process' for his partner. A man who in everyday life is perfectly open, jolly and friendly becomes stubbornly persistent when sitting at his drawing board. 'My page looks like a battlefield. Crossing-outs, erasures, various attempts and corrections... It's a maze of lines.'

Drawing is no walk in the park for Mézières. 'I often redo the first pages. The *Valerian* "engine" never turns over on the first try. I draw something, then I try something else until, at some point, it finally starts getting somewhere...' The truth is, Mézières faces difficulties commensurate with his demanding nature.

A DYNAMIC DUO

After forty years of intensive cooperation, Christin is still impressed. 'Working with him is always wild! He needs a lot of preparation phases to get in the right frame of mind. But the fireworks really begin as soon as my script arrives! It's too long... Too many characters... This doesn't make a good scene...!' There follows a long period that can at best be called four-hands creation and at worse a tug of war until the two partners eventually reach an agreement on the characters and the story's values. As for him, Mézières is prompt to defend his point of view. A comic isn't simply an accumulation of side-by-side drawings: the tempo, the motion are what matters. In other words, 'Christin writes the script and the dialogues – but I'm the director.' Despite the arguing and the difficult deliveries, there's one thing on which the two men agree entirely: high standards. 'Mézières never gives himself a free pass or an easy way out. I've never seen him give up when facing a difficulty,' says Christin. While Mézières comments, 'I only ever see my faults and my mistakes. So I always need to kickstart the mechanism again.'

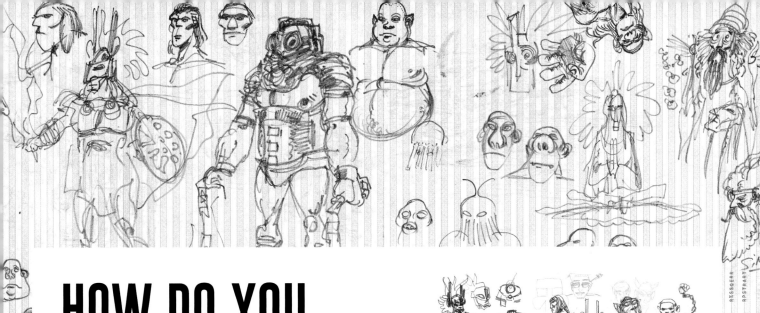

HOW DO YOU DRAW WHAT DOESN'T EXIST?

In his defence, you have to admit that it's a colossal task. Compared with other artists who accumulate masses of documentation and details, Mézières's job is considerably more difficult. How do you draw what doesn't exist?
'I started panicking from the very first panel of *Bad Dreams*,' recalls Mézières. 'All Pierre had written was "draw a nice big picture of the megalopolis"...' That's right! How do you illustrate Galaxity, Point Central, or any of the thousand other planets such as Solum, the world where everything constantly sinks into the ground, forming new strata?
How do you draw an alien, a plant, an animal or the landscapes of a planet you've never seen? What does a TümTüm from Lüm look like? Or a gumun, a furutz, a zypanon, a schniarfer? Mézières's problem isn't imitating – it's inventing. When you ask him how he goes about it, the answer comes in stages. According to him, it is first a question of personality: 'I don't like to copy photographs or pictures found on the Internet, as is too often the case in comics.'

***Preliminary studies and sketches for* Heroes of the Equinox.**

AND NEVER FORGET, VALERIAN, THAT YOU WILL BE BEARING EARTH'S COLOURS!
I SHALL BE WORTHY OF THE HONOUR YOU DO ME.

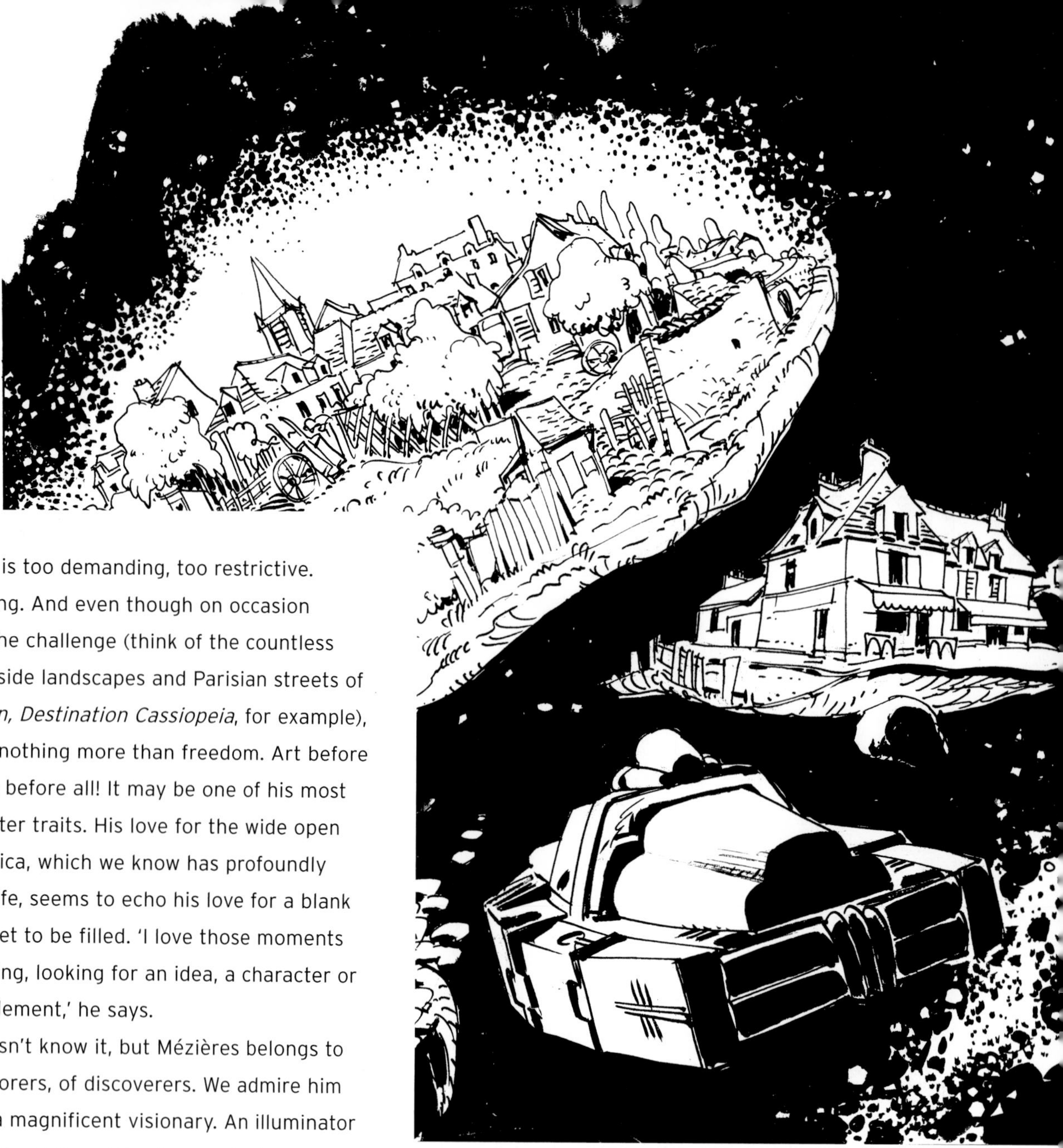

Reality, to him, is too demanding, too restrictive. Copying is boring. And even though on occasion he's accepted the challenge (think of the countless French countryside landscapes and Parisian streets of *Châtelet Station, Destination Cassiopeia*, for example), Mézières loves nothing more than freedom. Art before all! Imagination before all! It may be one of his most defining character traits. His love for the wide open spaces of America, which we know has profoundly influenced his life, seems to echo his love for a blank page that has yet to be filled. 'I love those moments of pure wandering, looking for an idea, a character or a background element,' he says.
Perhaps he doesn't know it, but Mézières belongs to the race of explorers, of discoverers. We admire him for what he is: a magnificent visionary. An illuminator of the unknown in all its subtle shapes. And we understand why Christin is the first to pay homage to him. As the writer and wordsmith puts it, 'I've often been awed when discovering my script in pictures.'
So have we, Pierre! So have we!

On the False Earths, ***page 98 (rejected art)***

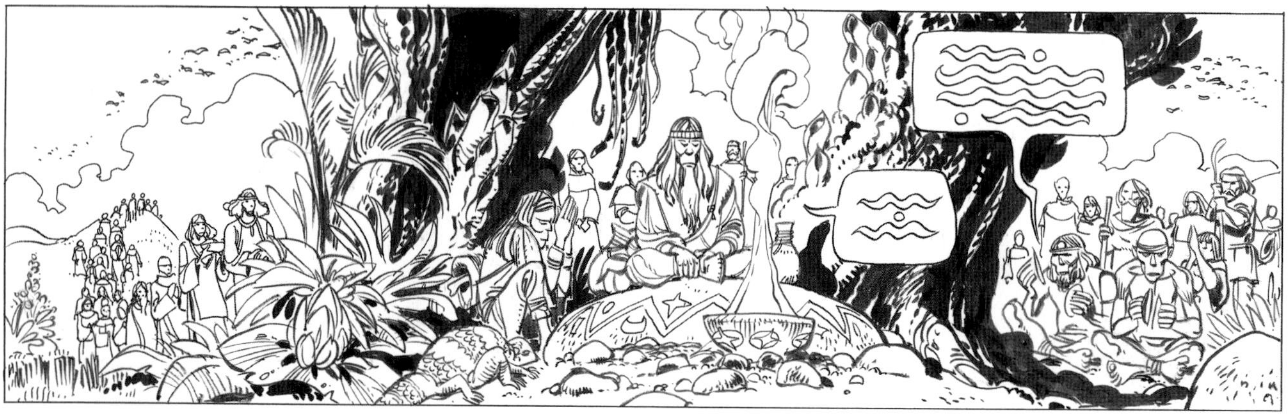

Heroes of the Equinox, ***page 129 (rejected art)***

‘ART REJECTED BECAUSE I WASN’T SATISFIED WITH IT OR BECAUSE OF A CHANGE IN PAGE LAYOUT. IN A FANTASY WORLD, NOTHING *HAS* TO BE HORIZONTAL OR VERTICAL, OR ROUND OR… YOU MUST TRY EVERYTHING, AND OFTEN REDO IT ALL!’

JEAN-CLAUDE MÉZIÈRES

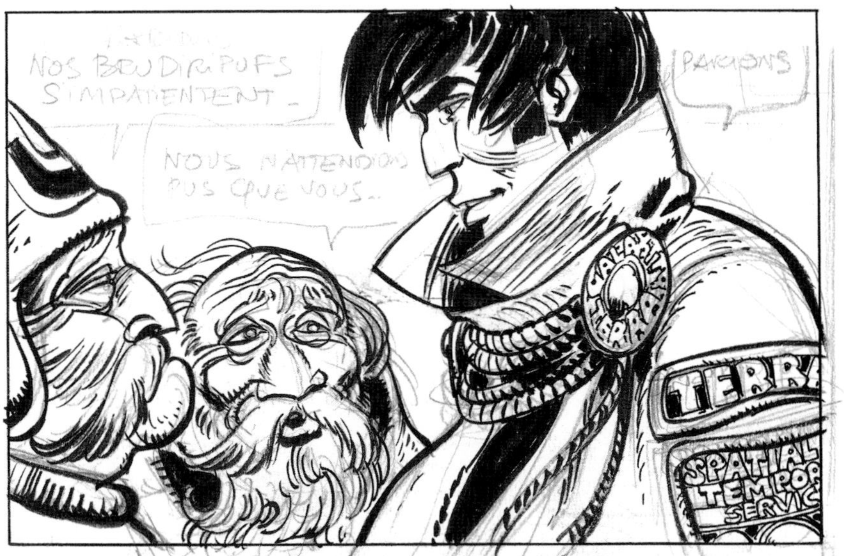
NOS BOUDIRIPUFS S'IMPATIENTENT_
NOUS N'ATTENDIONS PUS QUE VOUS..
PARTONS
TERRA
SPATIAL TEMPOR SERVIC

Heroes of the Equinox, ***page 132***

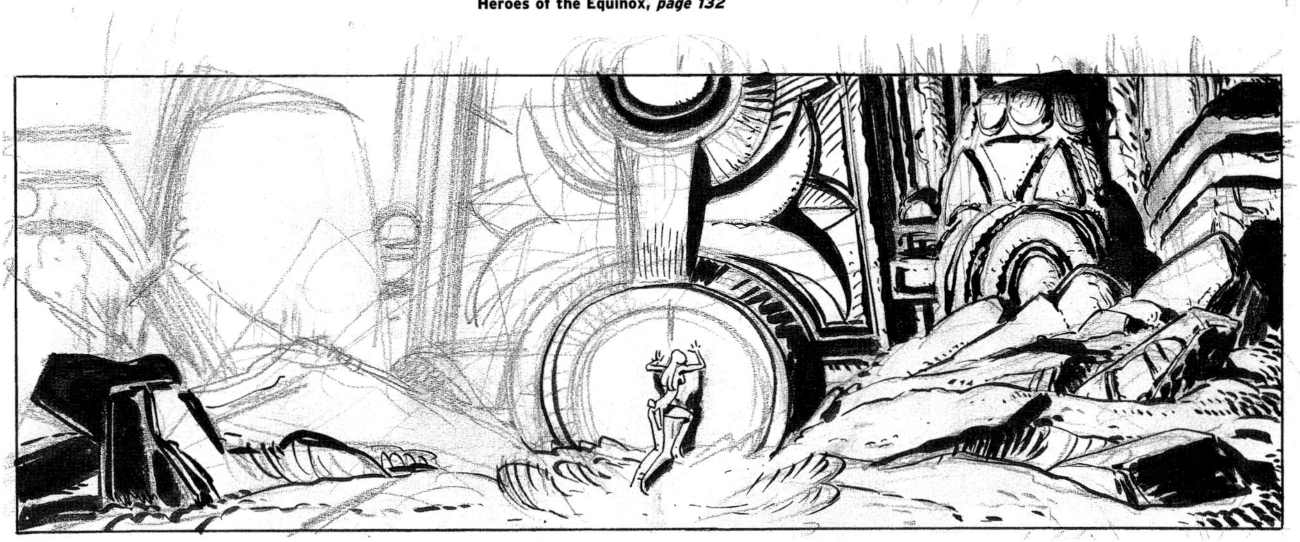

Ambassador of the Shadows, ***page 69***

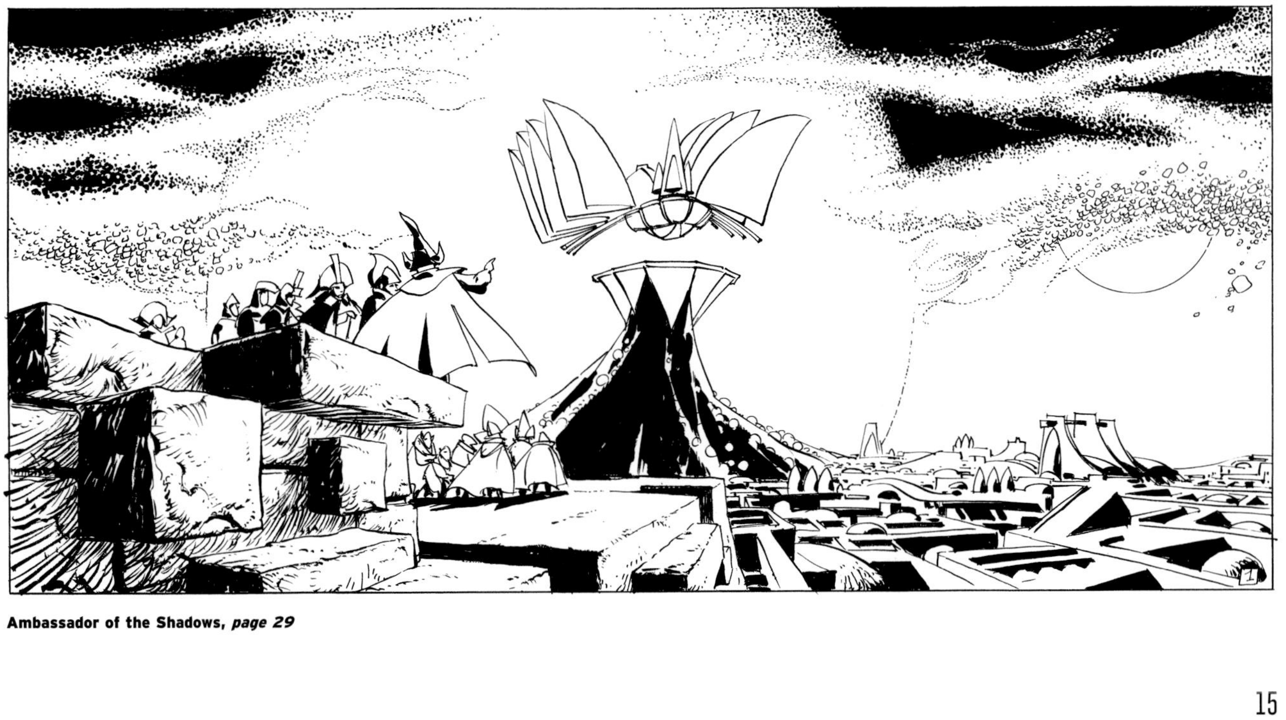

Ambassador of the Shadows, ***page 29***

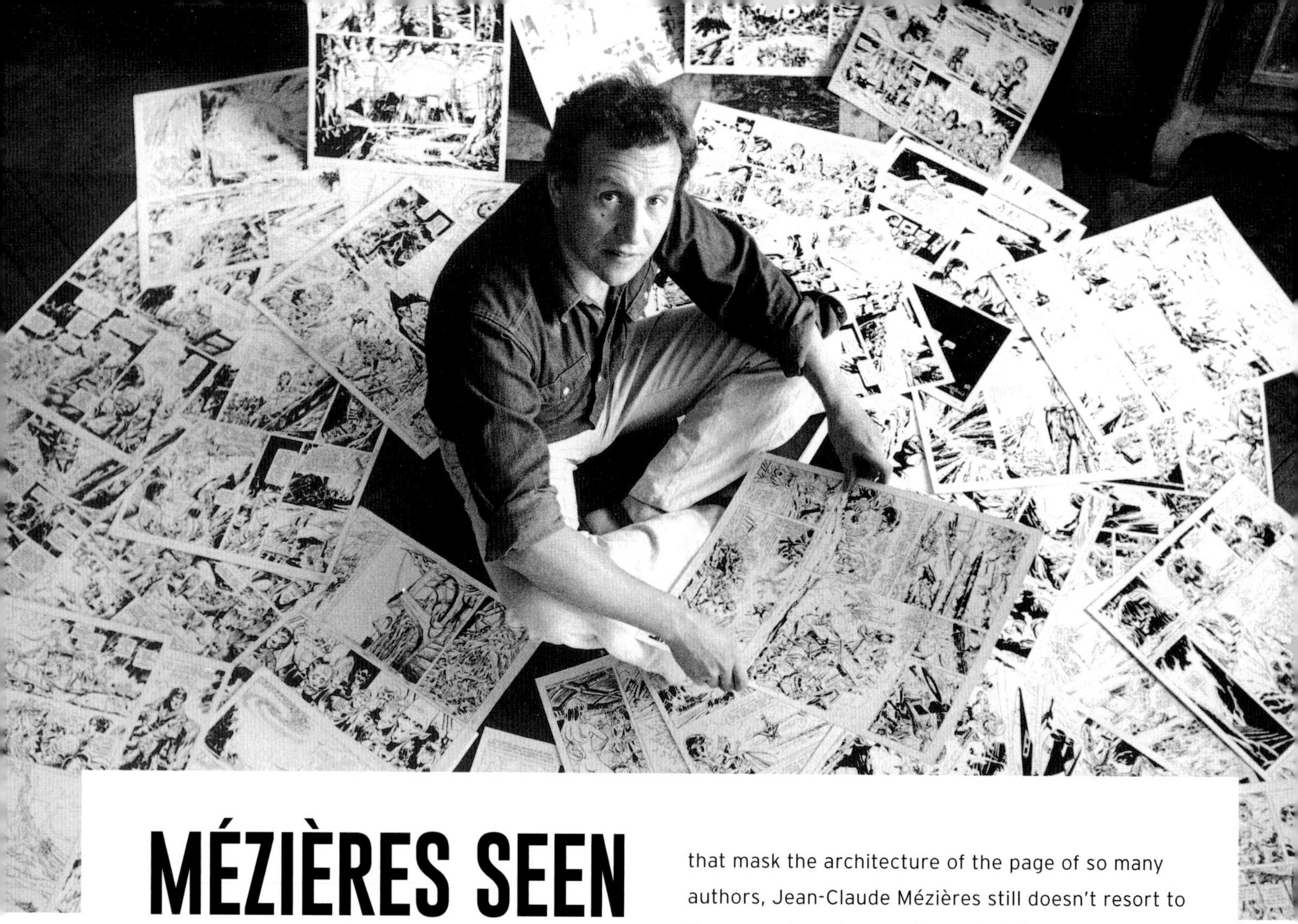

MÉZIÈRES SEEN BY CHRISTIN

'Never quite in fashion, never altogether stylish, never entirely legitimate, but also never completely forgotten, never hated, and in the end never outdated, "Mézières-esque" art, in its intense humility, is at the very heart of what *bandes dessinées* are in the 1980s. You might even posit that said art belongs to the realm of inescapable evidence: the framing is precise, unnecessary details are shunned, ornamental austerity is deliberate… Everything contributes to making it the archetype of a simple art – perhaps too simple for those easily dazzled by passing mannerisms. And yet… There is so much technical virtuosity in that stripped-down style, light-years from any naivety or innocence! Shunning the flamboyant excesses of a Druillet, the embeddings, arabesques, gargoyles and garlands that mask the architecture of the page of so many authors, Jean-Claude Mézières still doesn't resort to the pure, elegant, unreally perfect forms that remain the uncontested preserve of a Moebius. [...] Instead he proposes, discreetly yet infallibly, a new relation to the art object. A perfect knowledge of techniques, a taste for pictorial or cinematic quotes, a mastery of elaborate architectural language, a passion for all living or inert natural forms, a capacity for social analysis that rests on the fiercely realistic visual basis that is each panel – all those seemingly disparate elements come together to make Jean-Claude's art something homogenous and, in the end, beyond its apparent limpidity, something inimitable. In short, everything is simple because it's the simplicity of evidence. [...] At the same time, however, nothing is simple. Because beyond that seemingly transparent yet extremely lucid aspect of Jean-Claude Mézières's art, rational choices and opaque impulses, avowed commitments and concealed mysteries give the story life from inside.'

ÉVELYNE TRANLÉ: THE ONE BY WHOM THE COLOUR COMES

What is it that all of *Valerian*'s albums and some of *Blueberry*, *Asterix* and *Philemon* have in common? These various series are linked by the personality of a single artist, Évelyne Tranlé, who coloured them all. In truth, readers all too often forget that the artist delivers a black-and-white job. It is then the colourist's job to give life to the art. Such is the all-too-often overlooked* occupation that Évelyne chose. 'In my forty-year career, I've produced over sixty volumes – and three boys,' she admits with humility. True, the artist often gives instructions for colours or

moods, and keeps the choiciest morsels that are covers and 'direct colour' illustrations for themself. But if a Shingouz is of that particular colour, if a ship is red or blue, if a mood is gloomy or bright, it's all due to Évelyne. She who, by birth, was Mézières's little sister has also become, in her way, Valerian and Laureline's mother. And we thank her for it!

*An unfortunate state of affairs in France and Belgium, where for a long time colourists were hardly ever mentioned. Fans of American and British comics would be much more aware of their importance.

Original inked art.

Watercolour over blue outlines.

Final product after superimposition of inks over colours.

AND MEANWHILE...

HIS OWN AMERICA!

In 1974, as if to take a break between two *Valerian* albums, Mézières returned to the pages of *Pilote*. In a short story titled *Mon Amérique à moi* (*My Own America*), he went back over his past and the great founding experience that was his life in the Far West.

It begins like a fairy tale: 'When I was a little boy, I wasn't too smart...' And it leads to a candid story, filled with nostalgia and love, of that exotic adventure. Put yourself in the mindset of the '60s, when distances were still long and communications much slower. Imagine that penniless little Frenchy, and drop him into the canyons of Utah or the vast prairies of Wyoming. Finding such a complete change of scenery again today would require going to a very remote corner of the world indeed – or doing what Mézières did upon returning to France: attempting to follow Valerian to the far ends of space and time!

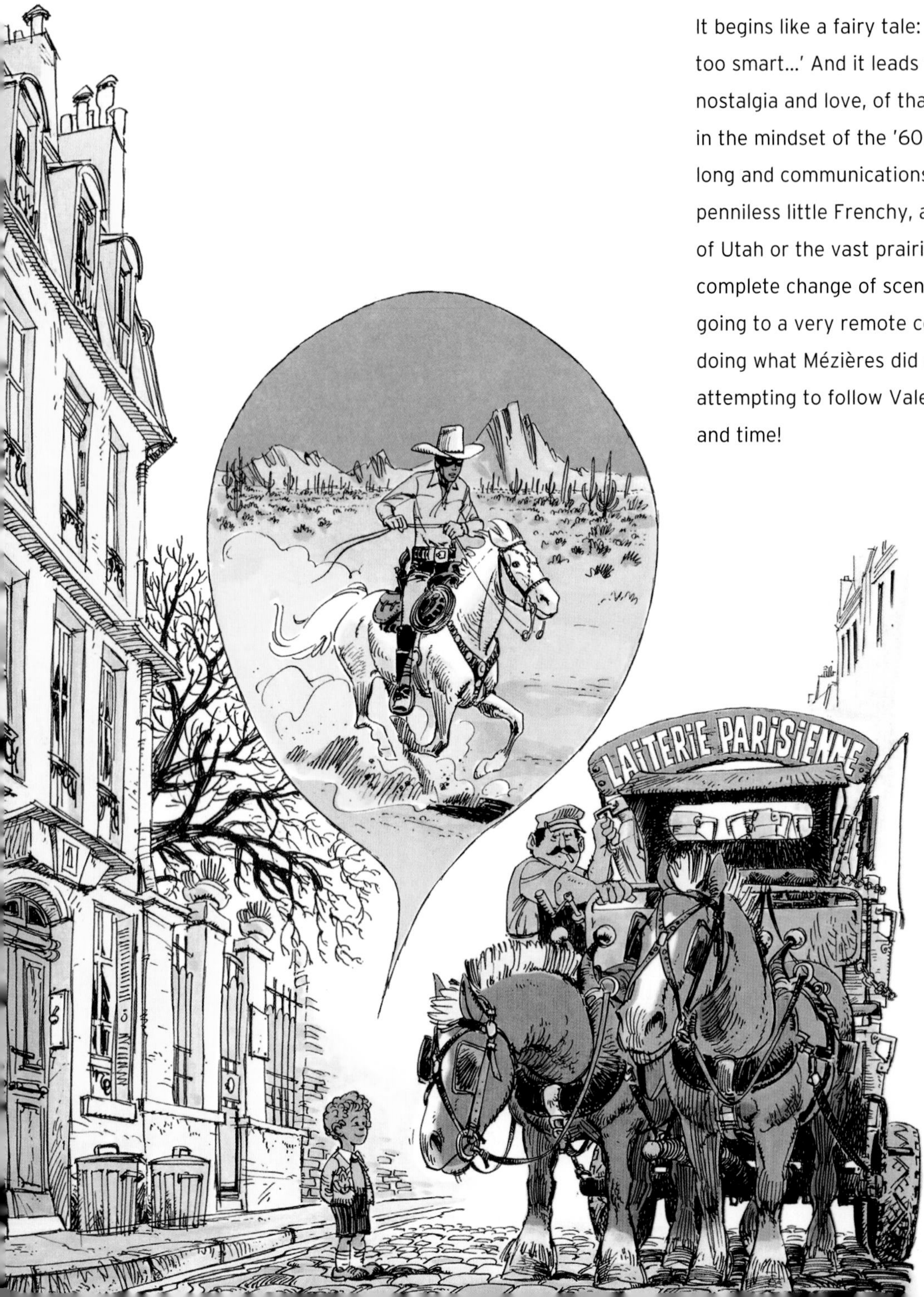
LAITERIE PARISIENNE

From* Mon Amérique à moi, *published in Pilote in 1974.

TWO METAL-RICH EPISODES

As I was, if not one of the actors, then at least one of the witnesses of the *Métal Hurlant* experiment, I will take the liberty of reminding the reader how much of a thunderclap the publishing of that magazine was in the small, closed world of '70s *bandes dessinées*. A wind of freedom like no other before blew over the periodical of Dionnet, Moebius and Druillet. The tone was radically new, and all graphical experiments were welcome. There was no way Mézières couldn't be part of it.

And so he was already in issue 7 with *Les baroudeurs de l'espace* (*Space Grunts*), a short but beautiful story set halfway between Earth and the stars. And three years later his second story, *Retour à la nature* (*Back to Nature*), was published in issue 41. In both cases, we (re)discovered a Mézières at the top of his game, happy in such sci-fi stories, without *Valerian*. And, most of all, he found in them the opportunity to leave the strict frame of conventional BD for the first time, and deliver outstanding work he coloured directly himself.

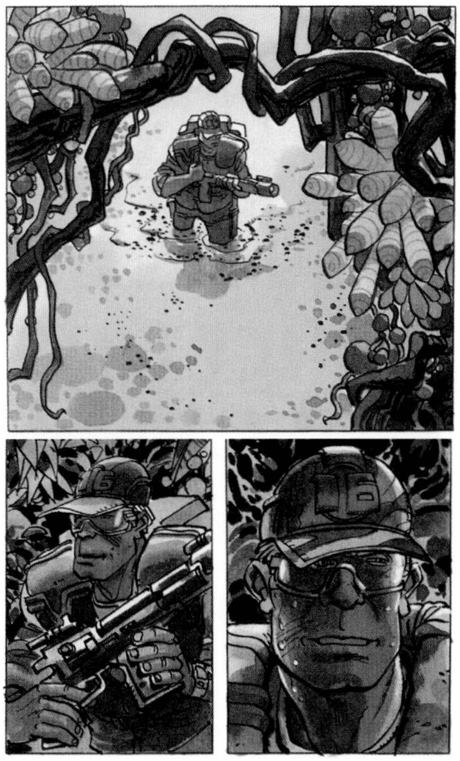

Above: From* Retour à la nature*, published in* Métal Hurlant *in 1979.
Below: Illustration from* Les Baroudeurs de l'espace*, published in* Métal Hurlant *in 1976.

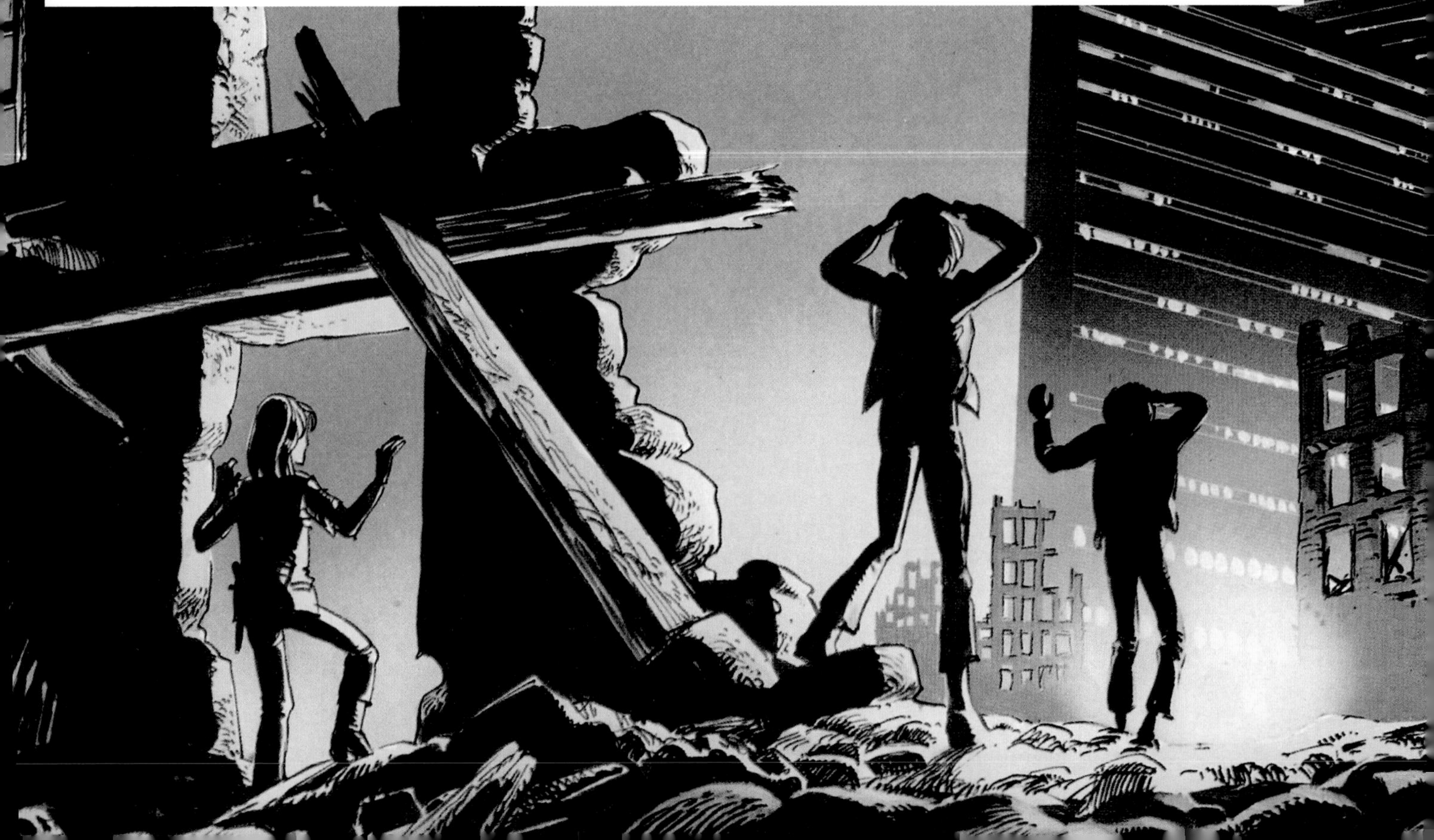

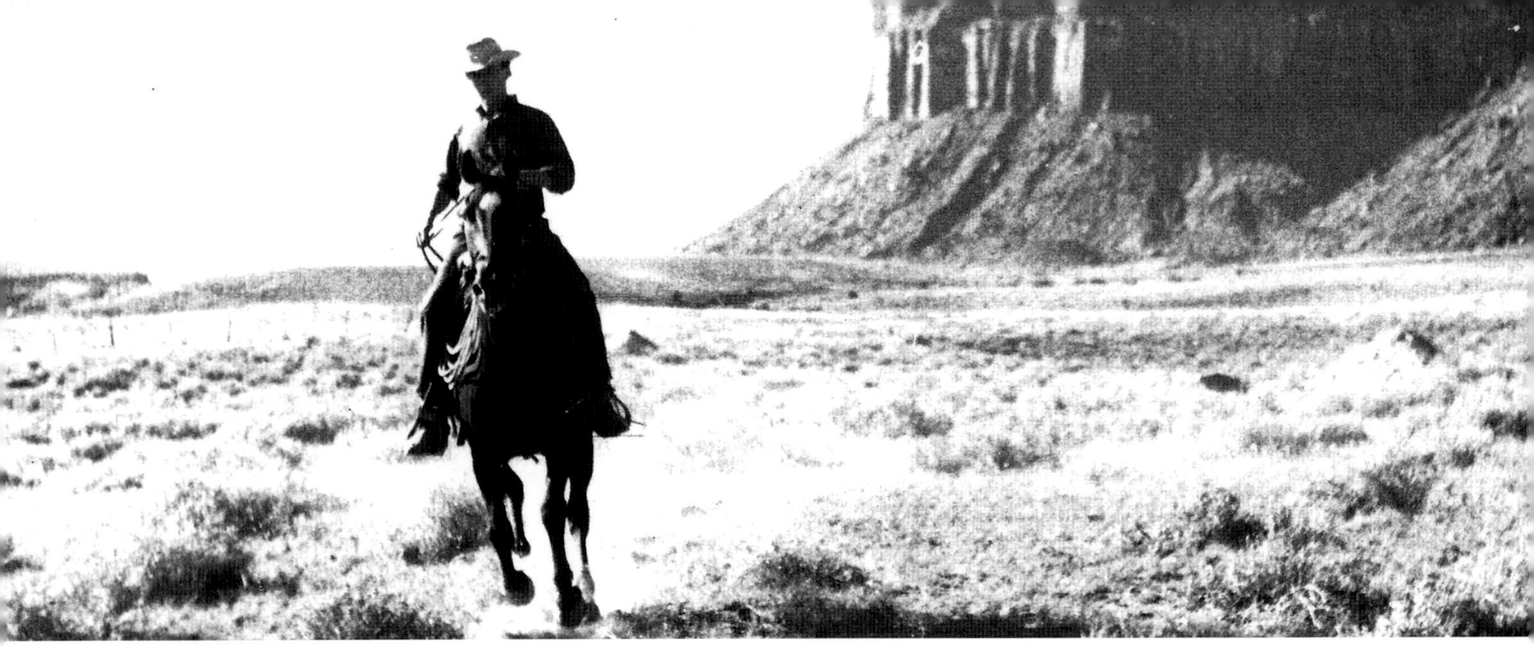

FAR WEST 67 – THE ADVENTURE OF A PARISIAN COWBOY

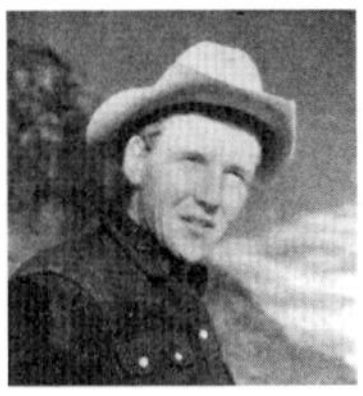

JEAN-CLAUDE MÉZIÈRES (PICTURED HERE), 28, HAS JUST SPENT A YEAR AND A HALF IN THE UNITED STATES, WHERE HE WORKED IN RANCHES ACROSS MONTANA, WYOMING AND UTAH. *PILOTE* HAS SECURED THE EXCLUSIVE RIGHTS TO THE FASCINATING RECOLLECTIONS OF THAT YOUNG FRENCHMAN, WHO WENT WEST LOOKING FOR ADVENTURE.

TEXTS AND PICTURES BY J.C. MÉZIÈRES

5 a.m. The big truck has been driving along the rutted track for over an hour. It's still quite dark outside. In the truck's cab, the hat-topped profiles of my three companions are visible only in the dashboard's lights. In the back, the horses, buffeted by the ride, scrape the metallic floor with their hooves. The sky brightens slightly in the east, revealing the black outline of the cliffs that overlook us. The track ends abruptly in a vast basin formed by several canyons. In the semi-darkness I can see an immense herd of cattle scattered through the bushes, grazing peacefully. Everyone leads his horse out of the truck and ties them up to the limb of a dead tree. It's March. A dry, cold wind blows softly. Al builds a fire, which we gather around to warm up. Lloyd is the ranch foreman; 50 years old, his rugged face made leathery and craggy by sun and wind, bearing the marks of the only job he knows: cowboy. Next to him, old Al, even slimmer, almost skinny, and Dennis - just turned 18, ginger hair, and face covered in freckles. They're all dressed the same, all wearing the uniform of the West: a felt hat - the wide brim rolled, the top creased with a punch, the ribbon stained with sweat and mud; a scarf knotted two or three times around the neck; a coat or jacket so worn out and faded that the colour can't be recognised, and which never shakes off the sharp smell of cattle and horse sweat; jeans and wide, brown leather chaps, frayed, torn and scratched by thorny bushes and rubbing against the lasso; boots with Cuban heels, caked with dust, their silver spurs scraping the ground with every step. The fire crackles. Muted mooing resonates from somewhere in the canyons. The horses, muzzles in their feedbags, finish their oats. The sky lightens - it's almost day now. Let's go!

I put the bit in my horse's mouth and, fingers stiff and clumsy with cold, check the bags and straps of my saddle. Like the others, I pull my hat down to my eyebrows. Dennis and I are off to round up the cattle that have scattered during the night.

The blazing red finger of the first ray of the sun touches the top of a strange stone monolith, 600 feet tall, while the rest of the valley remains in blue shade. On the other side of the canyon, two tiny cowboy shapes flush out group after group of frightened cows that run to rejoin the herd. Cantering across the rocks and the bushes, standing in the stirrups, holding the reins with my left hand and a lasso in the right, I guide my horse towards a small band of cattle. Yaaa... C'mon, cows... Yaaa... That pinto knows his business! Brown with large white spots, strong and incredibly sure-footed, he is trained to perfection, like all the horses of the ranch. He obeys the merest signal and, almost of his own will, cuts off the fugitives and finds the lost. The mooing of cows calling their calves, the shouts and whistles of the cowboys ring clear in the sharp morning wind. Soon, the reconstituted herd gets underway. For 4 days, spending 12 to 14 hours a day in the saddle, we're going to drive these 800 head of cattle to

their summer pasture, 100 miles away over the mountains, on the other side of the ranch. In the golden dust lifted by thousands of hooves, in the middle of this fabulous landscape, I'm suddenly filled with a wild joy as my old dream has finally come true: I'm a cowboy...

Casually, Lloyd twists in his saddle, turning to me:
- How're you doing, JC?
- OK, I'm doing fine...
And it's true that I'm doing fine!
Despite the saddle that's beginning to turn my backside to leather.

GO WEST, YOUNG MAN, GO WEST!

The American West! A fantastic legend we all know through books and movies. Endless open spaces, huge herds wandering across the prairie, the rough and dangerous life of pioneers - but a life of freedom in a untouched land!
But what is the Far West nowadays? Do cowboys still walk around with a Colt strapped to their leg, or are they hiding in the countless Westerns on American TV? Has the helicopter replaced the horse and modernity killed adventure? Are the empty landscapes now covered in highways, billboards and motels? Is the West dead, or is there still a way of life there that isn't quite in sync with the mechanised civilisation of the 20th century?

With a lot of enthusiasm but little money, I decided to try my luck and go see if the reality still fit the legend. I stayed in the United States for a year and a half. Having first spent a few months in New York and on the West Coast, I then spent fall season wandering from Montana to Arizona, taking buses or hitch-hiking. After wintering with hospitable friends in Salt Lake City, the snows melted and, with the temperature once again sufficient for spending the night in a ditch, I reacquainted myself with the hopeful gesture of the hitch-hiker. I had a specific goal in mind: to get hired as a cowboy.

I'd been sitting on my suitcase for several hours, watching out for the few (very few) cars that drove on some out-of-the-way road in southern Utah, when a park ranger's jeep stopped. Four hours later, the ranger dropped me off near a ranch where he thought I might find work.

At the bottom of a vast red rock canyon, hidden in a thicket, I found the ranch.

I walked through the tall wooden gate at the courtyard's entrance. On one side, two log cabins next to a corral holding a dozen horses. On the other side, a few whitewashed wooden or stone buildings. Parked under the trees, trucks, tractors and two or three jeeps. Not a soul in sight. Actually, yes: coming out of the corral, holding his heavy saddle in his arms, a cowboy was looking at me.

- Hi! I'm French. My name's JC (Jean-Claude being completely unpronounceable west of the Mississippi - not to mention entirely anachronistic). I'm looking for a job as cowboy - do you think there's one available?

He looks at me, spits on the ground once and, still carrying his saddle, heads to the stables. From the back of a stall he mutters something I barely understand:
- Well, depends... Can you ride a horse?
- Sure! I ride a fair bit in France...
Well, yes, I can handle a horse all right, but there might be a slight difference between French horses and those I can see in the corral: magnificent animals, powerful, with broad chests and thick, often scarred legs. Bah! We'll see how it goes.

He comes back towards me, starts chewing on a toothpick and grunts:
- Might be! Gotta see with the boss. Follow me!
Inside the dining hall, a long room with sea-green walls and lit by a single bulb, a young guy - probably the same age as me - is writing in some accounts books spread over a table corner. Weathered skin, bright blue eyes and short-cropped hair, he bursts out laughing when I tell him the reasons for my trip. His name is Bob. His father owns the biggest ranch in the area and has entrusted him with managing this part of their immense domain.
- I knew the French were mad about Westerns, but I had no idea it was this bad!
The deal is struck: $6 per day, full room and board. I can stay - there's plenty of work.
Bob points me towards my room, in another building. Two beds with sleeping bags, an unbelievable mess: pin-ups all over the walls, a muddy pair of old boots under a bed, dirty shirts, books, and in a corner, hanging from a pair of antlers, an old hat and a Winchester.
I put my suitcase and camera bag down on one of the

beds. A stocky young man comes in, with very brown skin and jet-black hair. He must have a Native American or Mexican grandmother. By 9 p.m. everyone is in bed. We smoke a last cigarette.

- It's enjoyable work here, Sam tells me. I'm a mechanic and a farmhand, but what I'd like to be is a ladies' hairstylist...

I have a hard time falling asleep. The next day, all of Hollywood's wild rides will become reality.

We're awakened by the bell at the entrance to the kitchen. It's 6 a.m.

The cook – a large woman who's constantly joking – brings out the enormous pot of coffee, the bacon and eggs, the porridge, the crackers... Everything we need to begin a hard day's work.

The meal over, the foreman and two cowboys head towards the corral. Bob has tasked Sam and me to put down some barbed wire in a canyon. We pile up steel and wooden posts, spades and pickaxes, and rolls of barbed wire into the back of a pickup. The cowboys saddle their horses. Dammit! I hope I'm not going to spend all my time in this ranch putting up fences! I want to ride horses and drive cattle! But barbed wire is part of the cowboy's life – which isn't all glamour. And the whole day long I hammer posts into the rocky ground and stretch between them uncooperative wire that keeps pricking my fingers even through the thick leather gloves.

After several days of miscellaneous, variously enjoyable tasks – miles of fences put down and repaired, the bed of arroyos cleared and deepened, hay bales stored, stables cleaned, and more – one night Bob tells me that the next day I'll be going on the cattle drive! Finally I'll be a full-blown cowboy...

VAST OPEN SPACES

Inside the stables, 4 a.m. Lloyd hands me a halter:

- Go get your horse – the pinto. You can take this saddle.

My saddle! The symbol of the West! A massive saddle, its leather polished by use, with a lasso fastened to the pommel and an Indian blanket.

A thin rain is falling from the dark, starless sky. In the corral, the moving shapes of horses skitter away as soon as I come near. I manage to locate my mount and, after a chase that lasts several minutes, place the halter on him. Next time I'll know that it's better to jiggle a few oats in a feedbag because, even though they're superbly trained, these horses aren't easily approached until they've been saddled.

The other guys have already led their horses inside the truck while I'm still struggling with the saddle's straps, unsure of how to tie them exactly. I finally manage it. I climb into the cab with Lloyd, Al and Dennis, and realise I've forgotten my saddlebags with the cameras! I run to the stables and retrieve them.

This time everything's ready. We're off!

We've been at it for several hours now. It's starting to get hot. The herd is advancing at a slow, regular pace, spread along over half a mile of the trail. The cattle follow that path up to the mountains, where water and pastures are more abundant in summer, then they come down in the fall, driven off by cold winds and the first snows. Lloyd and Al are riding

outside the middle of the herd. Dennis and I are pushing the rearguard forward.

Ahead of me, the thick, brown-red backs of the Herefords sway slowly through the dust. It's an English breed, with the face, hocks and tail extremity white.

Again and again, we have to urge on animals that have stopped to graze.

Often a calf or a group of cows escape. I spur my horse into a gallop and chase them until they return to the herd. At the back, Dennis and I ride side by side, chatting. He crosses the reins over his horse's neck, rolls a cigarette and lights a match with a flick of his thumb.

At the end of the plateau, a river runs into an arroyo. The leading cattle rush to drink. Soon it's a crush that has to be cleared. The rest of the herd are pushing forward, stomping, mooing, pressed flank to flank; they must be allowed to reach the river. Al whirls his lasso, up to his spurs in water. The

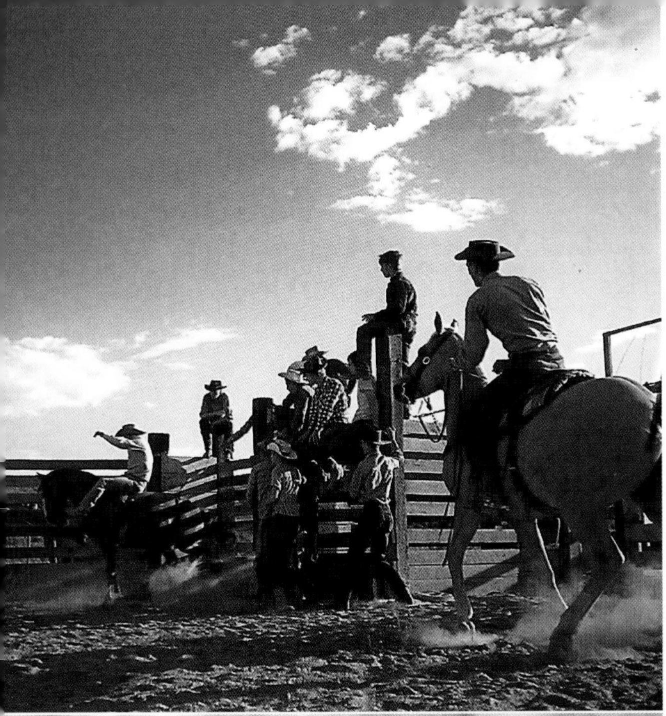

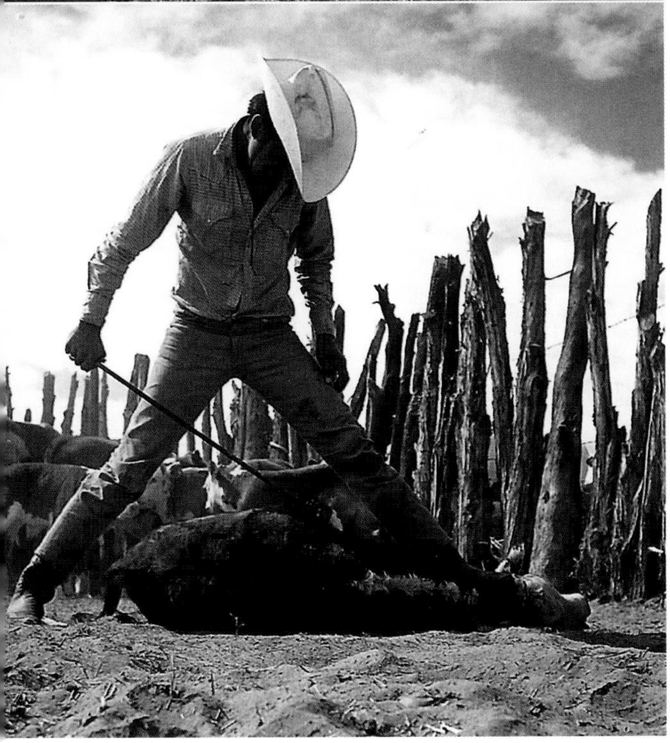

frightened cattle shy away and climb up the other bank while other cows take their place. The herd is across. The horses, lips drawn, drink. Underneath their hide glistening with sweat, a little ball travels up their neck with every gulp.

We let the cattle rest. It's time to eat, anyway. On the horizon, a plume of dust moves rapidly. Bob and his truck. The cows halt, lie down and chew the cud; others graze. The calves suck from their mother voraciously, head-butting the udders. We dismount. My legs are wobbly – I'm starting to understand the shuffling gait of cowboys! In a great cloud of dust the truck stops. Bob is right on time. He brings us sandwiches, a thermos full of coffee and – a touch of sophistication – small, brightly coloured paper napkins for everyone! In silence, sitting on the ground or on a rock, we enjoy a tuna-mayo sandwich in the middle of the Utah desert! Behind us the horses, reins dragging on the ground, eat their ration of oats. One last cup of coffee, then saddle up! We have to gather the herd again. The long, monotonous, wonderful drive resumes.

Way high in the deep blue, a falcon flies in wide circles above us. In the evening, the temperature drops. The whole landscape takes on a pink hue. The cows are tired. In the distance, we can see the cabin and the big corral. We'll have to lock the cattle in, take the horses to the waterhole, feed them and get a fire going before the sun disappears. We eat by the light of an oil lamp. By the stove, Lloyd and Al talk about horses, as always.

A HORSE, A SADDLE, A LASSO AND A HAT, CLOUDS OF DUST, SORE MUSCLES, THIRST, THE SUN AND THE RAIN, RED ROCKS, BLUE SKY, COWS, LOTS OF COWS ... AND $6 A DAY.

We've been travelling for three days now. Last night we slept under the stars. Our progression is slower. Lloyd killed a rattlesnake. It's scorching. Big grey clouds appear on the horizon. Suddenly, the storm breaks out; huge hailstones pelt us. My horse balks. The rain comes down in sheets, drenching me through my denim jacket. The herd turns its collective back to the storm and leaves the trail. Faces to the lashing rain, we try to make it change direction. We yell, we holler, we scream volleys of heartfelt insults against the entire bovine race. Nothing will do. It keeps going up an increasingly steep ground. I struggle with my horse, which is also trying to put his back to the storm. I curse and laugh at the same time.

The storm has passed. We retrieve the herd from among boulders and scree. I'm freezing. Fortunately, we spend that night in a furbished cave, where our clothes dry out through the night.

Last day of the cattle drive. We've made it to the paved road that leads to our destination: the ranch of Bob's father. The cows are exhausted. A large bull stops and lets out a plaintive, halting lowing. Often we walk, leading our horses. They've covered two or three times the actual distance travelled. The roadsides are littered with empty beer cans. We put a few rocks in and use them as rattles to scare stragglers and keep them moving.

In the evening, other cowboys from the ranch join us to take the cattle to their well-deserved pastures.

Our horses walk slowly, heads bent towards the ground. The orange sun dips towards the horizon; the wind lifts little swirling clouds of dust.

In the corral I take the saddle off my horse, stroke his neck. He bolts... He's probably not keen to go on such a trip again any time soon!

Me, I'm dead on my feet... But I'm ready to go again.

THE STORIES IN THIS BOOK

'THE SAGA CONTINUES WITH THE DISCOVERIES OF NEW WORLDS IN SPACE. IT ALSO INCLUDES A FIRST RETURN TO EARTH, LIKE A PRELUDE TO THE SECOND CYCLE OF THE SERIES, WHERE OUR PLANET FEATURES PROMINENTLY.' PIERRE CHRISTIN

AMBASSADOR OF THE SHADOWS – 1975

A new ambassador arrives at Point Central, meeting place of all of the galaxy's people. It's his turn, in the name of Earth, to preside over the Council. Unenthusiastic bodyguards, Valerian and Laureline escort him ... but are unable to prevent his kidnapping. Who gave the orders? Who are those Shadows who reject Earth's domination? On the trail of the abductors, Laureline explores this strange world... Warning: This is one of the great *Valerians*!

A magnificent tale in praise of diversity, and a masterpiece infused with a galaxy-spanning epic spirit. Mézières unleashes his artistic imagination, filling spectacular space-station sets with all sorts of strange creatures. And to visit this intergalactic UN (the Zools, the centaur-like Kamuniks, the protean Suffuss, the Bagulins, the massive, blind Groobos and their zuur jellyfish, the Gnarf-dreamers...), Christin has his most charming guide take centre stage. Yes, it's Laureline who will thwart Galaxity's imperialist plans, by pleading in favour of freedom and self-determination for all when faced with the Shadows' strange wisdom: 'For untold millennia, life here has passed by, day after similar day... Nothing is ever the same and yet everything remains unchanged.'

The series also gains a few colourful characters. Particularly wonderful are the Shingouz, a trio of venal spies, and the cute, grumpy transmuter from Bluxte - quite useful, but so very grumpy...

ON THE FALSE EARTHS – 1977

Back to Earth! An unknown party appears to be messing with our planet's past, and Valerian is tasked with putting a stop to it - or more accurately his clones are. The only problem is that they keep dying to accomplish their duty. Along with Galaxity agent Jadna, Laureline is forced to witness the carnage and cry for her companion's demise every time. And so we go from the conquest of India to a Victorian club in London, from San Francisco to the First World War... A strange volume, perhaps less spectacular than the previous titles but that admirably evokes the nature of reality and illusion in the manner of Philip K. Dick.

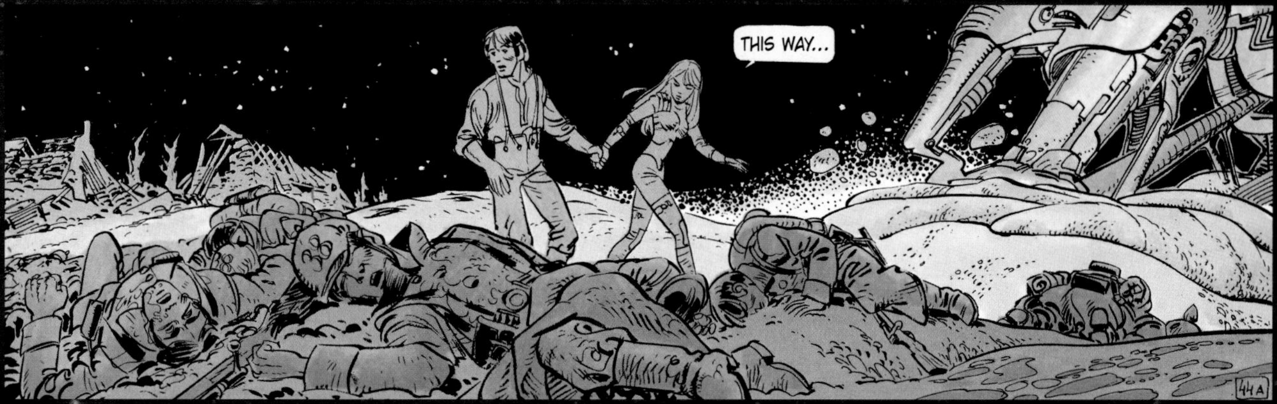
THIS WAY...
44A

All those fake-but-so-real Valerians follow one another until they induce a sort of metaphysical vertigo. What is History? Is there a meaning to it? Can it be rewritten? And how to choose between all of these parallel pasts? Far from the Great Falsifier's aesthetic diversions, Laureline offers her own answer with a nostalgic evocation of a long-gone happier time...

HEROES OF THE EQUINOX – 1978

Bearing 'the colours of Earth', Valerian is sent to a dying planet to regenerate it. Placed in competition with three other champions, he will have to follow a difficult path – part challenge, part rite of passage – until the final test that will reveal all of ... Laureline's wisdom. This story, one of the most accomplished in the series, combines all the charms of political fable and artistic achievement. At his drawing board, Mézières does wonders to describe Simlane, an ageing planet dotted with noble but decadent architecture; but he especially shines at showing in parallel the itineraries of the four champions, his efforts culminating in gorgeous, double-page spreads that literally explode when the stories converge. As for Christin, he's having a ball. Under the guise of a pastiche of Stan Lee-style superhero stories, he pits against each other three great ideologies – fascism, communism and spiritualism. The winner?...

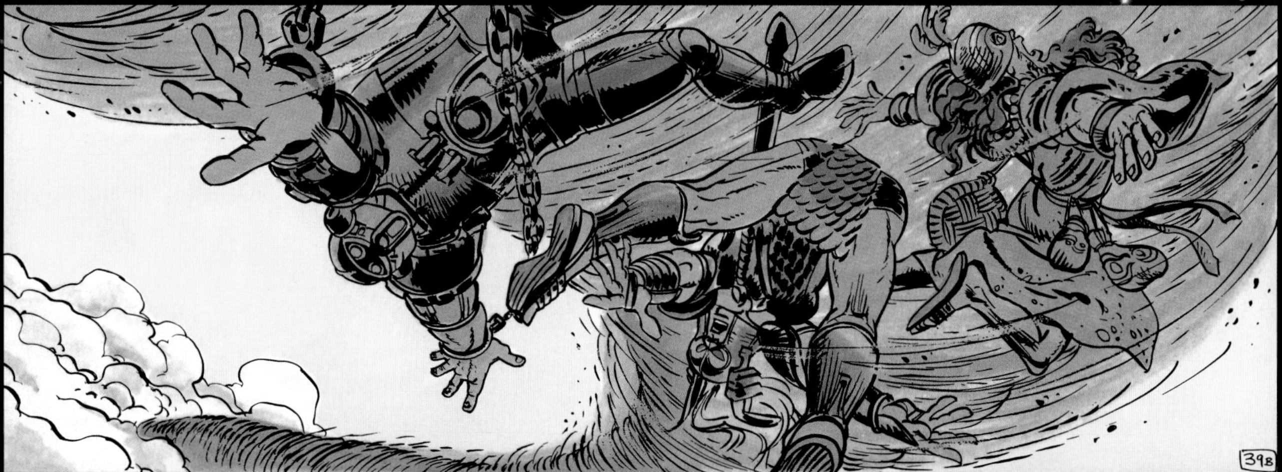
39B

AMBASSADOR OF
THE SHADOWS

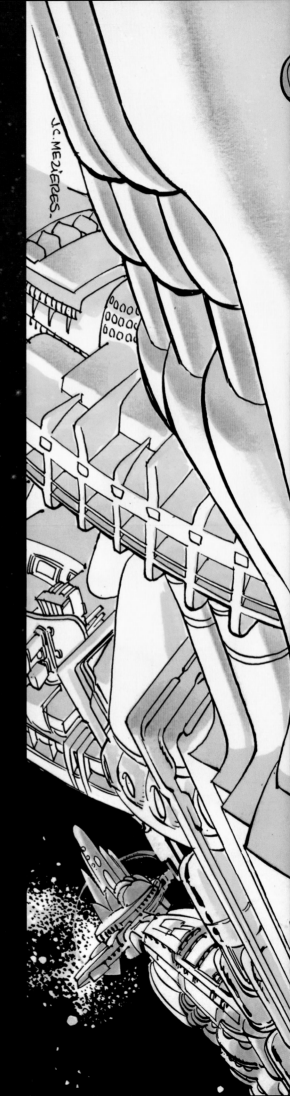

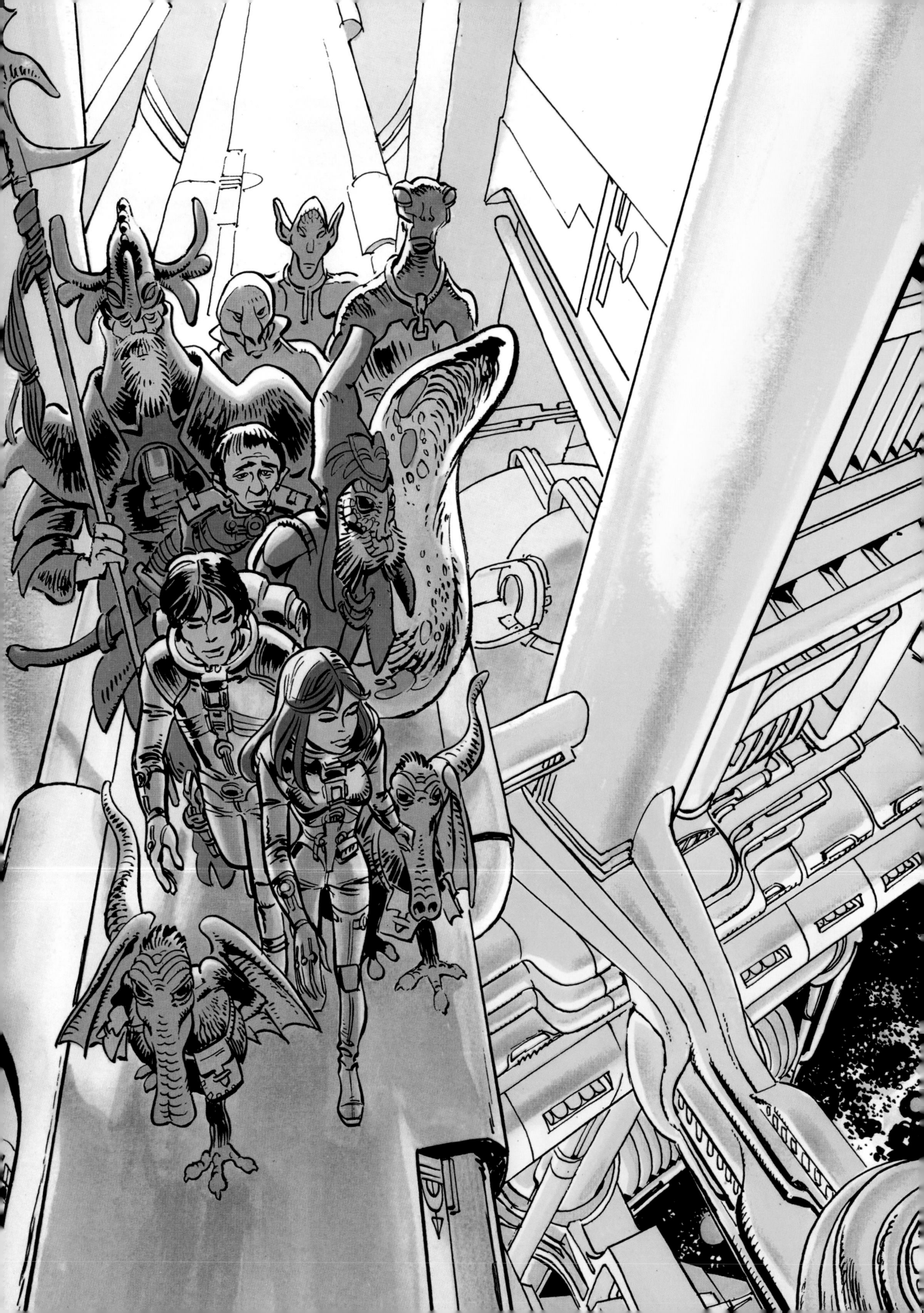

PERHAPS, IN THE IMMEASURABLE DEPTHS OF THE DISTANT PAST, SPACE WAS EMPTY OF LIFE...

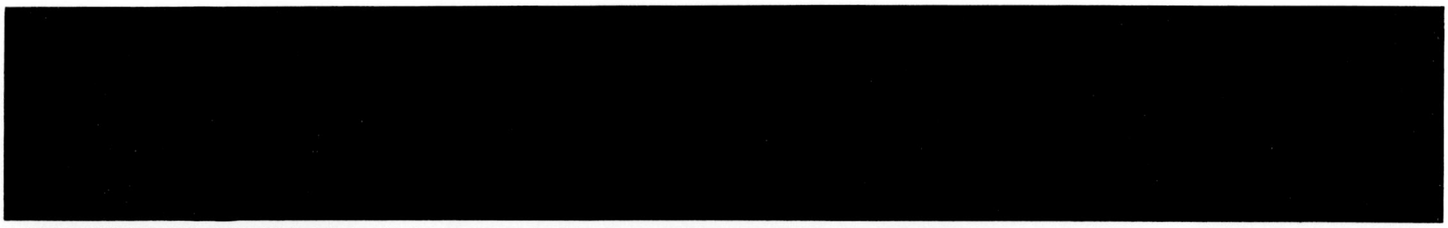

BUT COUNTLESS ARE THE MEMORIES, THE FOOTPRINTS LEFT BY CIVILISATIONS LOST IN ITS VASTNESS...

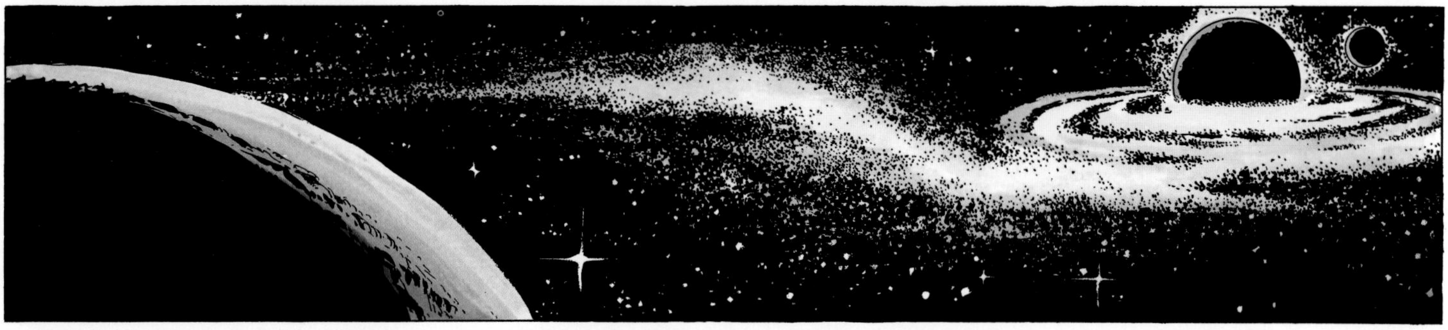

...IMPOSSIBLE TO TELL ARE THE STORIES OF WORLDS SOMETIMES DEAD FOR THOUSANDS OF CENTURIES...

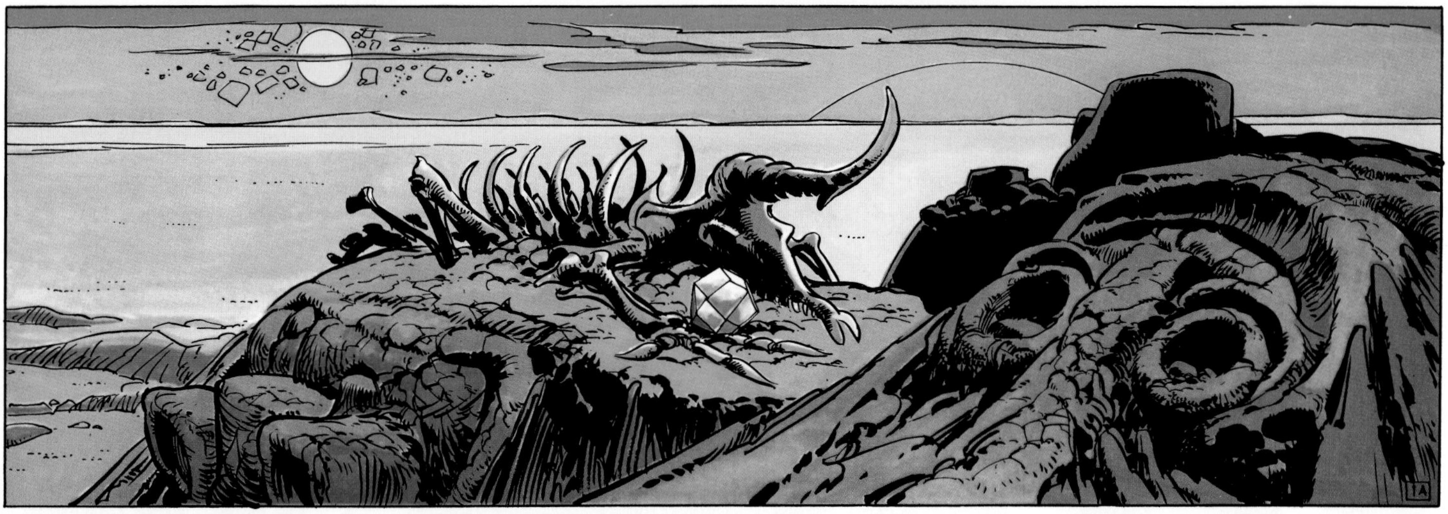

FOR WHEREVER SENTIENT BEINGS LIVED AND EVOLVED, ALWAYS THEY TURNED TOWARDS THE ENDLESS SKY TO EXPLORE IT...

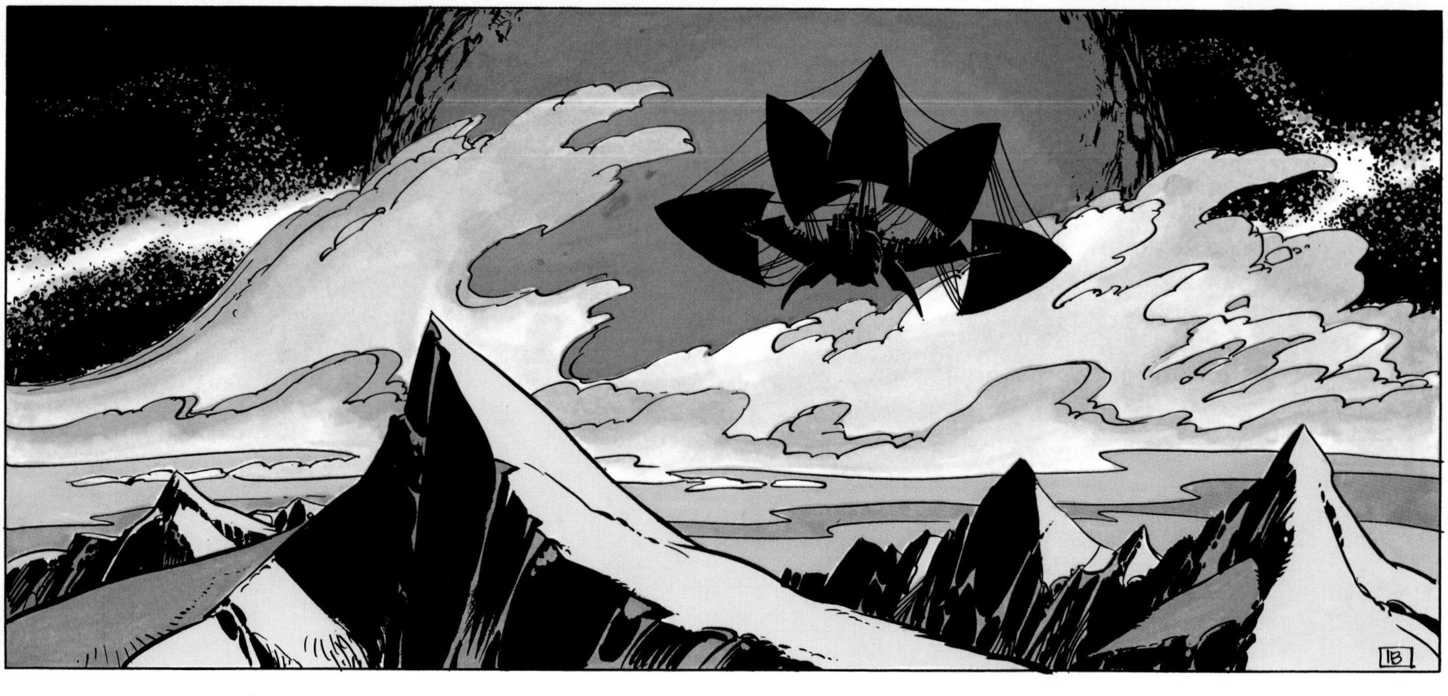

MANY AIMLESS QUESTS ENDED WITH NO ENCOUNTERS...

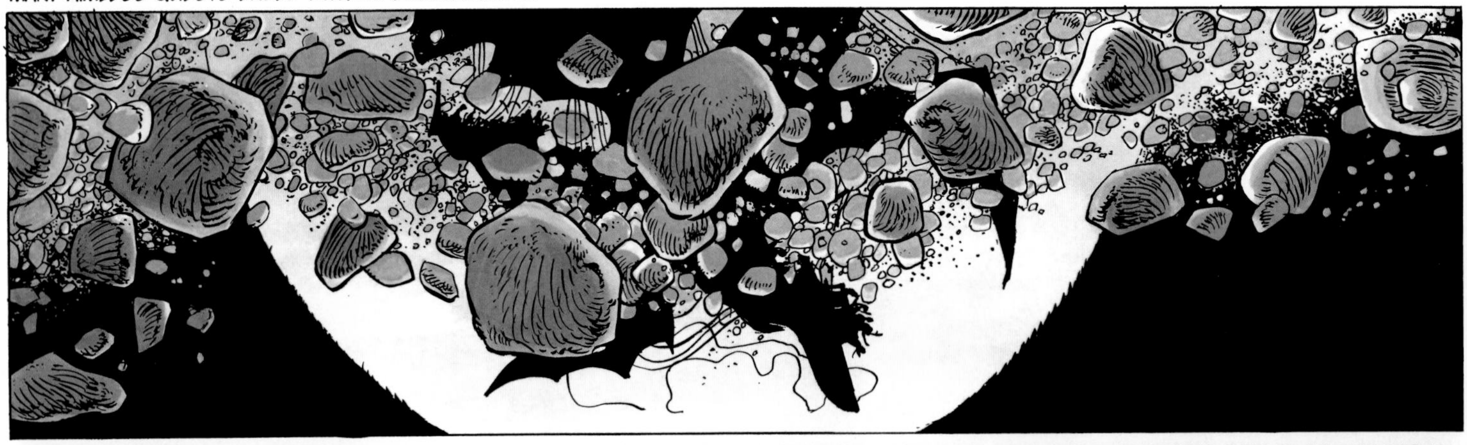

...YET THE OTHERS, THOSE THAT ALWAYS CAME FROM ELSEWHERE, WERE NEVERTHELESS THERE, THEY TOO LOOKING FOR SOMETHING THEY COULD NOT DEFINE.

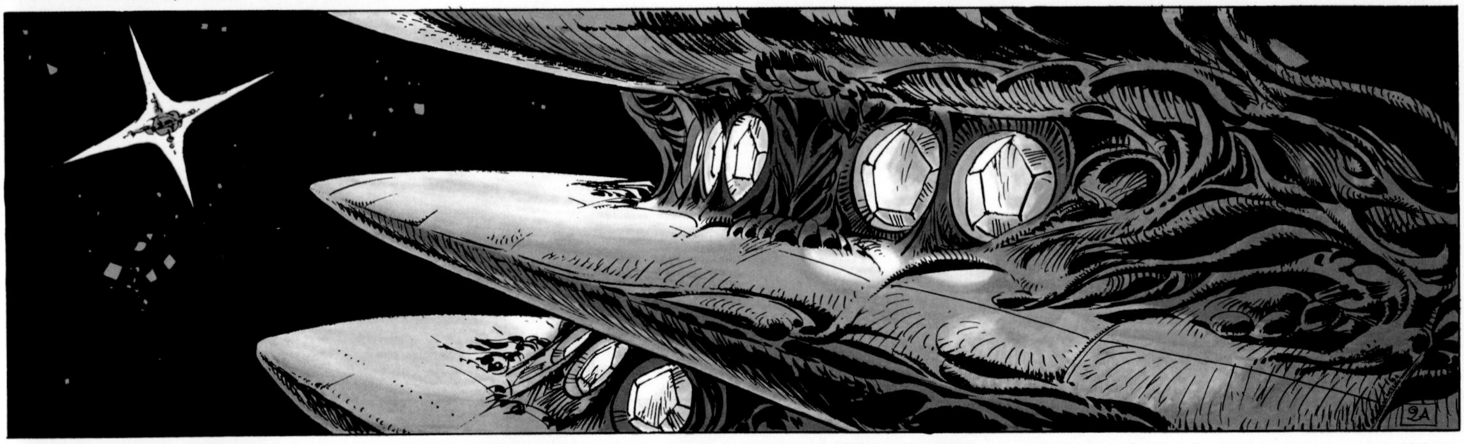

WHAT WERE THE FIRST ENCOUNTERS LIKE? UNFORGIVABLE WARS OR SPONTANEOUS FRATERNISATION?...

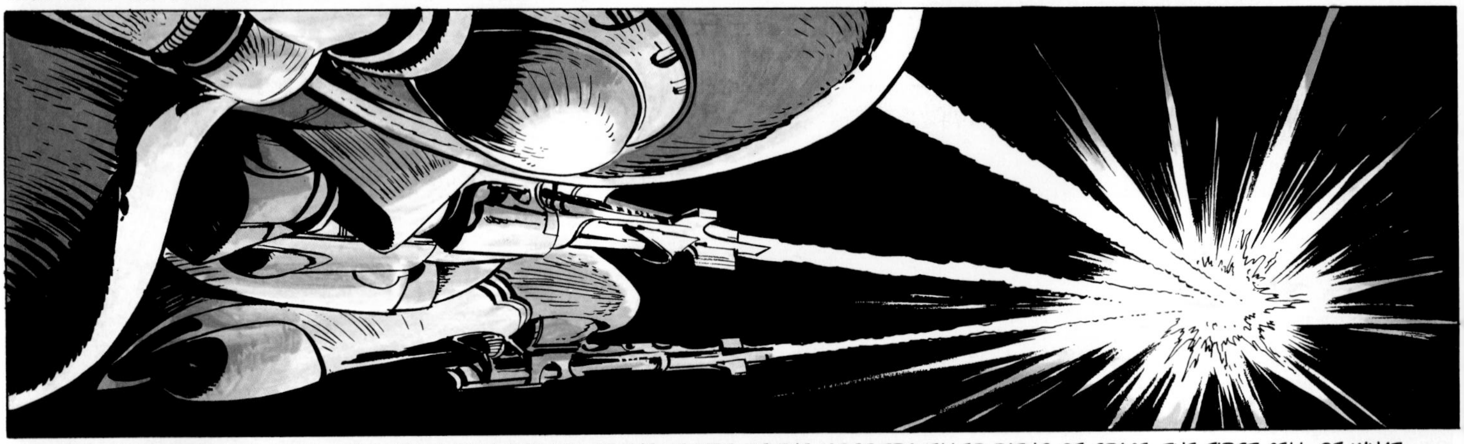

NO ONE REMEMBERS. THE ONLY CERTAINTY IS THAT ONE DAY, AT THE CENTRE OF THE MOST TRAVELLED PATHS OF SPACE, THE FIRST CELL OF WHAT WOULD BECOME **POINT CENTRAL** WAS ERECTED.

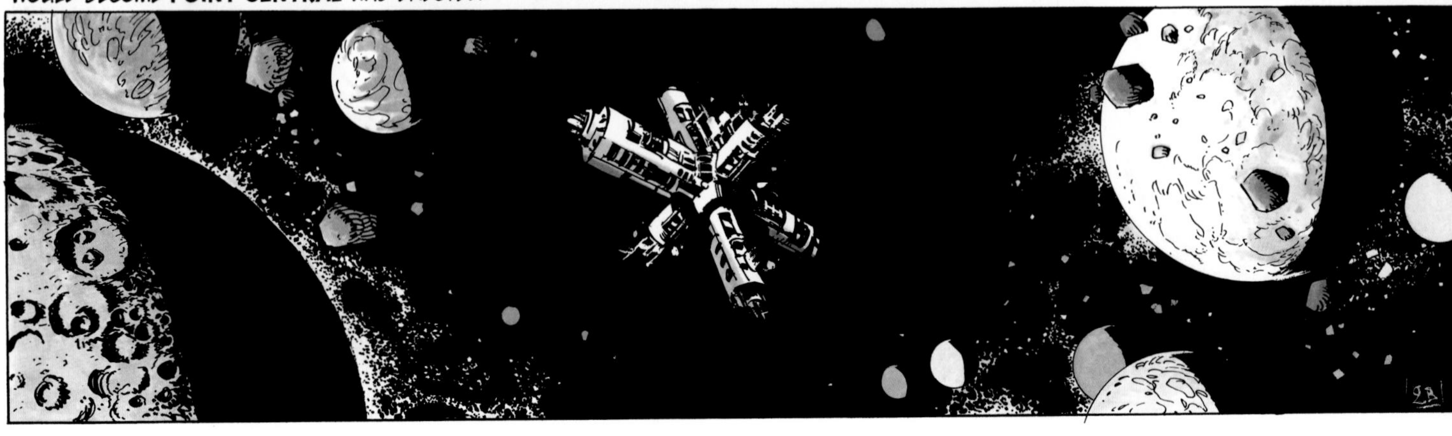

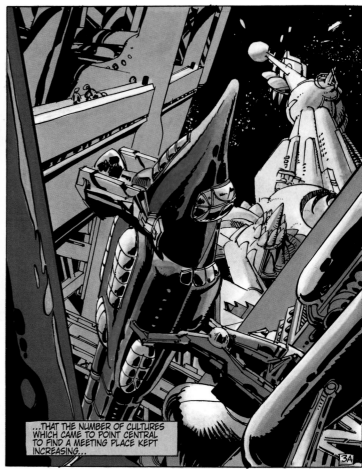

WHAT IS ALSO KNOWN IS THAT OTHER CELLS CAME TO BE ADDED TO THE INITIAL NUCLEUS...

...THAT THE NUMBER OF CULTURES WHICH CAME TO POINT CENTRAL TO FIND A MEETING PLACE KEPT INCREASING...

...SOMETIMES BRINGING A WHOLE CHUNK OF THEIR WORLD WITH THEM...

...AND THAT, LITTLE BY LITTLE, ALL OF THAT BECAME **POINT CENTRAL**...

31

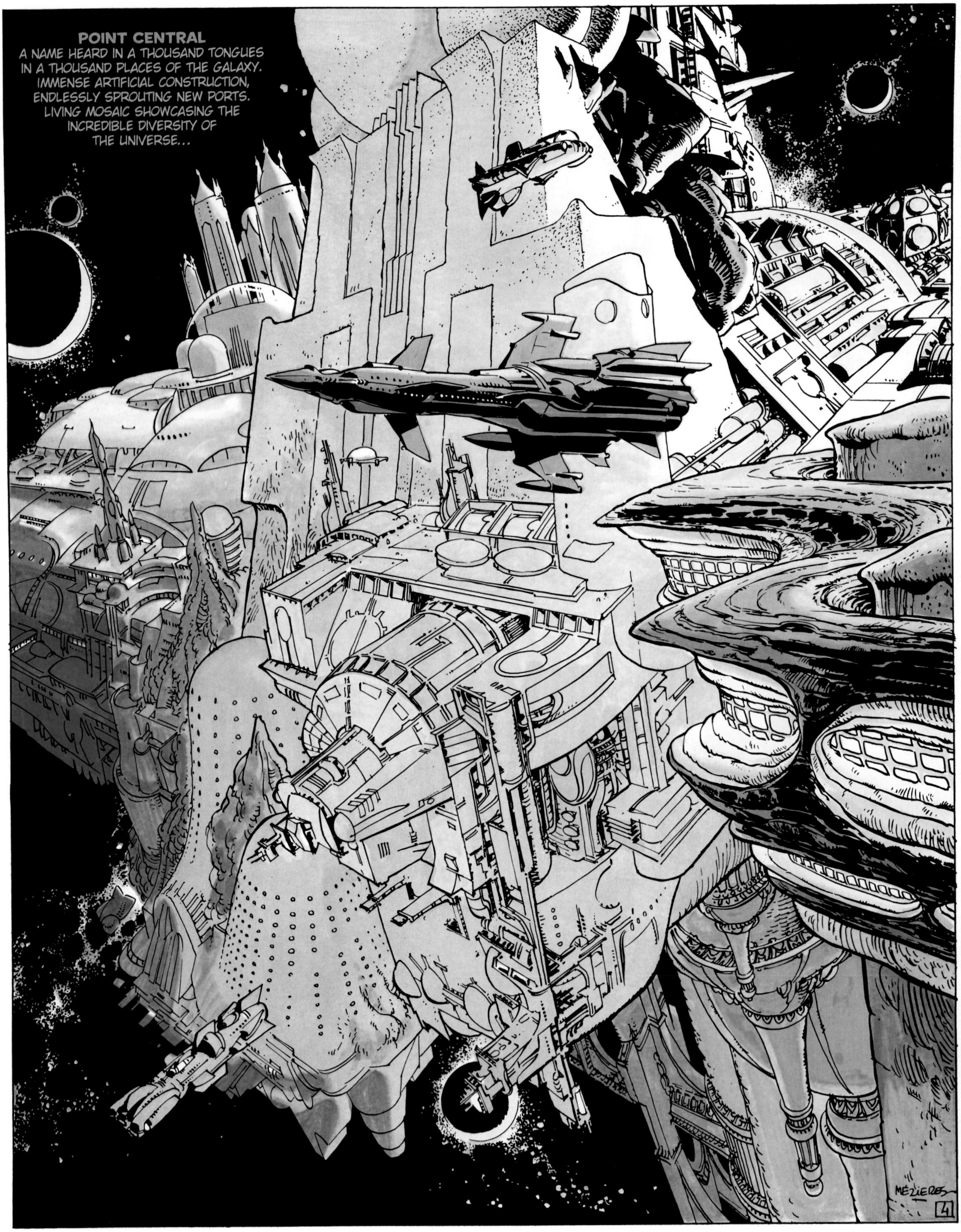
POINT CENTRAL
A NAME HEARD IN A THOUSAND TONGUES IN A THOUSAND PLACES OF THE GALAXY. IMMENSE ARTIFICIAL CONSTRUCTION, ENDLESSLY SPROUTING NEW PORTS. LIVING MOSAIC SHOWCASING THE INCREDIBLE DIVERSITY OF THE UNIVERSE...
MÉZIÈRES
4

NSIDE, AMONG A JUMBLE OF RECONSTITUTED ATMOSPHERES
ND ARTIFICIAL GRAVITIES, SEPARATED BY IMPREGNABLE
VALLS, SPECIES WITH NOTHING IN COMMON COEXIST: THE
ROORS, NATURAL MATHEMATICIANS WHOSE BODIES EXUDE
POISONS DEADLY TO ANY OTHER ORGANISM...

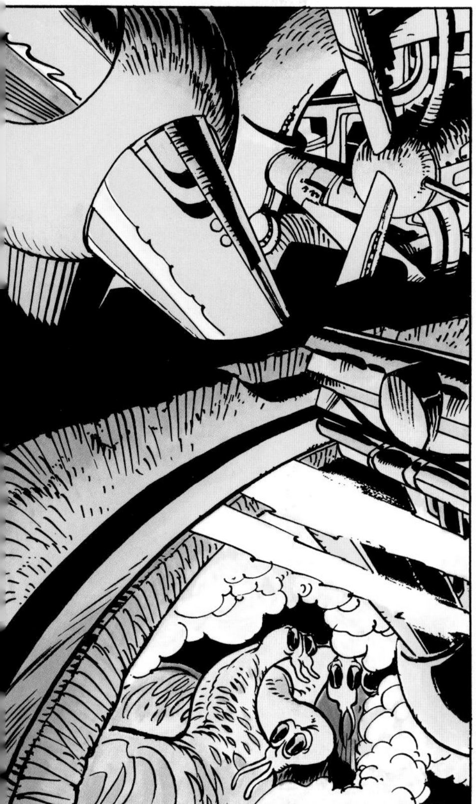

...THE MARMAKAS, FEARED FOR THEIR DREADFUL RADIOACTIVITY BUT FAMED FOR THEIR TALENT AS PSYCHOLOGISTS...

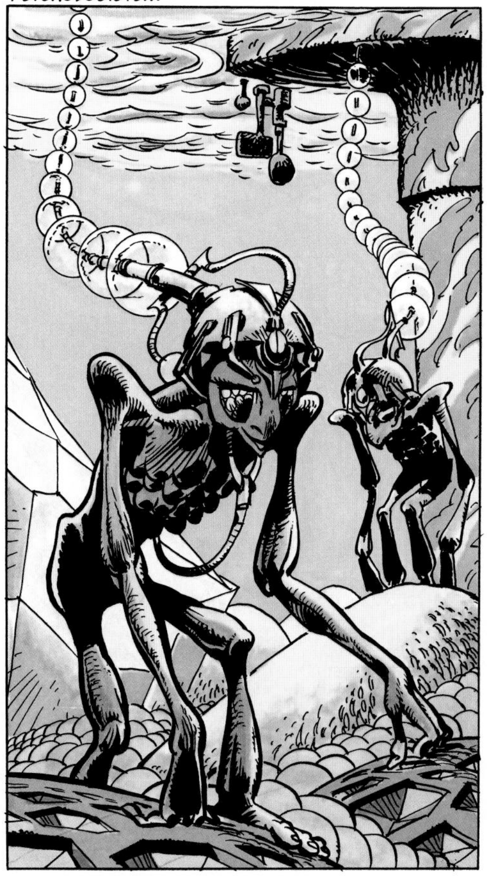

...THE PULPISSIMS, WHOSE FINE PRODUCTS ARE ALL THE RAGE IN MANY A CELL...

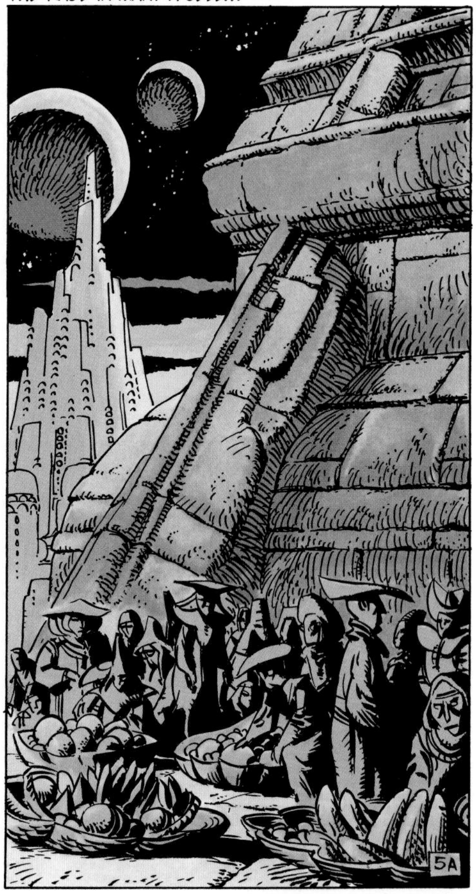
5A

...AND THE TAGLIANS, WHO ARE CONSULTED ON ALL THE THEOLOGICAL DISPUTES OF THE UNIVERSE.

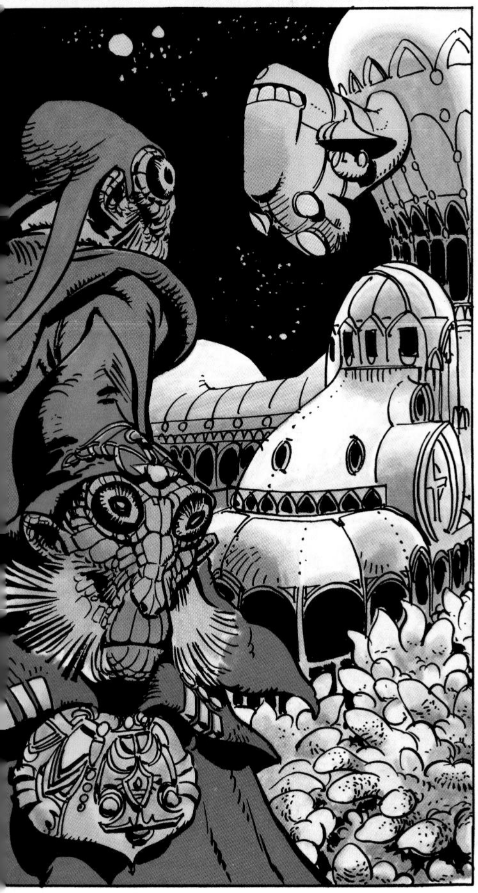

THERE IS NO CENTRAL AUTHORITY ON POINT CENTRAL. AMBASSADORS FROM ALL FOUR CORNERS OF SPACE TAKE TURNS PRESIDING OVER THE COUNCIL FROM THE GIGANTIC HALL OF SCREENS. AND IT'S THERE, IN THE LOW-LIT SILENCE, THAT EVERY CONFLICT TEARING AT THE GALAXY'S HISTORICAL FRAME EVENTUALLY EMERGES.

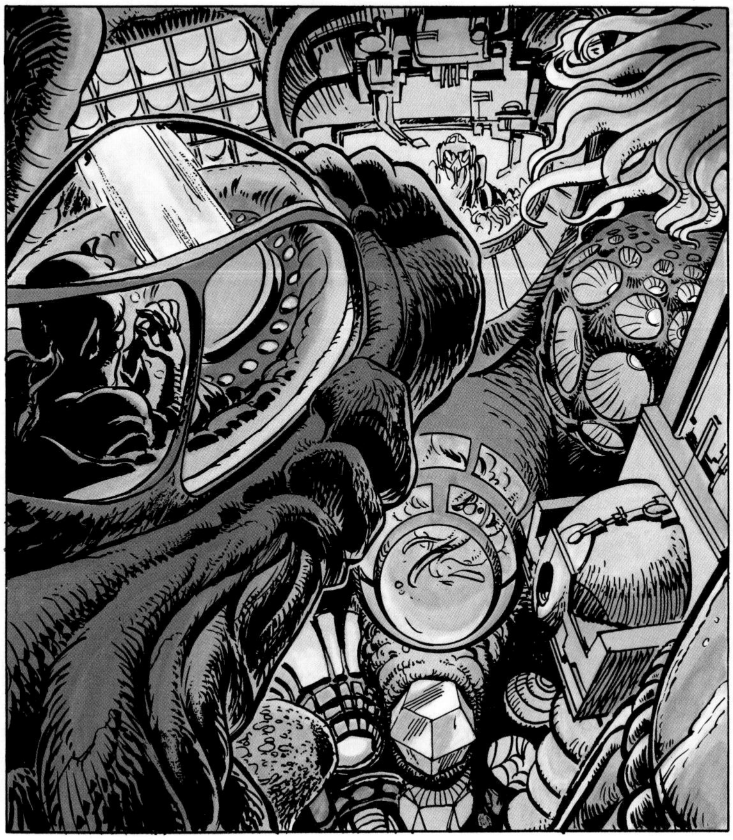

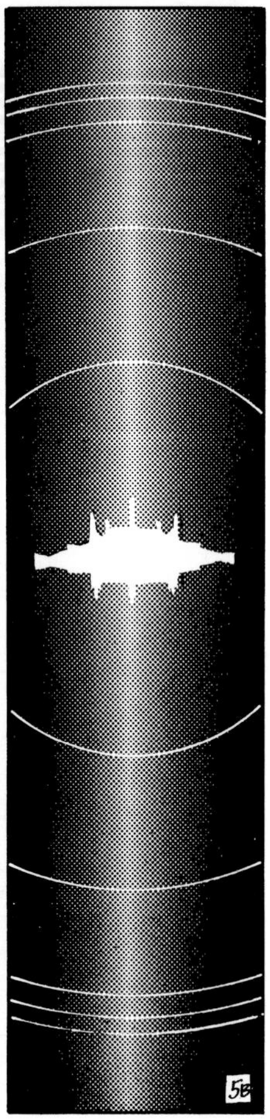
5B

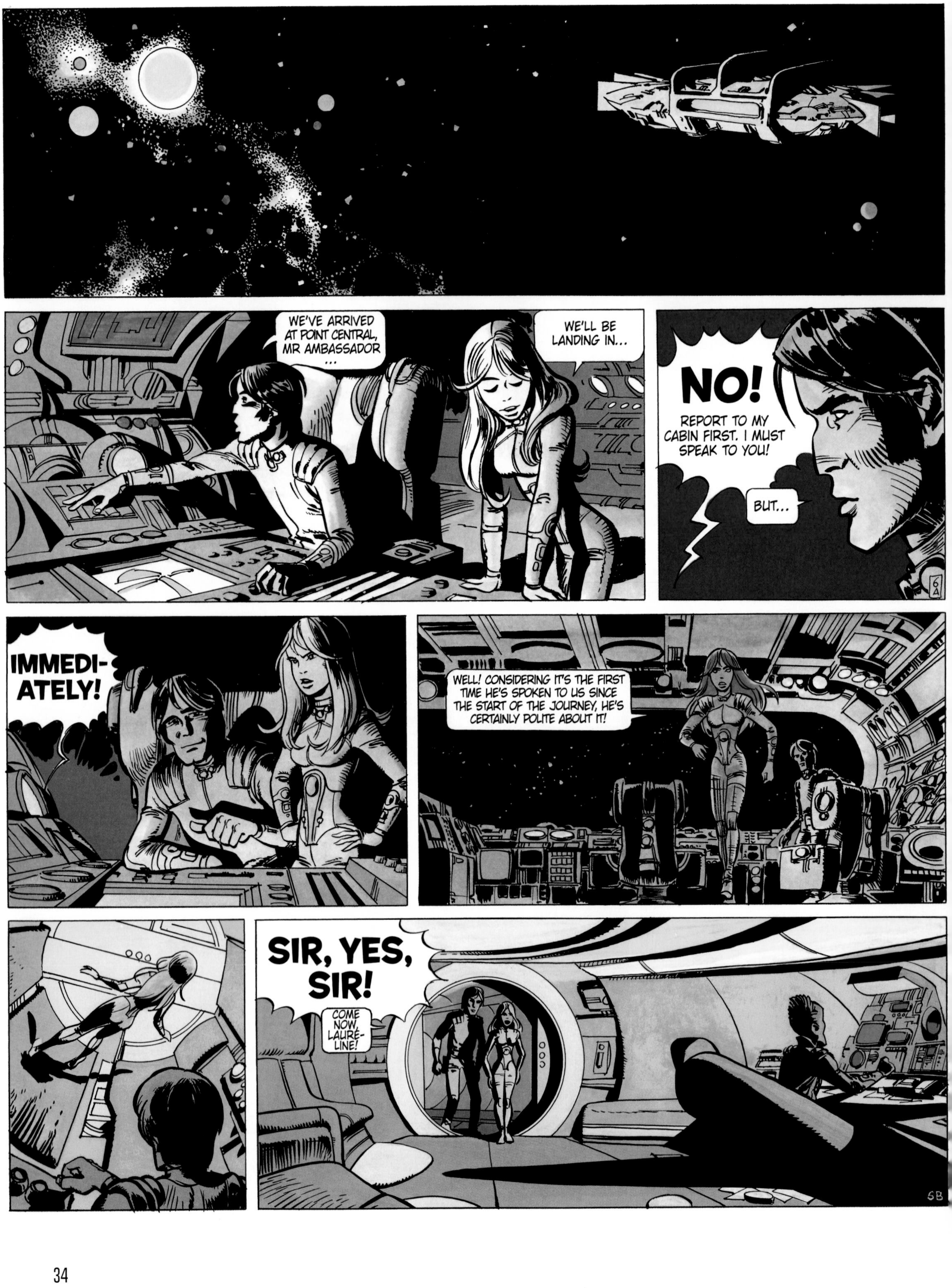
WE'VE ARRIVED AT POINT CENTRAL, MR AMBASSADOR ...
WE'LL BE LANDING IN...
NO!
REPORT TO MY CABIN FIRST. I MUST SPEAK TO YOU!
BUT...
IMMEDI-ATELY!
WELL! CONSIDERING IT'S THE FIRST TIME HE'S SPOKEN TO US SINCE THE START OF THE JOURNEY, HE'S CERTAINLY POLITE ABOUT IT!
SIR, YES, SIR!
COME NOW, LAURÉ-LINE!

DON'T BOTHER, VALERIAN! I'M AWARE OF YOUR REPUTATION, AND IF I CHOSE YOU TWO IT'S NOT OUT OF PERSONAL PREFERENCE...

...IT'S BECAUSE I NEED AGENTS FAMILIAR WITH ALIEN PSYCHES.

AS YOU'RE AWARE, FOR THE FIRST TIME IT'S EARTH'S TURN TO PRESIDE OVER POINT CENTRAL'S COUNCIL. NOW I'M READY TO STRIKE A DECISIVE BLOW! YOU KNOW AS WELL AS I DO HOW INCOHERENT AND CHAOTIC THE ADMINISTRATION OF SPACE IS. WELL, I INTEND TO BRING SOME ORDER TO IT...

WHAT DO YOU MEAN?

NO ONE TOLD US ABOUT THIS BEFORE WE LEFT!

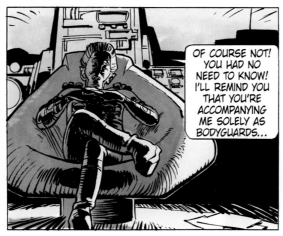

OF COURSE NOT! YOU HAD NO NEED TO KNOW! I'LL REMIND YOU THAT YOU'RE ACCOMPANYING ME SOLELY AS BODYGUARDS...

IN THAT CASE, IF I'M ONLY HERE TO SHIELD YOU WITH MY BODY, I'LL GO AND GRAB MY BLASTER!... NO NEED FOR A SPEECH...

STAY HERE!... AND LISTEN TO ME!

ER... I'M LISTENING, SIR...

HMM!... YES... IT'S IMPOSSIBLE TO TRADE IN PEACE OR TO ORGANISE METHODICAL EXPLORATION MISSIONS. SPACE ROUTES AREN'T SAFE, AND ALL SORTS OF CRANKS HAVE FAILED TO UNDERSTAND THAT THE EMERGENCE OF EARTH MARKED THE DAWN OF A NEW ERA...

OUR TECHNICAL POTENTIAL GIVES US ABSOLUTE SUPREMACY. I AM THEREFORE GOING TO PROPOSE THE CREATION OF A SORT OF FEDERATION, OF WHICH WE WOULD BE THE CORNERSTONE...

...AND THE POLICE!!

SPEAK RATHER OF A CIVILISING MISSION, MY GOOD FELLOW. TRUST ME, THERE ARE NUMEROUS PEOPLE WHO, EVEN UNCONSCIOUSLY, LONG FOR OUR ACTION...

UNCONSCIOUSLY? PFFF...

IT WILL BE A HARD SALE, EVEN THOUGH WE ALREADY HAVE A FEW ALLIES IN PLACE AND ... ER ... SOME EXTERNAL ASSETS!

35

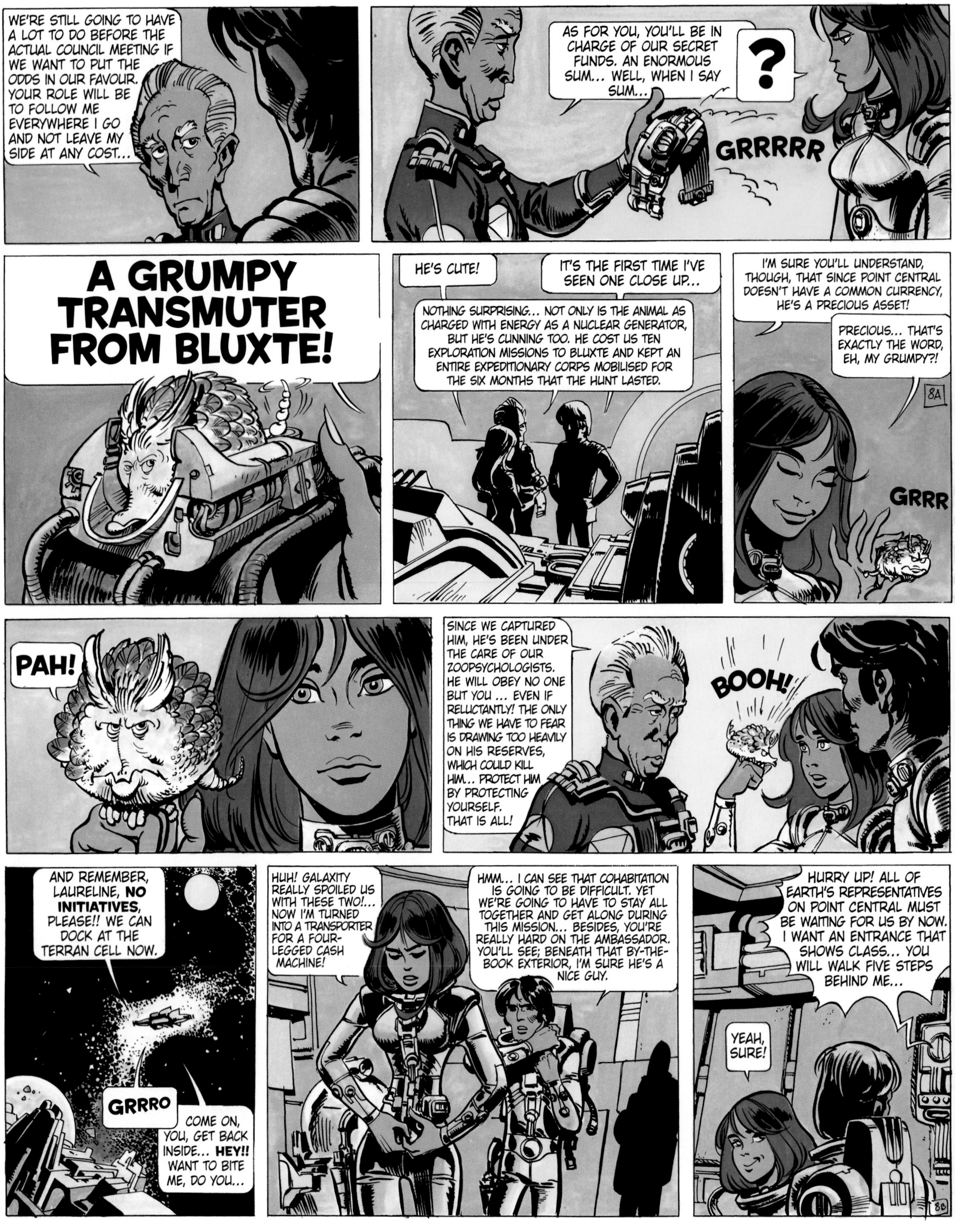
WE'RE STILL GOING TO HAVE A LOT TO DO BEFORE THE ACTUAL COUNCIL MEETING IF WE WANT TO PUT THE ODDS IN OUR FAVOUR. YOUR ROLE WILL BE TO FOLLOW ME EVERYWHERE I GO AND NOT LEAVE MY SIDE AT ANY COST...
AS FOR YOU, YOU'LL BE IN CHARGE OF OUR SECRET FUNDS. AN ENORMOUS SUM... WELL, WHEN I SAY SUM...
?
GRRRRR
A GRUMPY TRANSMUTER FROM BLUXTE!
HE'S CUTE!
IT'S THE FIRST TIME I'VE SEEN ONE CLOSE UP...
NOTHING SURPRISING... NOT ONLY IS THE ANIMAL AS CHARGED WITH ENERGY AS A NUCLEAR GENERATOR, BUT HE'S CUNNING TOO. HE COST US TEN EXPLORATION MISSIONS TO BLUXTE AND KEPT AN ENTIRE EXPEDITIONARY CORPS MOBILISED FOR THE SIX MONTHS THAT THE HUNT LASTED.
I'M SURE YOU'LL UNDERSTAND, THOUGH, THAT SINCE POINT CENTRAL DOESN'T HAVE A COMMON CURRENCY, HE'S A PRECIOUS ASSET!
PRECIOUS... THAT'S EXACTLY THE WORD, EH, MY GRUMPY?!
8A
GRRR
PAH!
SINCE WE CAPTURED HIM, HE'S BEEN UNDER THE CARE OF OUR ZOOPSYCHOLOGISTS. HE WILL OBEY NO ONE BUT YOU ... EVEN IF RELUCTANTLY! THE ONLY THING WE HAVE TO FEAR IS DRAWING TOO HEAVILY ON HIS RESERVES, WHICH COULD KILL HIM... PROTECT HIM BY PROTECTING YOURSELF. THAT IS ALL!
BOOH!
AND REMEMBER, LAURELINE, NO INITIATIVES, PLEASE!! WE CAN DOCK AT THE TERRAN CELL NOW.
GRRRO
COME ON, YOU, GET BACK INSIDE... HEY!! WANT TO BITE ME, DO YOU...
HUH! GALAXITY REALLY SPOILED US WITH THESE TWO!... NOW I'M TURNED INTO A TRANSPORTER FOR A FOUR-LEGGED CASH MACHINE!
HMM... I CAN SEE THAT COHABITATION IS GOING TO BE DIFFICULT. YET WE'RE GOING TO HAVE TO STAY ALL TOGETHER AND GET ALONG DURING THIS MISSION... BESIDES, YOU'RE REALLY HARD ON THE AMBASSADOR. YOU'LL SEE; BENEATH THAT BY-THE-BOOK EXTERIOR, I'M SURE HE'S A NICE GUY.
HURRY UP! ALL OF EARTH'S REPRESENTATIVES ON POINT CENTRAL MUST BE WAITING FOR US BY NOW. I WANT AN ENTRANCE THAT SHOWS CLASS... YOU WILL WALK FIVE STEPS BEHIND ME...
YEAH, SURE!
8B

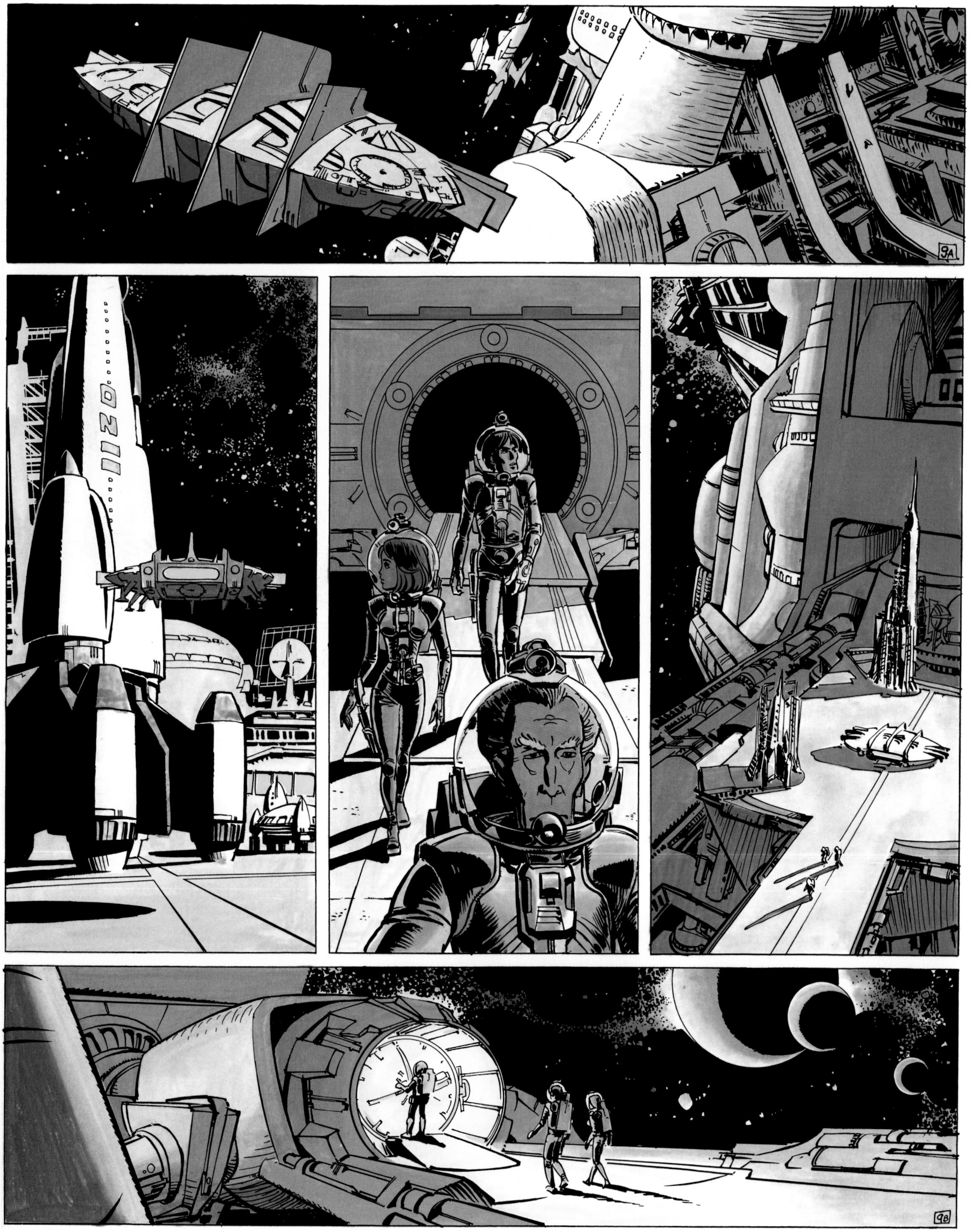

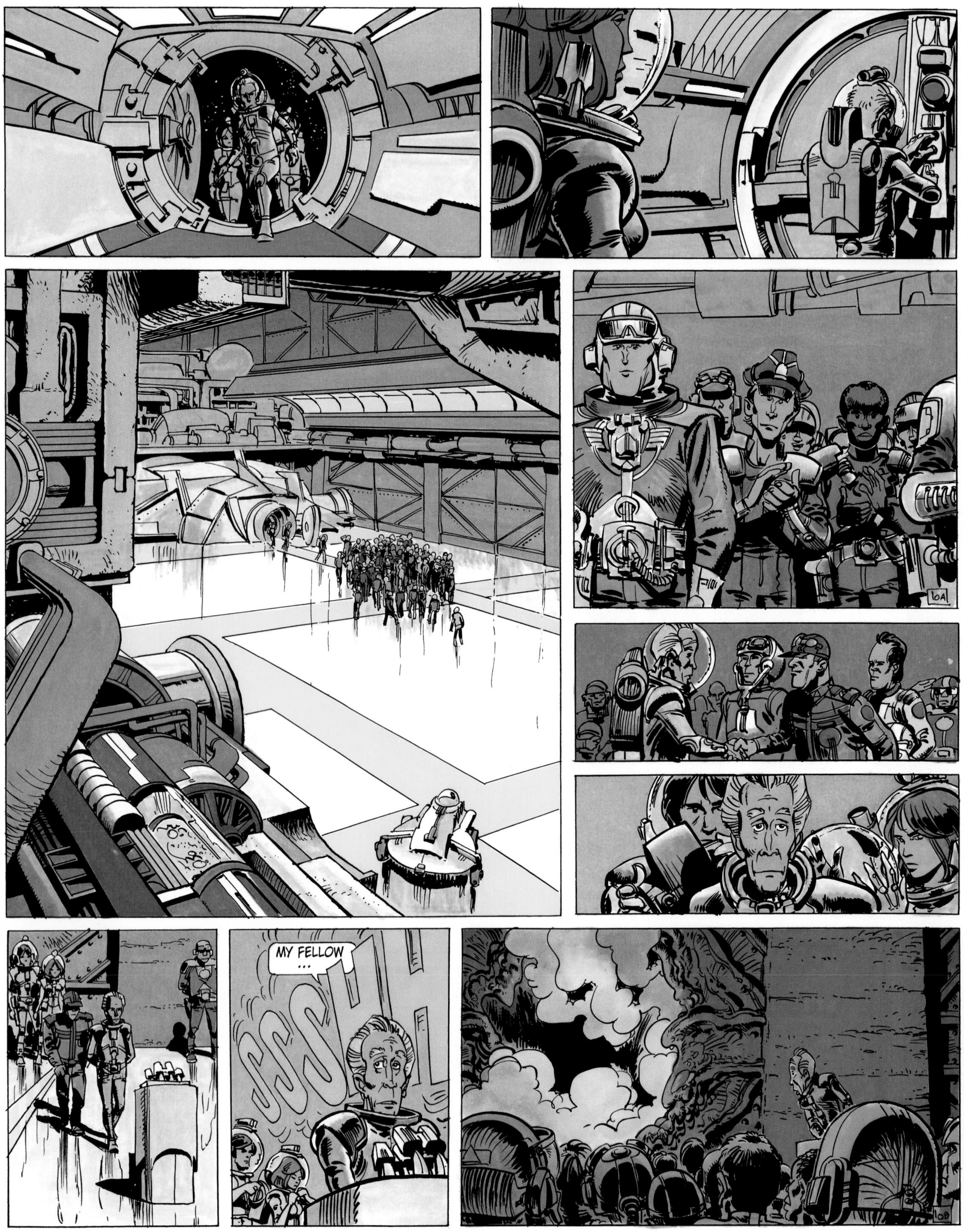
MY FELLOW
...

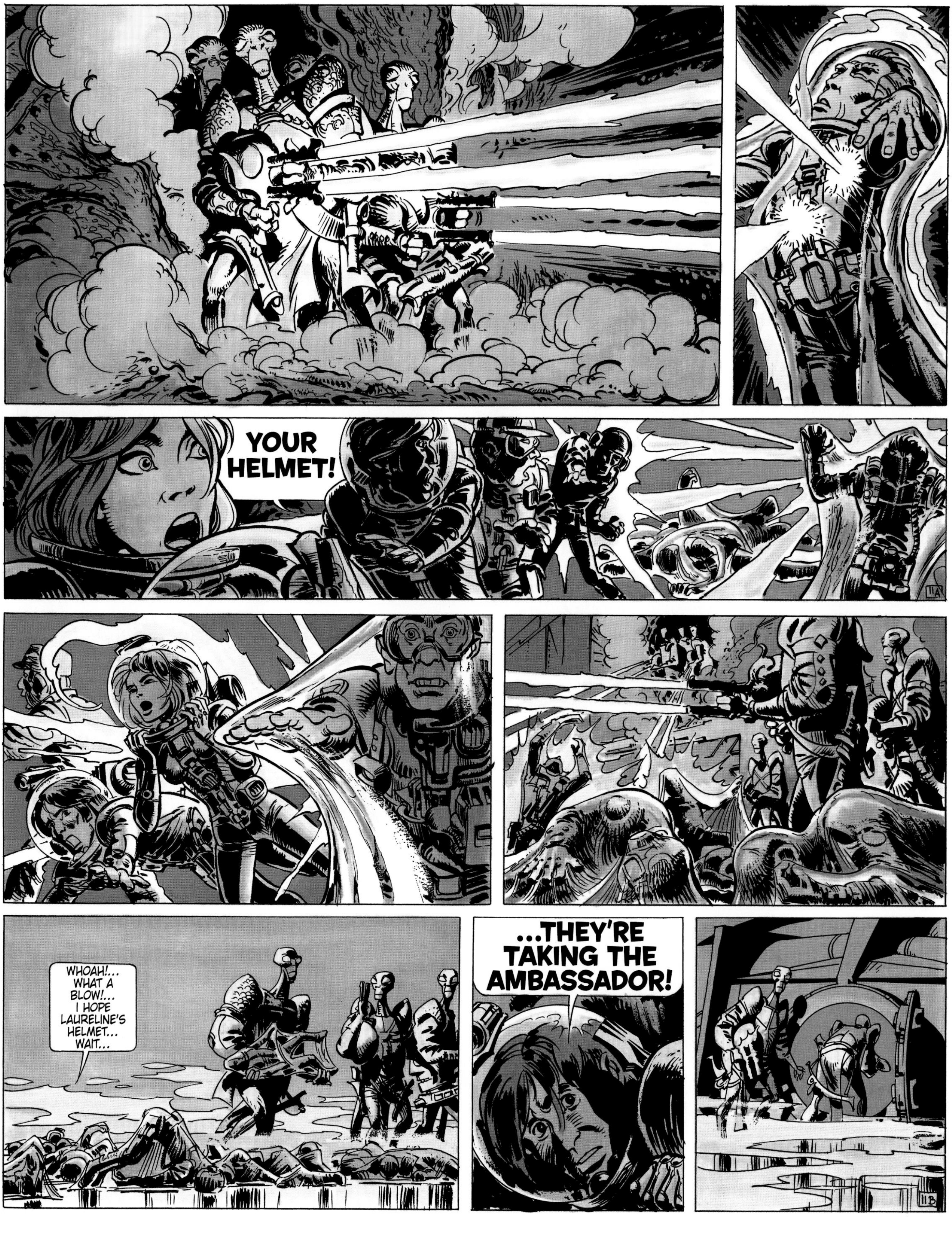
YOUR HELMET!
WHOAH!... WHAT A BLOW!... I HOPE LAURELINE'S HELMET... WAIT...
...THEY'RE TAKING THE AMBASSADOR!
11A
11B

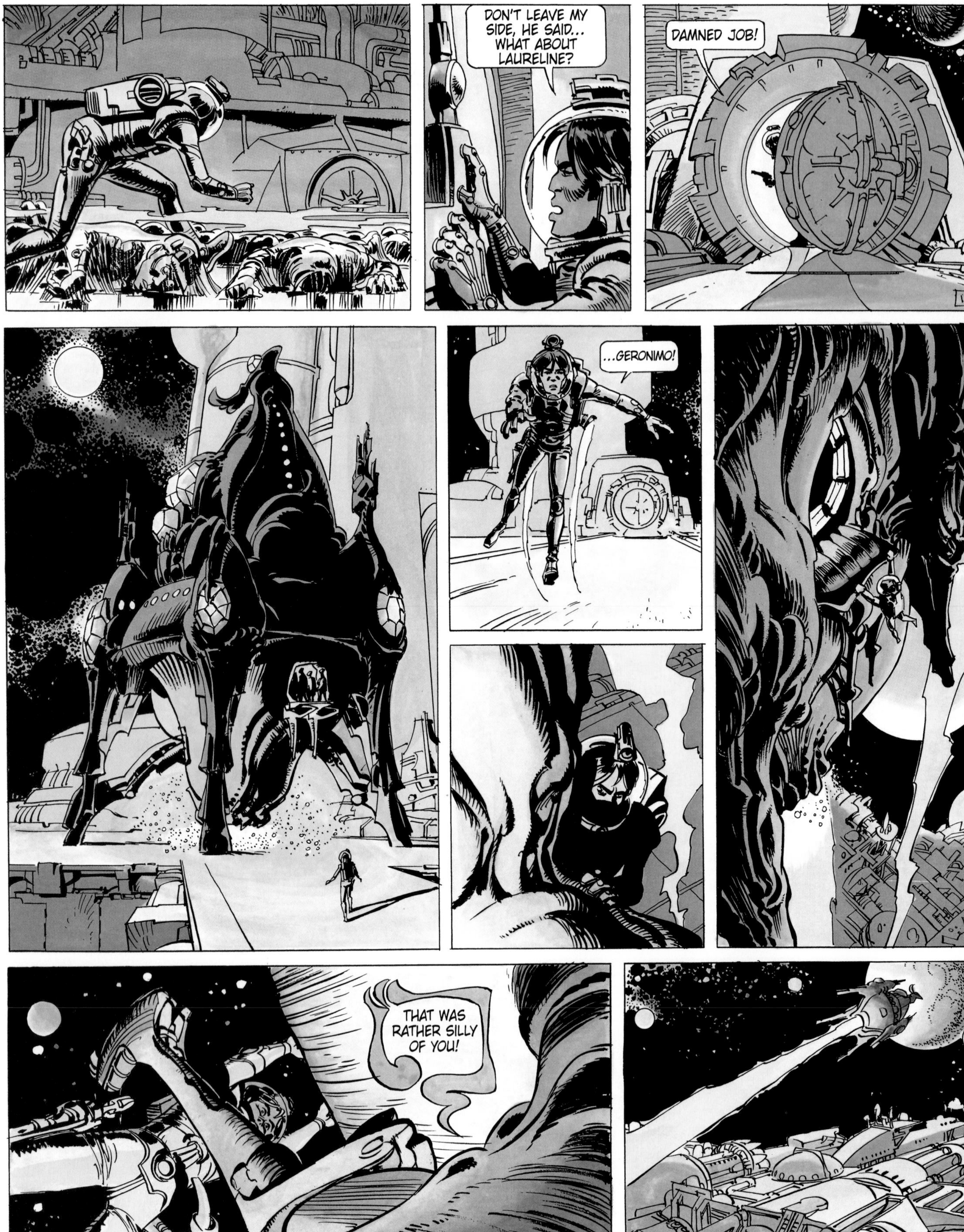
DON'T LEAVE MY SIDE, HE SAID... WHAT ABOUT LAURELINE?
DAMNED JOB!
12A
...GERONIMO!
THAT WAS RATHER SILLY OF YOU!
12C

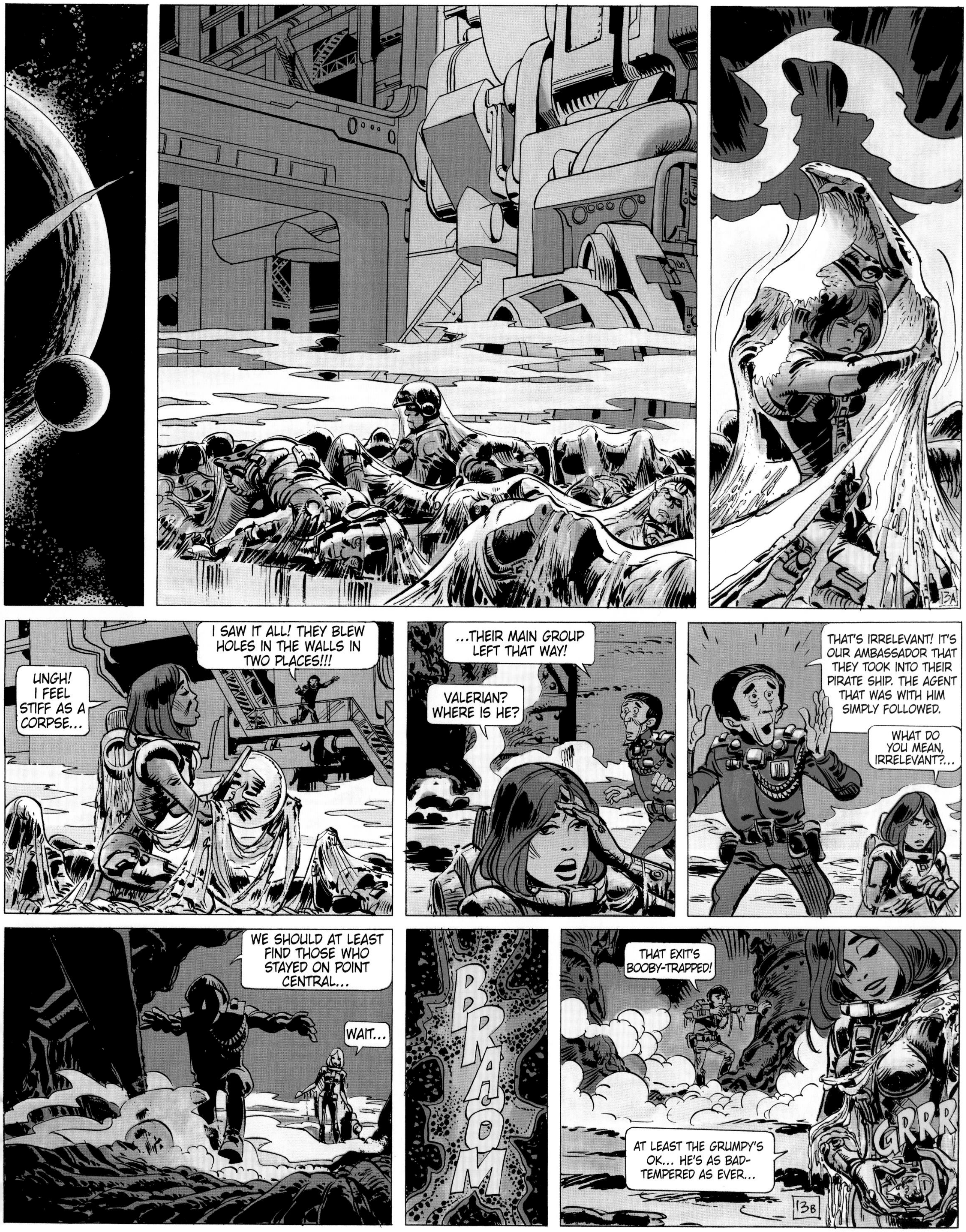

13A
UNGH! I FEEL STIFF AS A CORPSE...
I SAW IT ALL! THEY BLEW HOLES IN THE WALLS IN TWO PLACES!!!
...THEIR MAIN GROUP LEFT THAT WAY!
VALERIAN? WHERE IS HE?
THAT'S IRRELEVANT! IT'S OUR AMBASSADOR THAT THEY TOOK INTO THEIR PIRATE SHIP. THE AGENT THAT WAS WITH HIM SIMPLY FOLLOWED.
WHAT DO YOU MEAN, IRRELEVANT?...
WE SHOULD AT LEAST FIND THOSE WHO STAYED ON POINT CENTRAL...
WAIT...
BRAAOOM
THAT EXIT'S BOOBY-TRAPPED!
GRRR
AT LEAST THE GRUMPY'S OK... HE'S AS BAD-TEMPERED AS EVER...
13B

THE OTHER ONE MAYBE...

WHOA! IT'LL PROBABLY BE THE SAME THING, SO SETTLE DOWN! WHY DON'T YOU TELL ME WHO YOU ARE INSTEAD?...

ER... COLONEL DIOL, UNDER-CHIEF OF PROTOCOL. I WAS IN CHARGE OF WELCOMING THE AMBASSADOR TO THE BUFFET THAT WE PREPARED UPSTAIRS. I'M THE ONLY ONE LEFT... WHAT SHOULD I DO?...

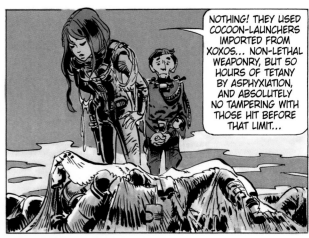

NOTHING! THEY USED COCOON-LAUNCHERS IMPORTED FROM XOXOS... NON-LETHAL WEAPONRY, BUT 50 HOURS OF TETANY BY ASPHYXIATION, AND ABSOLUTELY NO TAMPERING WITH THOSE HIT BEFORE THAT LIMIT...

AND THE SHIP? DO YOU KNOW WHICH DIRECTION IT TOOK?...

ER... DIDN'T THINK ABOUT IT. THE RADAR SCREENS ARE UP THERE... I'LL GO AND EXPLORE THE OTHER PASSAGE...

DO THAT.

BAM

THAT PASSAGE WAS BOOBY-TRAPPED TOO!

REALLY?... THAT PROVES THEY THOUGHT OF EVERYTHING AT ANY RATE: THEY EVEN HID EVERY TRACE OF THEIR DEPARTURE BY PLACING THEMSELVES UNDER AN ANTI-RADAR CLOAK... THEY LEFT NO CLUE...

THE AMBASSADOR... LOST... WHAT A DISASTER!!

DO YOU HAVE ANY IDEA WHO THE ATTACKERS WERE?

NONE! THERE ARE THOUSAND OF SPECIES ON POINT CENTRAL, AND MY JOB'S ORGANISING RECEPTIONS... MY BEAUTIFUL RECEPTION!... EVERYTHING WAS READY FOR THE AMBASSADOR!!!

WE HAVE TO TELL EARTH! CALL IN THE MILITARY!!!... BECAUSE ... POINT CENTRAL...

WHAT DO YOU ... CRUNCH ... MEAN?...

BAH! IT'S COMPLETE ANARCHY! NO ONE KNOWS ANYTHING ABOUT ANYTHING! EVERYWHERE IT'S A FREE-FOR-ALL... ONLY THE COUNCIL HAS A MEASURE OF POWER, BUT SINCE THERE WON'T BE A COUNCIL MEETING UNLESS WE FIND THE AMBASSADOR...

YES... I WONDER ... MUNCH ... WHAT...

BUZZZ

IT'S THEM! THEY'RE BACK! LET'S HIDE!...

YEAH, RIGHT! AND THEY'D POLITELY KNOCK ON THE DOOR OF THE MAIN HATCH?... BESIDES, LOOK...

WE'RE EXPECTED...

...THESE ONES ARE COMPLETELY DIFFERENT... WHY DON'T YOU SHOW ME HOW TO OPEN THE HATCH?...

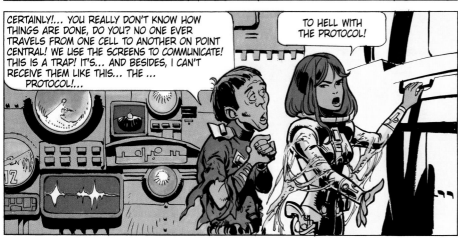

CERTAINLY!... YOU REALLY DON'T KNOW HOW THINGS ARE DONE, DO YOU? NO ONE EVER TRAVELS FROM ONE CELL TO ANOTHER ON POINT CENTRAL! WE USE THE SCREENS TO COMMUNICATE! THIS IS A TRAP! IT'S... AND BESIDES, I CAN'T RECEIVE THEM LIKE THIS... THE ... PROTOCOL!...

TO HELL WITH THE PROTOCOL!

43

DO YOU REPRESENT EARTH?...

ER, YES...

NO, NO...

IS IT YES OR NO?... BECAUSE WE'VE RECEIVED PROMISES...

YOU DON'T KNOW WHO WE ARE?... THE SHINGOUZ...

WE HAD A MEETING WITH THE AMBASSADOR TO SELL HIM SOME BITS OF INFORMATION... IS HE AROUND?...

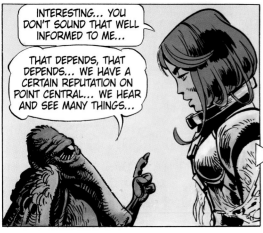

INTERESTING... YOU DON'T SOUND THAT WELL INFORMED TO ME...

THAT DEPENDS, THAT DEPENDS... WE HAVE A CERTAIN REPUTATION ON POINT CENTRAL... WE HEAR AND SEE MANY THINGS...

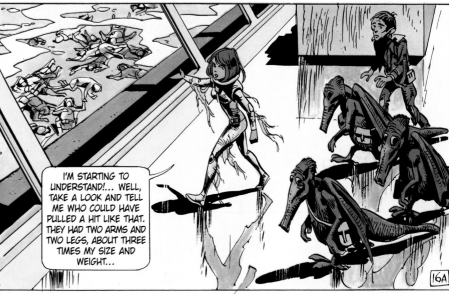

I'M STARTING TO UNDERSTAND!... WELL, TAKE A LOOK AND TELL ME WHO COULD HAVE PULLED A HIT LIKE THAT. THEY HAD TWO ARMS AND TWO LEGS, ABOUT THREE TIMES MY SIZE AND WEIGHT...

16A

BY THE TEN PURPLE MOONS! XOXOS COCOONS!! NEVER SEEN ANYTHING LIKE IT ON POINT CENTRAL!

AND THE ATTACK-ERS?...

BIG, TWO ARMS, TWO LEGS... YOU DON'T REALISE – THAT COULD BE ANYBODY...

MERCENARIES, PROBABLY, TO BE USING SUCH METHODS! NONE OF THE MAJOR SPECIES WOULD WANT TO BE MIXED UP IN THIS...

FOR 1,000 EBEBE PEARLS LIKE THIS ONE...

A THOUSAND EBEBE PEARLS?! IS THAT ALL?!

WHEN YOU'RE LUCKY ENOUGH TO OWN A TRANSMUTER, YOU SHOULDN'T BE STINGY... BESIDES, OUR INFORMATION IS WELL WORTH IT!

GRRR

IT'S NOT THE ONE WE CAME HERE TO SELL YOU, BUT IT'S STILL A GOOD PIECE OF INFORMATION FOR YOU, SINCE YOUR AMBASSADOR OBVIOUSLY DIDN'T SHARE ALL HIS BUSINESS WITH YOU...

...THIS HIT IS TOO RECENT FOR US TO KNOW WHO DID IT. BUT EARTH HAS SOME SECRET ALLIES, MERCENARIES THEMSELVES. SUCH PEOPLE KNOW EACH OTHER... YOU KNOW HOW IT IS: YOU WORK FOR ONE SIDE, THEN FOR ANOTHER...

HEEHEE

16B

BOOH

MORF
MORF
MORF

I'M LISTENING...

GO AND SEE THE KAMLINIKS! IF THOSE WARRIOR PEOPLE PLACED THEMSELVES IN THE SERVICE OF EARTH, IT'S BECAUSE THEY HAVE GREAT NEEDS...

THEY'LL TALK... IF YOU PAY THE PRICE.

HOW CAN I CONTACT THEM DISCREETLY?

ANOTHER 500 PEARLS...

...WILL BUY YOU A MAP OF POINT CENTRAL — VERY RARE...

YOU'RE WELL EQUIPPED! AND DRIVE A HARD BARGAIN TOO...

WHAT CAN I SAY? WE COME FROM A POOR PLANET AND LIFE IS DEAR ON POINT CENTRAL! YOU'VE GOT TO KNOW HOW TO SELL YOUR SKILLS...

SO, INTERESTED?

FIVE HUNDRED PEARLS! A STEAL...

THE KAMLINIKS ARE HERE!

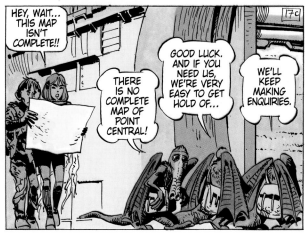

HEY, WAIT... THIS MAP ISN'T COMPLETE!!

THERE IS NO COMPLETE MAP OF POINT CENTRAL!

GOOD LUCK. AND IF YOU NEED US, WE'RE VERY EASY TO GET HOLD OF...

WE'LL KEEP MAKING ENQUIRIES.

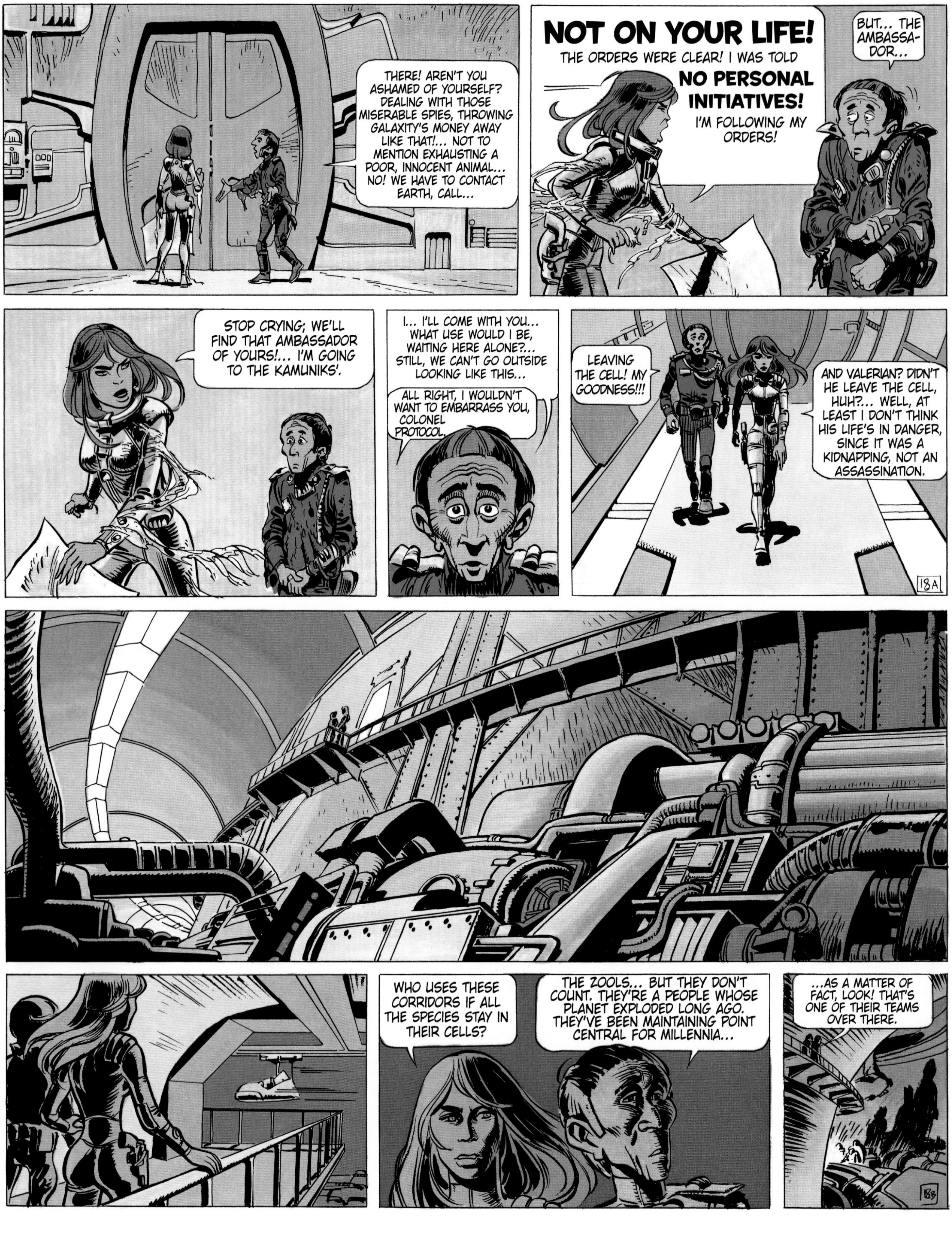
THERE! AREN'T YOU ASHAMED OF YOURSELF? DEALING WITH THOSE MISERABLE SPIES, THROWING GALAXITY'S MONEY AWAY LIKE THAT!... NOT TO MENTION EXHAUSTING A POOR, INNOCENT ANIMAL... NO! WE HAVE TO CONTACT EARTH, CALL...
NOT ON YOUR LIFE! THE ORDERS WERE CLEAR! I WAS TOLD NO PERSONAL INITIATIVES! I'M FOLLOWING MY ORDERS!
BUT... THE AMBASSADOR...
STOP CRYING; WE'LL FIND THAT AMBASSADOR OF YOURS!... I'M GOING TO THE KAMUNIKS'.
I... I'LL COME WITH YOU... WHAT USE WOULD I BE, WAITING HERE ALONE?... STILL, WE CAN'T GO OUTSIDE LOOKING LIKE THIS...
ALL RIGHT, I WOULDN'T WANT TO EMBARRASS YOU, COLONEL PROTOCOL.
LEAVING THE CELL! MY GOODNESS!!!
AND VALERIAN? DIDN'T HE LEAVE THE CELL, HUH?... WELL, AT LEAST I DON'T THINK HIS LIFE'S IN DANGER, SINCE IT WAS A KIDNAPPING, NOT AN ASSASSINATION.
18A
WHO USES THESE CORRIDORS IF ALL THE SPECIES STAY IN THEIR CELLS?
THE ZOOLS... BUT THEY DON'T COUNT. THEY'RE A PEOPLE WHOSE PLANET EXPLODED LONG AGO. THEY'VE BEEN MAINTAINING POINT CENTRAL FOR MILLENNIA...
...AS A MATTER OF FACT, LOOK! THAT'S ONE OF THEIR TEAMS OVER THERE.
18B

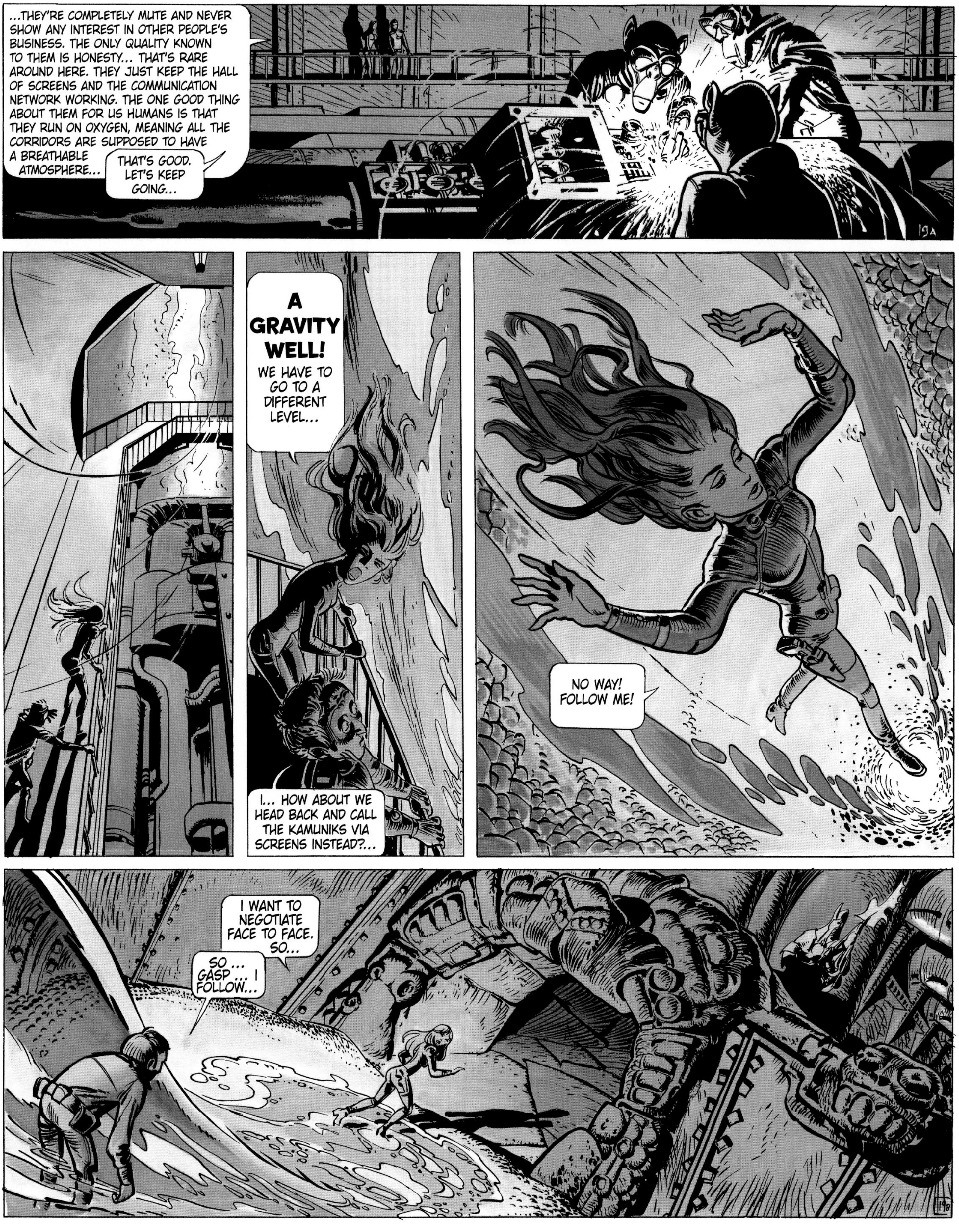

...THEY'RE COMPLETELY MUTE AND NEVER SHOW ANY INTEREST IN OTHER PEOPLE'S BUSINESS. THE ONLY QUALITY KNOWN TO THEM IS HONESTY... THAT'S RARE AROUND HERE. THEY JUST KEEP THE HALL OF SCREENS AND THE COMMUNICATION NETWORK WORKING. THE ONE GOOD THING ABOUT THEM FOR US HUMANS IS THAT THEY RUN ON OXYGEN, MEANING ALL THE CORRIDORS ARE SUPPOSED TO HAVE A BREATHABLE ATMOSPHERE...
THAT'S GOOD. LET'S KEEP GOING...
A GRAVITY WELL! WE HAVE TO GO TO A DIFFERENT LEVEL...
I... HOW ABOUT WE HEAD BACK AND CALL THE KAMUNIKS VIA SCREENS INSTEAD?...
NO WAY! FOLLOW ME!
I WANT TO NEGOTIATE FACE TO FACE. SO...
SO... GASP... I FOLLOW...

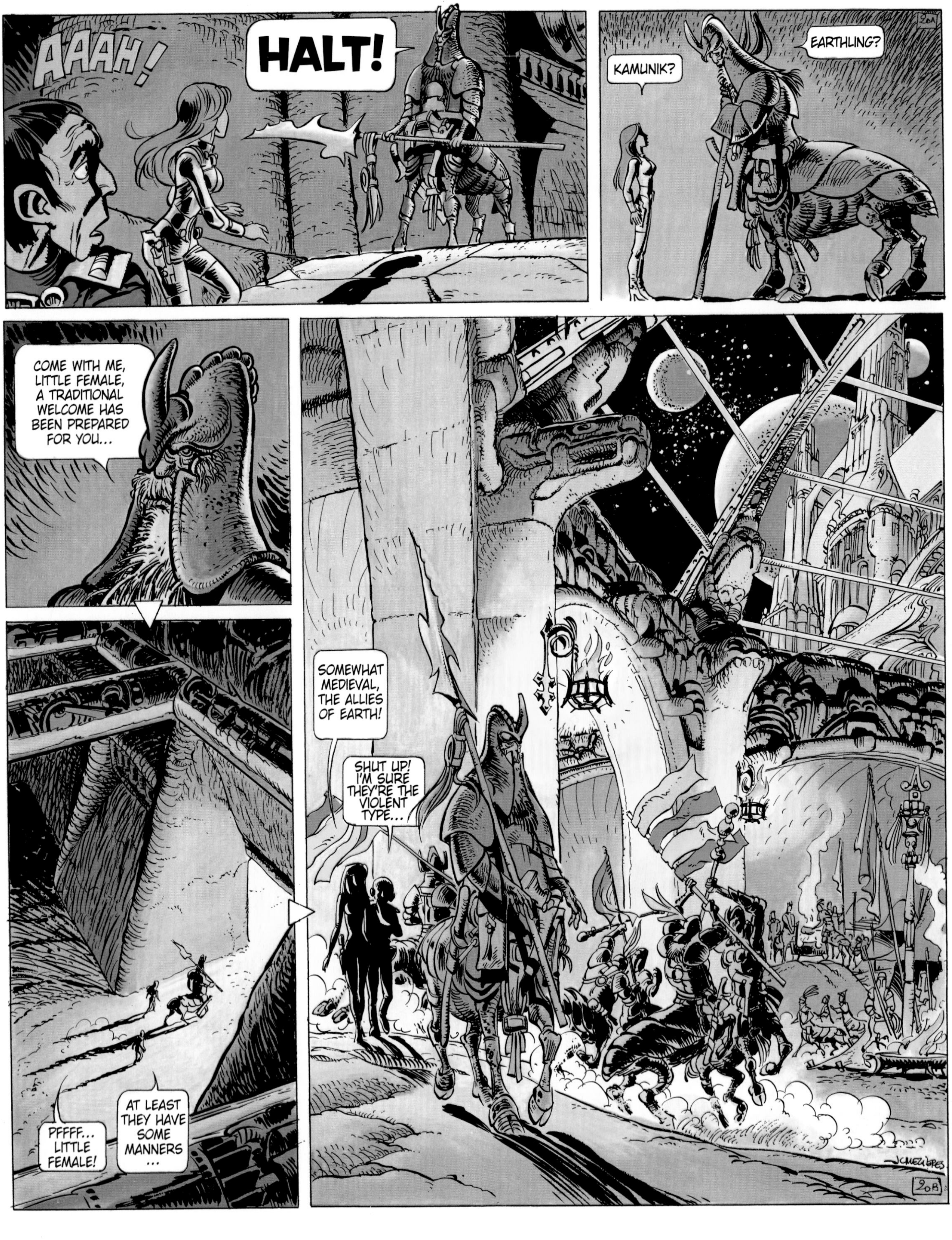

AAAH!
HALT!
KAMUNIK?
EARTHLING?
COME WITH ME, LITTLE FEMALE, A TRADITIONAL WELCOME HAS BEEN PREPARED FOR YOU...
PFFFF... LITTLE FEMALE!
AT LEAST THEY HAVE SOME MANNERS ...
SOMEWHAT MEDIEVAL, THE ALLIES OF EARTH!
SHUT UP! I'M SURE THEY'RE THE VIOLENT TYPE...

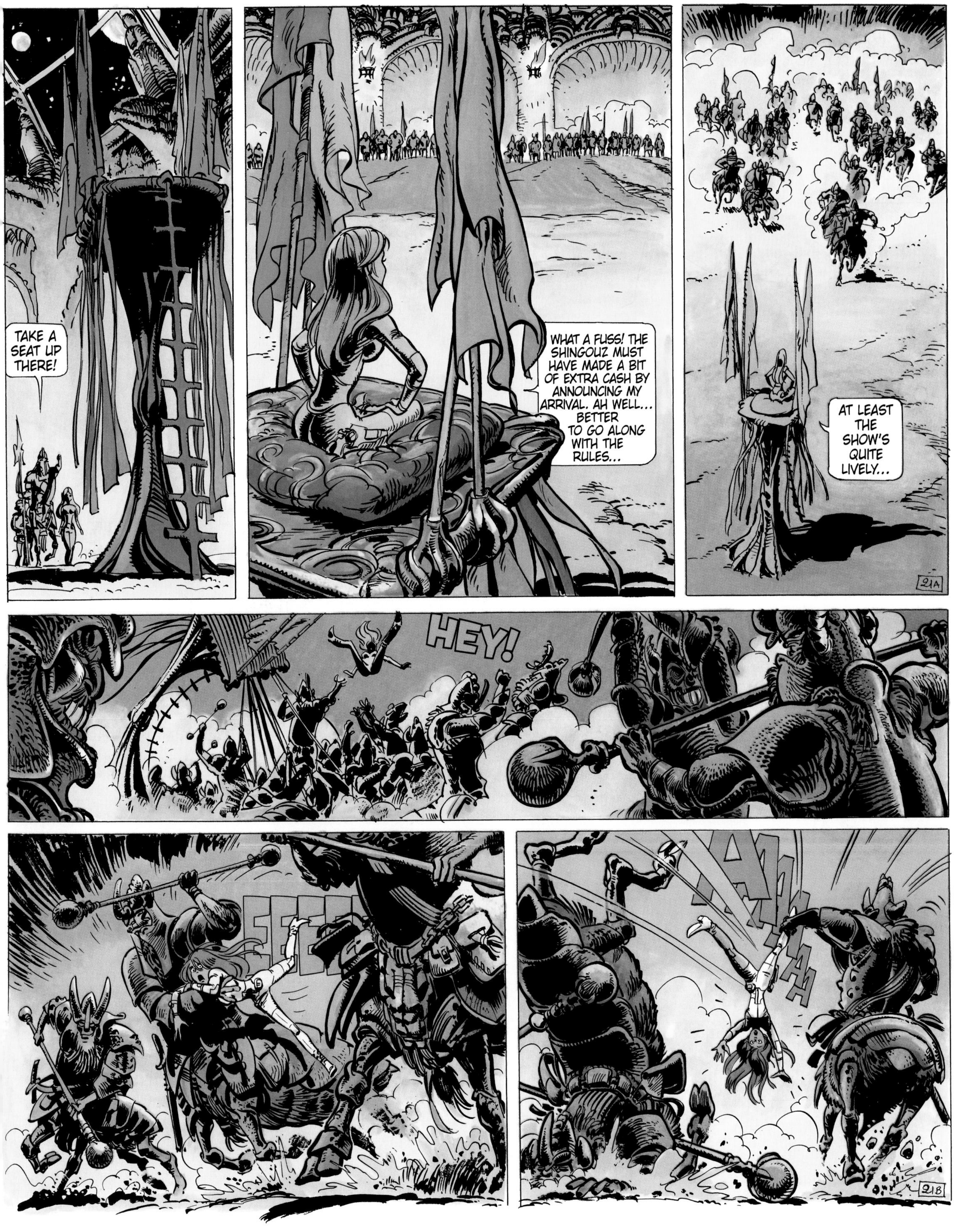
TAKE A SEAT UP THERE!
WHAT A FUSS! THE SHINGOUZ MUST HAVE MADE A BIT OF EXTRA CASH BY ANNOUNCING MY ARRIVAL. AH WELL... BETTER TO GO ALONG WITH THE RULES...
AT LEAST THE SHOW'S QUITE LIVELY...
21A
HEY!
21B

HERE'S THE GUEST!

COMPLIMENTS, BALDOUR! STILL THE BEST!

SO, WHAT DID YOU COME HERE FOR?

GOOD QUES- TION...

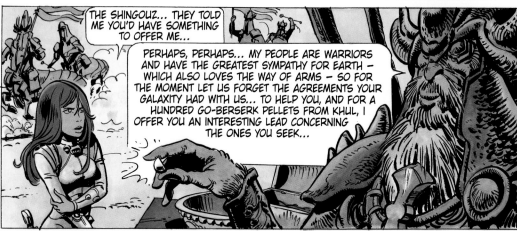

THE SHINGOUZ... THEY TOLD ME YOU'D HAVE SOMETHING TO OFFER ME...

PERHAPS, PERHAPS... MY PEOPLE ARE WARRIORS AND HAVE THE GREATEST SYMPATHY FOR EARTH – WHICH ALSO LOVES THE WAY OF ARMS – SO FOR THE MOMENT LET US FORGET THE AGREEMENTS YOUR GALAXY HAD WITH US... TO HELP YOU, AND FOR A HUNDRED GO-BERSERK PELLETS FROM KHUL, I OFFER YOU AN INTERESTING LEAD CONCERNING THE ONES YOU SEEK...

HMM! THAT CAN BE ARRANGED... COME HERE, GRUMPY, YOU'RE NEEDED...

GRRR

HEY?! OUCH!

YOU! NOW'S NOT THE TIME TO MESS WITH ME! GET IT?...

SWALLOW THIS AND GET TO WORK!

BAH!

I'M LISTENING...

AT THE SUFFLISS... ONE OF MY WARRIORS BACK FROM SEEING THEM TOLD ME ABOUT MANY BAGULINS FLOCKING THERE... BAGULINS AREN'T REAL WARRIORS, JUST BONEHEADED HERD ANIMALS, THUGS FOR DOING THE DIRTY WORK. THE KIND THAT WOULD USE XOXOS COCOON-LAUNCHERS ... IF YOU SEE WHAT I MEAN...

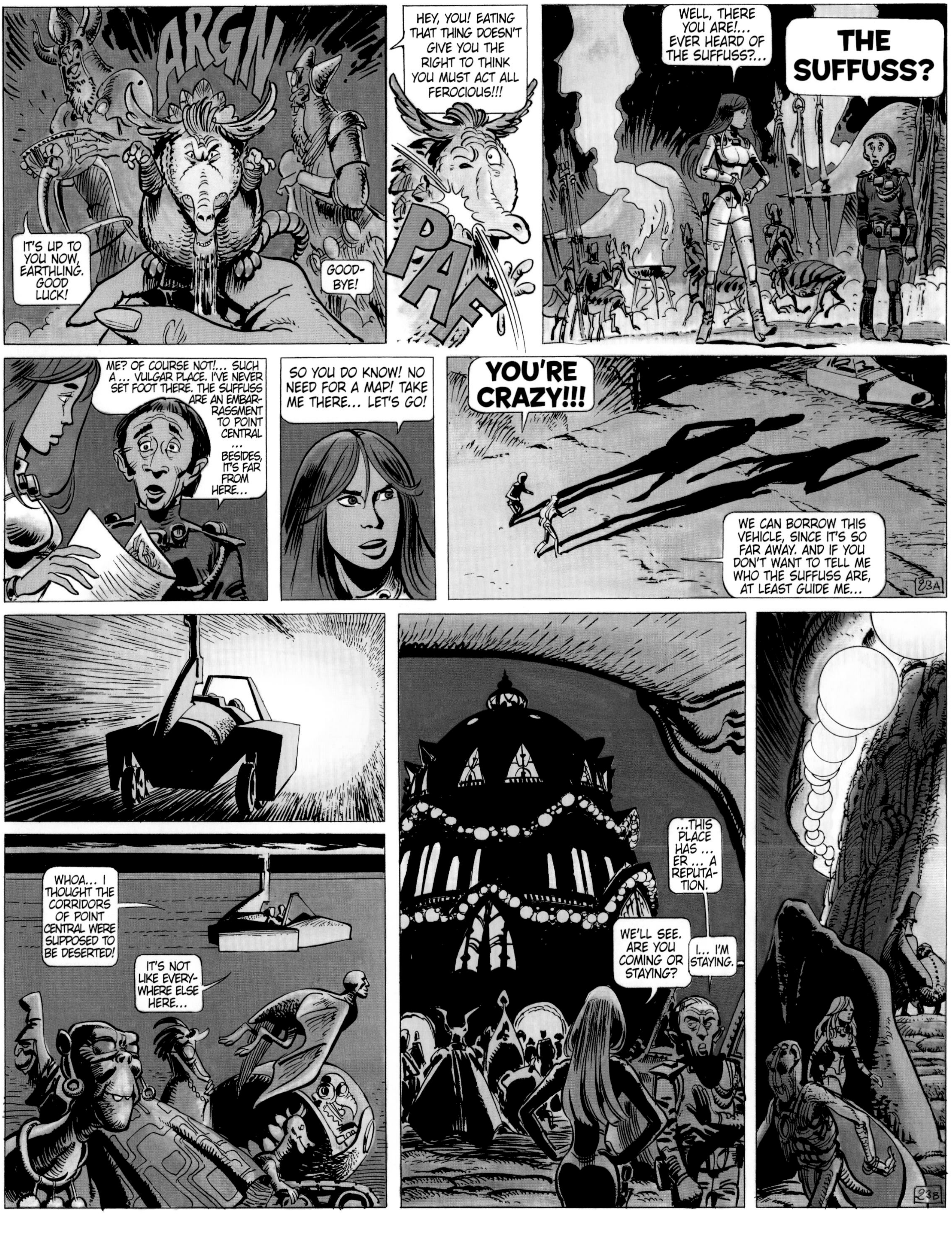
ARGN
IT'S UP TO YOU NOW, EARTHLING. GOOD LUCK!
GOOD-BYE!
HEY, YOU! EATING THAT THING DOESN'T GIVE YOU THE RIGHT TO THINK YOU MUST ACT ALL FEROCIOUS!!!
PAF
WELL, THERE YOU ARE!... EVER HEARD OF THE SUFFUSS?...
THE SUFFUSS?
ME? OF COURSE NOT!... SUCH A ... VULGAR PLACE. I'VE NEVER SET FOOT THERE. THE SUFFUSS ARE AN EMBARRASSMENT TO POINT CENTRAL ... BESIDES, IT'S FAR FROM HERE...
SO YOU DO KNOW! NO NEED FOR A MAP! TAKE ME THERE... LET'S GO!
YOU'RE CRAZY!!!
WE CAN BORROW THIS VEHICLE, SINCE IT'S SO FAR AWAY. AND IF YOU DON'T WANT TO TELL ME WHO THE SUFFUSS ARE, AT LEAST GUIDE ME...
23A
WHOA... I THOUGHT THE CORRIDORS OF POINT CENTRAL WERE SUPPOSED TO BE DESERTED!
IT'S NOT LIKE EVERYWHERE ELSE HERE...
...THIS PLACE HAS ... ER ... A REPUTATION.
WE'LL SEE. ARE YOU COMING OR STAYING?
I... I'M STAYING.
23B

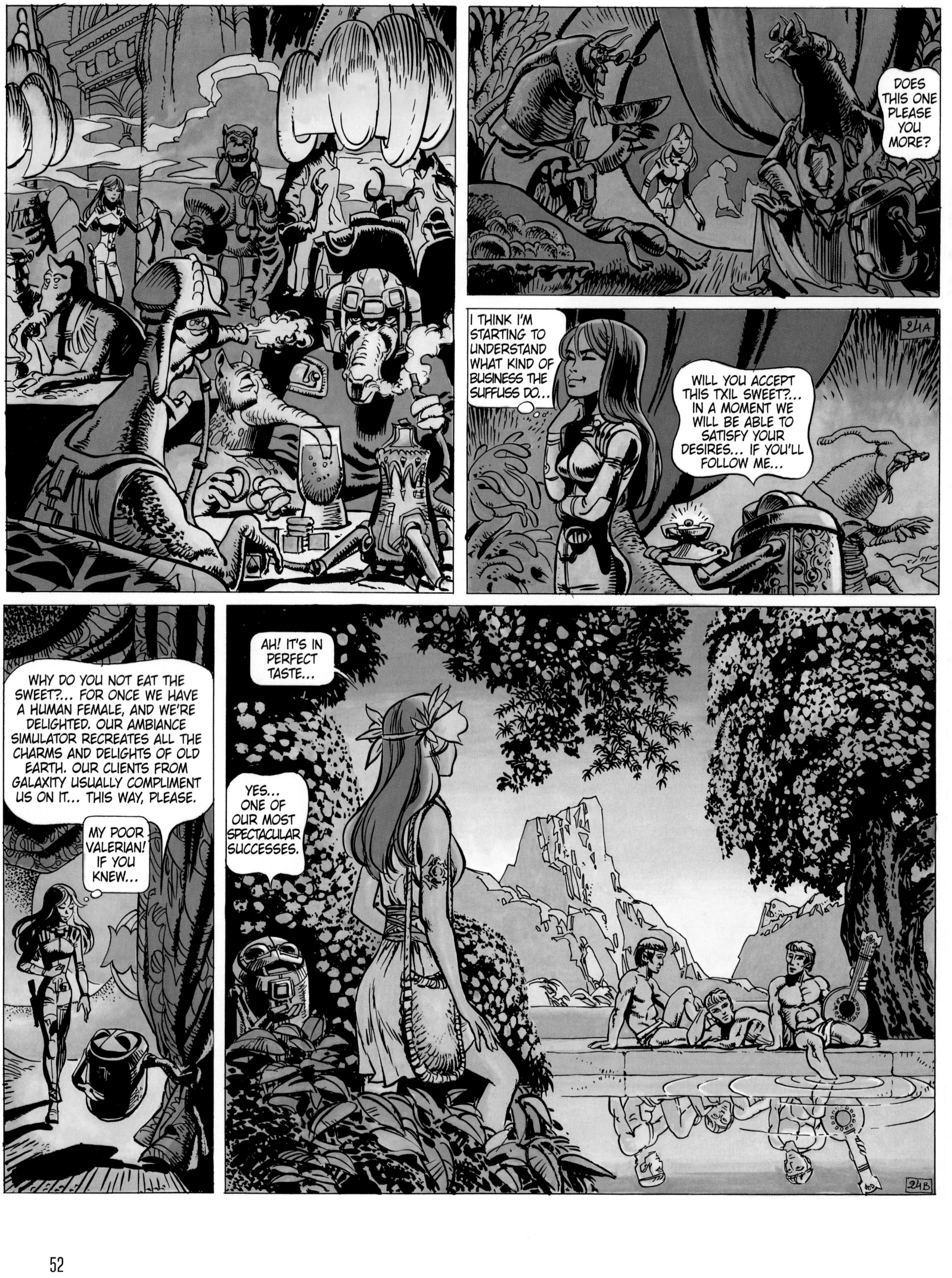
DOES THIS ONE PLEASE YOU MORE?
I THINK I'M STARTING TO UNDERSTAND WHAT KIND OF BUSINESS THE SUFFUSS DO...
WILL YOU ACCEPT THIS TXIL SWEET?... IN A MOMENT WE WILL BE ABLE TO SATISFY YOUR DESIRES... IF YOU'LL FOLLOW ME...
24A
WHY DO YOU NOT EAT THE SWEET?... FOR ONCE WE HAVE A HUMAN FEMALE, AND WE'RE DELIGHTED. OUR AMBIANCE SIMULATOR RECREATES ALL THE CHARMS AND DELIGHTS OF OLD EARTH. OUR CLIENTS FROM GALAXITY USUALLY COMPLIMENT US ON IT... THIS WAY, PLEASE.
MY POOR VALERIAN! IF YOU KNEW...
AH! IT'S IN PERFECT TASTE...
YES... ONE OF OUR MOST SPECTACULAR SUCCESSES.
24B

MAYBE IF I HAD SOME FREE TIME...

HMM...

WHERE... WHERE DID MY GUN GO WITH ALL THIS? AH, HERE IT IS...

BUT DON'T YOU KNOW THAT THE SUFFUSS CELL IS NEUTRAL TERRITORY?

NEVER MIND THAT... I DIDN'T COME HERE LOOKING FOR ILLUSIONS!

LET'S GET OUT OF THIS MAS-QUERADE.

FINE. IF YOU INSIST...

ALL RIGHT, MY HANDSOME FRIEND, THAT'S ENOUGH! BUT... UP!

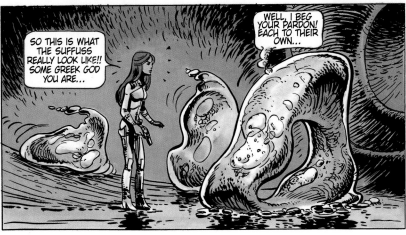

SO THIS IS WHAT THE SUFFUSS REALLY LOOK LIKE!! SOME GREEK GOD YOU ARE...

WELL, I BEG YOUR PARDON! EACH TO THEIR OWN...

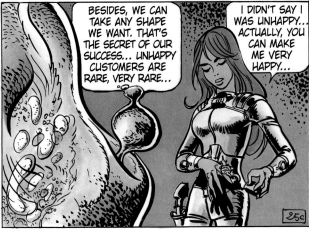

BESIDES, WE CAN TAKE ANY SHAPE WE WANT. THAT'S THE SECRET OF OUR SUCCESS... UNHAPPY CUSTOMERS ARE RARE, VERY RARE...

I DIDN'T SAY I WAS UNHAPPY... ACTUALLY, YOU CAN MAKE ME VERY HAPPY...

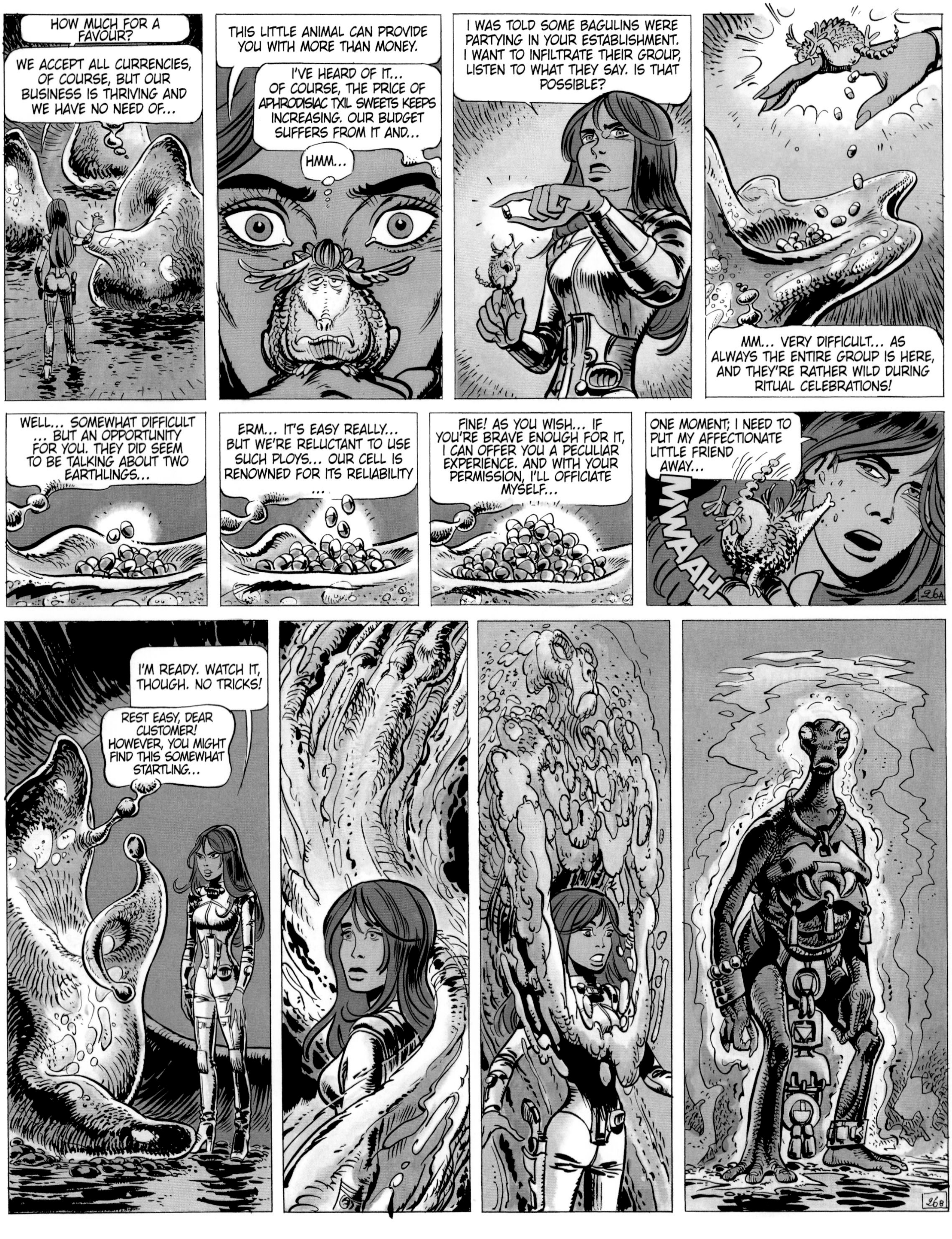
HOW MUCH FOR A FAVOUR?
WE ACCEPT ALL CURRENCIES, OF COURSE, BUT OUR BUSINESS IS THRIVING AND WE HAVE NO NEED OF...
THIS LITTLE ANIMAL CAN PROVIDE YOU WITH MORE THAN MONEY.
I'VE HEARD OF IT... OF COURSE, THE PRICE OF APHRODISIAC TXIL SWEETS KEEPS INCREASING. OUR BUDGET SUFFERS FROM IT AND...
HMM...
I WAS TOLD SOME BAGULINS WERE PARTYING IN YOUR ESTABLISHMENT. I WANT TO INFILTRATE THEIR GROUP, LISTEN TO WHAT THEY SAY. IS THAT POSSIBLE?
MM... VERY DIFFICULT... AS ALWAYS THE ENTIRE GROUP IS HERE, AND THEY'RE RATHER WILD DURING RITUAL CELEBRATIONS!
WELL... SOMEWHAT DIFFICULT ... BUT AN OPPORTUNITY FOR YOU. THEY DID SEEM TO BE TALKING ABOUT TWO EARTHLINGS...
ERM... IT'S EASY REALLY... BUT WE'RE RELUCTANT TO USE SUCH PLOYS... OUR CELL IS RENOWNED FOR ITS RELIABILITY ...
FINE! AS YOU WISH... IF YOU'RE BRAVE ENOUGH FOR IT, I CAN OFFER YOU A PECULIAR EXPERIENCE. AND WITH YOUR PERMISSION, I'LL OFFICIATE MYSELF...
ONE MOMENT; I NEED TO PUT MY AFFECTIONATE LITTLE FRIEND AWAY...
MWAAAH
26A
I'M READY. WATCH IT, THOUGH. NO TRICKS!
REST EASY, DEAR CUSTOMER! HOWEVER, YOU MIGHT FIND THIS SOMEWHAT STARTLING...
26B

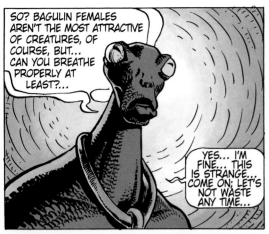

SO? BAGULIN FEMALES AREN'T THE MOST ATTRACTIVE OF CREATURES, OF COURSE, BUT... CAN YOU BREATHE PROPERLY AT LEAST?...

YES... I'M FINE... THIS IS STRANGE... COME ON; LET'S NOT WASTE ANY TIME...

WE'RE ALMOST THERE!

I HEAR THAT! LET'S HURRY...

BAH! THEY'LL BE HERE FOR DAYS AND DAYS, AS ALWAYS AFTER ONE OF THEIR DIRTY JOBS...

...AND THEY'RE DRUNK AS LORDS AS USUAL, LISTENING TO THEIR STORYTELLER'S BALDERDASH...

OH YES? THAT'S INTERESTING. GET CLOSER...

AS YOU WISH — YOU'RE THE CUSTOMER. BUT WE'RE NOT GOING UNNOTICED, YOU KNOW...

COME HERE, MY BEAUTY!

WELL, YOU AREN'T, ANYWAY! I'D HAVE PREFERRED A MORE DISCREET ENTRANCE...

HEY, HAVE A DRINK WITH ME...

OUR STORY-TELLER IS GOING TO CONTINUE HIS TALE!

SHHHH!

NEAR OUR FAIR PLANET... THEY COME... I CAN HEAR BUT NOT YET SEE...

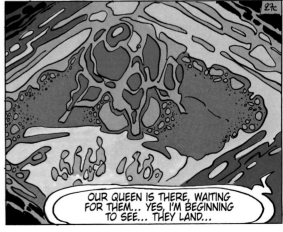

OUR QUEEN IS THERE, WAITING FOR THEM... YES, I'M BEGINNING TO SEE... THEY LAND...

THEY COME OUT AND OUR QUEEN IS SATISFIED...

...BUT ONE OF THEM IS SUPERFLUOUS... SHOULD HE BE STRICKEN DEAD?

OUR QUEEN PONDERS WITH HER CUSTOMARY MAGNANIMITY... SHE OBSERVES THE SEEMINGLY SLEEPING EARTHLING...

VALERIAN! WHAT HAPPENED TO HIM?!...

BE QUIET!

?!

TIME IS SHORT, FOR IN THE LAKE OF FRAGRANT WATERS...

...THE GROOBOS WAIT TO GO WHERE THEY MUST...

OUR QUEEN HAS MADE HER DECISION: THE EXTRA MAN'S LIFE IS SPARED...

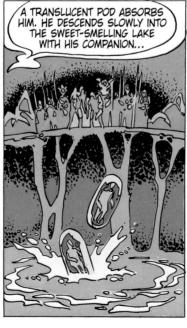

A TRANSLUCENT POD ABSORBS HIM. HE DESCENDS SLOWLY INTO THE SWEET-SMELLING LAKE WITH HIS COMPANION...

OUR BELOVED QUEEN CONGRATULATES THE HEROES. AND THE LAKE PARTS TO LET THE GROOBOS AND THEIR BURDEN DEPART.

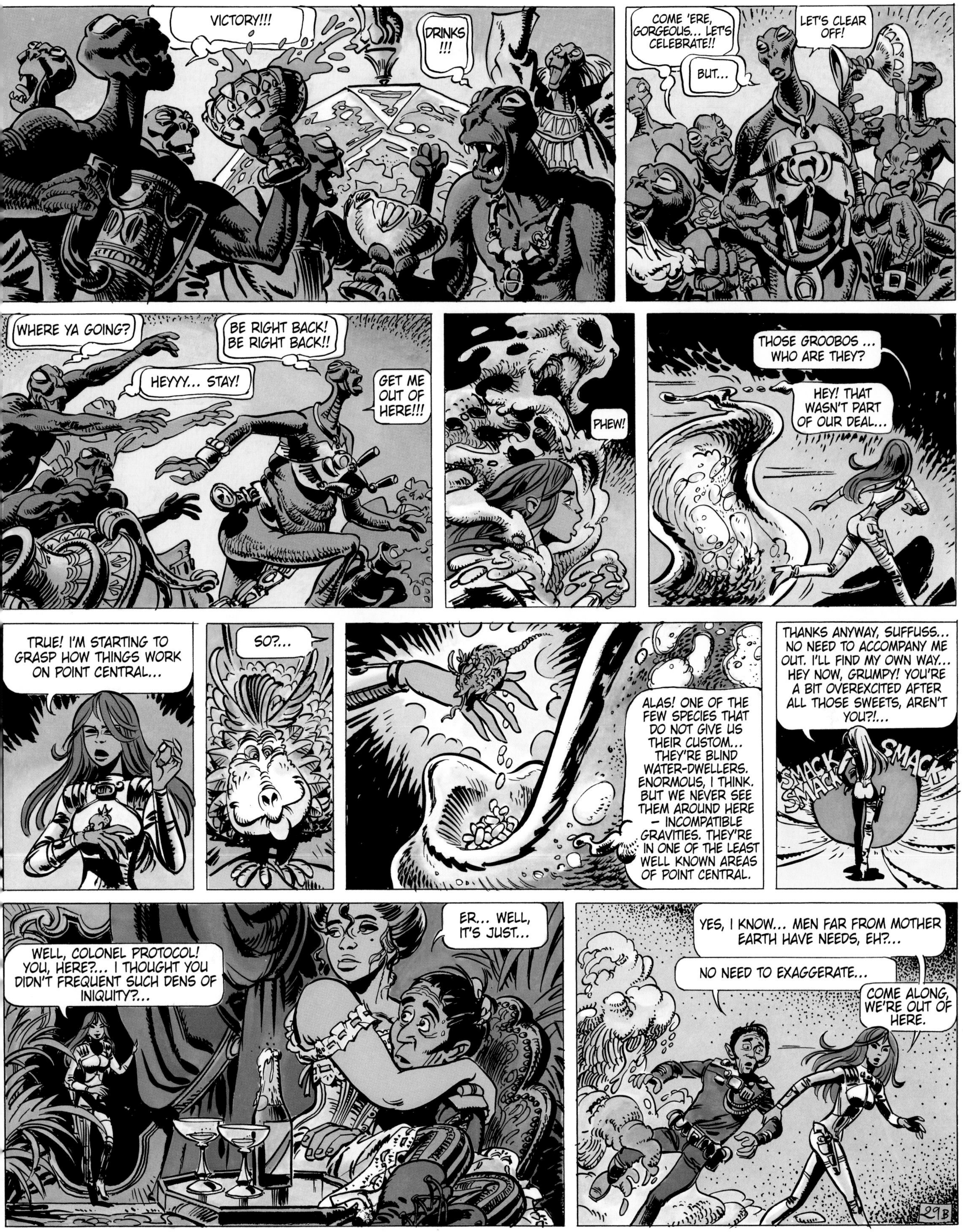
VICTORY!!!
DRINKS !!!
COME 'ERE, GORGEOUS... LET'S CELEBRATE!!
BUT...
LET'S CLEAR OFF!
WHERE YA GOING?
BE RIGHT BACK! BE RIGHT BACK!!
HEYYY... STAY!
GET ME OUT OF HERE!!!
PHEW!
THOSE GROOBOS ... WHO ARE THEY?
HEY! THAT WASN'T PART OF OUR DEAL...
TRUE! I'M STARTING TO GRASP HOW THINGS WORK ON POINT CENTRAL...
SO?...
ALAS! ONE OF THE FEW SPECIES THAT DO NOT GIVE US THEIR CUSTOM... THEY'RE BLIND WATER-DWELLERS. ENORMOUS, I THINK. BUT WE NEVER SEE THEM AROUND HERE – INCOMPATIBLE GRAVITIES. THEY'RE IN ONE OF THE LEAST WELL KNOWN AREAS OF POINT CENTRAL.
THANKS ANYWAY, SUFFUSS... NO NEED TO ACCOMPANY ME OUT. I'LL FIND MY OWN WAY... HEY NOW, GRUMPY! YOU'RE A BIT OVEREXCITED AFTER ALL THOSE SWEETS, AREN'T YOU?!...
SMACK SMACK SMACK
WELL, COLONEL PROTOCOL! YOU, HERE?... I THOUGHT YOU DIDN'T FREQUENT SUCH DENS OF INIQUITY?...
ER... WELL, IT'S JUST...
YES, I KNOW... MEN FAR FROM MOTHER EARTH HAVE NEEDS, EH?...
NO NEED TO EXAGGERATE...
COME ALONG, WE'RE OUT OF HERE.
29B

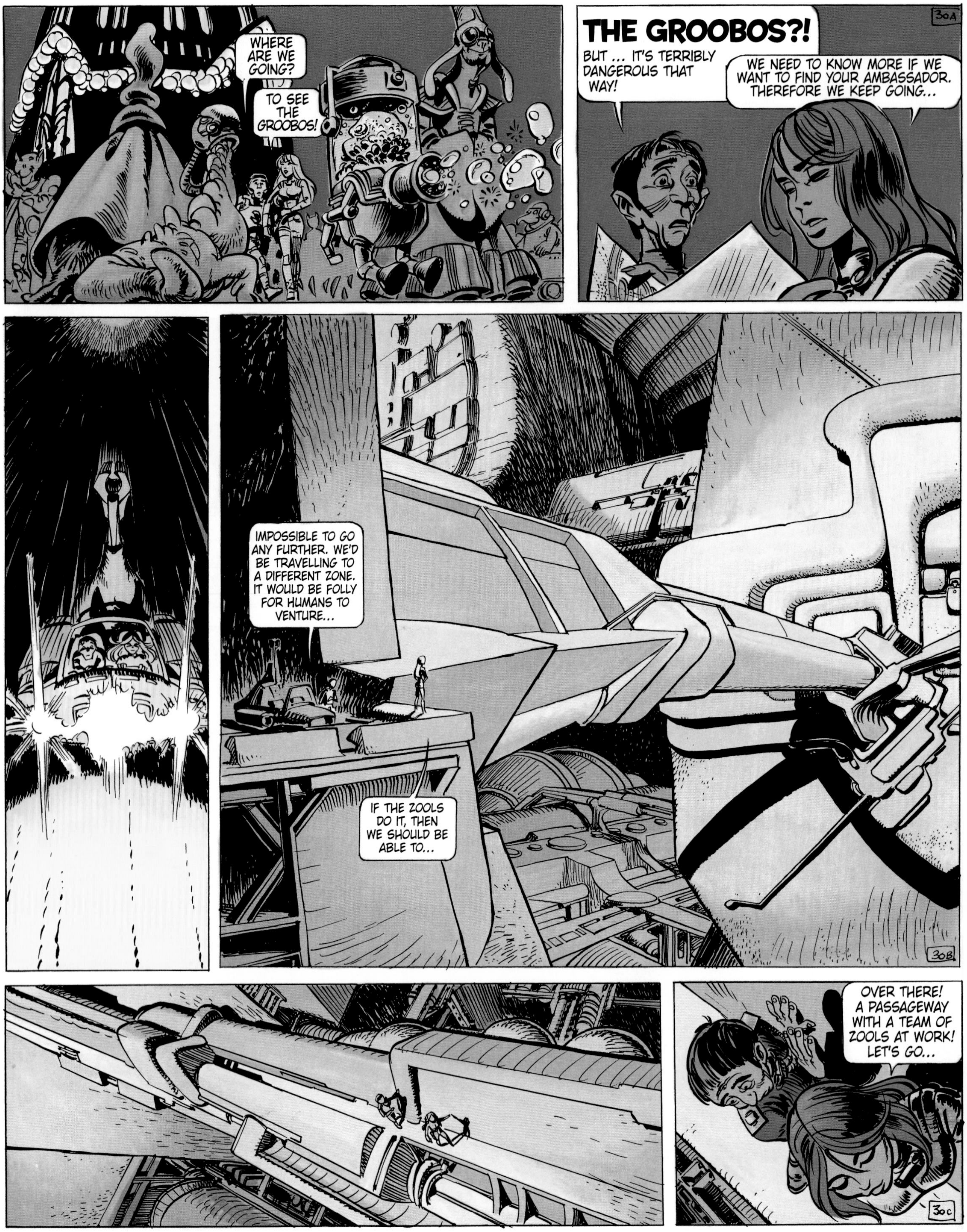
WHERE ARE WE GOING?
TO SEE THE GROOBOS!
THE GROOBOS?!
BUT ... IT'S TERRIBLY DANGEROUS THAT WAY!
WE NEED TO KNOW MORE IF WE WANT TO FIND YOUR AMBASSADOR. THEREFORE WE KEEP GOING...
IMPOSSIBLE TO GO ANY FURTHER. WE'D BE TRAVELLING TO A DIFFERENT ZONE. IT WOULD BE FOLLY FOR HUMANS TO VENTURE...
IF THE ZOOLS DO IT, THEN WE SHOULD BE ABLE TO...
OVER THERE! A PASSAGEWAY WITH A TEAM OF ZOOLS AT WORK! LET'S GO...

THEY REALLY AREN'T VERY INQUISITIVE... **HEY!** DO YOU KNOW HOW WE CAN CONTACT THE GROOBOS?...

PFFF... LEAVE IT. THEY WON'T ANSWER!

CLICK
EARTHLINGS!

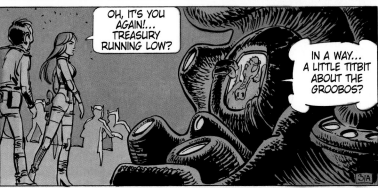

OH, IT'S YOU AGAIN!... TREASURY RUNNING LOW?

IN A WAY... A LITTLE TITBIT ABOUT THE GROOBOS?

...FOR 1,000 EBEBE PEARLS CASH, A MEANS OF KNOWING WHAT GOES ON IN THEIR UNIQUE MINDS...

HOW AM I SUPPOSED TO PAY YOU?

YOUR CREATURE CAN, IF IT WISHES, RECONSTITUTE SOMETHING IT'S ALREADY PRODUCED, WITHOUT A NEW MODEL. BIG ENERGY EXPENDITURE, OF COURSE...

MEH!

WILL YOU BE ABLE TO DO THAT, YOU POOR THING?

THE GROOBOS ARE A UNIQUE FORM OF PSYCHIC ENTITY. BLIND, AND FOR ALL WE KNOW PERHAPS COMPLETELY DUMB. IT'S THEIR PILOT ZUURS — A SORT OF PEDUNCULATED JELLYFISH — THAT KEEP THEM INFORMED OF EVERYTHING AROUND THEM. WHEN IN CONTACT WITH ANY LIFE FORM, THEY FUNCTION BY TELEPATHY. IF YOU'RE QUICK, YOU CAN GRAB A ZUUR AND KNOW WHAT'S HAPPENING ANYWHERE THERE ARE GROOBOS. YOU'LL HAVE TO BE SWIFT: ZUURS ONLY LIVE FOR A FEW SECONDS OUT OF THE WATER...

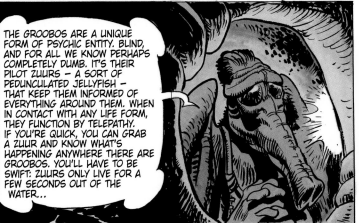

AND HOW DO I GET INSIDE THE GROOBOS' CELL?

WELL, YOU'RE A GOOD CUSTOMER... AS A FRIENDLY GESTURE, I SUGGEST ONE OF THE ARMOURED MAINTENANCE SUBS YOU'LL FIND ON THE GREEN CANAL.

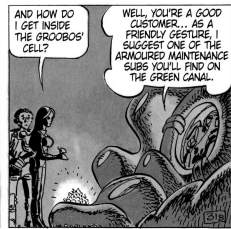

59

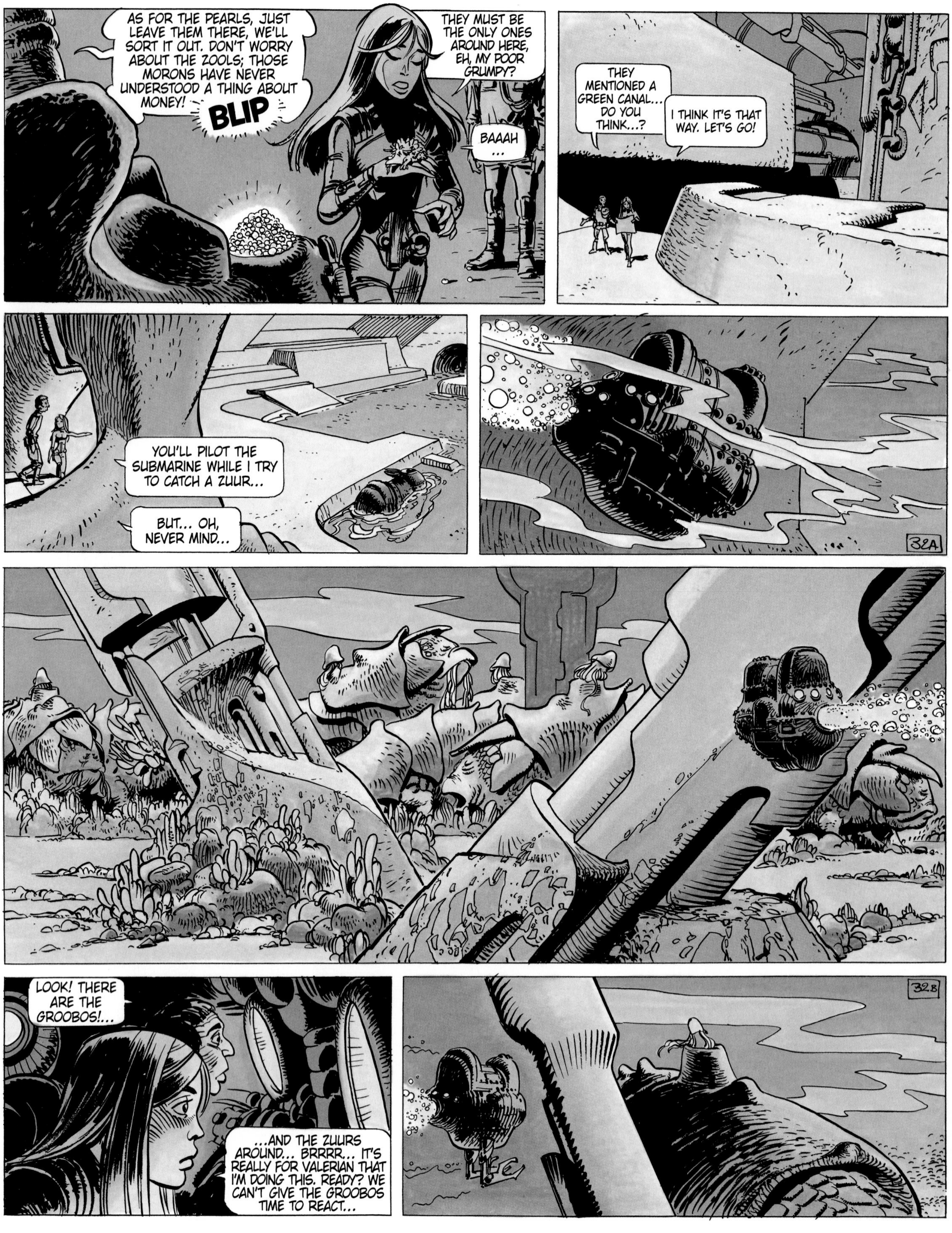
AS FOR THE PEARLS, JUST LEAVE THEM THERE, WE'LL SORT IT OUT. DON'T WORRY ABOUT THE ZOOLS; THOSE MORONS HAVE NEVER UNDERSTOOD A THING ABOUT MONEY!
BLIP
THEY MUST BE THE ONLY ONES AROUND HERE, EH, MY POOR GRUMPY?
BAAAH ...
THEY MENTIONED A GREEN CANAL... DO YOU THINK...?
I THINK IT'S THAT WAY. LET'S GO!
YOU'LL PILOT THE SUBMARINE WHILE I TRY TO CATCH A ZUUR...
BUT... OH, NEVER MIND...
32A
32B
LOOK! THERE ARE THE GROOBOS!...
...AND THE ZUURS AROUND... BRRRR... IT'S REALLY FOR VALERIAN THAT I'M DOING THIS. READY? WE CAN'T GIVE THE GROOBOS TIME TO REACT...

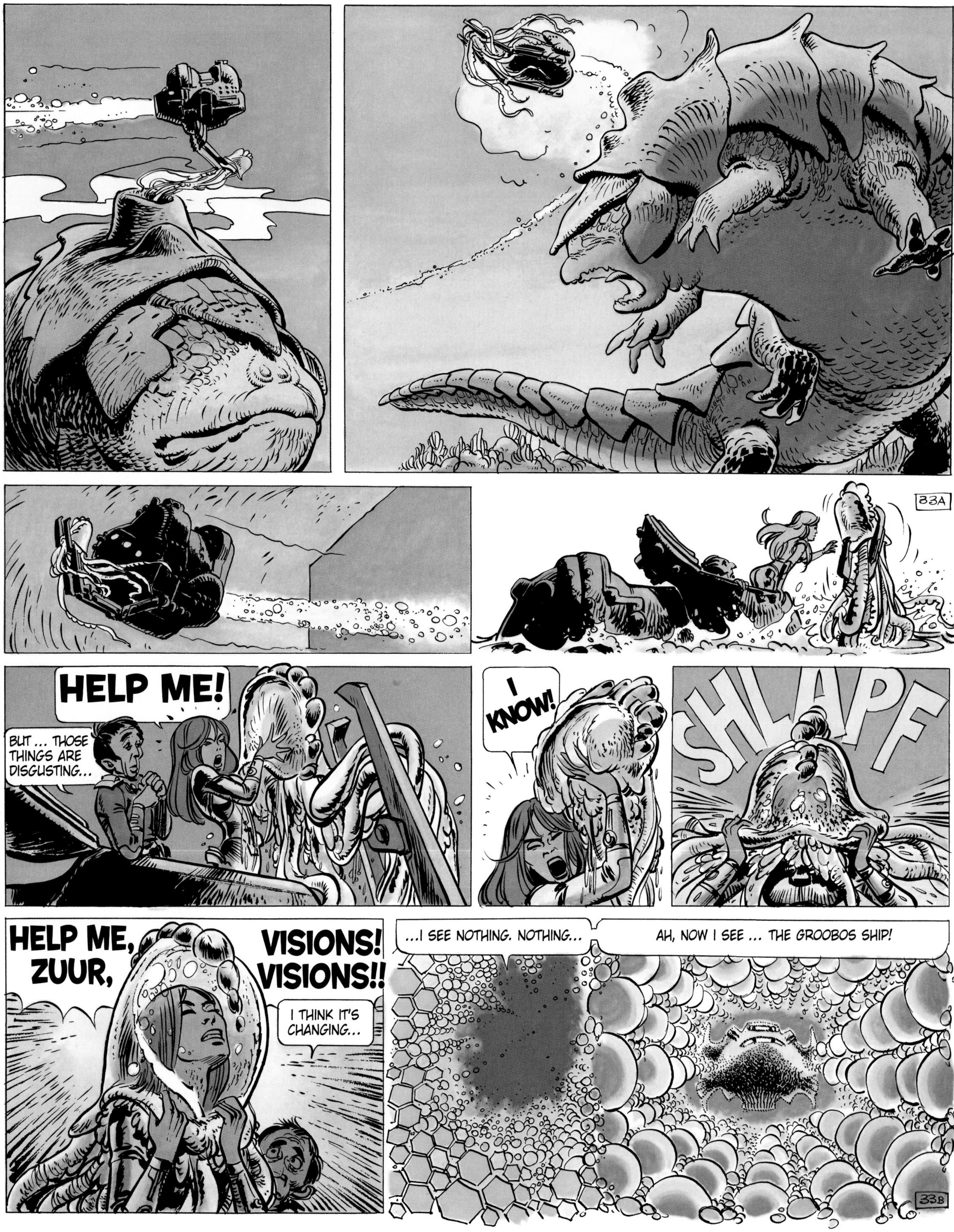
33A
HELP ME!
BUT ... THOSE THINGS ARE DISGUSTING...
I KNOW!
SHLAPF
HELP ME, ZUUR,
VISIONS! VISIONS!!
I THINK IT'S CHANGING...
...I SEE NOTHING. NOTHING...
AH, NOW I SEE ... THE GROOBOS SHIP!
33B

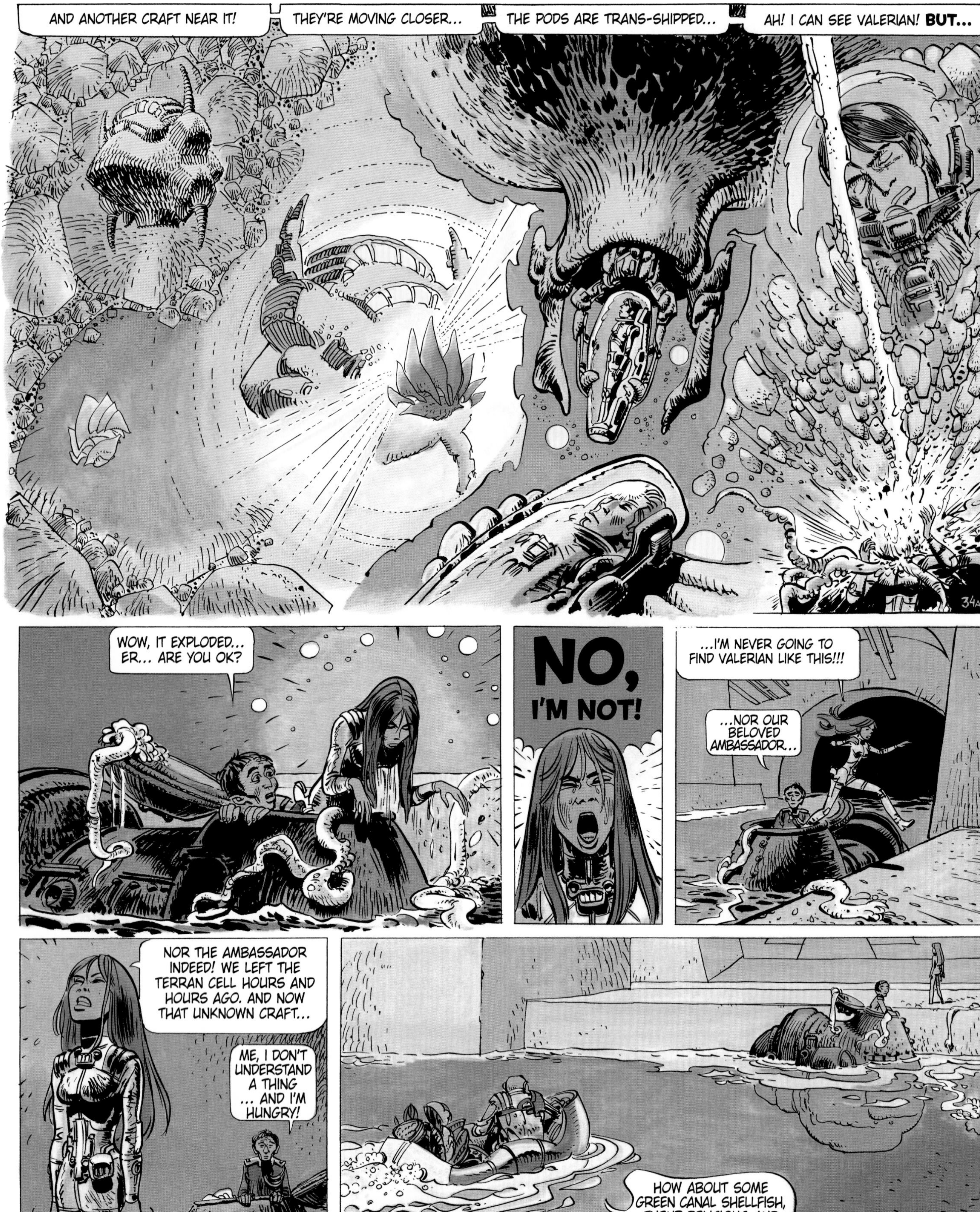
AND ANOTHER CRAFT NEAR IT!
THEY'RE MOVING CLOSER...
THE PODS ARE TRANS-SHIPPED...
AH! I CAN SEE VALERIAN! BUT...
34A
WOW, IT EXPLODED... ER... ARE YOU OK?
NO, I'M NOT!
...I'M NEVER GOING TO FIND VALERIAN LIKE THIS!!!
...NOR OUR BELOVED AMBASSADOR...
NOR THE AMBASSADOR INDEED! WE LEFT THE TERRAN CELL HOURS AND HOURS AGO. AND NOW THAT UNKNOWN CRAFT...
ME, I DON'T UNDERSTAND A THING ... AND I'M HUNGRY!
HOW ABOUT SOME GREEN CANAL SHELLFISH, THEN? DELICIOUS AND CHEAP...
34B

WHO... WHO ARE YOU?

BAH... THERE'S A LITTLE OF EVERYTHING ON POINT CENTRAL, AND THIS PLACE IS PERFECT FOR FISHING. WHEN YOU'RE DOWN TO YOUR LAST BLUTOK LIKE I AM, THERE'S NO SUCH THING AS A BAD JOB...

BUT... DO YOU LIVE HERE ALONE?

OH, YEAH!... A LONG TIME AGO, I LOST MY SHIP GAMBLING AND I WAS THROWN OUT OF THE SERVICE, EXPELLED FROM MY CELL... SINCE THEN I'VE BEEN MOSTLY GETTING BY; BUT I'M FLAT BROKE RIGHT NOW... SO, INTERESTED IN MY SHELLFISH?

GIVE ME YOUR LAST BLUTOK.

HEY! I'M THE ONE ASKING YOU FOR SOME OF THOSE!

WAIT, YOU'LL UNDERSTAND... HE'S TIRED, BUT FOR A SMALL AMOUNT... COME ON, GRUMPY, WAKE UP!

"PFUUU..."

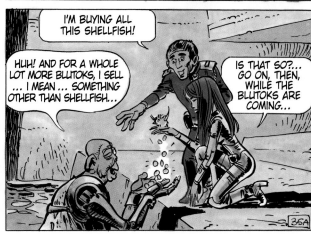

I'M BUYING ALL THIS SHELLFISH!

HUH! AND FOR A WHOLE LOT MORE BLUTOKS, I SELL ... I MEAN ... SOMETHING OTHER THAN SHELLFISH...

IS THAT SO?... GO ON, THEN, WHILE THE BLUTOKS ARE COMING...

35A

LOOKING FOR SOMEONE? THEN COME ABOARD! MAYBE MY FRIENDS THE GNARF-DREAMERS – I SELL THEM SEASHELLS SOMETIMES – WILL AGREE TO HELP YOU... BUT IT'S A LONG WAY AWAY...

WHAT IS IT THEY CAN DO, THOSE GNARF-DREAMERS OF YOURS?

OH! THEY HAVE THIS VERY FANCY EQUIPMENT THAT CAN PROJECT YOU INTO THE MIND OF YOUR CHOICE AS YOU DREAM – FOR A PRICE, OF COURSE...

...OF COURSE! WELL, LET'S GO...

AND YOU, COLONEL PROTOCOL, STOP GORGING YOURSELF LIKE A PIG!!

ALL RIGHT, ALL RIGHT...

35B

63

SO YOU HAVE BLUTOKS TO SPEND? LOTS OF BLUTOKS? WE'RE DELIGHTED TO HAVE YOU AS A CUSTOMER, PRETTY LADY...

I BRING YOU SOMEONE INTERESTED IN YOUR TALENTS...

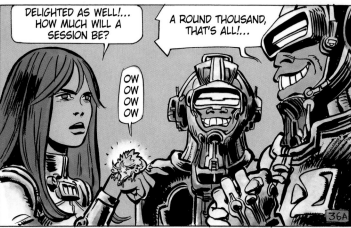

DELIGHTED AS WELL!... HOW MUCH WILL A SESSION BE?

A ROUND THOUSAND, THAT'S ALL!...

OW OW OW OW

DREAMS ARE EXPENSIVE, YOU KNOW! WE'RE CONSTANTLY IMPROVING OUR TECHNIQUES AND WE NEED TO INVEST HEAVILY. THERE'S DEPRECIATION AND OBSOLESCENCE OF EQUIPMENT, MARKETING EXPENSES AND BRANDING...

YOU SEEM RATHER ORGANISED FOR A BUNCH OF DREAMERS...

DING DILING

LET'S LEAVE YOUR ANIMAL TO ITS REMARKABLE, IF SOMEWHAT SLOW, WORK, AND ALLOW ME TO GET YOU SETTLED IN. THIS WAY...

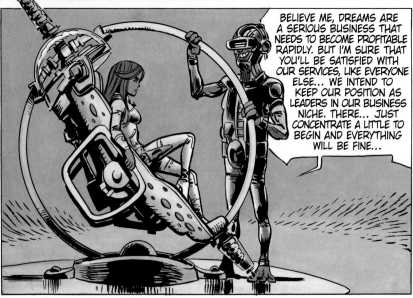

BELIEVE ME, DREAMS ARE A SERIOUS BUSINESS THAT NEEDS TO BECOME PROFITABLE RAPIDLY. BUT I'M SURE THAT YOU'LL BE SATISFIED WITH OUR SERVICES, LIKE EVERYONE ELSE... WE INTEND TO KEEP OUR POSITION AS LEADERS IN OUR BUSINESS NICHE. THERE... JUST CONCENTRATE A LITTLE TO BEGIN AND EVERYTHING WILL BE FINE...

VALERIAN
MY SWEET VALERIAN

BLASTED CASE! NEVER SEEN THE LIKES OF THIS MATERIAL! AT LEAST THEY DIDN'T FIND MY MICRO-EQUIPMENT...

THE AMBASSADOR! I CAN GET HIM OUT OF THIS NOW. IT'S BEEN OVER 50 HOURS... IT SHOULD BE SAFE.

I HOPE THE ORDEAL DIDN'T TAKE TOO MUCH OUT OF HIM, POOR OLD FELLOW...

NO! I'M PERFECTLY FINE, AND I ADVISE YOU TO WATCH YOUR LANGUAGE!!!

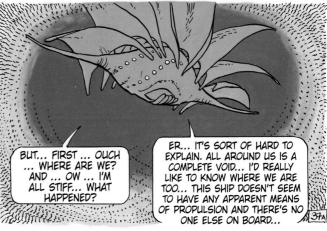

BUT... FIRST ... OUCH ... WHERE ARE WE? AND ... OW ... I'M ALL STIFF... WHAT HAPPENED?

ER... IT'S SORT OF HARD TO EXPLAIN. ALL AROUND US IS A COMPLETE VOID... I'D REALLY LIKE TO KNOW WHERE WE ARE TOO... THIS SHIP DOESN'T SEEM TO HAVE ANY APPARENT MEANS OF PROPULSION AND THERE'S NO ONE ELSE ON BOARD...

THIS IS UNACCEPTABLE! MY SPEECH TO THE GALACTIC COUNCIL IS SUPPOSED TO TAKE PLACE IN LESS THAN THREE HOURS!!!

...NOT TO MENTION THE 10,000 TERRAN CRUISERS THAT ARE AWAITING MY ORDERS TO SURROUND POINT CENTRAL!!!

WHAT!? WHAT THE HELL ARE YOU TALKING ABOUT!?!

EARTHLINGS FORGET YOUR DISPUTES! YOU ARE ABOUT TO PASS INTO THE SHADOWS' WORLD! NO HARM WILL BEFALL YOU! COME TO US...

LOOK OUT!

ORDERS!? I WILL NOT TOLERATE...

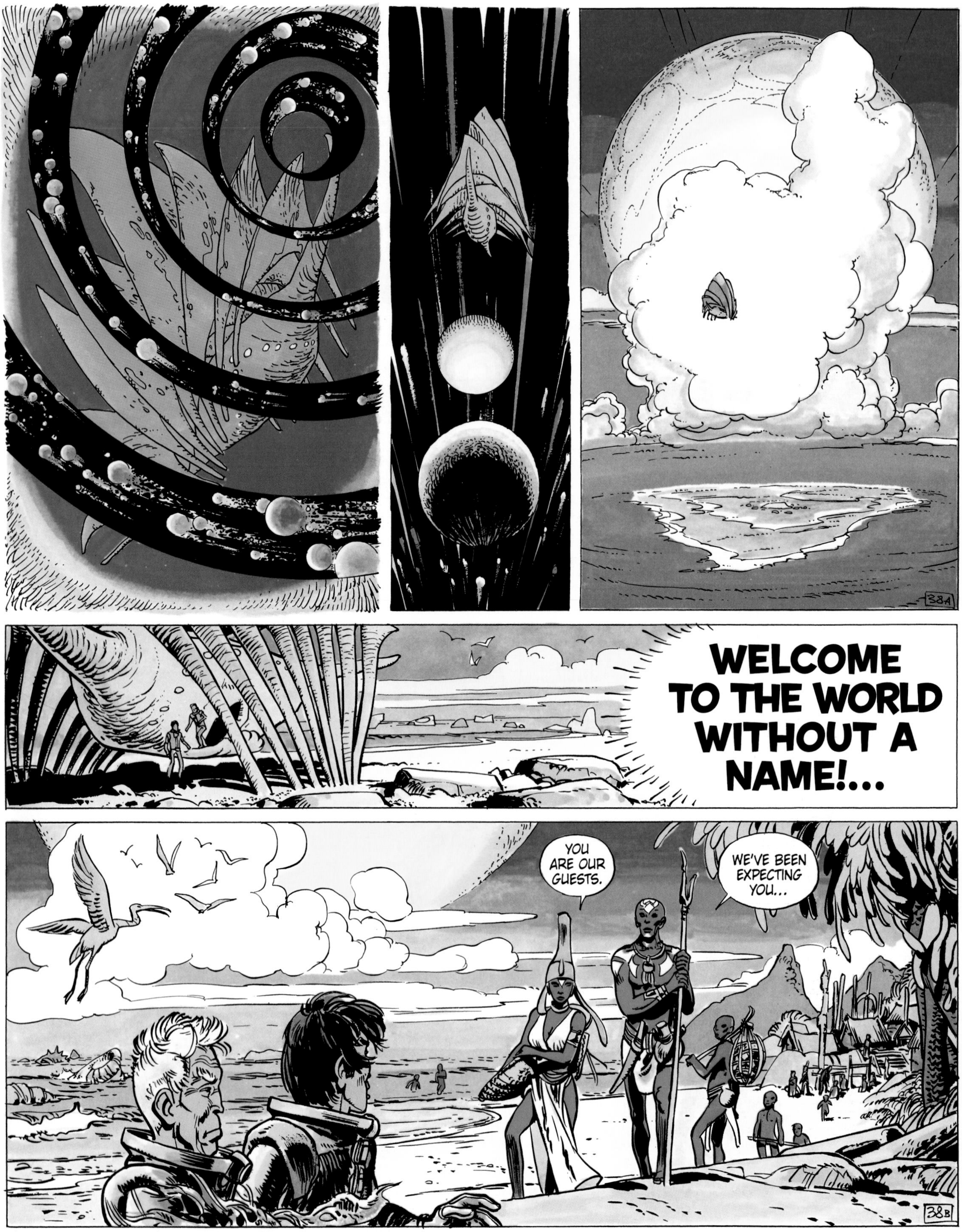
38A
WELCOME TO THE WORLD WITHOUT A NAME!...
YOU ARE OUR GUESTS.
WE'VE BEEN EXPECTING YOU...
38B

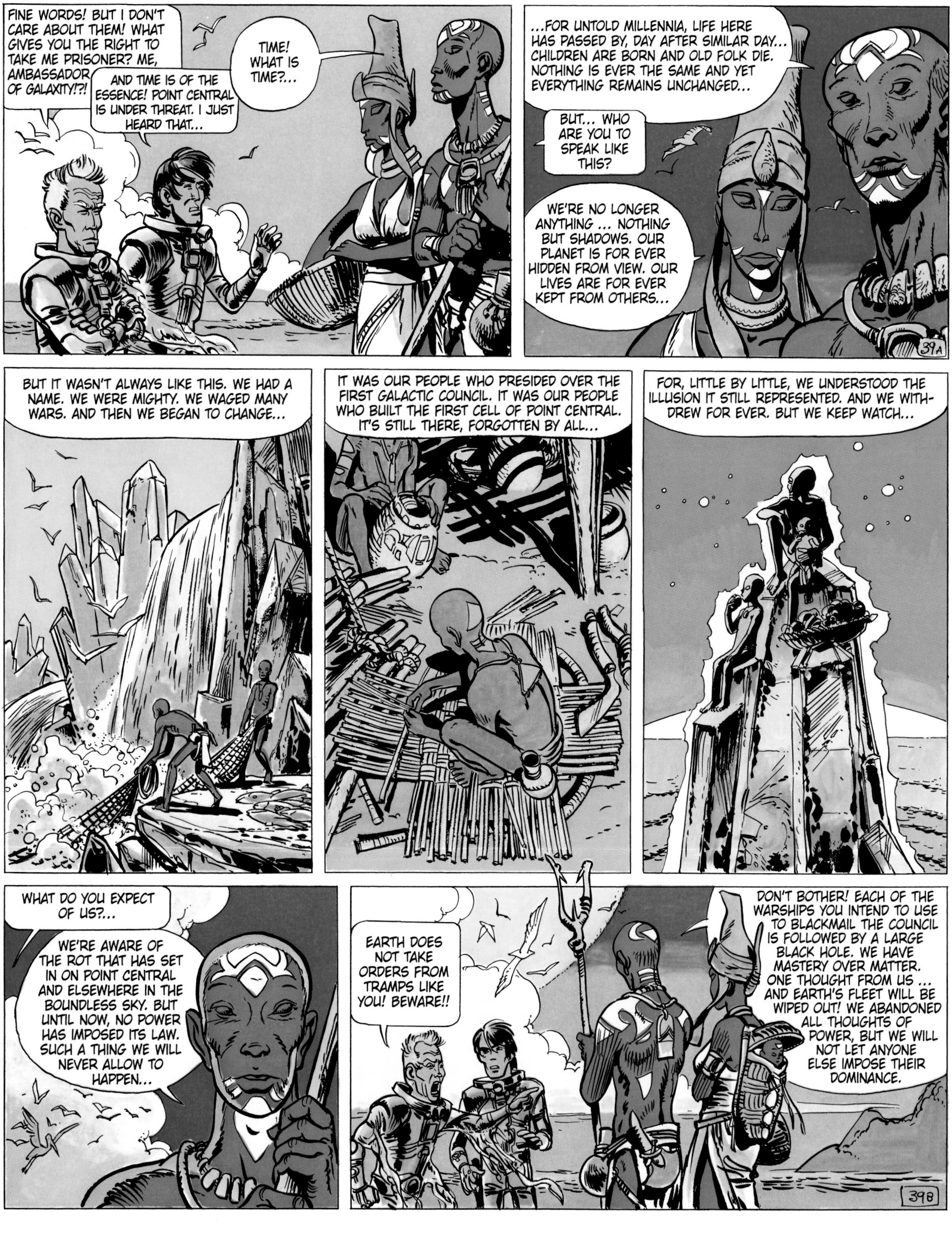
FINE WORDS! BUT I DON'T CARE ABOUT THEM! WHAT GIVES YOU THE RIGHT TO TAKE ME PRISONER? ME, AMBASSADOR OF GALAXITY!?!
AND TIME IS OF THE ESSENCE! POINT CENTRAL IS UNDER THREAT. I JUST HEARD THAT...
TIME! WHAT IS TIME?...
...FOR UNTOLD MILLENNIA, LIFE HERE HAS PASSED BY, DAY AFTER SIMILAR DAY... CHILDREN ARE BORN AND OLD FOLK DIE. NOTHING IS EVER THE SAME AND YET EVERYTHING REMAINS UNCHANGED...
BUT... WHO ARE YOU TO SPEAK LIKE THIS?
WE'RE NO LONGER ANYTHING ... NOTHING BUT SHADOWS. OUR PLANET IS FOR EVER HIDDEN FROM VIEW. OUR LIVES ARE FOR EVER KEPT FROM OTHERS...
39A
BUT IT WASN'T ALWAYS LIKE THIS. WE HAD A NAME. WE WERE MIGHTY. WE WAGED MANY WARS. AND THEN WE BEGAN TO CHANGE...
IT WAS OUR PEOPLE WHO PRESIDED OVER THE FIRST GALACTIC COUNCIL. IT WAS OUR PEOPLE WHO BUILT THE FIRST CELL OF POINT CENTRAL. IT'S STILL THERE, FORGOTTEN BY ALL...
FOR, LITTLE BY LITTLE, WE UNDERSTOOD THE ILLUSION IT STILL REPRESENTED. AND WE WITH-DREW FOR EVER. BUT WE KEEP WATCH...
WHAT DO YOU EXPECT OF US?...
WE'RE AWARE OF THE ROT THAT HAS SET IN ON POINT CENTRAL AND ELSEWHERE IN THE BOUNDLESS SKY. BUT UNTIL NOW, NO POWER HAS IMPOSED ITS LAW. SUCH A THING WE WILL NEVER ALLOW TO HAPPEN...
EARTH DOES NOT TAKE ORDERS FROM TRAMPS LIKE YOU! BEWARE!!
DON'T BOTHER! EACH OF THE WARSHIPS YOU INTEND TO USE TO BLACKMAIL THE COUNCIL IS FOLLOWED BY A LARGE BLACK HOLE. WE HAVE MASTERY OVER MATTER. ONE THOUGHT FROM US ... AND EARTH'S FLEET WILL BE WIPED OUT! WE ABANDONED ALL THOUGHTS OF POWER, BUT WE WILL NOT LET ANYONE ELSE IMPOSE THEIR DOMINANCE.
39B

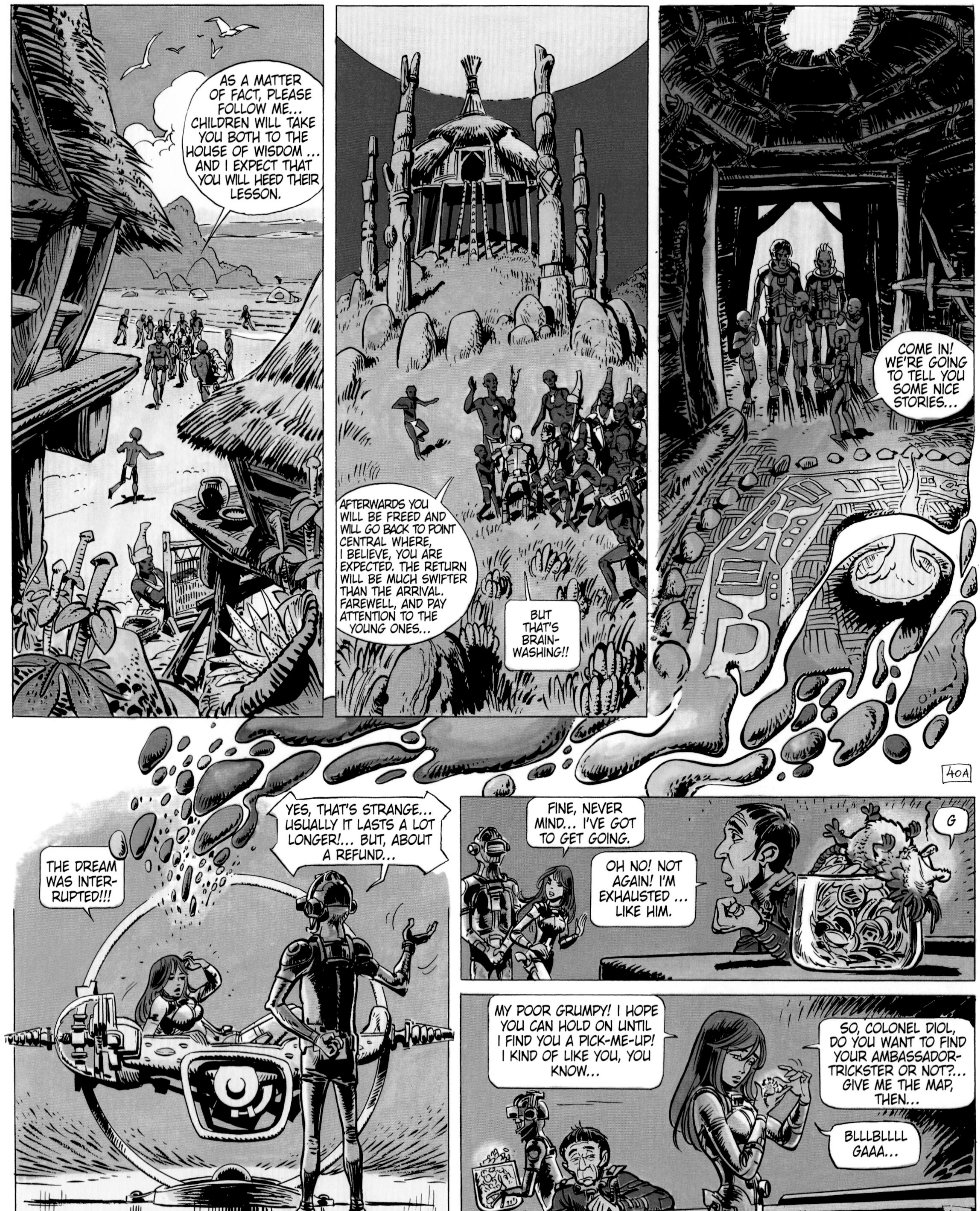
AS A MATTER OF FACT, PLEASE FOLLOW ME... CHILDREN WILL TAKE YOU BOTH TO THE HOUSE OF WISDOM ... AND I EXPECT THAT YOU WILL HEED THEIR LESSON.
AFTERWARDS YOU WILL BE FREED AND WILL GO BACK TO POINT CENTRAL WHERE, I BELIEVE, YOU ARE EXPECTED. THE RETURN WILL BE MUCH SWIFTER THAN THE ARRIVAL. FAREWELL, AND PAY ATTENTION TO THE YOUNG ONES...
BUT THAT'S BRAIN-WASHING!!
COME IN! WE'RE GOING TO TELL YOU SOME NICE STORIES...
40A
THE DREAM WAS INTER-RUPTED!!!
YES, THAT'S STRANGE... USUALLY IT LASTS A LOT LONGER!... BUT, ABOUT A REFUND...
FINE, NEVER MIND... I'VE GOT TO GET GOING.
OH NO! NOT AGAIN! I'M EXHAUSTED ... LIKE HIM.
G
MY POOR GRUMPY! I HOPE YOU CAN HOLD ON UNTIL I FIND YOU A PICK-ME-UP! I KIND OF LIKE YOU, YOU KNOW...
SO, COLONEL DIOL, DO YOU WANT TO FIND YOUR AMBASSADOR-TRICKSTER OR NOT?... GIVE ME THE MAP, THEN...
BLLLBLLLL GAAA...
40B

I THINK I'VE WORKED OUT WHAT'S GOING TO HAPPEN. WE HAVE TO FIND THE INITIAL SHADOWS CELL ... THERE!

AND YOU WANT TO GO **THERE**?!... NO WAY! I'M DONE!

YOUR CALL! BUT I'M WARNING YOU, COLONEL, THERE'LL BE A LACK OF PROTOCOL TO GREET THE AMBASSADOR...

HEY! WAIT FOR ME! WHAT ARE YOU TALKING ABOUT, THE AMBASSADOR? WHAT WOULD HE BE DOING IN A PLACE LIKE THAT?

COME ON ... TELL ME...

NO TIME! YOU TELL ME INSTEAD: WHAT ARE ALL THOSE GROUPS OF ZOOLS DOING?

HOW THE HECK SHOULD I KNOW? I'VE NEVER SEEN SO MANY AT THE SAME TIME...

ANYWAY, WHERE WE'RE GOING, I'M PRETTY SURE WE WON'T MEET ANYONE...

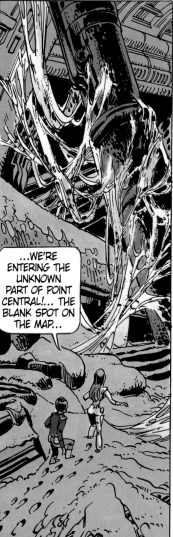

...WE'RE ENTERING THE UNKNOWN PART OF POINT CENTRAL!... THE BLANK SPOT ON THE MAP...

RUINS EVERYWHERE! AND THE AIR IS GETTING ALMOST UN-BREATHABLE...

WAIT... OVER THERE!!! THE DOOR TO AN INTACT CELL!!

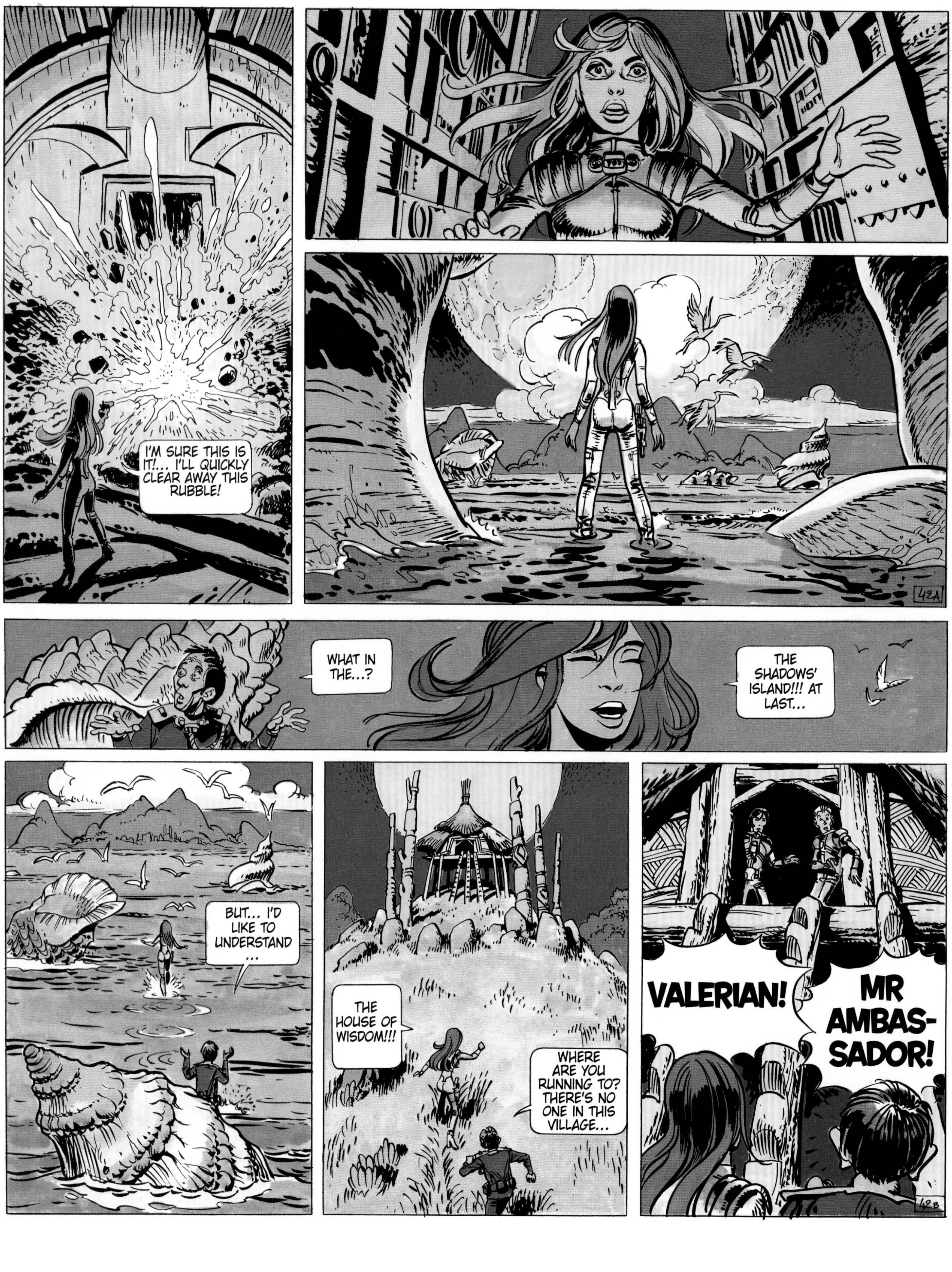

I'M SURE THIS IS IT!... I'LL QUICKLY CLEAR AWAY THIS RUBBLE!
42A
WHAT IN THE...?
THE SHADOWS' ISLAND!!! AT LAST...
BUT... I'D LIKE TO UNDERSTAND ...
THE HOUSE OF WISDOM!!!
WHERE ARE YOU RUNNING TO? THERE'S NO ONE IN THIS VILLAGE...
VALERIAN!
MR AMBAS-SADOR!
42B

MR AMBASSADOR! ALLOW ME TO WELCOME YOU TO POINT CENTRAL AND OFFER MY BEST WISHES FOR EARTH'S TRIUMPH, WHICH CANNOT FAIL TO...

THANK YOU, COLONEL DIOL, THANK YOU... BUT I'M AFRAID YOUR EXCELLENT SPEECH IS A LITTLE DATED, YOU SEE. WOULD YOU BE SO KIND AS TO TAKE ME TO THE HALL OF SCREENS?... I'M BACK JUST IN TIME FOR THE COUNCIL.

I WAS SORT OF WORRIED, YOU KNOW...

OHHH, YOU SHOULDN'T HAVE BEEN! OF COURSE, THERE WAS SOME DANGER ... BUT YOU KNOW YOUR VALERIAN ALWAYS PULLS THROUGH LIKE A CHAMP!...

AHEM!... QUICKLY PLEASE, MY FRIENDS. I CANNOT WAIT TO EXPLAIN EARTH'S PEACEFUL STANCE...

LAURELINE, WAIT! WHAT IS IT? ARE YOU SULKING?...

43A

WE CAN PLAY AN ENORMOUS ROLE, I CAN FEEL IT... I'LL EXPLAIN THE CHANGE OF TACTICS TO GALAXITY LATER...

DIOL, HELP ME GET OUT OF THIS SPACESUIT. I MUST PRESENT MYSELF BEFORE THE COUNCIL IN DRESS UNIFORM...

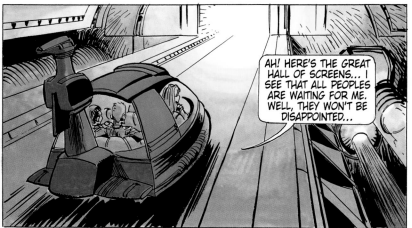
AH! HERE'S THE GREAT HALL OF SCREENS... I SEE THAT ALL PEOPLES ARE WAITING FOR ME. WELL, THEY WON'T BE DISAPPOINTED...

LEAVE ME, MY FRIENDS. I NO LONGER NEED YOUR LOYAL HELP...

43B

71

I'M RIGHT BEHIND YOU! I'M STARVING AFTER THIS WHOLE BUSINESS...

NOT THE MOST EVENTFUL JOB, THOUGH, WAS IT?

WELL, I'M GOING TO GO CHECK ON MY BUFFET...

PSSSSST... I HAVE SOME INFORMATION...

44A

...SOMETHING BIG. FOR LET'S SAY ... 500 EBEBE PEARLS...

YOU AGAIN!
SORRY, BUDDY, NO MORE!... BESIDES, MY LITTLE BEASTIE IS DYING...

A SHAME. IT'S TOO LATE, ANYWAY...

WELL, IF IT'S TOO LATE, THAT INFORMATION OF YOURS IS USELESS! SO JUST GIVE IT TO ME...

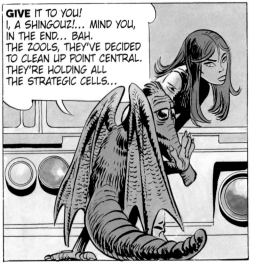

GIVE IT TO YOU! I, A SHINGOUZ!... MIND YOU, IN THE END... BAH. THE ZOOLS, THEY'VE DECIDED TO CLEAN UP POINT CENTRAL. THEY'RE HOLDING ALL THE STRATEGIC CELLS...

THOSE IDIOTS WANT TO RESTORE THE COUNCIL'S ORIGINAL INTEGRITY, KICK OUT THE PROFITEERS...

THEY'D BEEN PREPARING FOR IT FOR CENTURIES, BUT IT WAS YOUR AMBASSADOR'S SHADY DEALINGS THAT TRIGGERED THEIR MOVE... SERIOUSLY, WASN'T POINT CENTRAL FINE THE WAY IT WAS?... AND ... WAIT...

44B

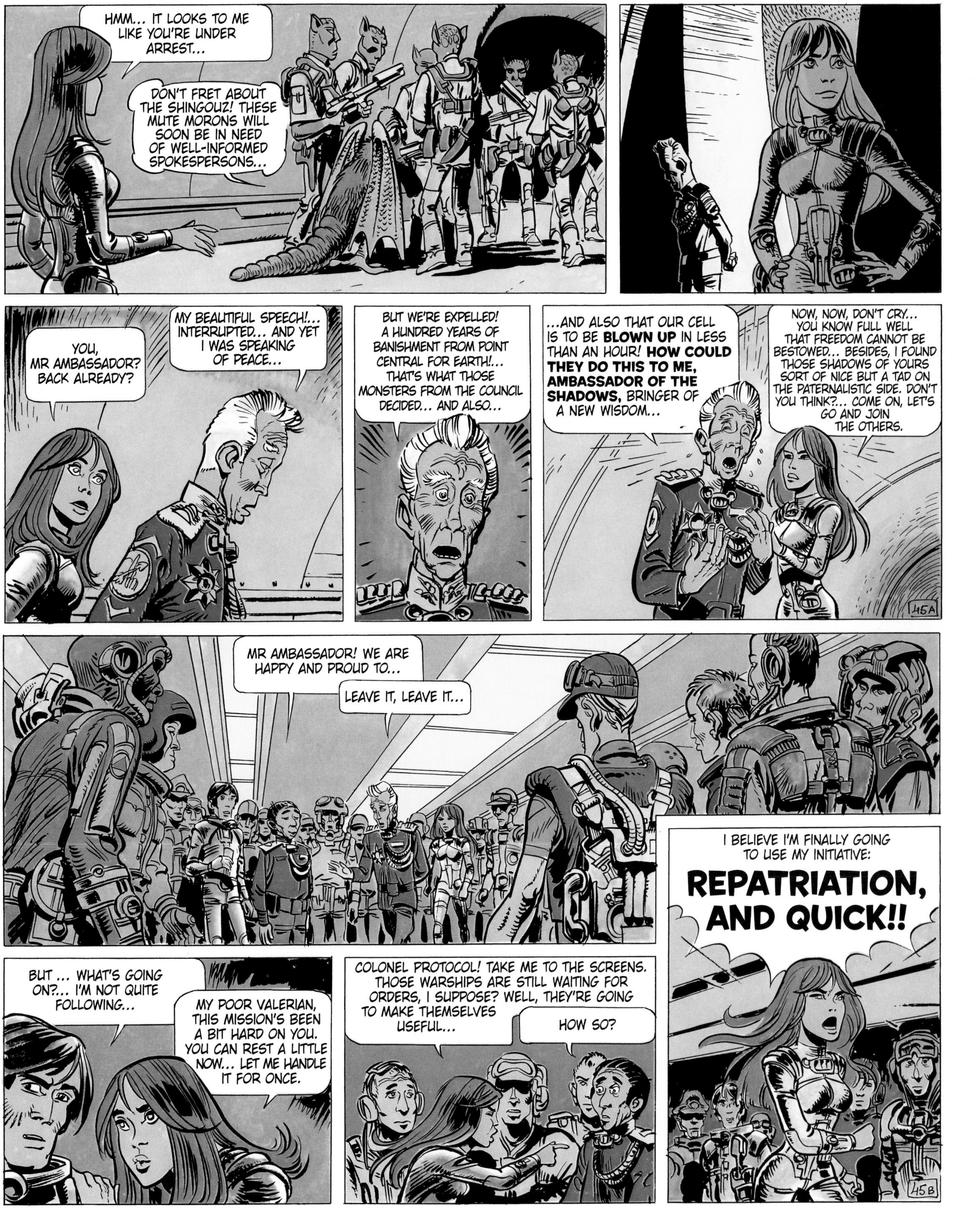

HMM... IT LOOKS TO ME LIKE YOU'RE UNDER ARREST...
DON'T FRET ABOUT THE SHINGOUZ! THESE MUTE MORONS WILL SOON BE IN NEED OF WELL-INFORMED SPOKESPERSONS...
YOU, MR AMBASSADOR? BACK ALREADY?
MY BEAUTIFUL SPEECH!... INTERRUPTED... AND YET I WAS SPEAKING OF PEACE...
BUT WE'RE EXPELLED! A HUNDRED YEARS OF BANISHMENT FROM POINT CENTRAL FOR EARTH!... THAT'S WHAT THOSE MONSTERS FROM THE COUNCIL DECIDED... AND ALSO...
...AND ALSO THAT OUR CELL IS TO BE **BLOWN UP** IN LESS THAN AN HOUR! **HOW COULD THEY DO THIS TO ME, AMBASSADOR OF THE SHADOWS,** BRINGER OF A NEW WISDOM...
NOW, NOW, DON'T CRY... YOU KNOW FULL WELL THAT FREEDOM CANNOT BE BESTOWED... BESIDES, I FOUND THOSE SHADOWS OF YOURS SORT OF NICE BUT A TAD ON THE PATERNALISTIC SIDE. DON'T YOU THINK?... COME ON, LET'S GO AND JOIN THE OTHERS.
45A
MR AMBASSADOR! WE ARE HAPPY AND PROUD TO...
LEAVE IT, LEAVE IT...
BUT ... WHAT'S GOING ON?... I'M NOT QUITE FOLLOWING...
MY POOR VALERIAN, THIS MISSION'S BEEN A BIT HARD ON YOU. YOU CAN REST A LITTLE NOW... LET ME HANDLE IT FOR ONCE.
COLONEL PROTOCOL! TAKE ME TO THE SCREENS. THOSE WARSHIPS ARE STILL WAITING FOR ORDERS, I SUPPOSE? WELL, THEY'RE GOING TO MAKE THEMSELVES USEFUL...
HOW SO?
I BELIEVE I'M FINALLY GOING TO USE MY INITIATIVE:
REPATRIATION, AND QUICK!!
45B

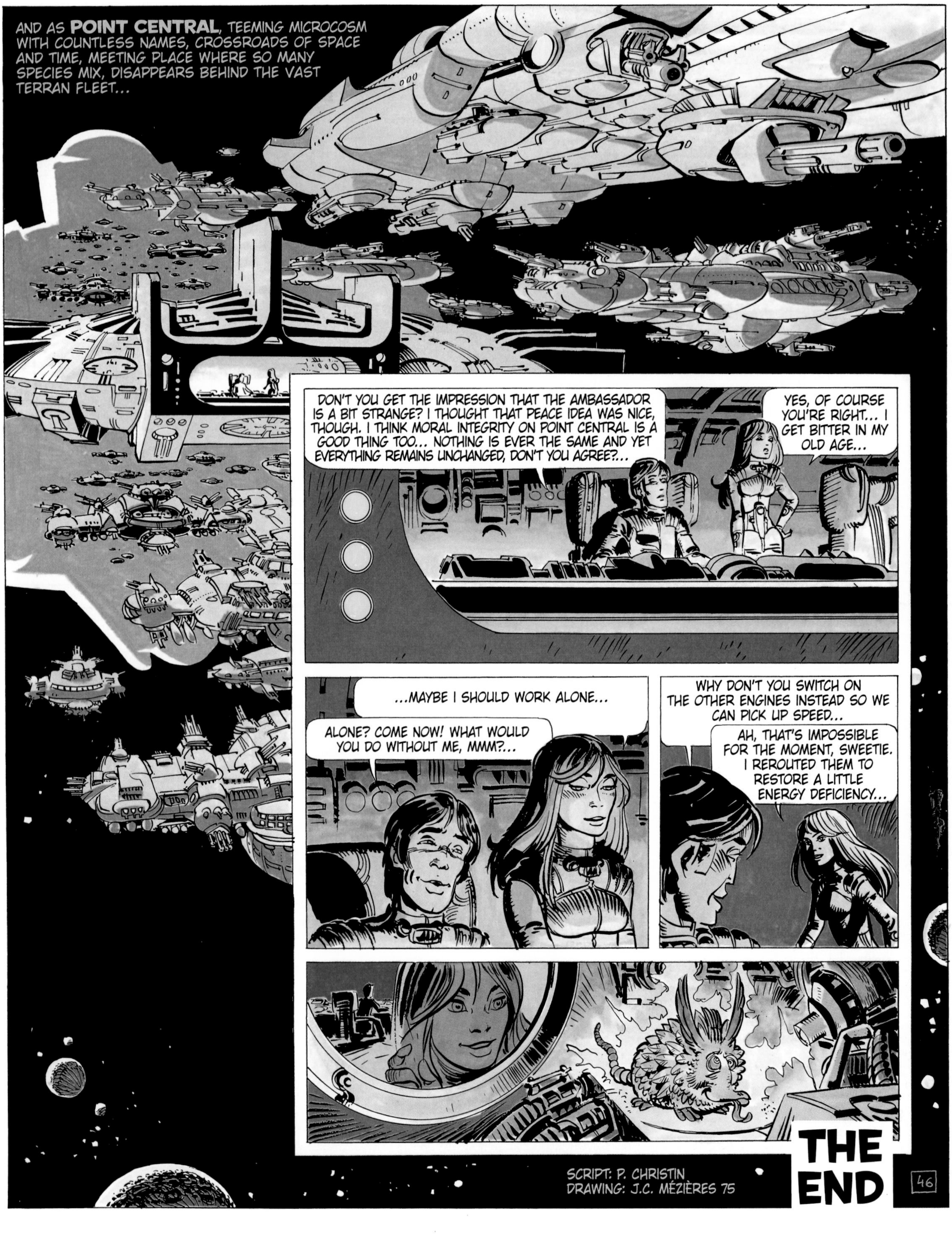
AND AS POINT CENTRAL, TEEMING MICROCOSM WITH COUNTLESS NAMES, CROSSROADS OF SPACE AND TIME, MEETING PLACE WHERE SO MANY SPECIES MIX, DISAPPEARS BEHIND THE VAST TERRAN FLEET...
DON'T YOU GET THE IMPRESSION THAT THE AMBASSADOR IS A BIT STRANGE? I THOUGHT THAT PEACE IDEA WAS NICE, THOUGH. I THINK MORAL INTEGRITY ON POINT CENTRAL IS A GOOD THING TOO... NOTHING IS EVER THE SAME AND YET EVERYTHING REMAINS UNCHANGED, DON'T YOU AGREE?...
YES, OF COURSE YOU'RE RIGHT... I GET BITTER IN MY OLD AGE...
...MAYBE I SHOULD WORK ALONE...
ALONE? COME NOW! WHAT WOULD YOU DO WITHOUT ME, MMM?...
WHY DON'T YOU SWITCH ON THE OTHER ENGINES INSTEAD SO WE CAN PICK UP SPEED...
AH, THAT'S IMPOSSIBLE FOR THE MOMENT, SWEETIE. I REROUTED THEM TO RESTORE A LITTLE ENERGY DEFICIENCY...
THE END
SCRIPT: P. CHRISTIN
DRAWING: J.C. MÉZIÈRES 75
46

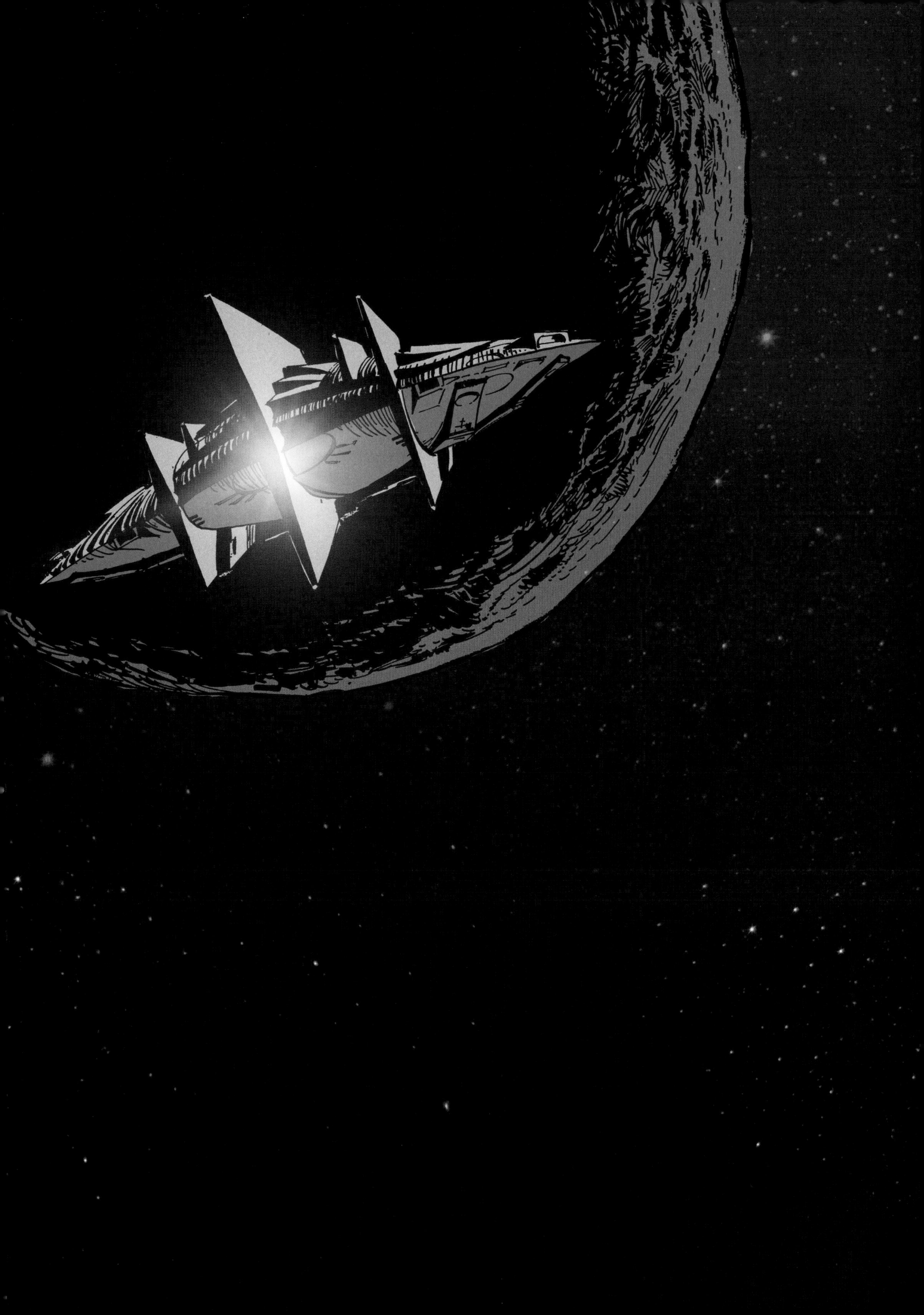

ON THE FALSE EARTHS

....

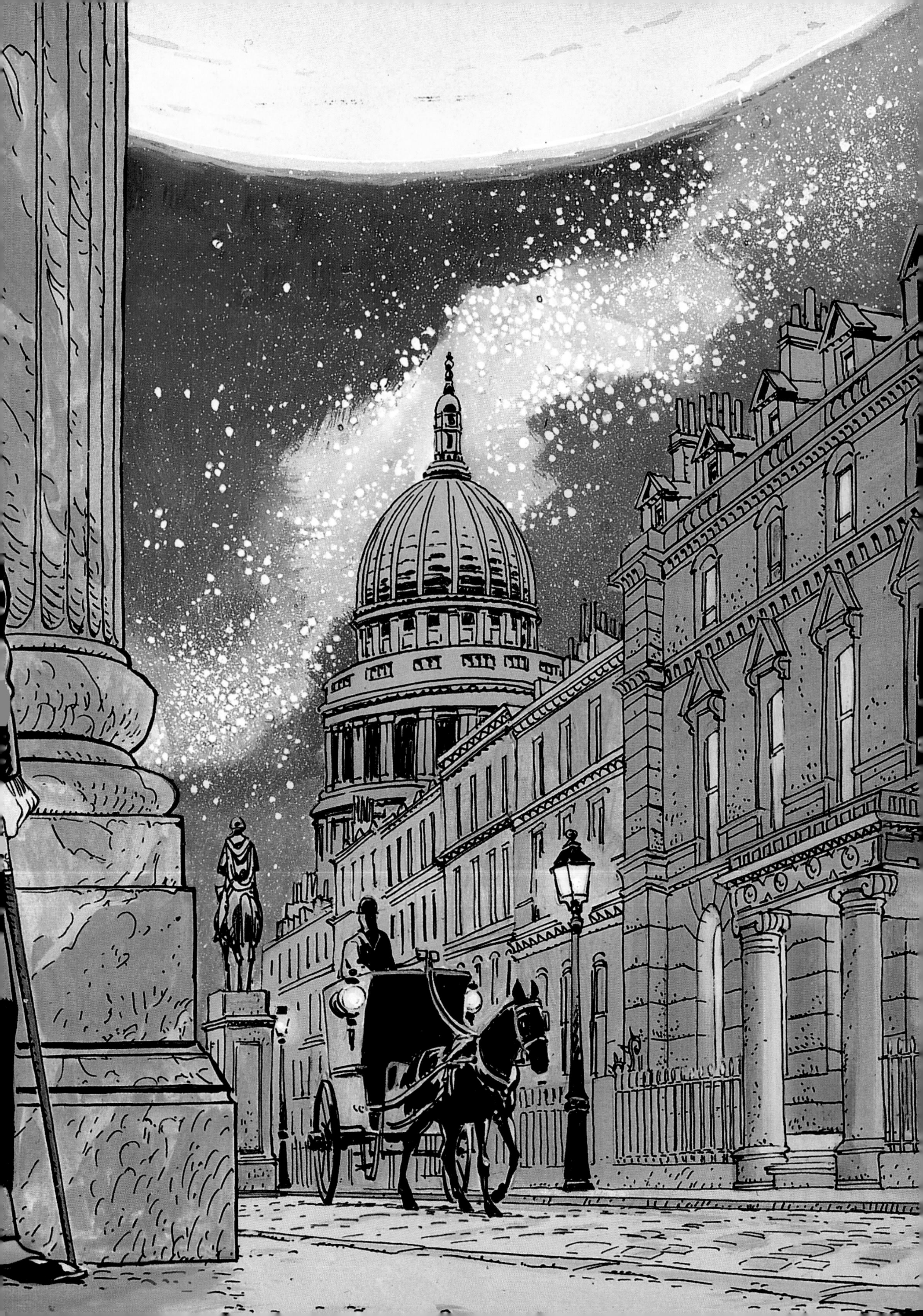

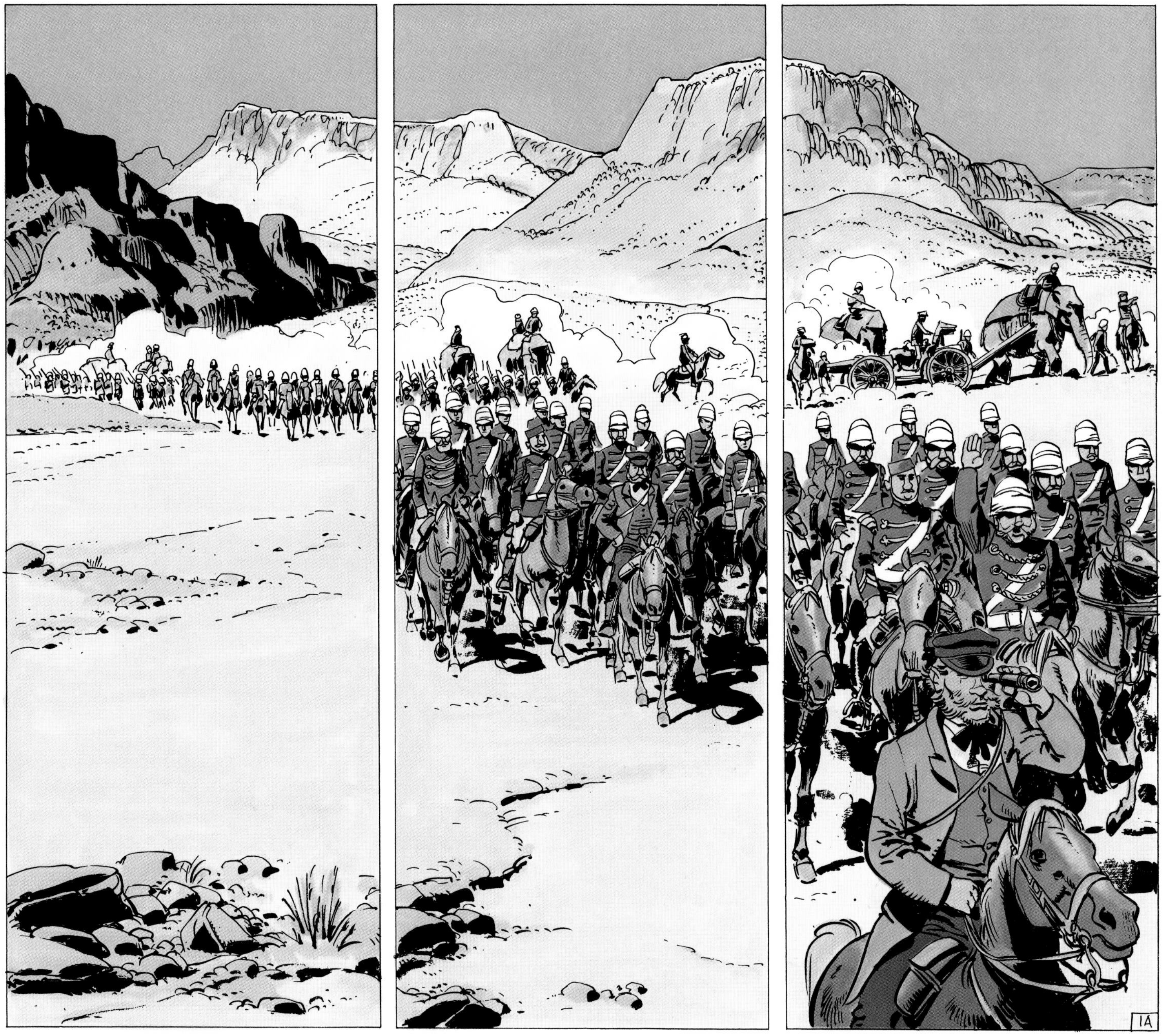
1A

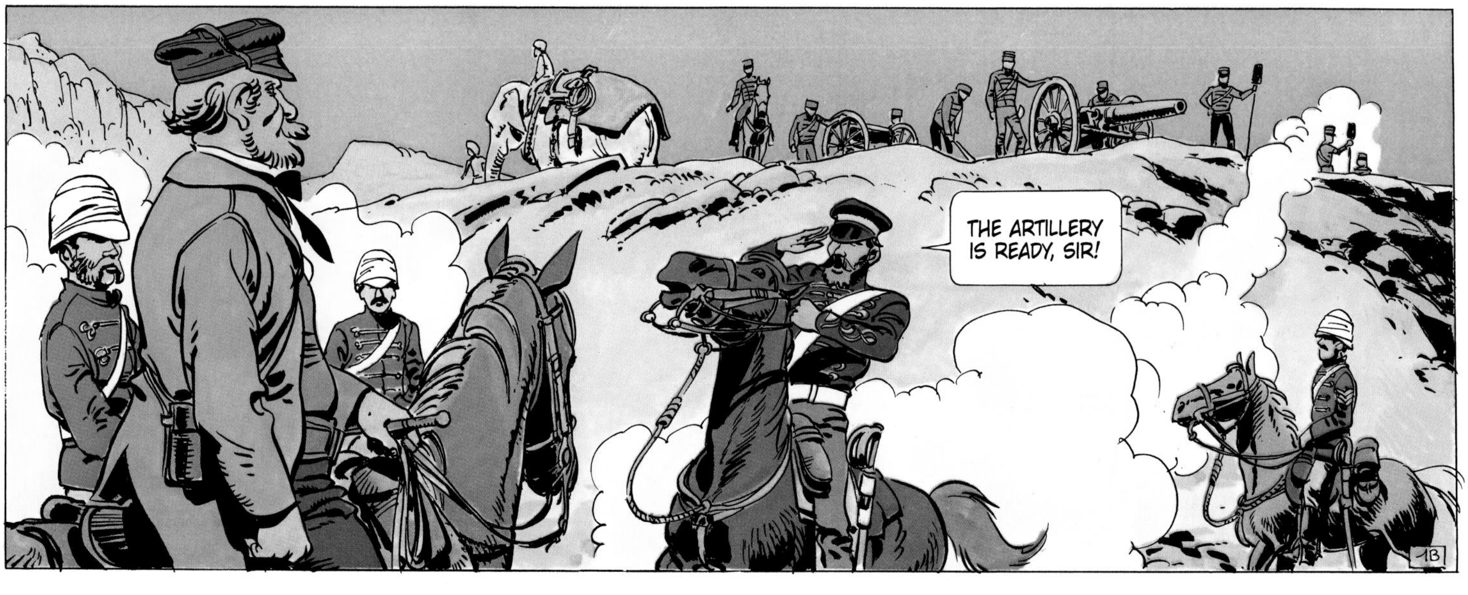
THE ARTILLERY IS READY, SIR!
1B

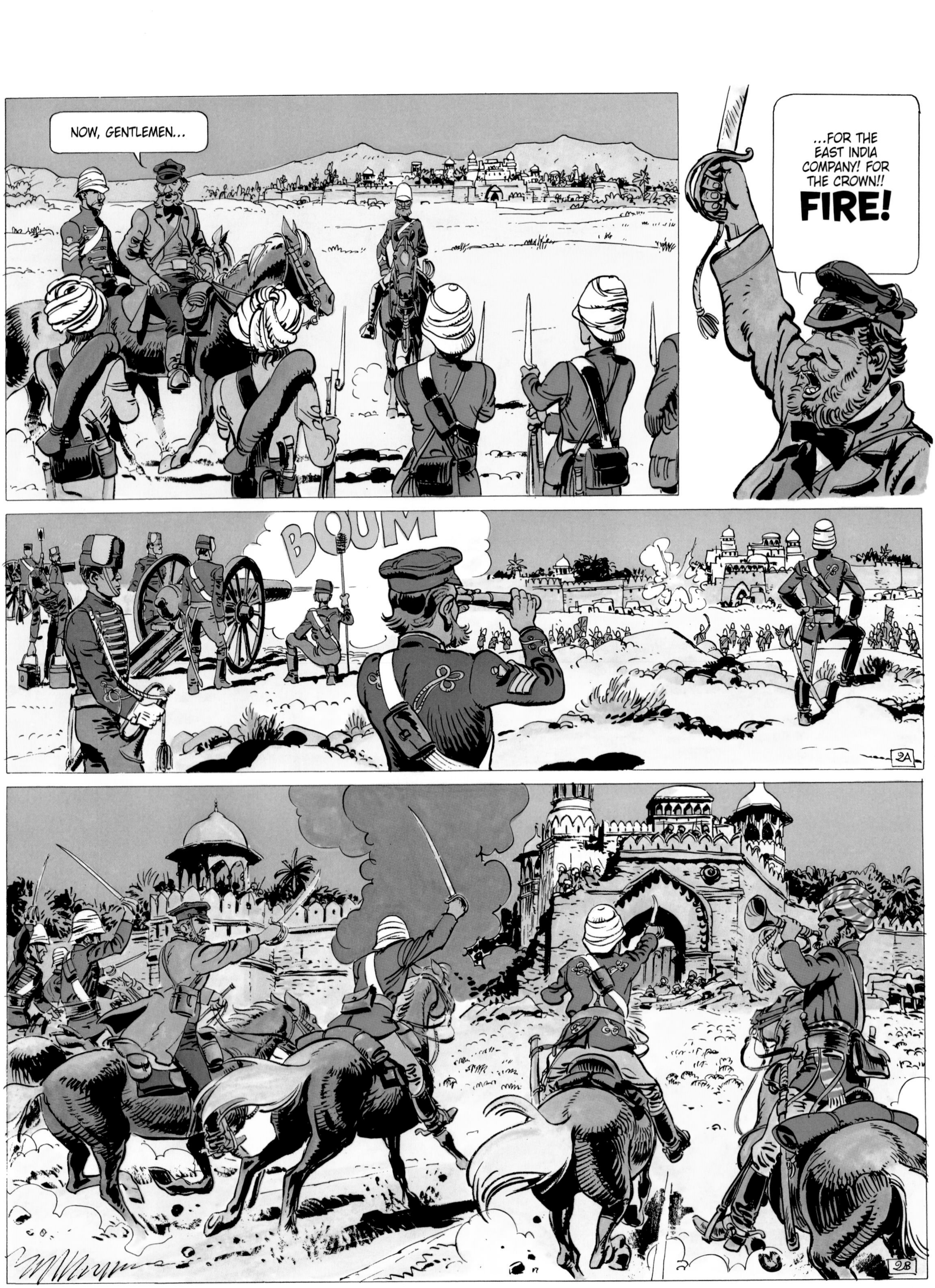
NOW, GENTLEMEN…
…FOR THE EAST INDIA COMPANY! FOR THE CROWN!! FIRE!
BOUM

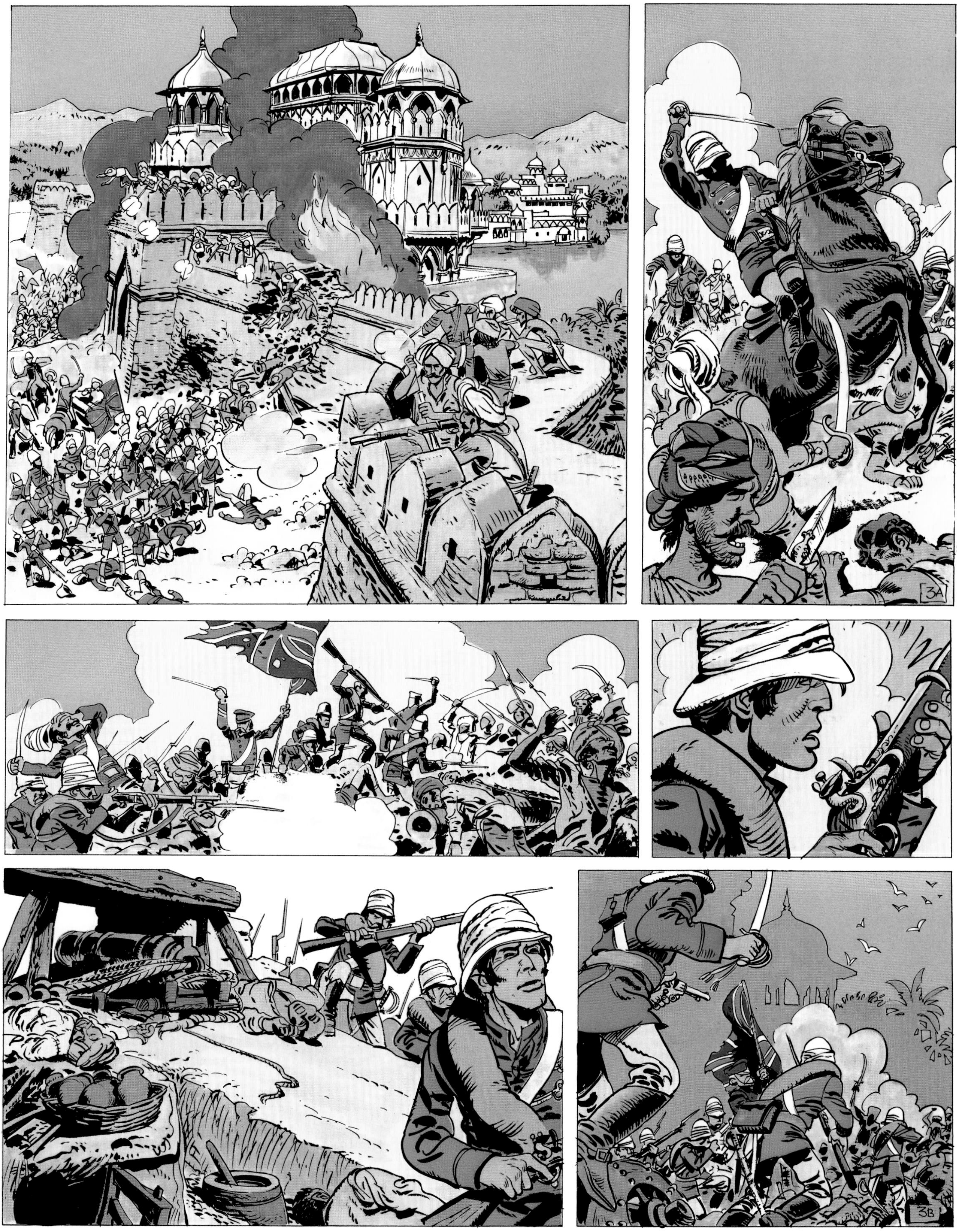
3A
3B

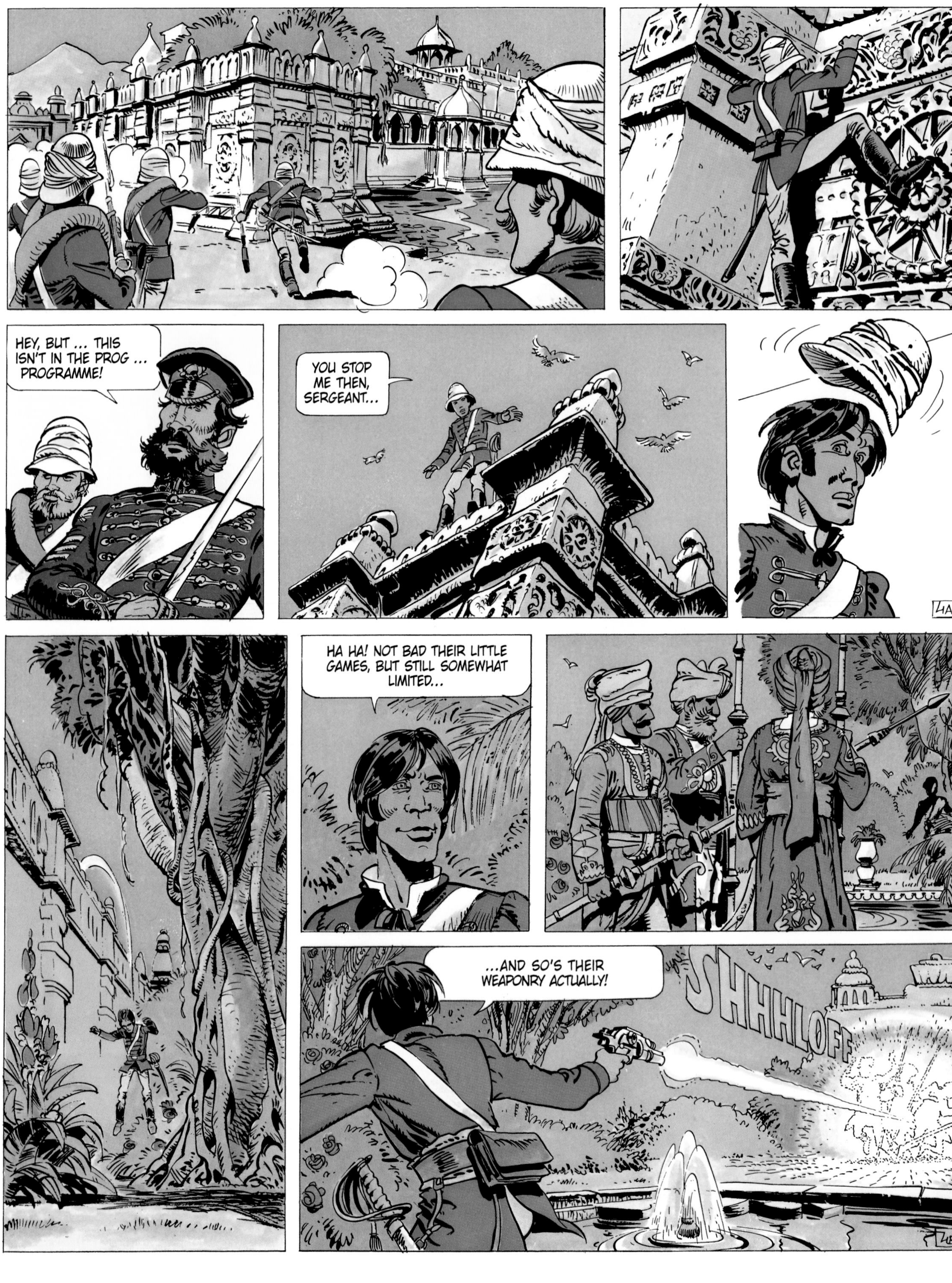
HEY, BUT ... THIS ISN'T IN THE PROG ... PROGRAMME!
YOU STOP ME THEN, SERGEANT...
HA HA! NOT BAD THEIR LITTLE GAMES, BUT STILL SOMEWHAT LIMITED...
...AND SO'S THEIR WEAPONRY ACTUALLY!
SHHHLOFF

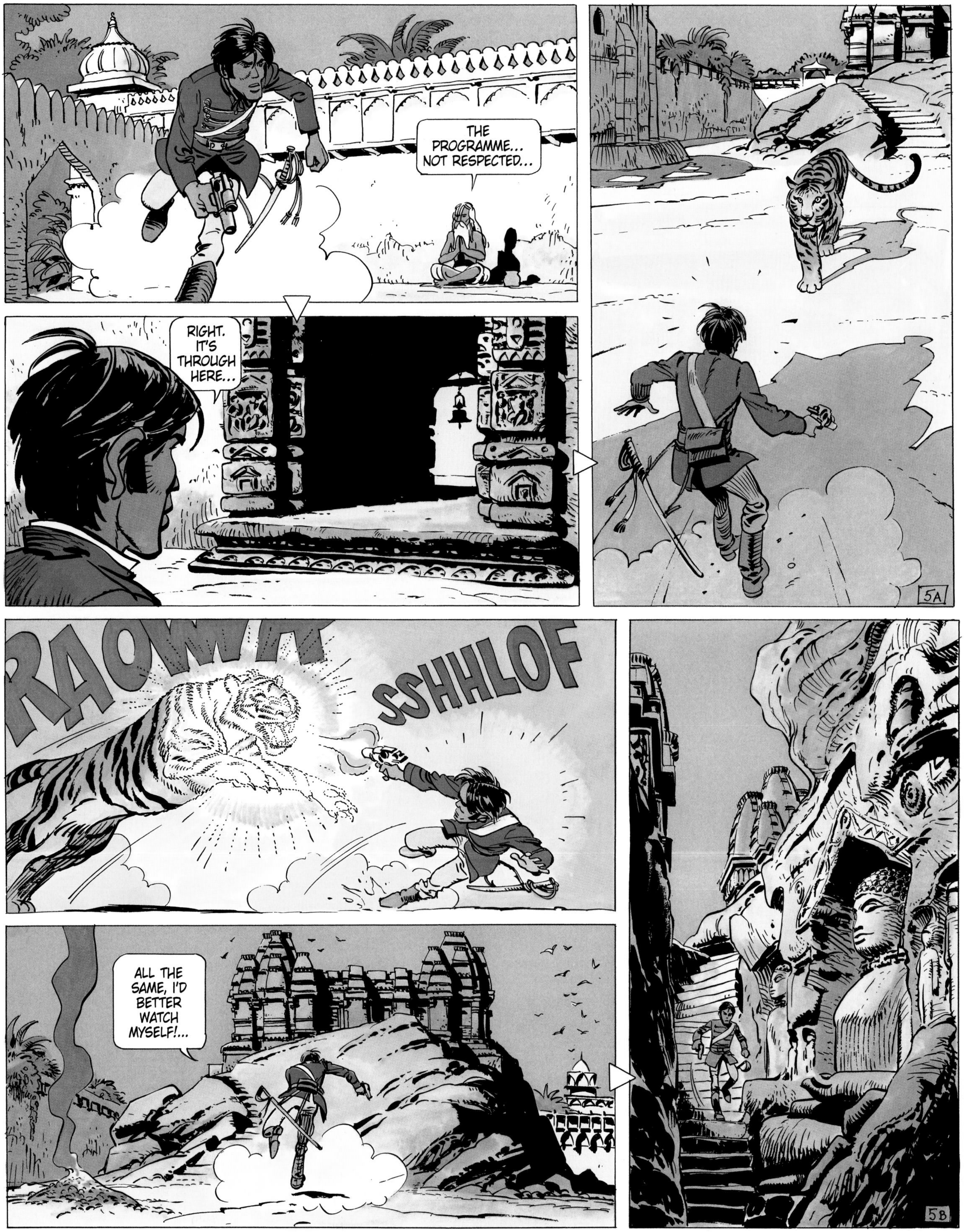
THE PROGRAMME... NOT RESPECTED...
RIGHT. IT'S THROUGH HERE...
5A
RAOWR
SSHHLOF
ALL THE SAME, I'D BETTER WATCH MYSELF!...
5B

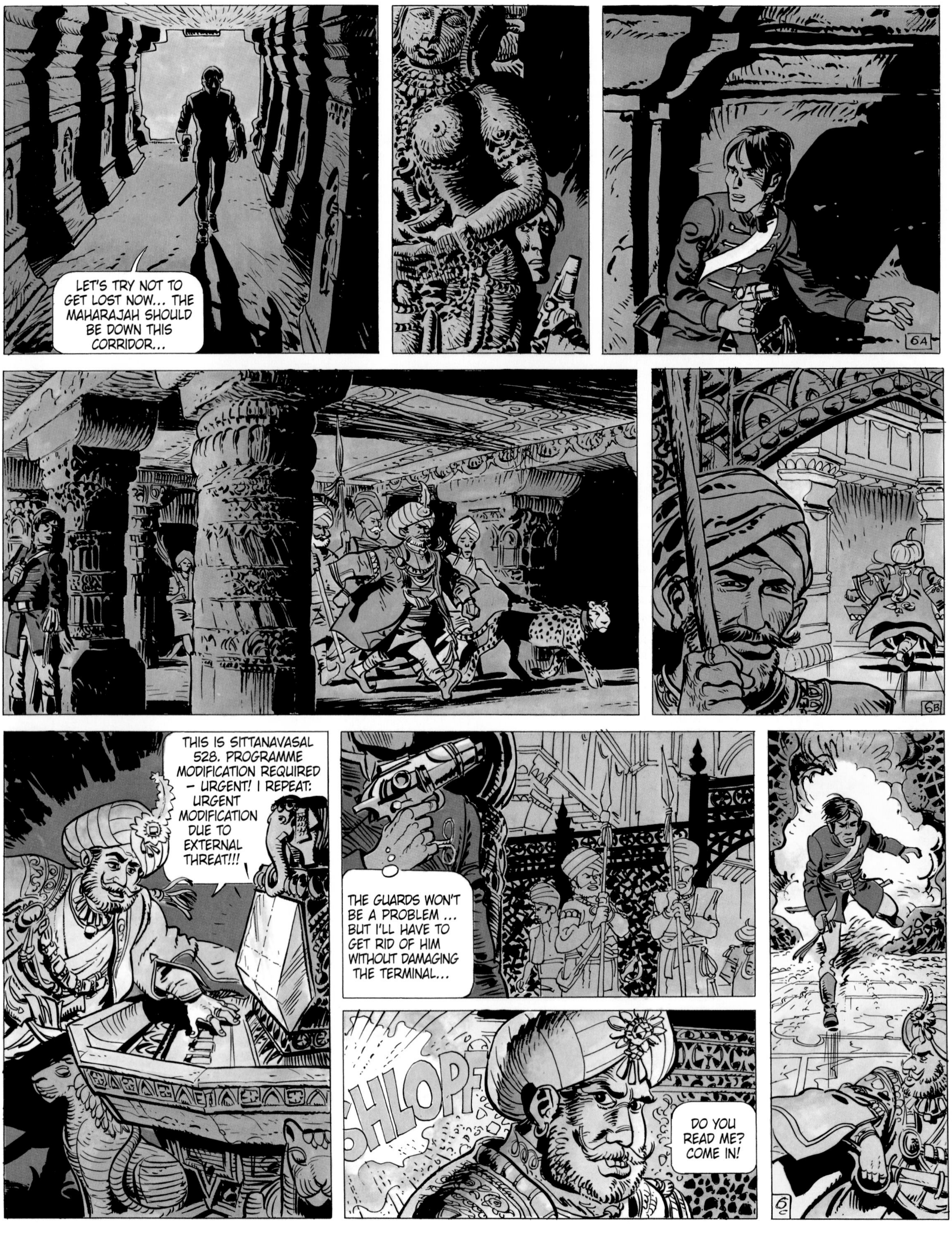
LET'S TRY NOT TO GET LOST NOW... THE MAHARAJAH SHOULD BE DOWN THIS CORRIDOR...
6A
6B
THIS IS SITTANAVASAL 528. PROGRAMME MODIFICATION REQUIRED – URGENT! I REPEAT: URGENT MODIFICATION DUE TO EXTERNAL THREAT!!!
THE GUARDS WON'T BE A PROBLEM ... BUT I'LL HAVE TO GET RID OF HIM WITHOUT DAMAGING THE TERMINAL...
SHLOPF
DO YOU READ ME? COME IN!
6C

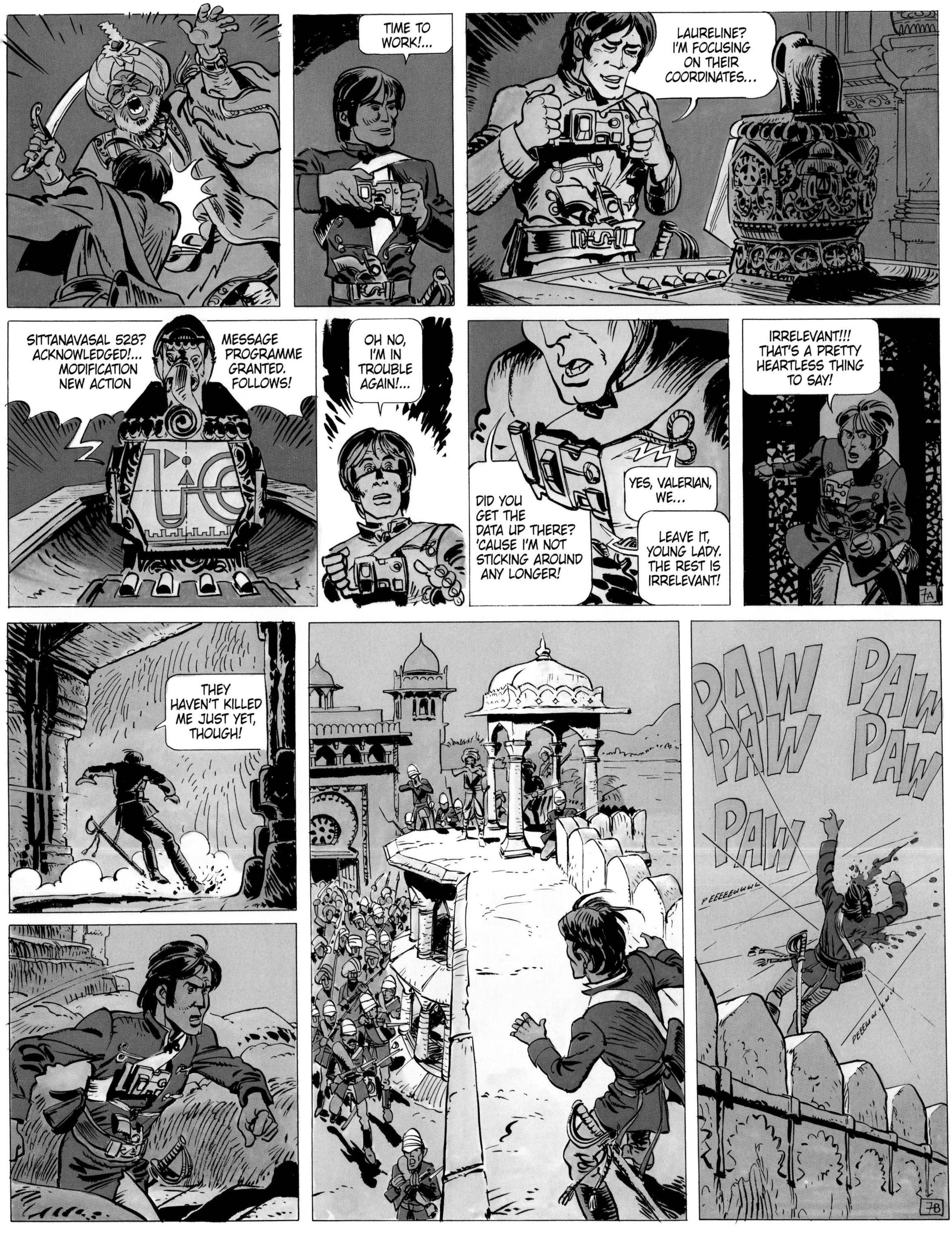
TIME TO WORK!...
LAURELINE? I'M FOCUSING ON THEIR COORDINATES...
SITTANAVASAL 528? ACKNOWLEDGED!... MODIFICATION NEW ACTION
MESSAGE PROGRAMME GRANTED. FOLLOWS!
OH NO, I'M IN TROUBLE AGAIN!...
DID YOU GET THE DATA UP THERE? 'CAUSE I'M NOT STICKING AROUND ANY LONGER!
YES, VALERIAN, WE...
LEAVE IT, YOUNG LADY. THE REST IS IRRELEVANT!
IRRELEVANT!!! THAT'S A PRETTY HEARTLESS THING TO SAY!
7A
THEY HAVEN'T KILLED ME JUST YET, THOUGH!
PAW PAW PAW PAW PAW PAW PAW
7B

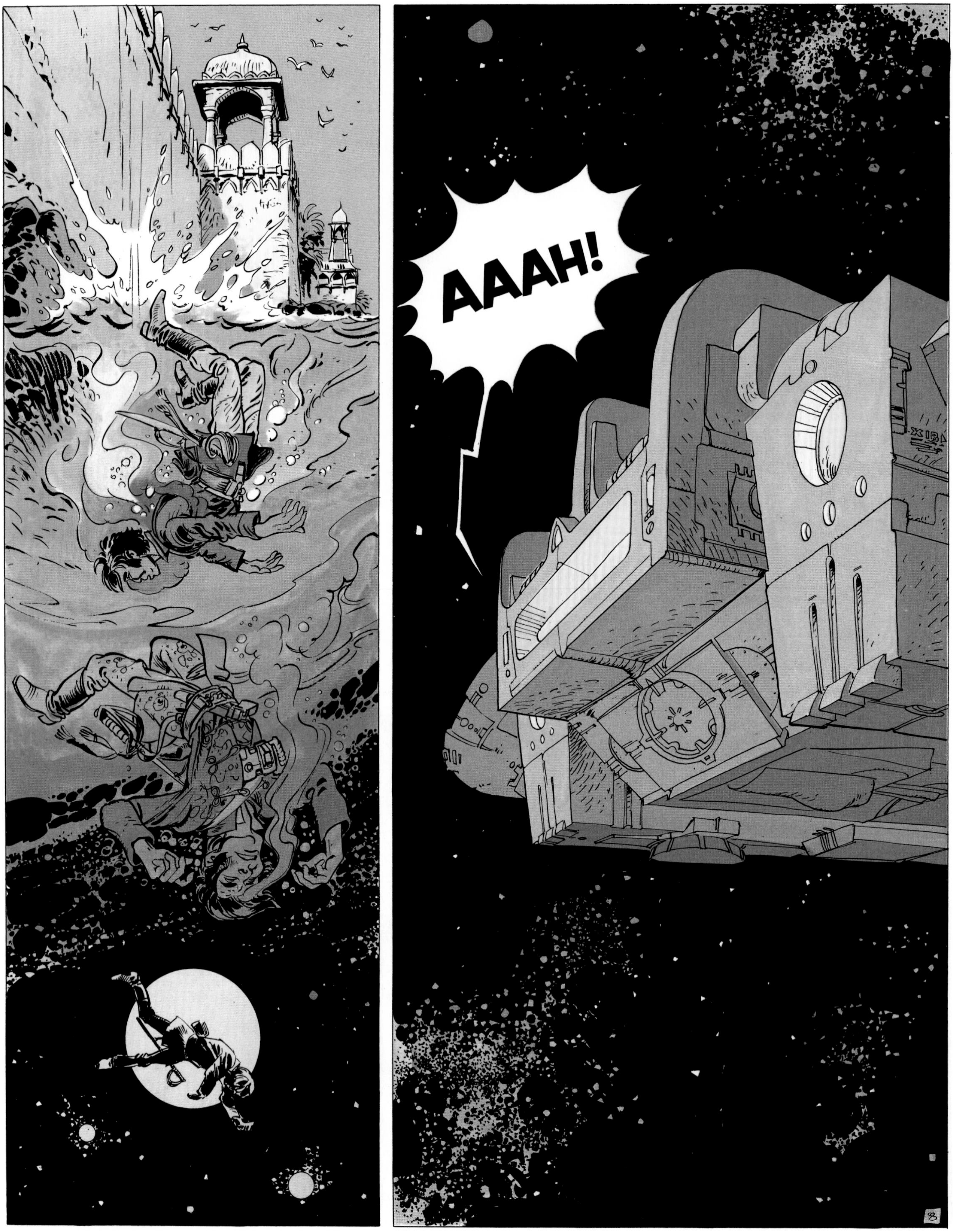
AAAH!

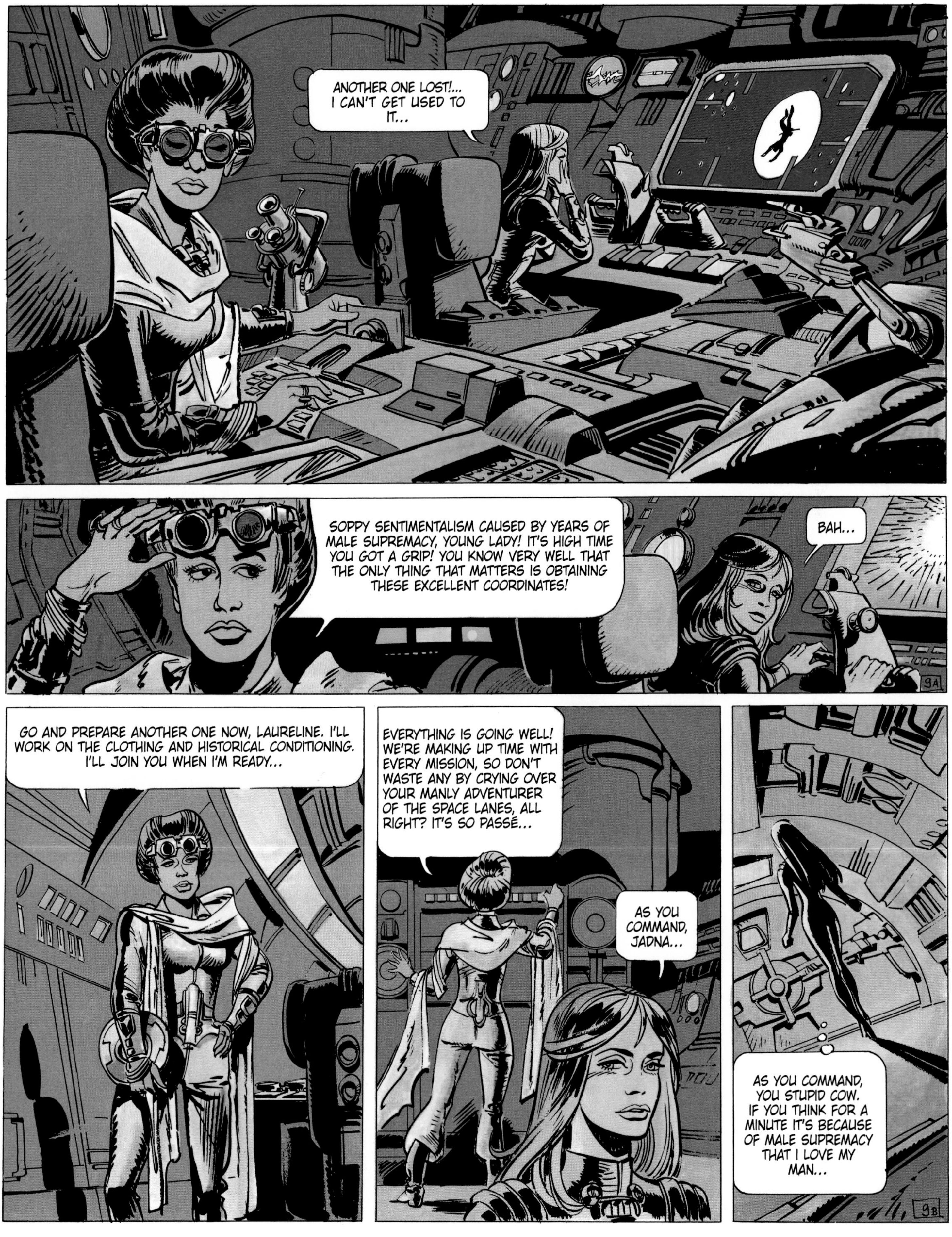
ANOTHER ONE LOST!... I CAN'T GET USED TO IT...
SOPPY SENTIMENTALISM CAUSED BY YEARS OF MALE SUPREMACY, YOUNG LADY! IT'S HIGH TIME YOU GOT A GRIP! YOU KNOW VERY WELL THAT THE ONLY THING THAT MATTERS IS OBTAINING THESE EXCELLENT COORDINATES!
BAH...
9A
GO AND PREPARE ANOTHER ONE NOW, LAURELINE. I'LL WORK ON THE CLOTHING AND HISTORICAL CONDITIONING. I'LL JOIN YOU WHEN I'M READY...
EVERYTHING IS GOING WELL! WE'RE MAKING UP TIME WITH EVERY MISSION, SO DON'T WASTE ANY BY CRYING OVER YOUR MANLY ADVENTURER OF THE SPACE LANES, ALL RIGHT? IT'S SO PASSÉ...
AS YOU COMMAND, JADNA...
AS YOU COMMAND, YOU STUPID COW. IF YOU THINK FOR A MINUTE IT'S BECAUSE OF MALE SUPREMACY THAT I LOVE MY MAN...
9B

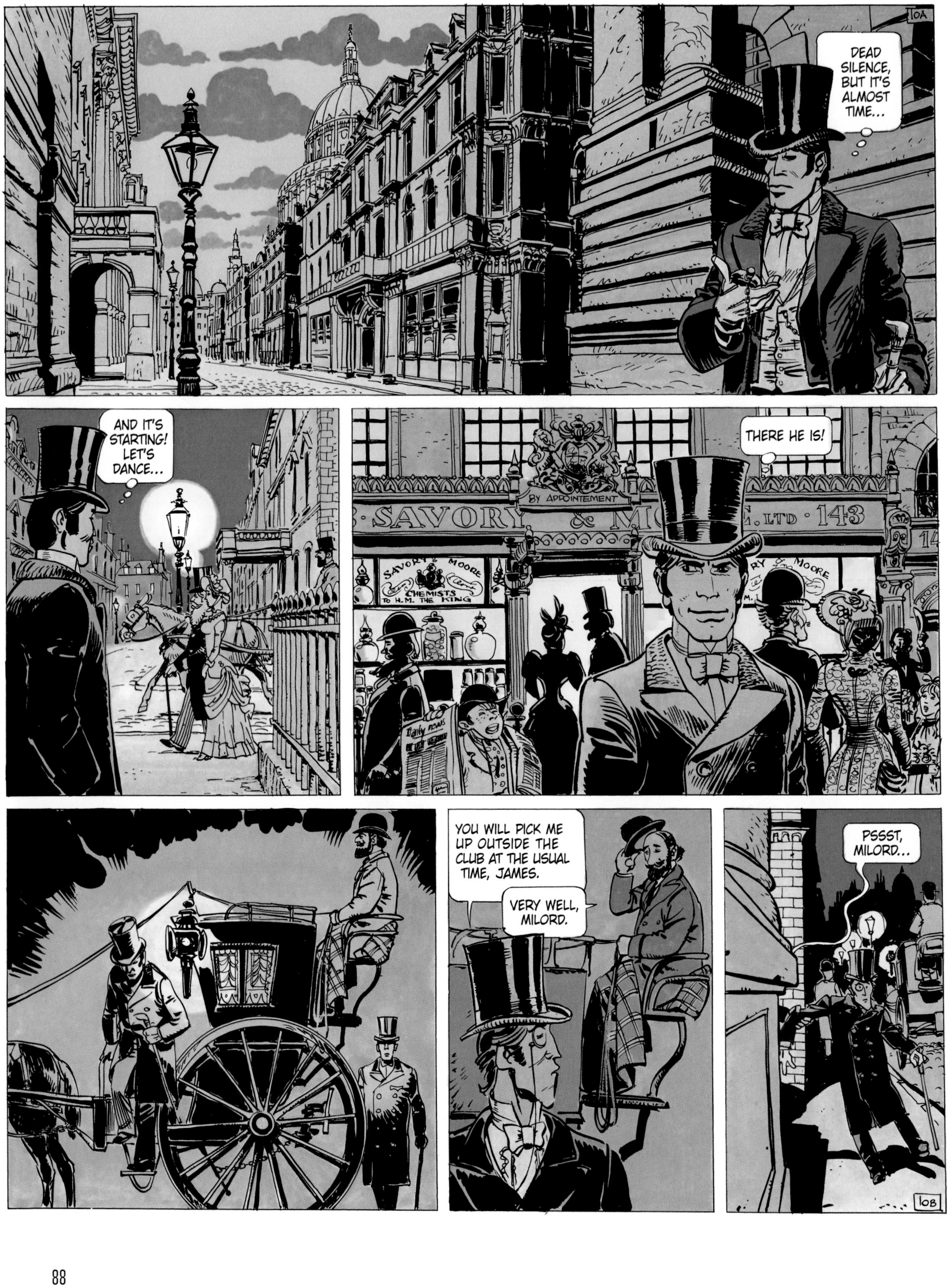
DEAD SILENCE, BUT IT'S ALMOST TIME...
AND IT'S STARTING! LET'S DANCE...
BY APPOINTEMENT
SAVORY & MOORE LTD 143
SAVORY & MOORE CHEMISTS TO H.M. THE KING
THERE HE IS!
YOU WILL PICK ME UP OUTSIDE THE CLUB AT THE USUAL TIME, JAMES.
VERY WELL, MILORD.
PSSST, MILORD...

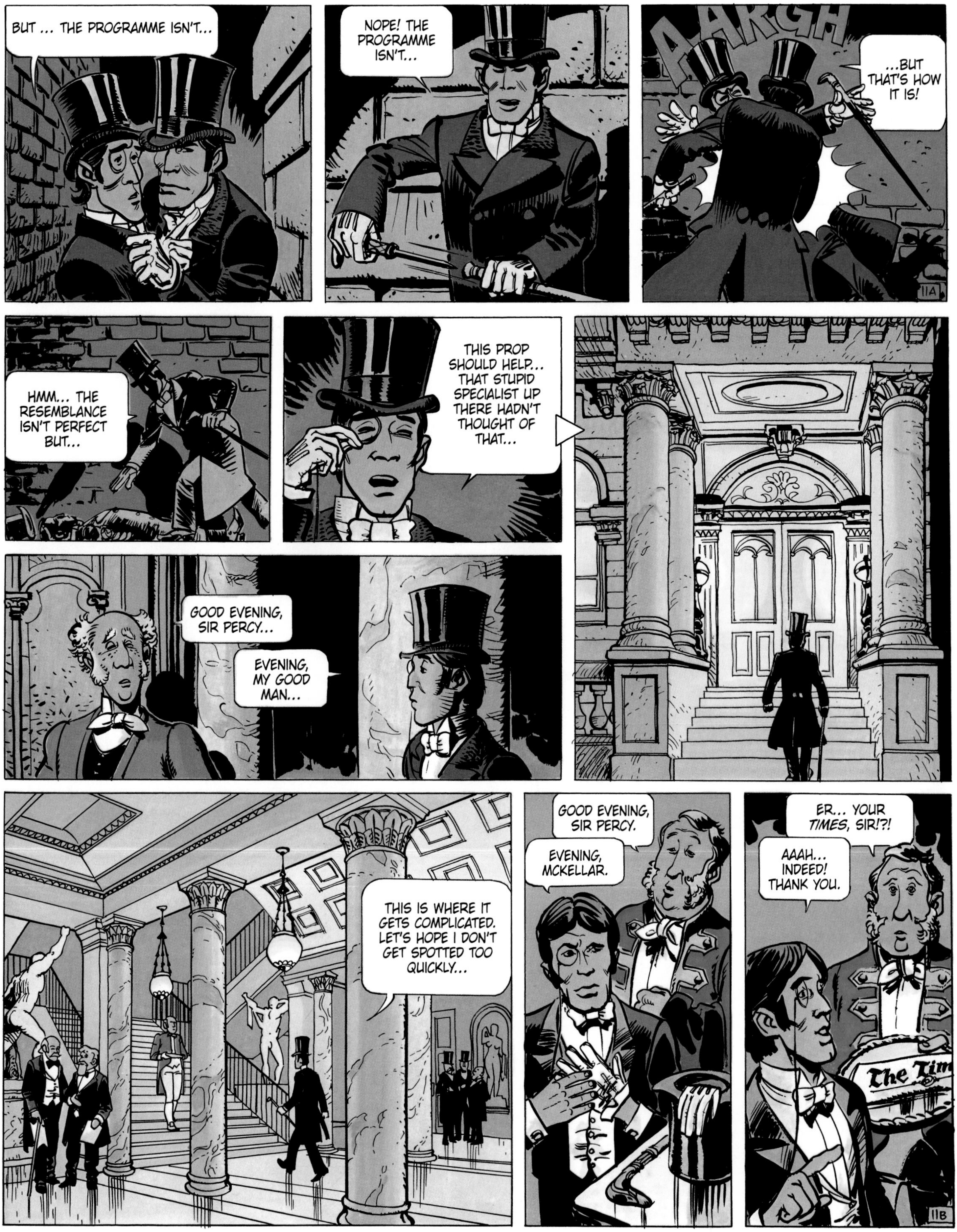
BUT ... THE PROGRAMME ISN'T...
NOPE! THE PROGRAMME ISN'T...
AARGH
...BUT THAT'S HOW IT IS!
11A
HMM... THE RESEMBLANCE ISN'T PERFECT BUT...
THIS PROP SHOULD HELP... THAT STUPID SPECIALIST UP THERE HADN'T THOUGHT OF THAT...
GOOD EVENING, SIR PERCY...
EVENING, MY GOOD MAN...
THIS IS WHERE IT GETS COMPLICATED. LET'S HOPE I DON'T GET SPOTTED TOO QUICKLY...
GOOD EVENING, SIR PERCY.
EVENING, MCKELLAR.
ER... YOUR *TIMES*, SIR!?!
AAAH... INDEED! THANK YOU.
The Tim
11B

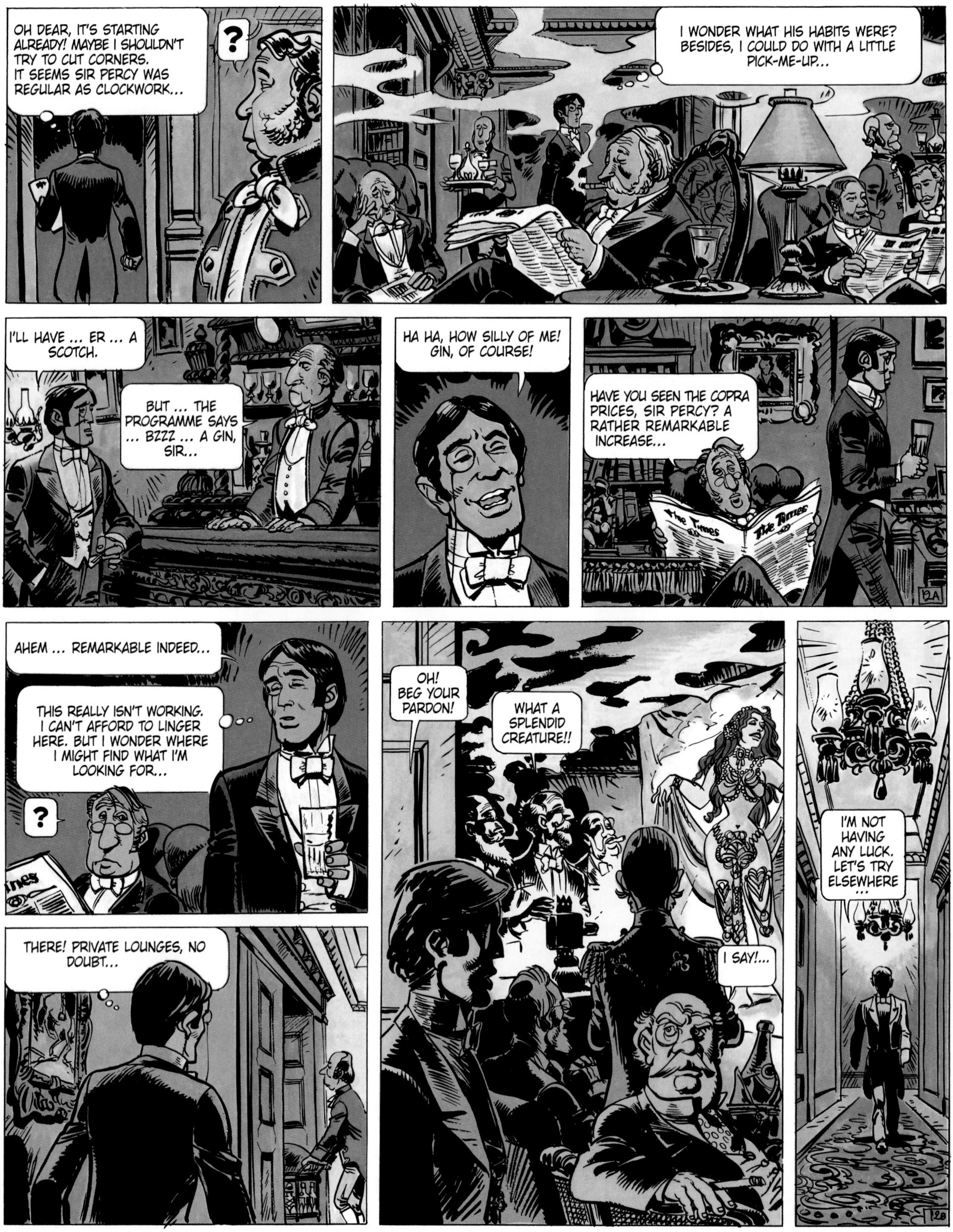
OH DEAR, IT'S STARTING ALREADY! MAYBE I SHOULDN'T TRY TO CUT CORNERS. IT SEEMS SIR PERCY WAS REGULAR AS CLOCKWORK...
?
I WONDER WHAT HIS HABITS WERE? BESIDES, I COULD DO WITH A LITTLE PICK-ME-UP...
I'LL HAVE ... ER ... A SCOTCH.
BUT ... THE PROGRAMME SAYS ... BZZZ ... A GIN, SIR...
HA HA, HOW SILLY OF ME! GIN, OF COURSE!
HAVE YOU SEEN THE COPRA PRICES, SIR PERCY? A RATHER REMARKABLE INCREASE...
The Times
12A
AHEM ... REMARKABLE INDEED...
THIS REALLY ISN'T WORKING. I CAN'T AFFORD TO LINGER HERE. BUT I WONDER WHERE I MIGHT FIND WHAT I'M LOOKING FOR...
?
THERE! PRIVATE LOUNGES, NO DOUBT...
OH! BEG YOUR PARDON!
WHAT A SPLENDID CREATURE!!
I SAY!...
I'M NOT HAVING ANY LUCK. LET'S TRY ELSEWHERE ...
12B

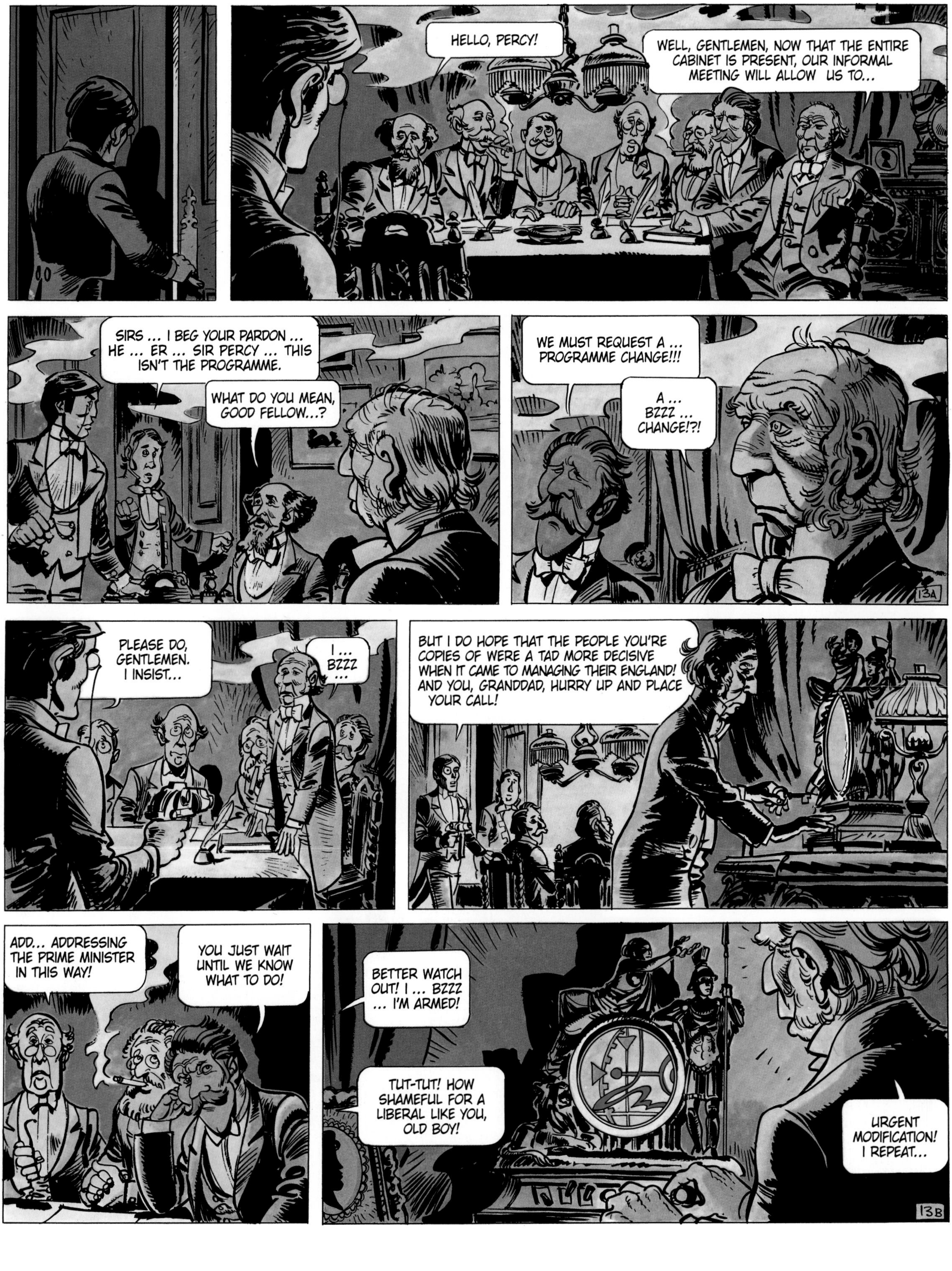
HELLO, PERCY!
WELL, GENTLEMEN, NOW THAT THE ENTIRE CABINET IS PRESENT, OUR INFORMAL MEETING WILL ALLOW US TO...
SIRS ... I BEG YOUR PARDON ... HE ... ER ... SIR PERCY ... THIS ISN'T THE PROGRAMME.
WHAT DO YOU MEAN, GOOD FELLOW...?
WE MUST REQUEST A ... PROGRAMME CHANGE!!!
A ... BZZZ ... CHANGE!?!
PLEASE DO, GENTLEMEN. I INSIST...
I ... BZZZ ...
BUT I DO HOPE THAT THE PEOPLE YOU'RE COPIES OF WERE A TAD MORE DECISIVE WHEN IT CAME TO MANAGING THEIR ENGLAND! AND YOU, GRANDDAD, HURRY UP AND PLACE YOUR CALL!
ADD... ADDRESSING THE PRIME MINISTER IN THIS WAY!
YOU JUST WAIT UNTIL WE KNOW WHAT TO DO!
BETTER WATCH OUT! I ... BZZZ ... I'M ARMED!
TUT-TUT! HOW SHAMEFUL FOR A LIBERAL LIKE YOU, OLD BOY!
URGENT MODIFICATION! I REPEAT...

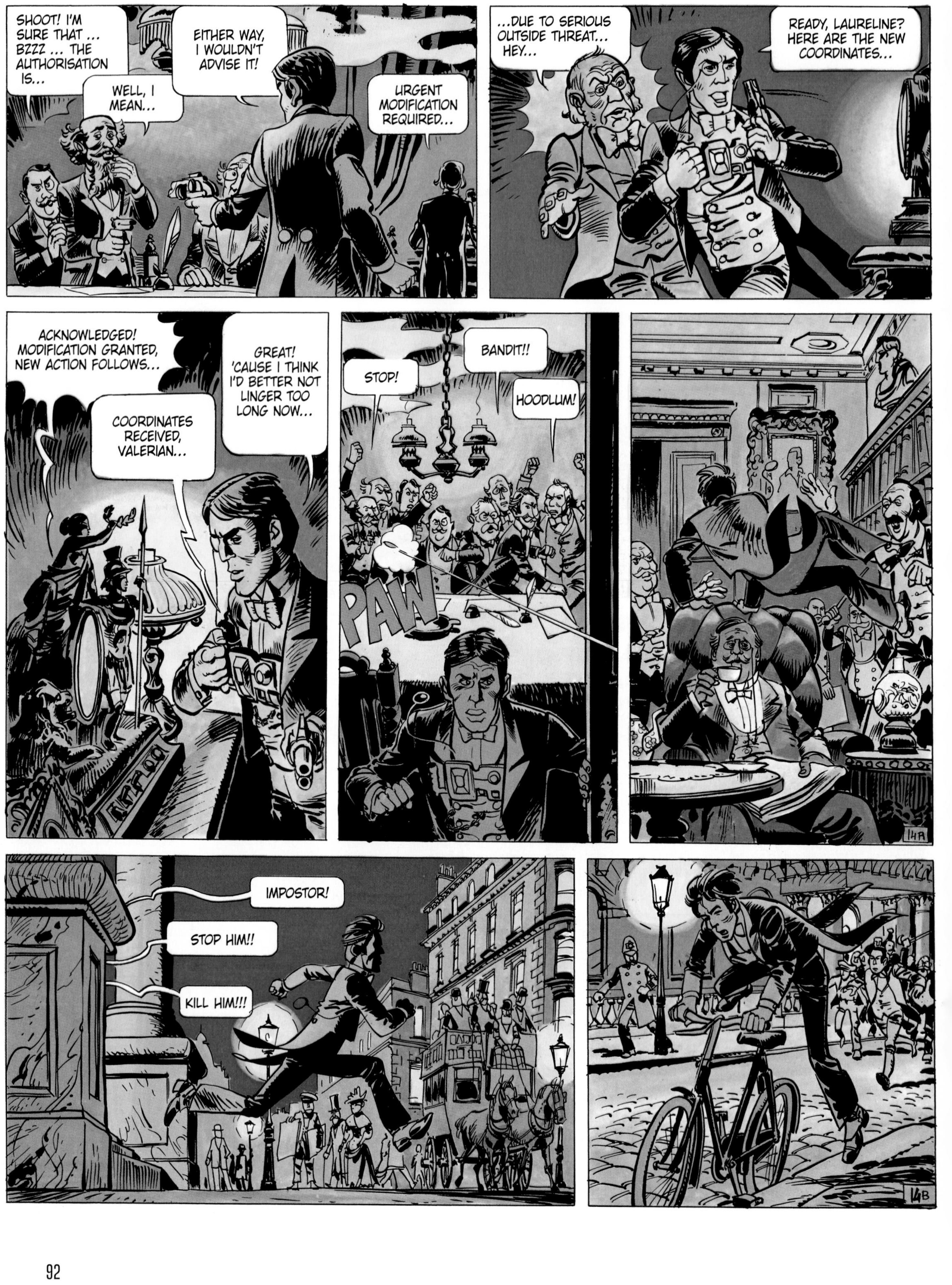
SHOOT! I'M SURE THAT ... BZZZ ... THE AUTHORISATION IS...
WELL, I MEAN...
EITHER WAY, I WOULDN'T ADVISE IT!
URGENT MODIFICATION REQUIRED...
...DUE TO SERIOUS OUTSIDE THREAT... HEY...
READY, LAURELINE? HERE ARE THE NEW COORDINATES...
ACKNOWLEDGED! MODIFICATION GRANTED, NEW ACTION FOLLOWS...
COORDINATES RECEIVED, VALERIAN...
GREAT! 'CAUSE I THINK I'D BETTER NOT LINGER TOO LONG NOW...
STOP!
BANDIT!!
HOODLUM!
PAW
IMPOSTOR!
STOP HIM!!
KILL HIM!!!

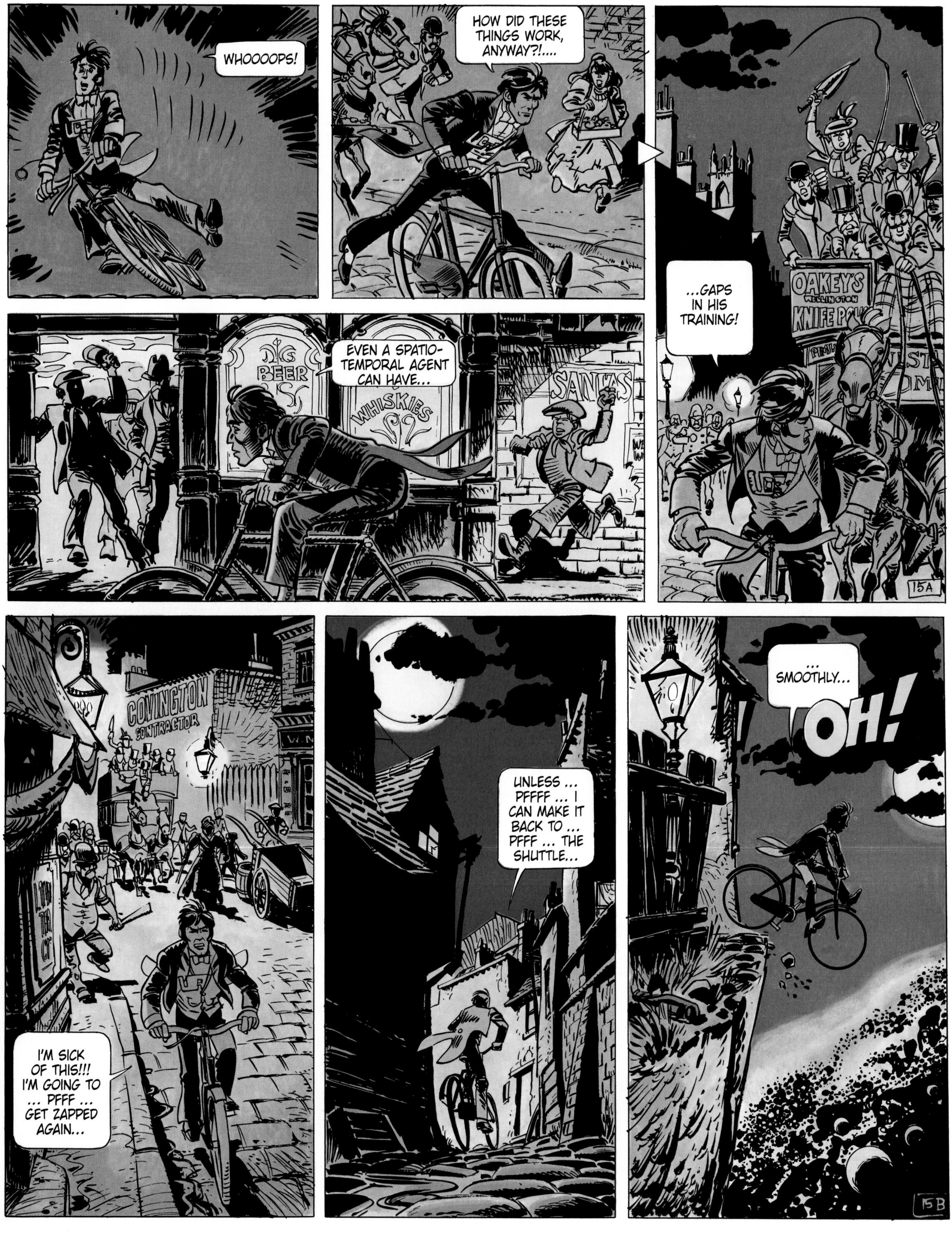
WHOOOOPS!
HOW DID THESE THINGS WORK, ANYWAY?!....
OAKEY'S WELLINGTON KNIFE PO
EVEN A SPATIO-TEMPORAL AGENT CAN HAVE...
BEER
WHISKIES
...GAPS IN HIS TRAINING!
15A
COVINGTON CONTRACTOR
I'M SICK OF THIS!!! I'M GOING TO ... PFFF ... GET ZAPPED AGAIN...
UNLESS ... PFFFF ... I CAN MAKE IT BACK TO ... PFFF ... THE SHUTTLE...
... SMOOTHLY...
OH!
15B

THOSE GALACTIC HEROES! ALWAYS INTO ACTION FOR ACTION'S SAKE! YOUR PARTNER KEEPS WASTING VALUABLE TIME FOR US WITH HIS POINTLESS HEROICS!

AAAH!

WHY WAS HE CHOSEN, THEN, HUH!?! HE MAY BE AN IDIOT, BUT HE'S A BRAVE IDIOT, AND THAT'S EXACTLY WHY...

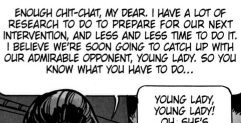

ENOUGH CHIT-CHAT, MY DEAR. I HAVE A LOT OF RESEARCH TO DO TO PREPARE FOR OUR NEXT INTERVENTION, AND LESS AND LESS TIME TO DO IT. I BELIEVE WE'RE SOON GOING TO CATCH UP WITH OUR ADMIRABLE OPPONENT, YOUNG LADY. SO YOU KNOW WHAT YOU HAVE TO DO...

YOUNG LADY, YOUNG LADY! OH, SHE'S ANNOYING!

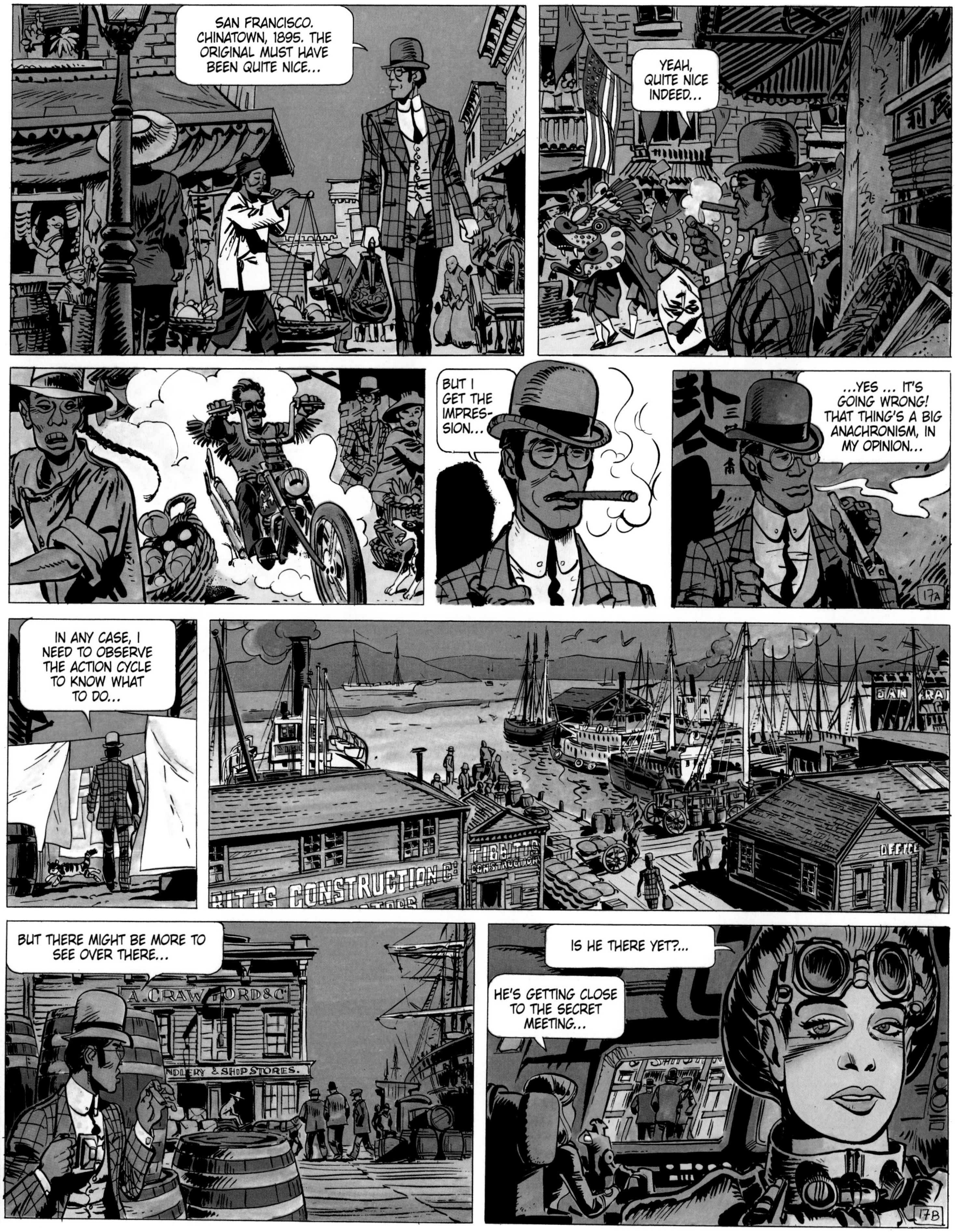

SAN FRANCISCO. CHINATOWN, 1895. THE ORIGINAL MUST HAVE BEEN QUITE NICE...
YEAH, QUITE NICE INDEED...
BUT I GET THE IMPRES-SION...
...YES ... IT'S GOING WRONG! THAT THING'S A BIG ANACHRONISM, IN MY OPINION...
17A
IN ANY CASE, I NEED TO OBSERVE THE ACTION CYCLE TO KNOW WHAT TO DO...
TIBBITTS CONSTRUCTION
OFFICE
BUT THERE MIGHT BE MORE TO SEE OVER THERE...
A. CRAWFORD & C°
IS HE THERE YET?...
HE'S GETTING CLOSE TO THE SECRET MEETING...
17B

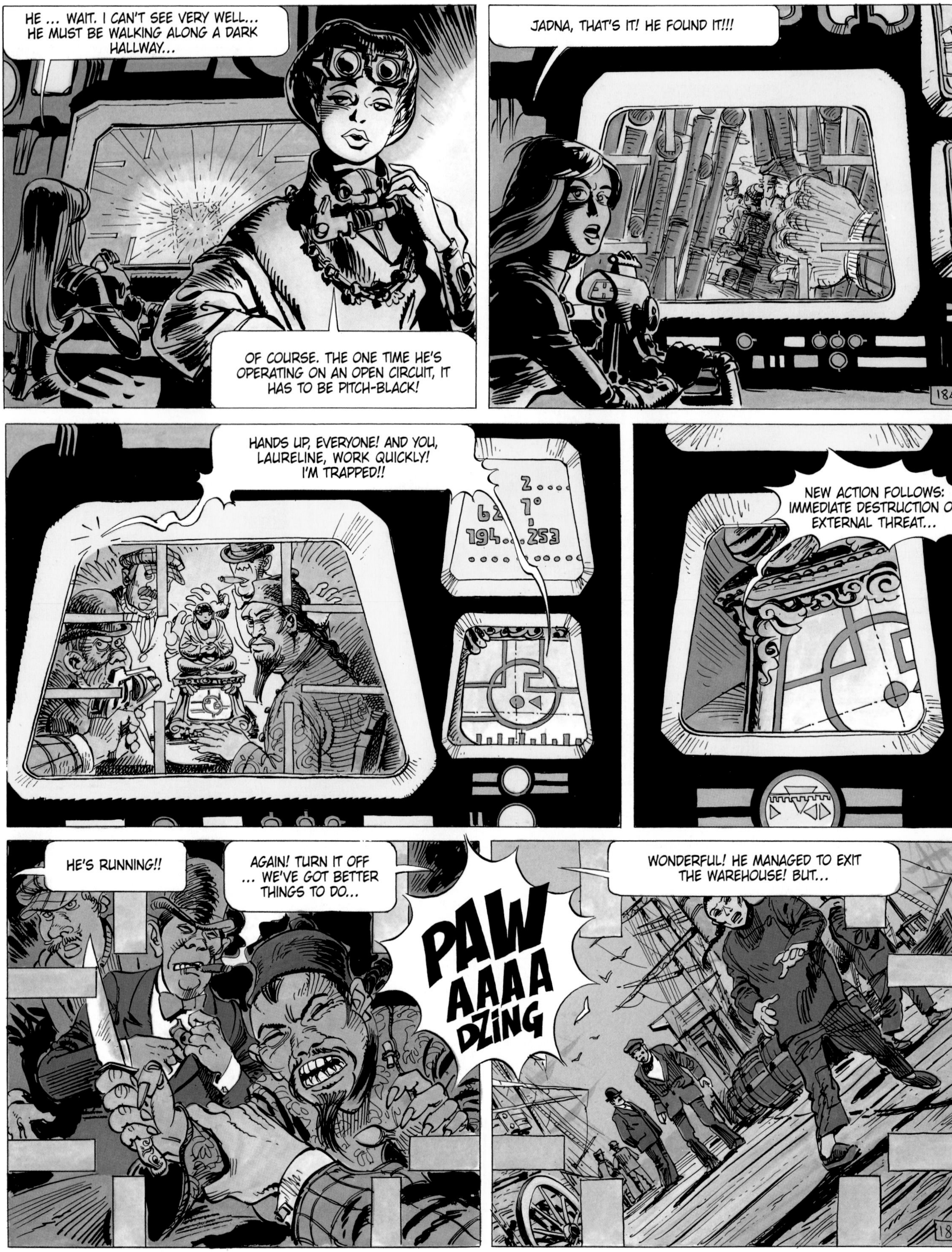
HE ... WAIT. I CAN'T SEE VERY WELL... HE MUST BE WALKING ALONG A DARK HALLWAY...
OF COURSE. THE ONE TIME HE'S OPERATING ON AN OPEN CIRCUIT, IT HAS TO BE PITCH-BLACK!
JADNA, THAT'S IT! HE FOUND IT!!!
18A
HANDS UP, EVERYONE! AND YOU, LAURELINE, WORK QUICKLY! I'M TRAPPED!!
NEW ACTION FOLLOWS: IMMEDIATE DESTRUCTION OF EXTERNAL THREAT...
HE'S RUNNING!!
AGAIN! TURN IT OFF ... WE'VE GOT BETTER THINGS TO DO...
PAW AAAA DZING
WONDERFUL! HE MANAGED TO EXIT THE WAREHOUSE! BUT...
18B

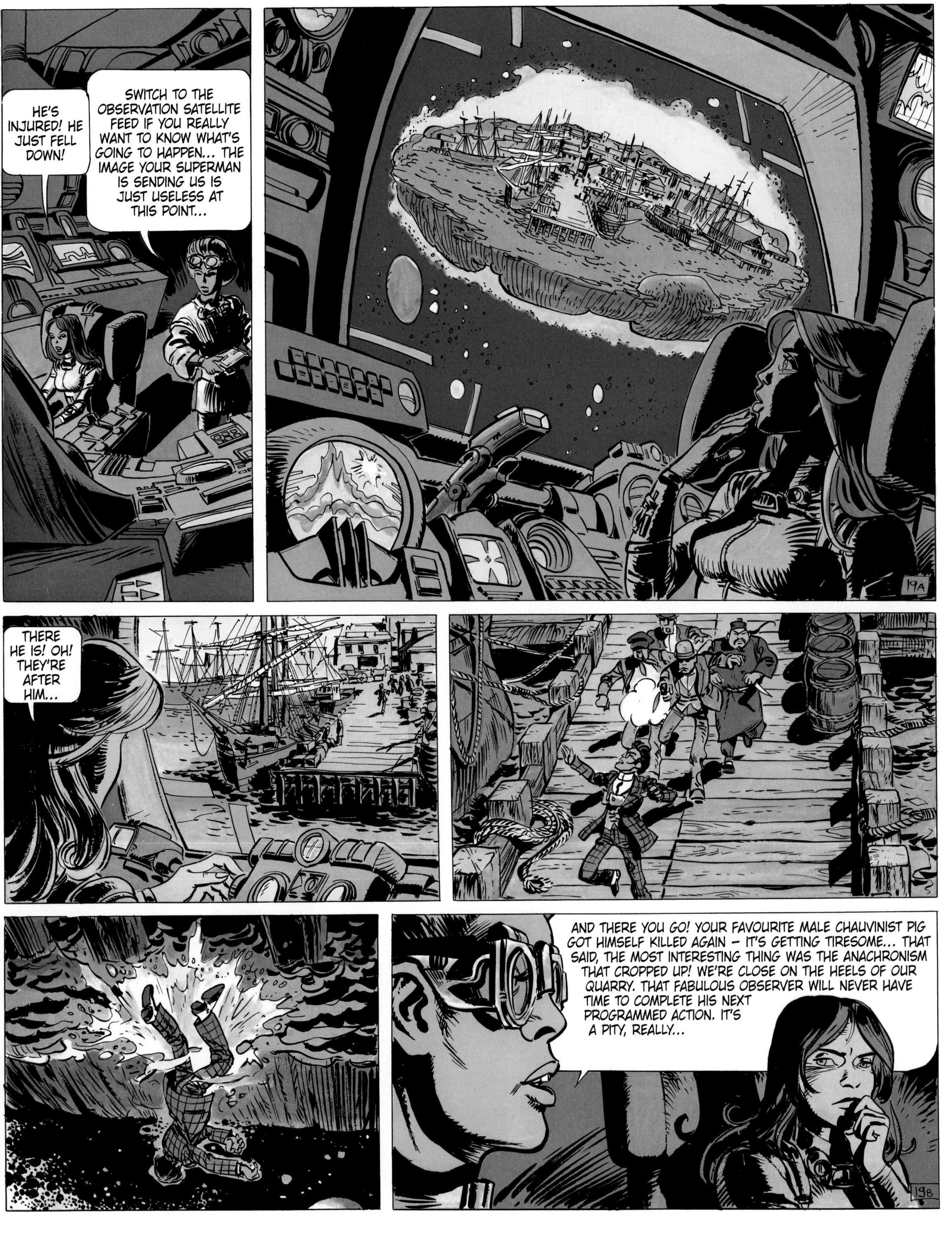
HE'S INJURED! HE JUST FELL DOWN!
SWITCH TO THE OBSERVATION SATELLITE FEED IF YOU REALLY WANT TO KNOW WHAT'S GOING TO HAPPEN... THE IMAGE YOUR SUPERMAN IS SENDING US IS JUST USELESS AT THIS POINT...
19A
THERE HE IS! OH! THEY'RE AFTER HIM...
AND THERE YOU GO! YOUR FAVOURITE MALE CHAUVINIST PIG GOT HIMSELF KILLED AGAIN – IT'S GETTING TIRESOME... THAT SAID, THE MOST INTERESTING THING WAS THE ANACHRONISM THAT CROPPED UP! WE'RE CLOSE ON THE HEELS OF OUR QUARRY. THAT FABULOUS OBSERVER WILL NEVER HAVE TIME TO COMPLETE HIS NEXT PROGRAMMED ACTION. IT'S A PITY, REALLY...
19B

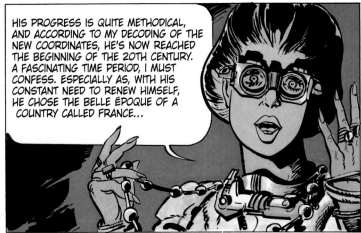

HIS PROGRESS IS QUITE METHODICAL, AND ACCORDING TO MY DECODING OF THE NEW COORDINATES, HE'S NOW REACHED THE BEGINNING OF THE 20TH CENTURY. A FASCINATING TIME PERIOD, I MUST CONFESS. ESPECIALLY AS, WITH HIS CONSTANT NEED TO RENEW HIMSELF, HE CHOSE THE BELLE ÉPOQUE OF A COUNTRY CALLED FRANCE...

AN ARTIST WITH REFINED TASTE, TRULY. ANYWAY, THIS MAY NOT BE OF ANY INTEREST TO PEOPLE LIKE YOU, SO GO AND THAW OUT ANOTHER ONE OF YOUR FAVOURITE HEROES, WILL YOU?

SU-U-RE! WHAT'S ANOTHER ONE AFTER ALL?...

NOW TO GET MY BEARINGS ... AND QUICK!

98

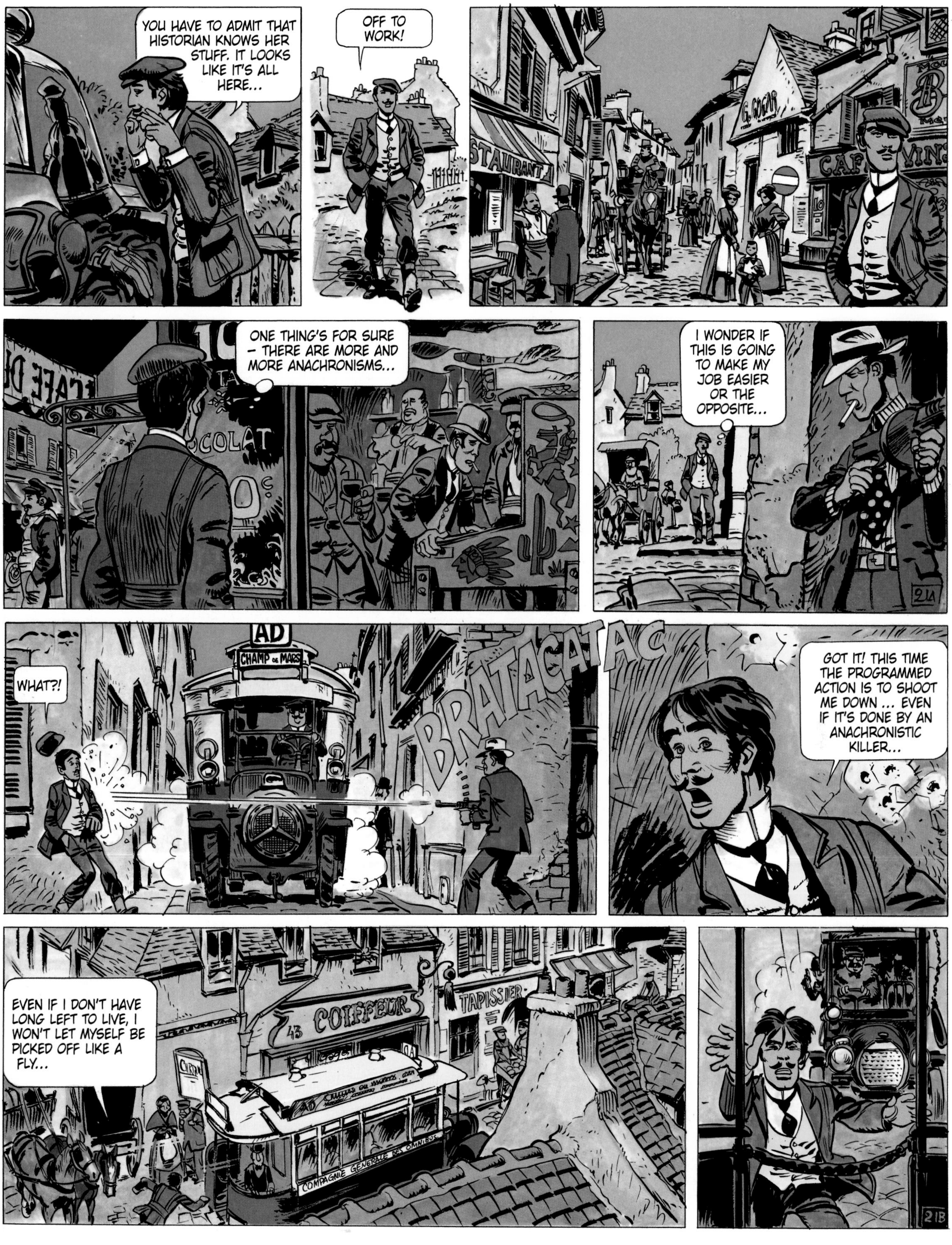
YOU HAVE TO ADMIT THAT HISTORIAN KNOWS HER STUFF. IT LOOKS LIKE IT'S ALL HERE...
OFF TO WORK!
ONE THING'S FOR SURE – THERE ARE MORE AND MORE ANACHRONISMS...
I WONDER IF THIS IS GOING TO MAKE MY JOB EASIER OR THE OPPOSITE...
WHAT?!
AD
CHAMP DE MARS
BRATACATAC
GOT IT! THIS TIME THE PROGRAMMED ACTION IS TO SHOOT ME DOWN ... EVEN IF IT'S DONE BY AN ANACHRONISTIC KILLER...
EVEN IF I DON'T HAVE LONG LEFT TO LIVE, I WON'T LET MYSELF BE PICKED OFF LIKE A FLY...
COIFFEUR
TAPISSIER
COMPAGNIE GENERALE DES OMNIBUS

OH GREAT! HE GOT HIMSELF AMBUSHED LIKE AN AMATEUR, YOUR TOUGH GUY!

VERY FUNNY! BECAUSE **YOU** HAD PREDICTED THE NEW SCRIPT, HADN'T YOU?

NO NEED TO DWELL ON THE PAST! WE MUST GO AND GET ANOTHER ONE – A QUICK PREPARATION WILL BE ENOUGH. IT'S OBVIOUS OUR MAGNIFICENT FOE CAUGHT ON TO OUR METHOD. SO THIS TIME, DARLING, WE'LL SEE WHAT STUFF YOUR VALERIAN'S REALLY MADE OF!

FIRST OF ALL, HE'S NOT REALLY MY VALERIAN, AND SECOND, I'M NOT YOUR D...

YES, YES, WE KNOW! I'M GOING WITH YOU, YOUNG LADY. BECAUSE WE MUST BE QUICK, VERY QUICK. I CAN FEEL IT...

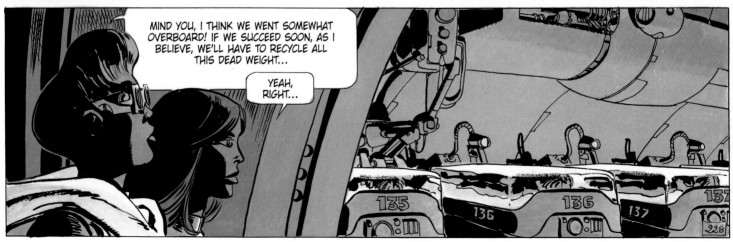

MIND YOU, I THINK WE WENT SOMEWHAT OVERBOARD! IF WE SUCCEED SOON, AS I BELIEVE, WE'LL HAVE TO RECYCLE ALL THIS DEAD WEIGHT...

YEAH, RIGHT...

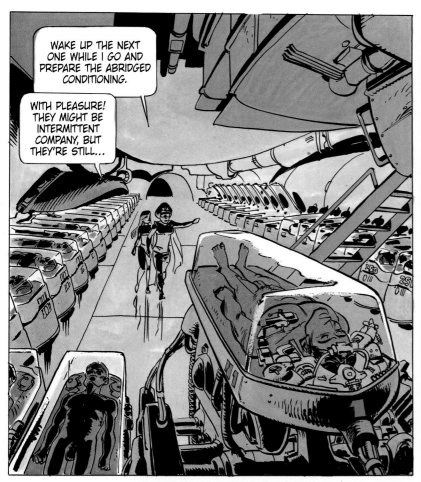

WAKE UP THE NEXT ONE WHILE I GO AND PREPARE THE ABRIDGED CONDITIONING.

WITH PLEASURE! THEY MIGHT BE INTERMITTENT COMPANY, BUT THEY'RE STILL...

...BETTER THAN OTHERS.

HI!

WHOHAA... OH!? WHAT AM...

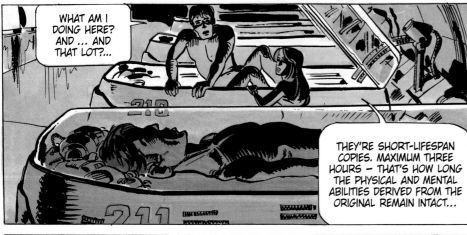

WHAT AM I DOING HERE? AND ... AND THAT LOT?...

THEY'RE SHORT-LIFESPAN COPIES. MAXIMUM THREE HOURS – THAT'S HOW LONG THE PHYSICAL AND MENTAL ABILITIES DERIVED FROM THE ORIGINAL REMAIN INTACT...

OH, RIGHT... IT'S COMING BACK TO ME, ACTUALLY. BUT EVEN THOUGH I'M THE ORIGINAL, I STILL DON'T FEEL TOO GOOD.

YOU POOR DEAR... YOU'RE NOT THE ORIGINAL...

WH... WHAT!?!

REMEMBER, THAT'S THE REAL ONE OVER THERE. YOU AND THE OTHERS WERE CREATED BY CLONING BECAUSE OF THE SPECIAL CHARACTERISTICS OF THE MISSION.

THE MISSION? AH, YES...

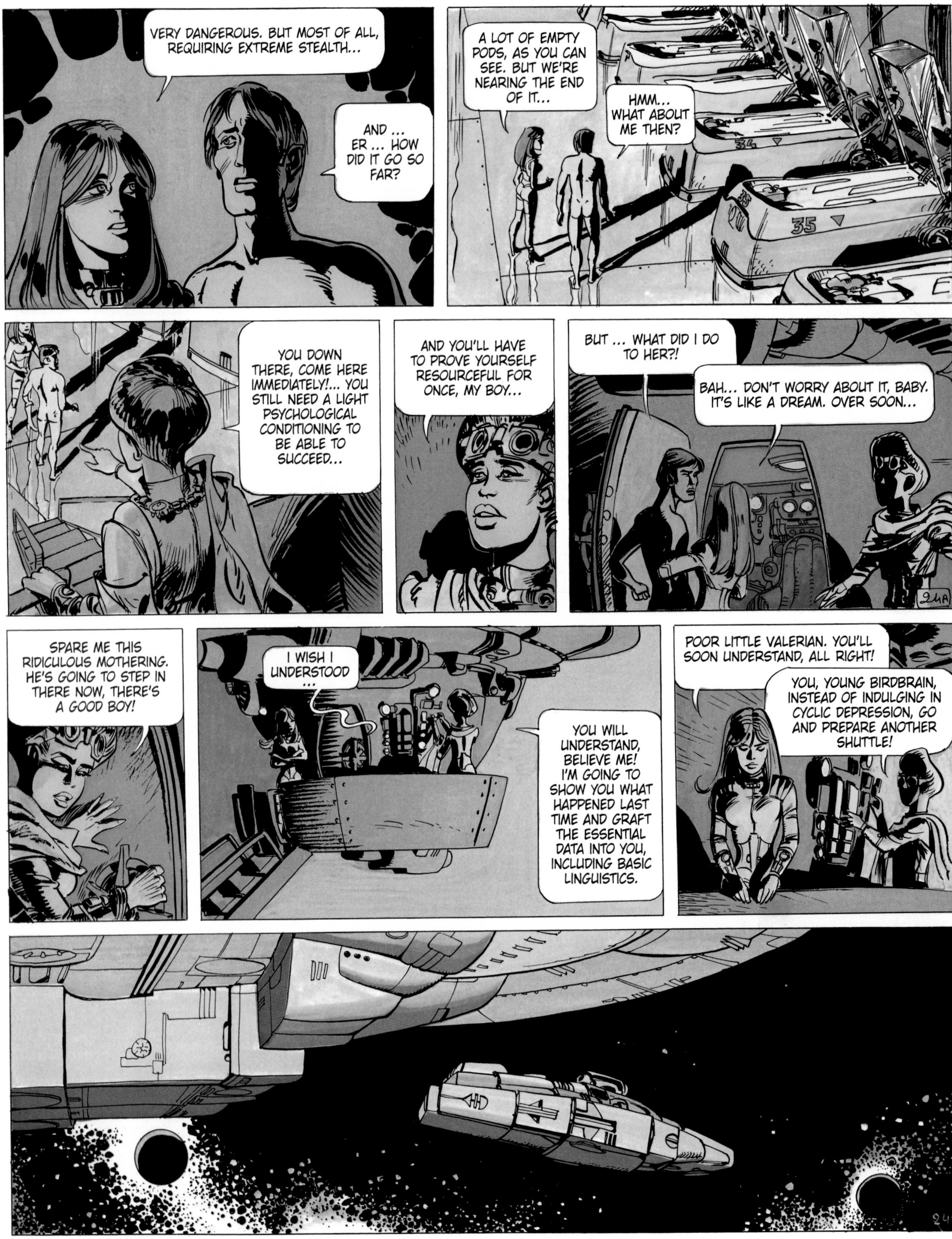
VERY DANGEROUS. BUT MOST OF ALL, REQUIRING EXTREME STEALTH...
AND ... ER ... HOW DID IT GO SO FAR?
A LOT OF EMPTY PODS, AS YOU CAN SEE. BUT WE'RE NEARING THE END OF IT...
HMM... WHAT ABOUT ME THEN?
YOU DOWN THERE, COME HERE IMMEDIATELY!... YOU STILL NEED A LIGHT PSYCHOLOGICAL CONDITIONING TO BE ABLE TO SUCCEED...
AND YOU'LL HAVE TO PROVE YOURSELF RESOURCEFUL FOR ONCE, MY BOY...
BUT ... WHAT DID I DO TO HER?!
BAH... DON'T WORRY ABOUT IT, BABY. IT'S LIKE A DREAM. OVER SOON...
SPARE ME THIS RIDICULOUS MOTHERING. HE'S GOING TO STEP IN THERE NOW, THERE'S A GOOD BOY!
I WISH I UNDERSTOOD ...
YOU WILL UNDERSTAND, BELIEVE ME! I'M GOING TO SHOW YOU WHAT HAPPENED LAST TIME AND GRAFT THE ESSENTIAL DATA INTO YOU, INCLUDING BASIC LINGUISTICS.
POOR LITTLE VALERIAN. YOU'LL SOON UNDERSTAND, ALL RIGHT!
YOU, YOUNG BIRDBRAIN, INSTEAD OF INDULGING IN CYCLIC DEPRESSION, GO AND PREPARE ANOTHER SHUTTLE!

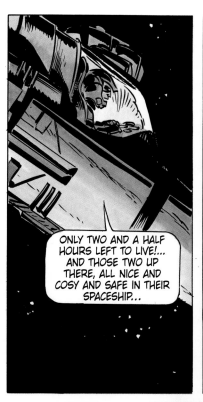

ONLY TWO AND A HALF HOURS LEFT TO LIVE!... AND THOSE TWO UP THERE, ALL NICE AND COSY AND SAFE IN THEIR SPACESHIP...

THIS IS SOMETHING ELSE! HOW MANY TIMES HAVE I DIED BY NOW?

WELL, WHEN I SAY 'I' ... I KNOW VERY WELL MY REAL ME ISN'T THE ME HERE... OH, AND SCREW THEM AND THEIR MISSION, ANYWAY! FIRST, I'LL AVENGE MY PREDECESSOR, THEN I'LL TRY TO MAKE IT OUT ALIVE. THERE'S GOT TO BE A WAY, DAMMIT!...

VALERIAN! IT IS PREFERABLE FOR YOU TO OPERATE ON AN OPEN CIRCUIT, BUT DO SPARE US YOUR MONOLOGUES, MY BOY. THEY'RE ALWAYS THE SAME, YOU KNOW! YOUR HEROISM MUST BE EXCLUSIVELY AIMED AT OBTAINING THE COORDINATES... IS THAT UNDERSTOOD!?!

YOU DON'T SAY! IF THAT'S THE WAY YOU FEEL, MIKE OFF, DUCHESS. THERE!...

AH, THIS IS WHERE MY UNFORTUNATE DOUBLE WAS GUNNED DOWN! THE KILLER MUST BE HIDDEN CLOSE BY...

HERE'S THE BUS!

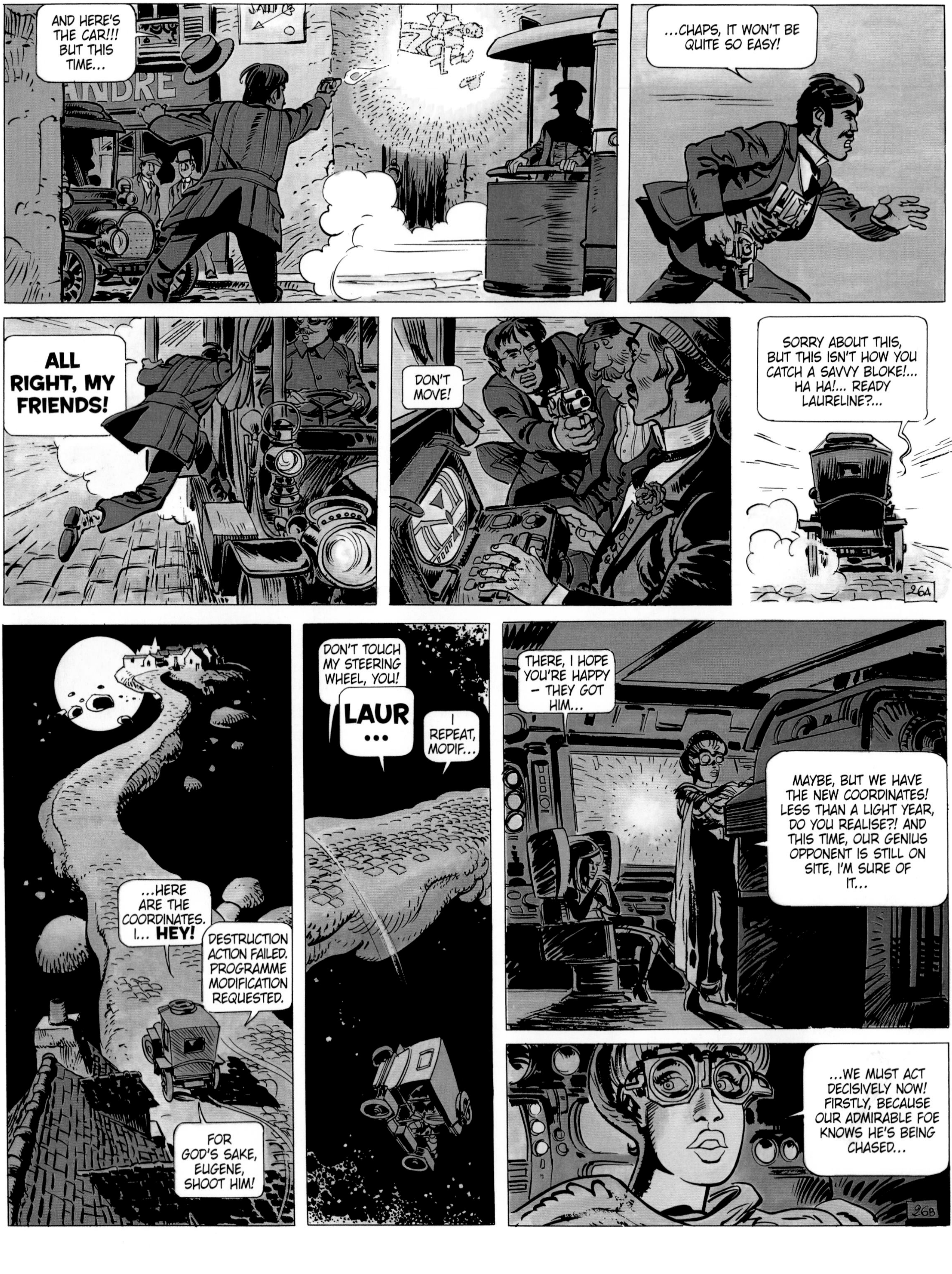

AND HERE'S THE CAR!!! BUT THIS TIME...
...CHAPS, IT WON'T BE QUITE SO EASY!
ALL RIGHT, MY FRIENDS!
DON'T MOVE!
SORRY ABOUT THIS, BUT THIS ISN'T HOW YOU CATCH A SAVVY BLOKE!... HA HA!... READY LAURELINE?...
26A
...HERE ARE THE COORDINATES. I... HEY!
DESTRUCTION ACTION FAILED. PROGRAMME MODIFICATION REQUESTED.
FOR GOD'S SAKE, EUGENE, SHOOT HIM!
DON'T TOUCH MY STEERING WHEEL, YOU!
LAUR ...
I REPEAT, MODIF...
THERE, I HOPE YOU'RE HAPPY – THEY GOT HIM...
MAYBE, BUT WE HAVE THE NEW COORDINATES! LESS THAN A LIGHT YEAR, DO YOU REALISE?! AND THIS TIME, OUR GENIUS OPPONENT IS STILL ON SITE, I'M SURE OF IT...
...WE MUST ACT DECISIVELY NOW! FIRSTLY, BECAUSE OUR ADMIRABLE FOE KNOWS HE'S BEING CHASED...
26B

...SECONDLY, BECAUSE THERE'S NO NEED TO USE CUNNING ANY MORE. HE'LL NEVER HAVE TIME TO CREATE HIS NEXT EARTH. QUITE REGRETTABLE, ACTUALLY, BECAUSE ACCORDING TO MY ROUGH DECODING, HE WAS ABOUT TO STAGE THE FIRST WORLD WAR! A MAGNIFICENT DISPLAY, NO DOUBT...

AH WELL; THE PLEASURE OF MEETING THIS MARVELLOUS CREATOR WILL MORE THAN MAKE UP FOR MY STYMIED CURIOSITY. IT'S UP TO YOU TO LET US CATCH UP WITH HIM, MY DEAR...

IS IT REALLY UP TO ME, JADNA?

LET'S GO THEN!

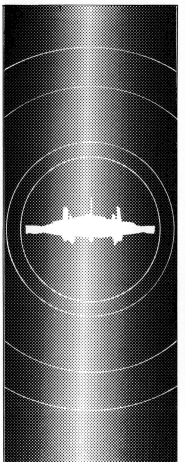

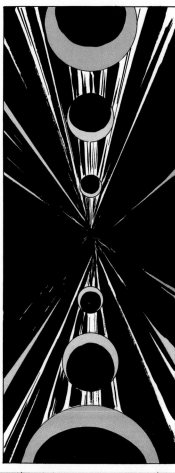

LOOK!

HE'S HERE!!!

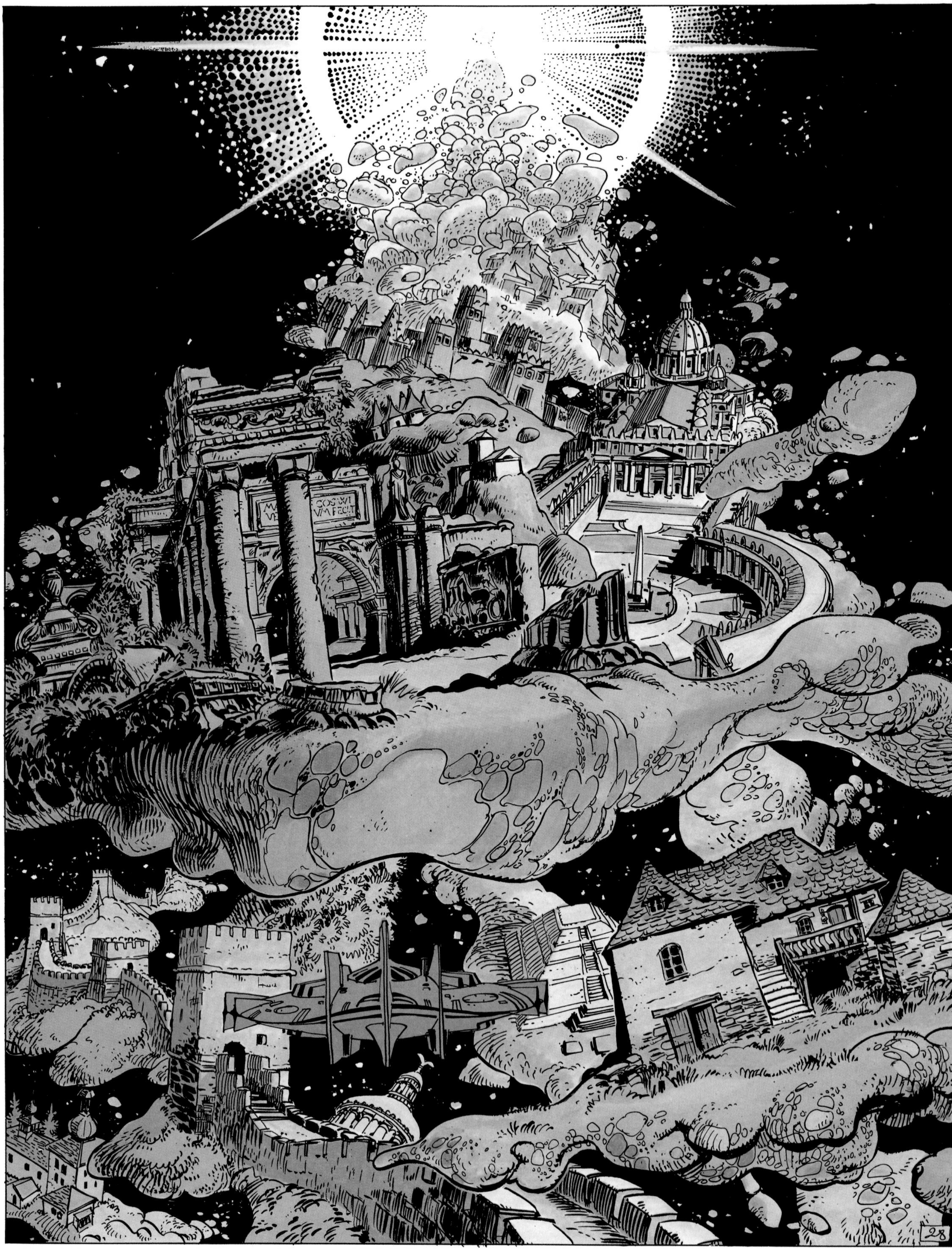

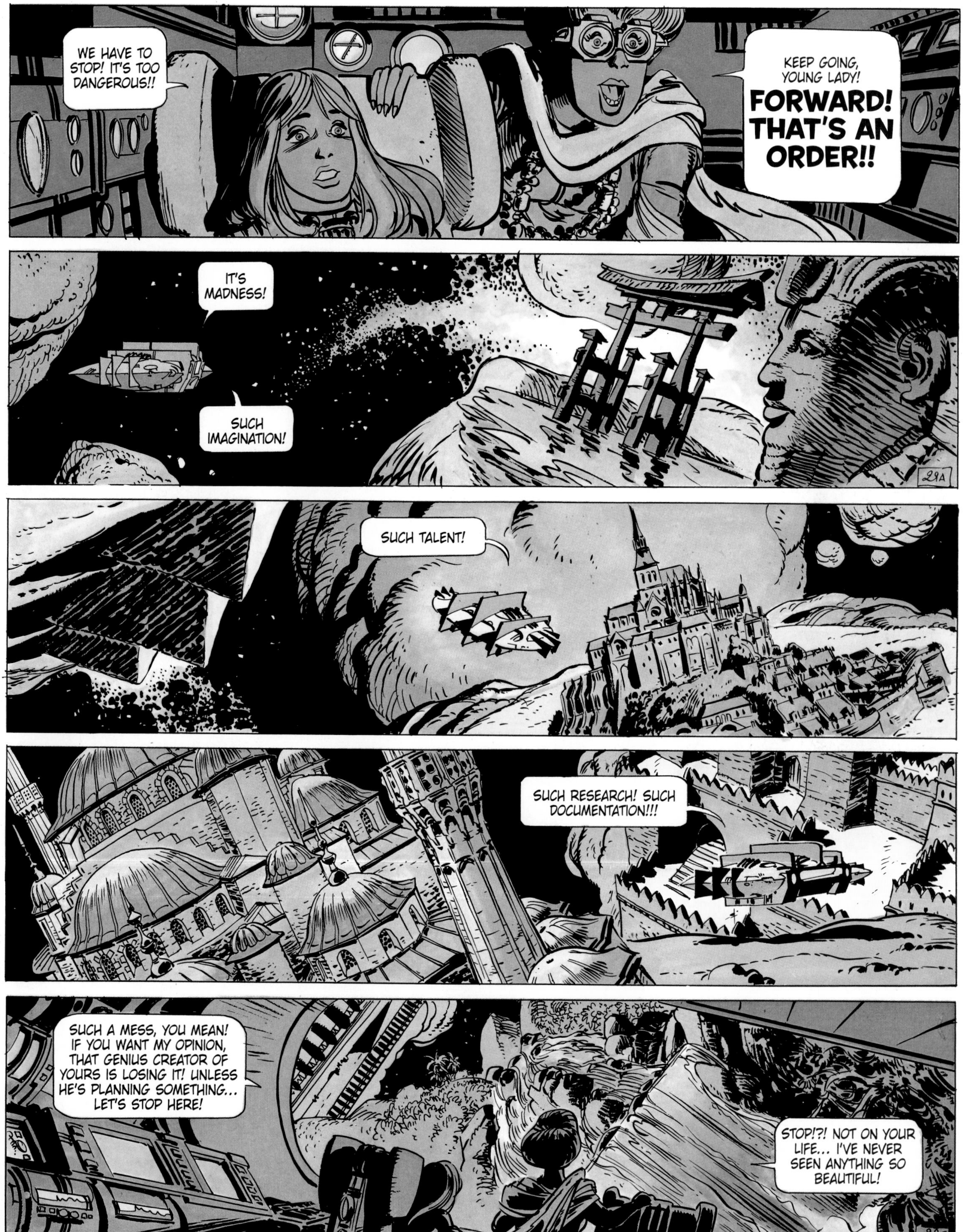
WE HAVE TO STOP! IT'S TOO DANGEROUS!!
KEEP GOING, YOUNG LADY!
FORWARD! THAT'S AN ORDER!!
IT'S MADNESS!
SUCH IMAGINATION!
29A
SUCH TALENT!
SUCH RESEARCH! SUCH DOCUMENTATION!!!
SUCH A MESS, YOU MEAN! IF YOU WANT MY OPINION, THAT GENIUS CREATOR OF YOURS IS LOSING IT! UNLESS HE'S PLANNING SOMETHING... LET'S STOP HERE!
STOP!?! NOT ON YOUR LIFE... I'VE NEVER SEEN ANYTHING SO BEAUTIFUL!
29B

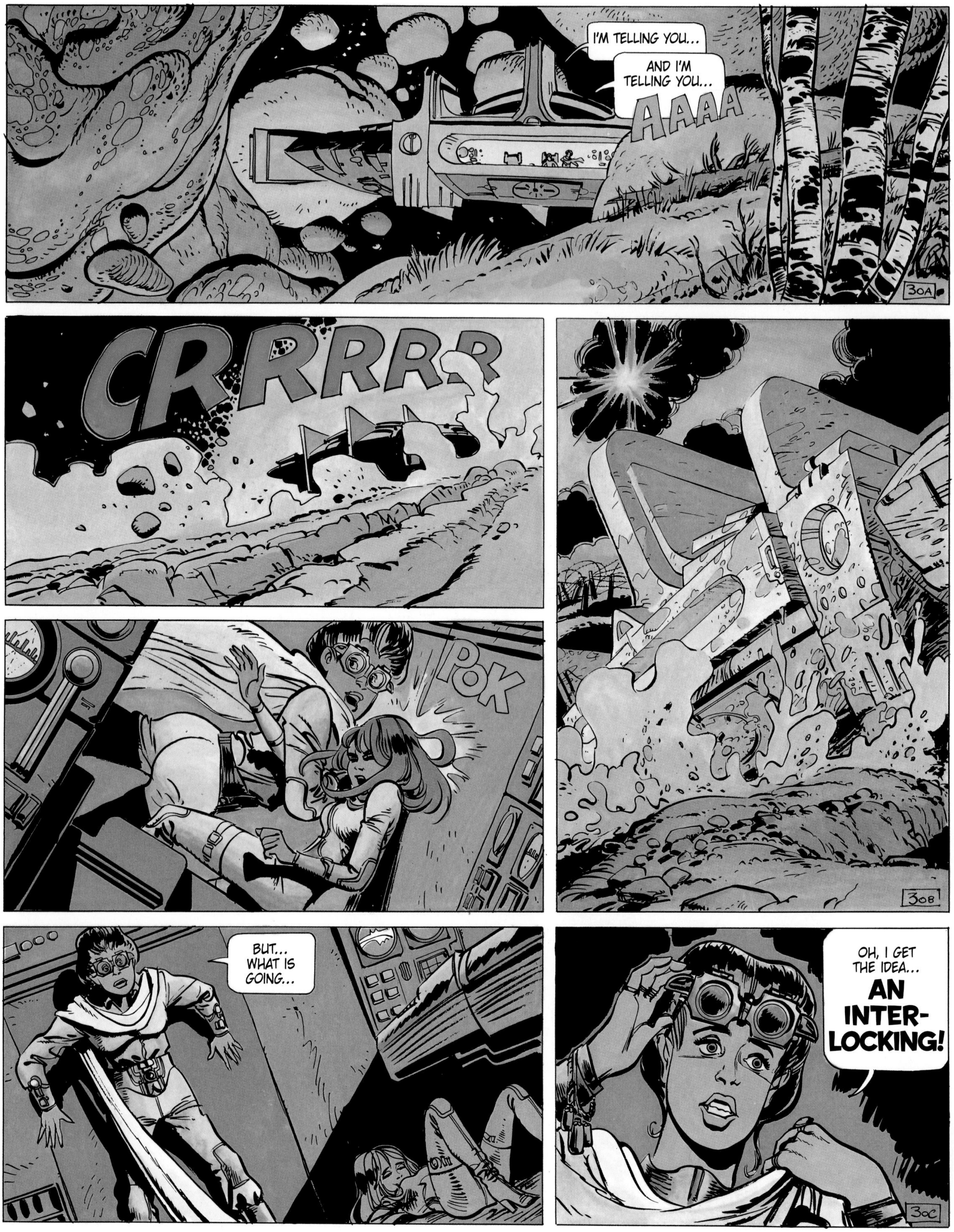
I'M TELLING YOU...
AND I'M TELLING YOU...
AAAA
30A
CRRRRR
POK
30B
BUT... WHAT IS GOING...
OH, I GET THE IDEA... **AN INTER-LOCKING!**
30C

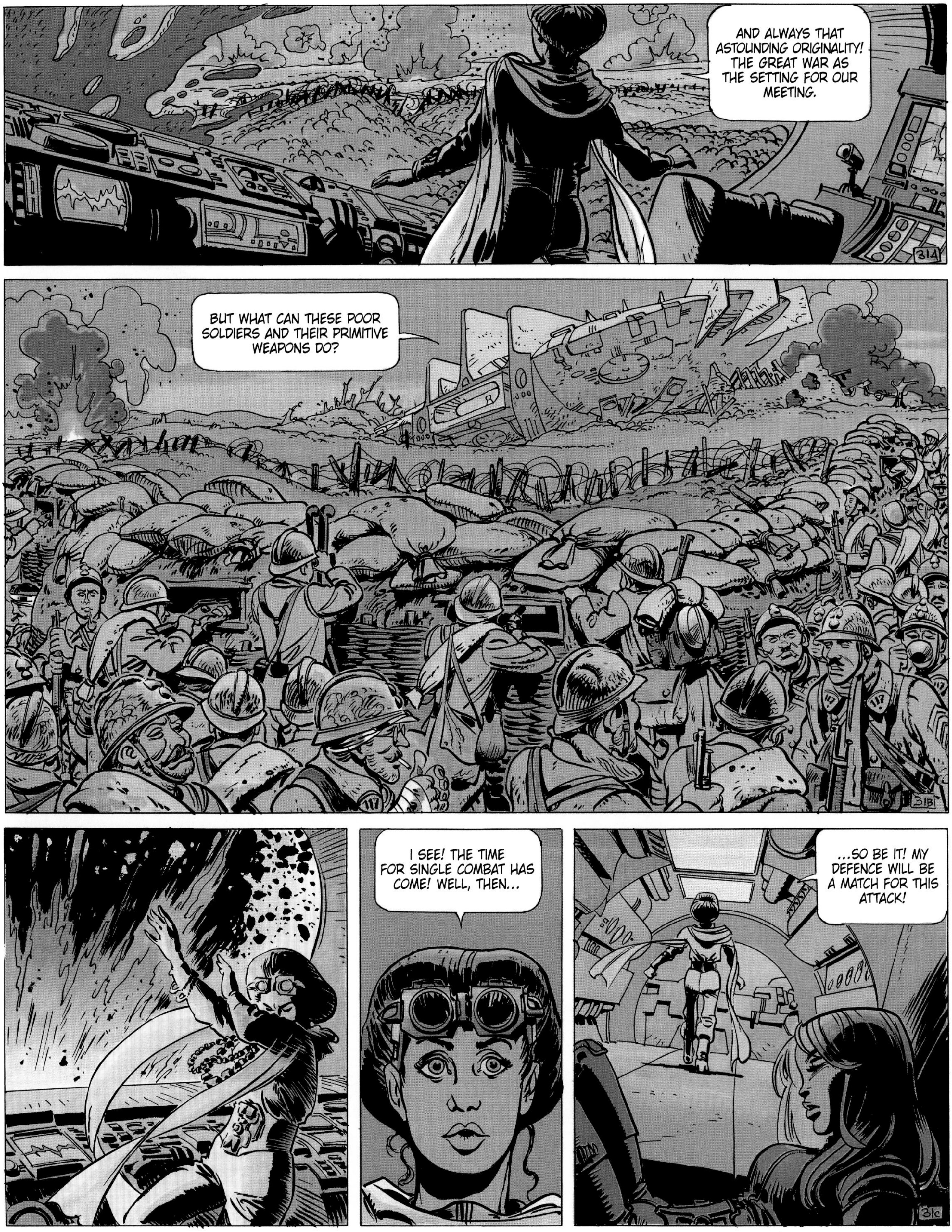
AND ALWAYS THAT ASTOUNDING ORIGINALITY! THE GREAT WAR AS THE SETTING FOR OUR MEETING.
BUT WHAT CAN THESE POOR SOLDIERS AND THEIR PRIMITIVE WEAPONS DO?
I SEE! THE TIME FOR SINGLE COMBAT HAS COME! WELL, THEN...
...SO BE IT! MY DEFENCE WILL BE A MATCH FOR THIS ATTACK!

WAKE UP, YOU LAYABOUTS! ALL OF YOU!

SINCE OUR FOE HAS CHOSEN THE WINNER'S SIDE, YOU SHALL BE MY PRUSSIAN TROOPS. IT FALLS TO YOU TO GLORIOUSLY REWRITE HISTORY!

WHAT DID SHE SAY?

HUH?

WHAT'S GOING ON?

WHAT?

ER...

I... I DON'T UNDERSTAND!

ALL OF YOU, I SAID!

THIS WAY FOR A LITTLE HYPNO-TEACHING SESSION ON THE SITUATION ... AND TO PICK UP YOUR ACCESSORIES.

HEY!

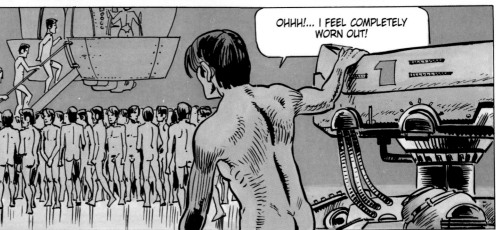

OHHH!... I FEEL COMPLETELY WORN OUT!

HURRY UP, HURRY UP! THE FRENCH ATTACK IS INTENSIFYING!

ATTACK! WHAT ATTACK?

HEY, YOUR HEL-MET!

WHO'RE YOU?

MY WHAT?

AND YOU? HAVEN'T WE MET SOMEWHERE BEFORE?

D'YOU HEAR THAT RACKET OUT THERE!

HA HA, WHAT A GET-UP!

LOOK WHO'S TALKING!

PFFF... I'VE GOT NO ENERGY AT ALL TODAY...

110

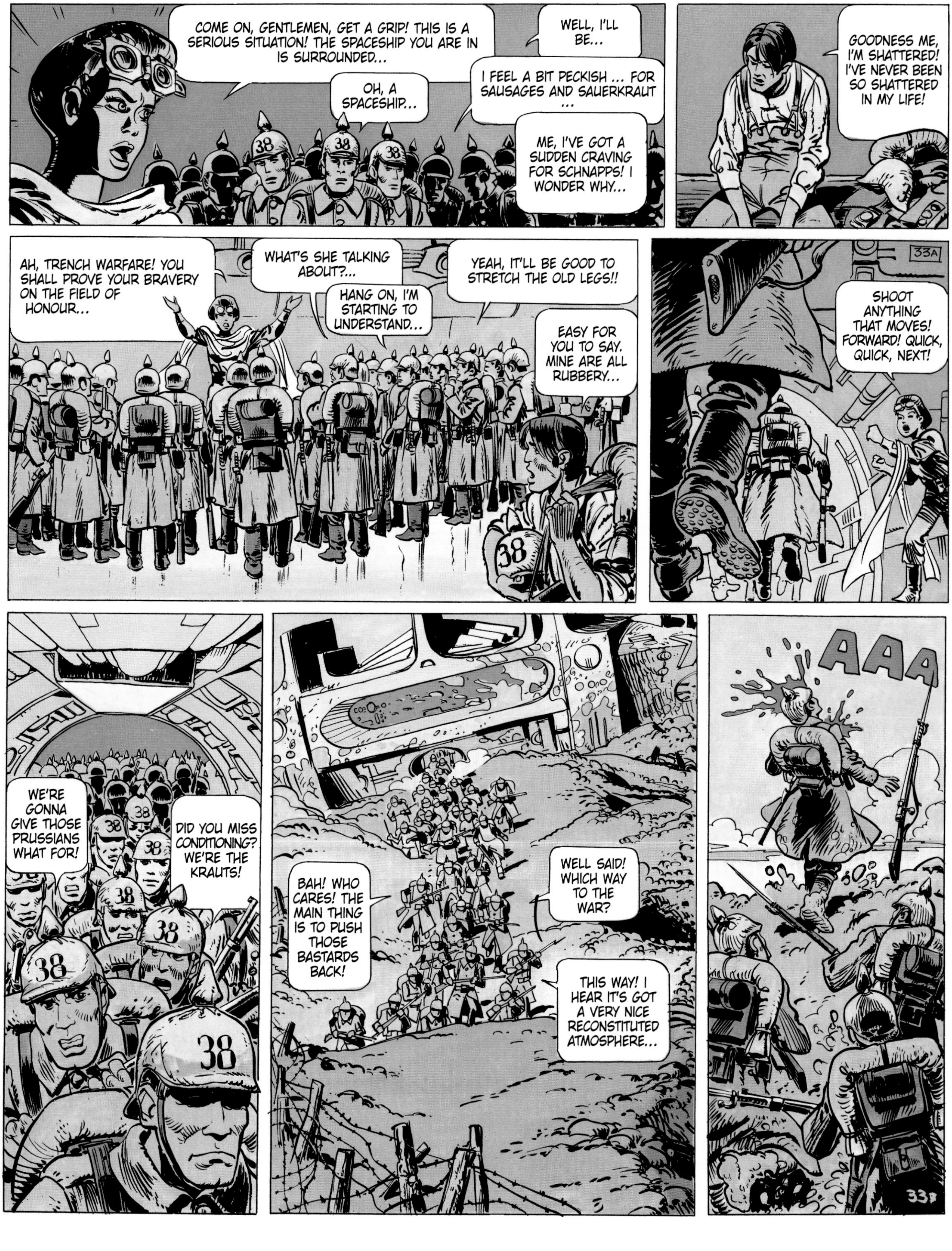
COME ON, GENTLEMEN, GET A GRIP! THIS IS A SERIOUS SITUATION! THE SPACESHIP YOU ARE IN IS SURROUNDED...
OH, A SPACESHIP...
WELL, I'LL BE...
I FEEL A BIT PECKISH ... FOR SAUSAGES AND SAUERKRAUT ...
ME, I'VE GOT A SUDDEN CRAVING FOR SCHNAPPS! I WONDER WHY...
GOODNESS ME, I'M SHATTERED! I'VE NEVER BEEN SO SHATTERED IN MY LIFE!
AH, TRENCH WARFARE! YOU SHALL PROVE YOUR BRAVERY ON THE FIELD OF HONOUR...
WHAT'S SHE TALKING ABOUT?...
HANG ON, I'M STARTING TO UNDERSTAND...
YEAH, IT'LL BE GOOD TO STRETCH THE OLD LEGS!!
EASY FOR YOU TO SAY. MINE ARE ALL RUBBERY...
33A
SHOOT ANYTHING THAT MOVES! FORWARD! QUICK, QUICK, NEXT!
WE'RE GONNA GIVE THOSE PRUSSIANS WHAT FOR!
DID YOU MISS CONDITIONING? WE'RE THE KRAUTS!
BAH! WHO CARES! THE MAIN THING IS TO PUSH THOSE BASTARDS BACK!
WELL SAID! WHICH WAY TO THE WAR?
THIS WAY! I HEAR IT'S GOT A VERY NICE RECONSTITUTED ATMOSPHERE...
AAA
33B

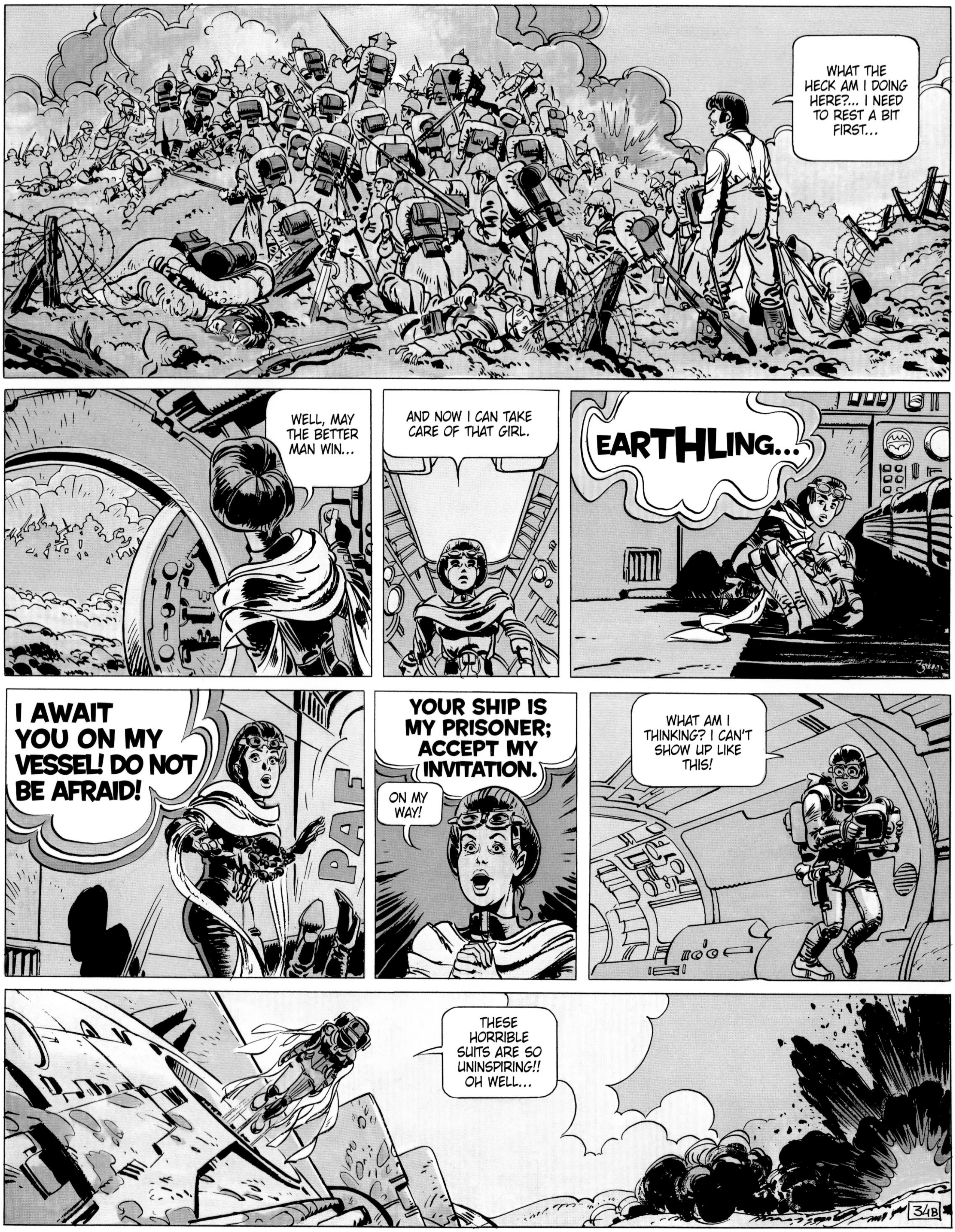
WHAT THE HECK AM I DOING HERE?... I NEED TO REST A BIT FIRST...
WELL, MAY THE BETTER MAN WIN...
AND NOW I CAN TAKE CARE OF THAT GIRL.
EARTHLING...
I AWAIT YOU ON MY VESSEL! DO NOT BE AFRAID!
YOUR SHIP IS MY PRISONER; ACCEPT MY INVITATION.
ON MY WAY!
WHAT AM I THINKING? I CAN'T SHOW UP LIKE THIS!
THESE HORRIBLE SUITS ARE SO UNINSPIRING!! OH WELL...
34B

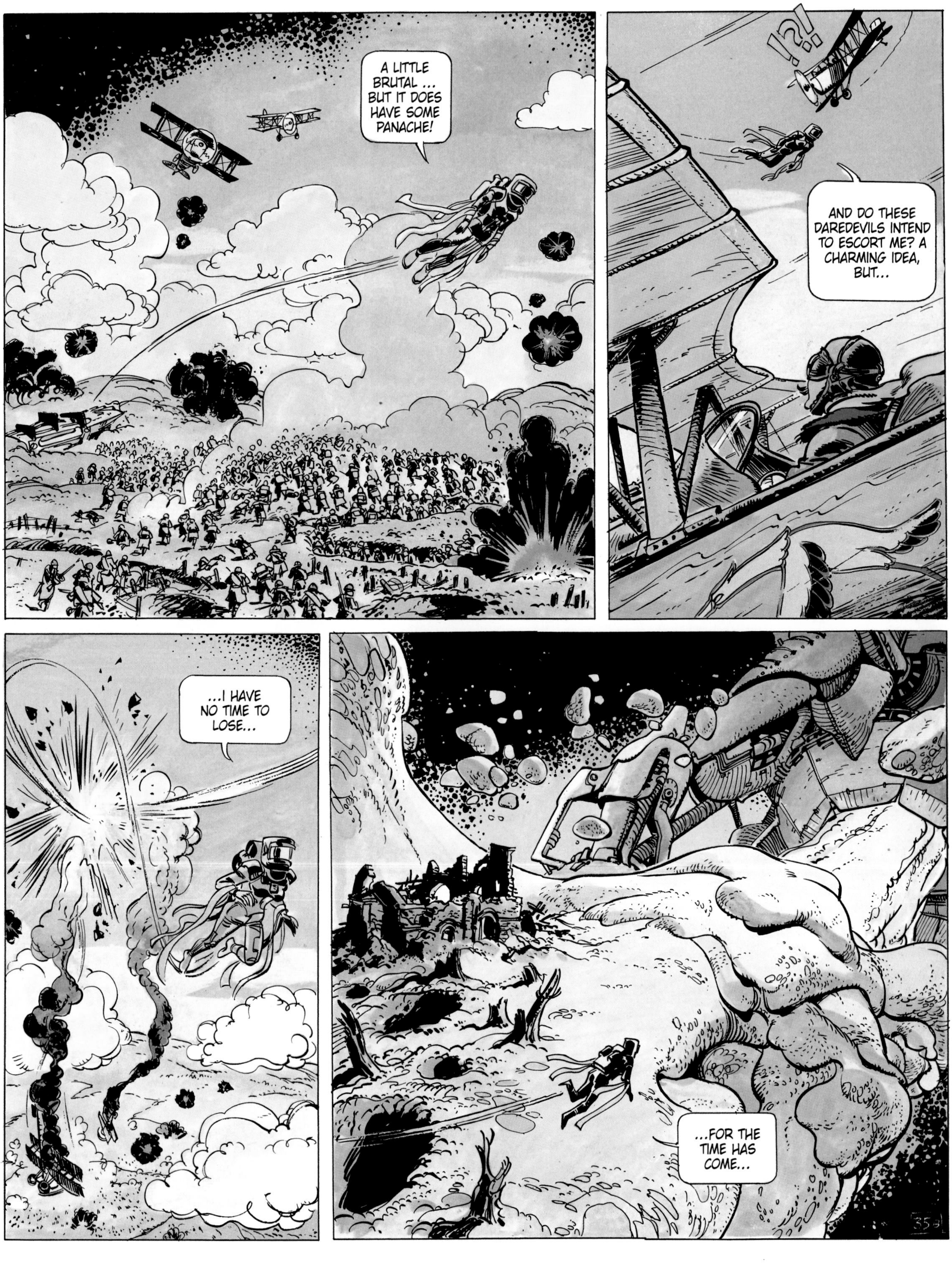
A LITTLE BRUTAL ... BUT IT DOES HAVE SOME PANACHE!
!?!
AND DO THESE DAREDEVILS INTEND TO ESCORT ME? A CHARMING IDEA, BUT...
...I HAVE NO TIME TO LOSE...
...FOR THE TIME HAS COME...

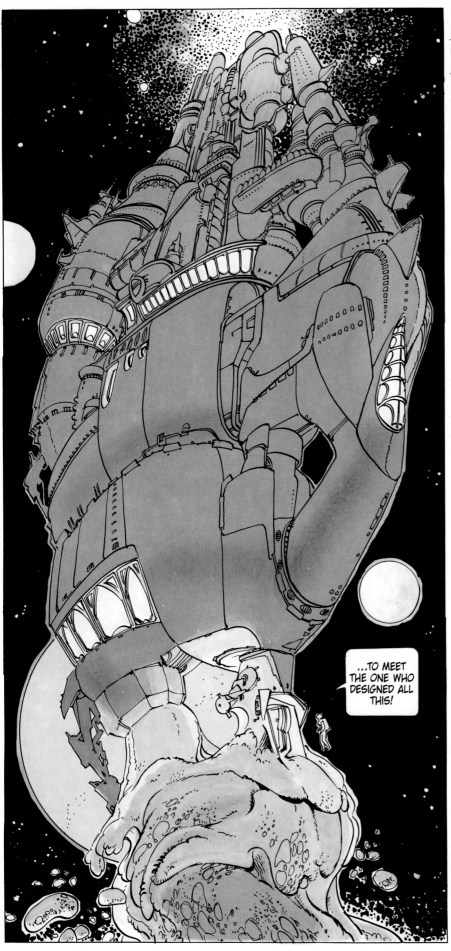

...TO MEET THE ONE WHO DESIGNED ALL THIS!

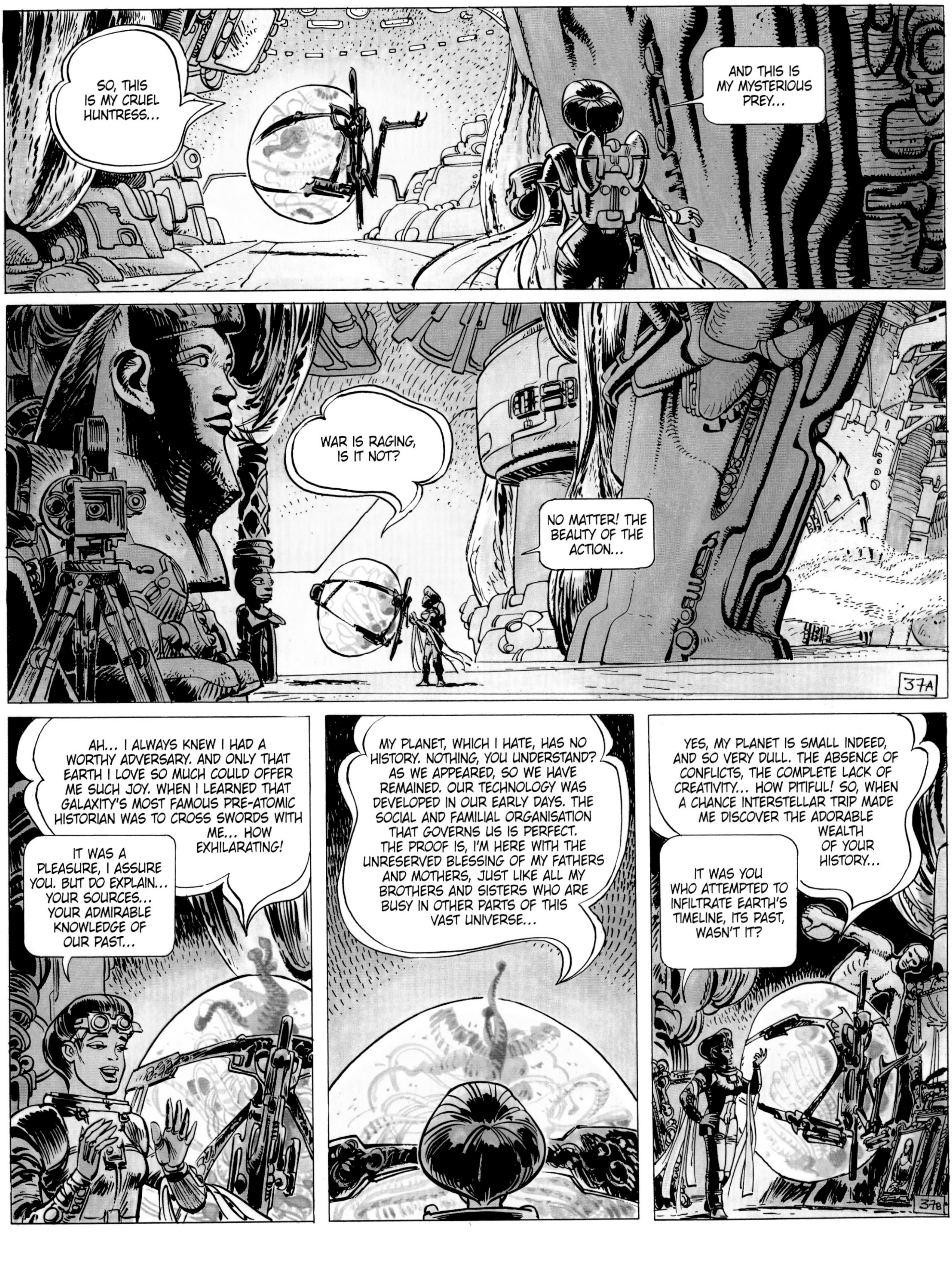
SO, THIS IS MY CRUEL HUNTRESS...
AND THIS IS MY MYSTERIOUS PREY...
WAR IS RAGING, IS IT NOT?
NO MATTER! THE BEAUTY OF THE ACTION...
37A
AH... I ALWAYS KNEW I HAD A WORTHY ADVERSARY. AND ONLY THAT EARTH I LOVE SO MUCH COULD OFFER ME SUCH JOY. WHEN I LEARNED THAT GALAXITY'S MOST FAMOUS PRE-ATOMIC HISTORIAN WAS TO CROSS SWORDS WITH ME... HOW EXHILARATING!
IT WAS A PLEASURE, I ASSURE YOU. BUT DO EXPLAIN... YOUR SOURCES... YOUR ADMIRABLE KNOWLEDGE OF OUR PAST...
MY PLANET, WHICH I HATE, HAS NO HISTORY. NOTHING, YOU UNDERSTAND? AS WE APPEARED, SO WE HAVE REMAINED. OUR TECHNOLOGY WAS DEVELOPED IN OUR EARLY DAYS. THE SOCIAL AND FAMILIAL ORGANISATION THAT GOVERNS US IS PERFECT. THE PROOF IS, I'M HERE WITH THE UNRESERVED BLESSING OF MY FATHERS AND MOTHERS, JUST LIKE ALL MY BROTHERS AND SISTERS WHO ARE BUSY IN OTHER PARTS OF THIS VAST UNIVERSE...
YES, MY PLANET IS SMALL INDEED, AND SO VERY DULL. THE ABSENCE OF CONFLICTS, THE COMPLETE LACK OF CREATIVITY... HOW PITIFUL! SO, WHEN A CHANCE INTERSTELLAR TRIP MADE ME DISCOVER THE ADORABLE WEALTH OF YOUR HISTORY...
IT WAS YOU WHO ATTEMPTED TO INFILTRATE EARTH'S TIMELINE, ITS PAST, WASN'T IT?
37B

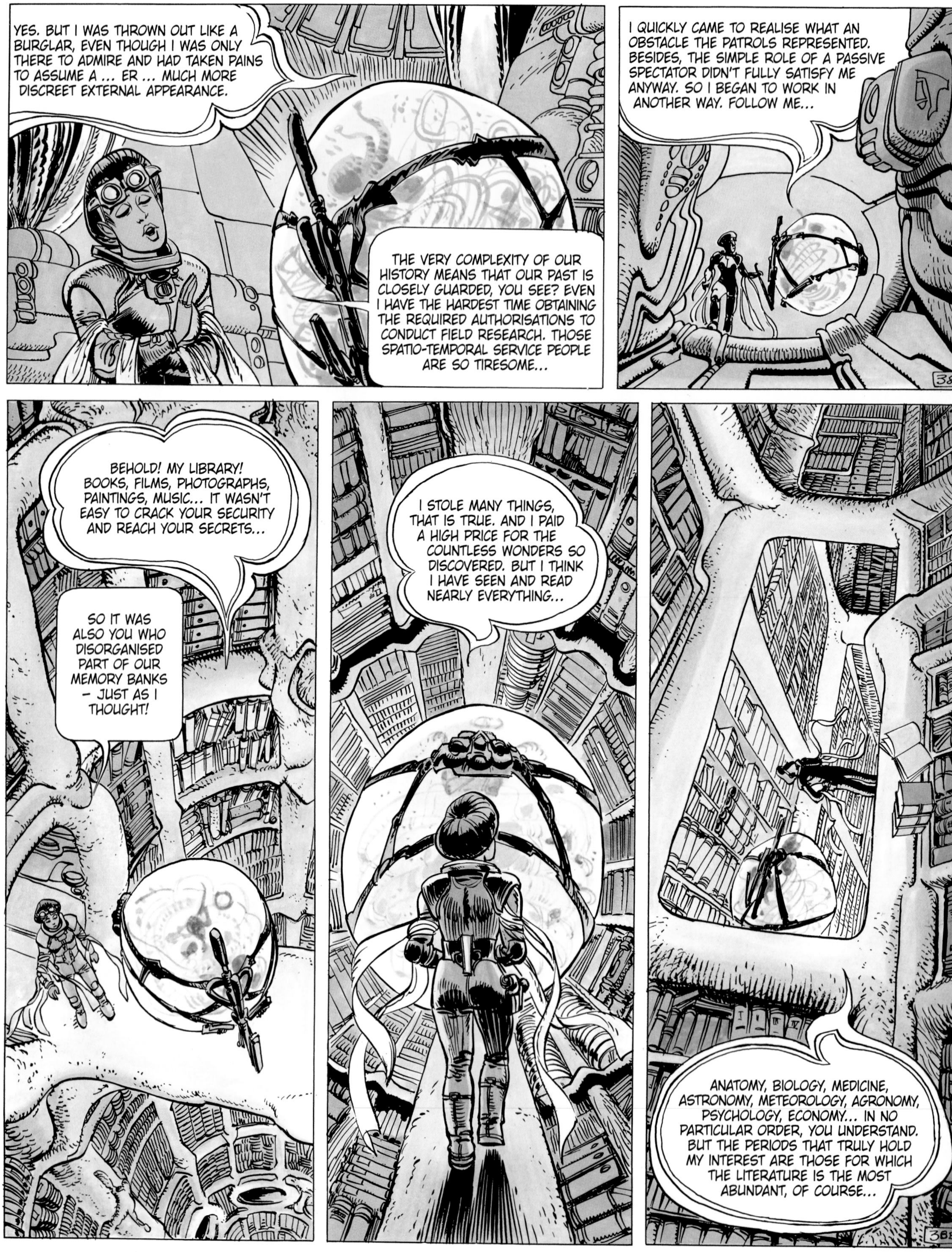
YES. BUT I WAS THROWN OUT LIKE A BURGLAR, EVEN THOUGH I WAS ONLY THERE TO ADMIRE AND HAD TAKEN PAINS TO ASSUME A ... ER ... MUCH MORE DISCREET EXTERNAL APPEARANCE.
THE VERY COMPLEXITY OF OUR HISTORY MEANS THAT OUR PAST IS CLOSELY GUARDED, YOU SEE? EVEN I HAVE THE HARDEST TIME OBTAINING THE REQUIRED AUTHORISATIONS TO CONDUCT FIELD RESEARCH. THOSE SPATIO-TEMPORAL SERVICE PEOPLE ARE SO TIRESOME...
I QUICKLY CAME TO REALISE WHAT AN OBSTACLE THE PATROLS REPRESENTED. BESIDES, THE SIMPLE ROLE OF A PASSIVE SPECTATOR DIDN'T FULLY SATISFY ME ANYWAY. SO I BEGAN TO WORK IN ANOTHER WAY. FOLLOW ME...
38A
BEHOLD! MY LIBRARY! BOOKS, FILMS, PHOTOGRAPHS, PAINTINGS, MUSIC... IT WASN'T EASY TO CRACK YOUR SECURITY AND REACH YOUR SECRETS...
SO IT WAS ALSO YOU WHO DISORGANISED PART OF OUR MEMORY BANKS – JUST AS I THOUGHT!
I STOLE MANY THINGS, THAT IS TRUE. AND I PAID A HIGH PRICE FOR THE COUNTLESS WONDERS SO DISCOVERED. BUT I THINK I HAVE SEEN AND READ NEARLY EVERYTHING...
ANATOMY, BIOLOGY, MEDICINE, ASTRONOMY, METEOROLOGY, AGRONOMY, PSYCHOLOGY, ECONOMY... IN NO PARTICULAR ORDER, YOU UNDERSTAND. BUT THE PERIODS THAT TRULY HOLD MY INTEREST ARE THOSE FOR WHICH THE LITERATURE IS THE MOST ABUNDANT, OF COURSE...
38B

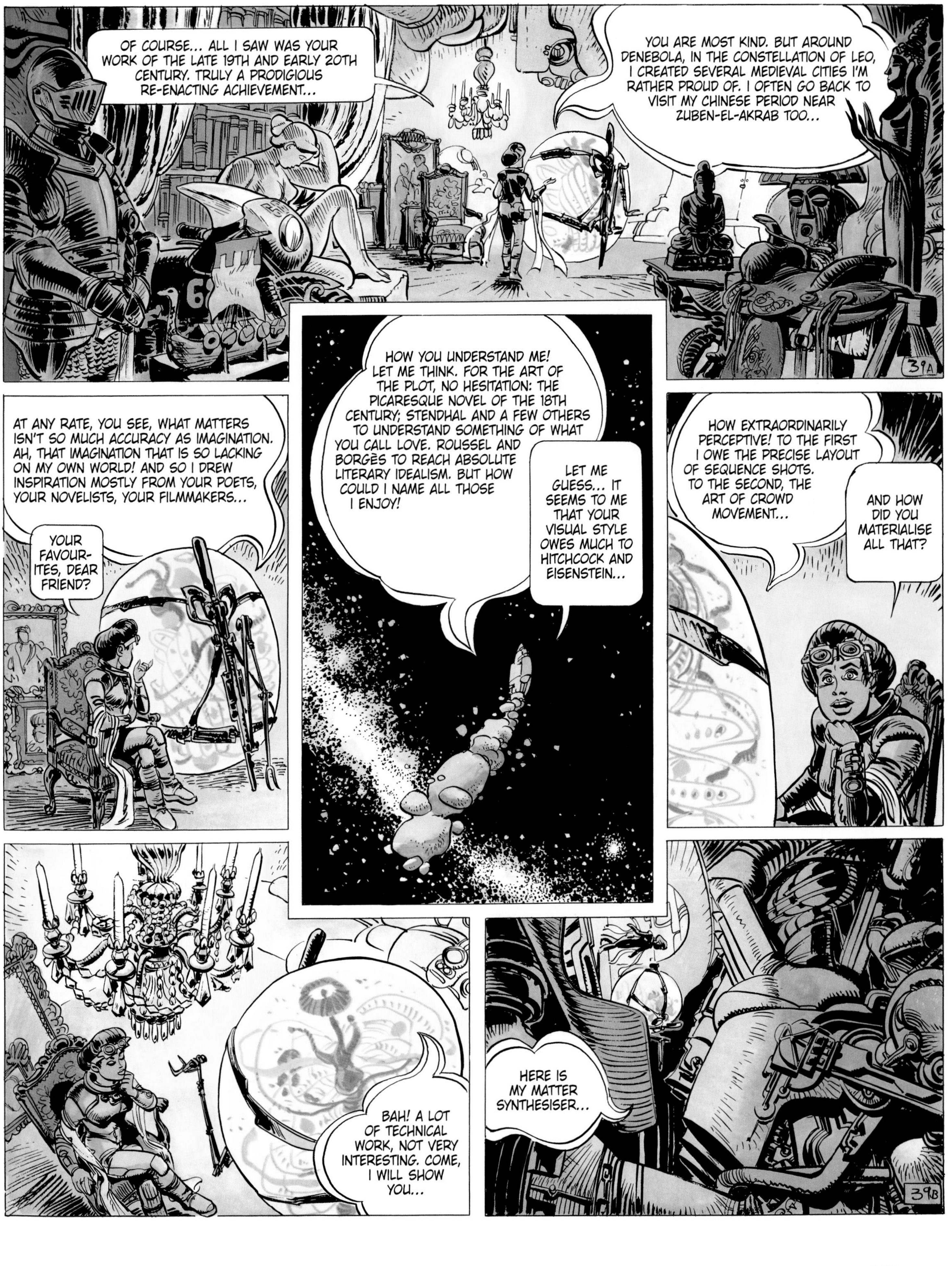
OF COURSE... ALL I SAW WAS YOUR WORK OF THE LATE 19TH AND EARLY 20TH CENTURY. TRULY A PRODIGIOUS RE-ENACTING ACHIEVEMENT...
YOU ARE MOST KIND. BUT AROUND DENEBOLA, IN THE CONSTELLATION OF LEO, I CREATED SEVERAL MEDIEVAL CITIES I'M RATHER PROUD OF. I OFTEN GO BACK TO VISIT MY CHINESE PERIOD NEAR ZUBEN-EL-AKRAB TOO...
39A
AT ANY RATE, YOU SEE, WHAT MATTERS ISN'T SO MUCH ACCURACY AS IMAGINATION. AH, THAT IMAGINATION THAT IS SO LACKING ON MY OWN WORLD! AND SO I DREW INSPIRATION MOSTLY FROM YOUR POETS, YOUR NOVELISTS, YOUR FILMMAKERS...
YOUR FAVOURITES, DEAR FRIEND?
HOW YOU UNDERSTAND ME! LET ME THINK. FOR THE ART OF THE PLOT, NO HESITATION: THE PICARESQUE NOVEL OF THE 18TH CENTURY; STENDHAL AND A FEW OTHERS TO UNDERSTAND SOMETHING OF WHAT YOU CALL LOVE. ROUSSEL AND BORGÈS TO REACH ABSOLUTE LITERARY IDEALISM. BUT HOW COULD I NAME ALL THOSE I ENJOY!
LET ME GUESS... IT SEEMS TO ME THAT YOUR VISUAL STYLE OWES MUCH TO HITCHCOCK AND EISENSTEIN...
HOW EXTRAORDINARILY PERCEPTIVE! TO THE FIRST I OWE THE PRECISE LAYOUT OF SEQUENCE SHOTS. TO THE SECOND, THE ART OF CROWD MOVEMENT...
AND HOW DID YOU MATERIALISE ALL THAT?
BAH! A LOT OF TECHNICAL WORK, NOT VERY INTERESTING. COME, I WILL SHOW YOU...
HERE IS MY MATTER SYNTHESISER...
39B

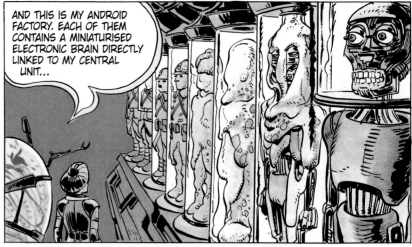

THE DIFFICULTY LIES IN CREATING THE HOLOGRAPHIC MODELS! THE REST IS MERE LOGISTICS...

AND THIS IS MY ANDROID FACTORY. EACH OF THEM CONTAINS A MINIATURISED ELECTRONIC BRAIN DIRECTLY LINKED TO MY CENTRAL UNIT...

BUT THE COMPLEXITY OF THE ACTIONS FORCES ME TO LIMIT THE DURATION OF THE PROGRAMMES. USUALLY NINETY MINUTES – AS IN THAT CLASSIC CINEMA WE BOTH LOVE SO MUCH...

MOREOVER, THE RANGE OF THE ACTORS' FREE WILL IS VERY LIMITED, AS YOU SAW FOR YOURSELF, EVEN THOUGH I TOOK THE PRECAUTION OF PLACING ONE SUBJECT WITH MORE EXTENDED CAPABILITIES ON EACH OF MY WORLDS, SO THAT I COULD BE CONTACTED AT ANY TIME...

THE ARRIVAL OF YOUR SPIES THEREFORE OFFERED ME FASCINATING SCRIPTING PROBLEMS! IT TOOK ME A FAIR AMOUNT OF TIME TO DISCOVER YOUR REMARKABLE APPROACH AND DEVISE NEW PROGRAMMED ACTIONS...

YES! GALAXITY GOT WORRIED AFTER ONE OF YOUR FALSE EARTHS WAS DISCOVERED BY CHANCE. AFTER THAT, THOSE IMBECILES WANTED TO DESTROY YOU, PLAIN AND SIMPLE. BUT I BELIEVED YOU WOULD BE ON YOUR GUARD, AND THAT A MISSION IN FORCE WOULD HAVE DRIVEN YOU TO DISAPPEAR FOR GOOD – WHICH WOULD HAVE BEEN A TERRIBLE LOSS TO THE WORLDS OF ARTS AND SCIENCE...

BESIDES, IT WAS OBVIOUS TO ME THAT THE ONLY WAY TO LOCATE YOU WAS TO FOLLOW YOUR CREATIVE PROCESS BY COLLECTING SUCCESSIVE COORDINATES AND GET EVER NEARER TO YOU BEFORE YOU REALISED IT. I THEREFORE DEEMED IT PREFERABLE TO USE ONE OF THEIR AGENTS AS I SAW FIT TO TRACK YOU...

YOU ARE TOO KIND.

WHAT A PITY!

HOW CLEVER! ALAS, OUR CHASE HAS OVERTAXED MY ENGINES. YOU ARE MY PRISONER, BUT MY SHIP HAS USED THE LAST OF ITS ENERGY. A LAMENTABLE STATE OF AFFAIRS, AS I WAS PLANNING TO BEGIN WORK ON AFRICAN AGRO-PASTORAL CIVILISATIONS...

118

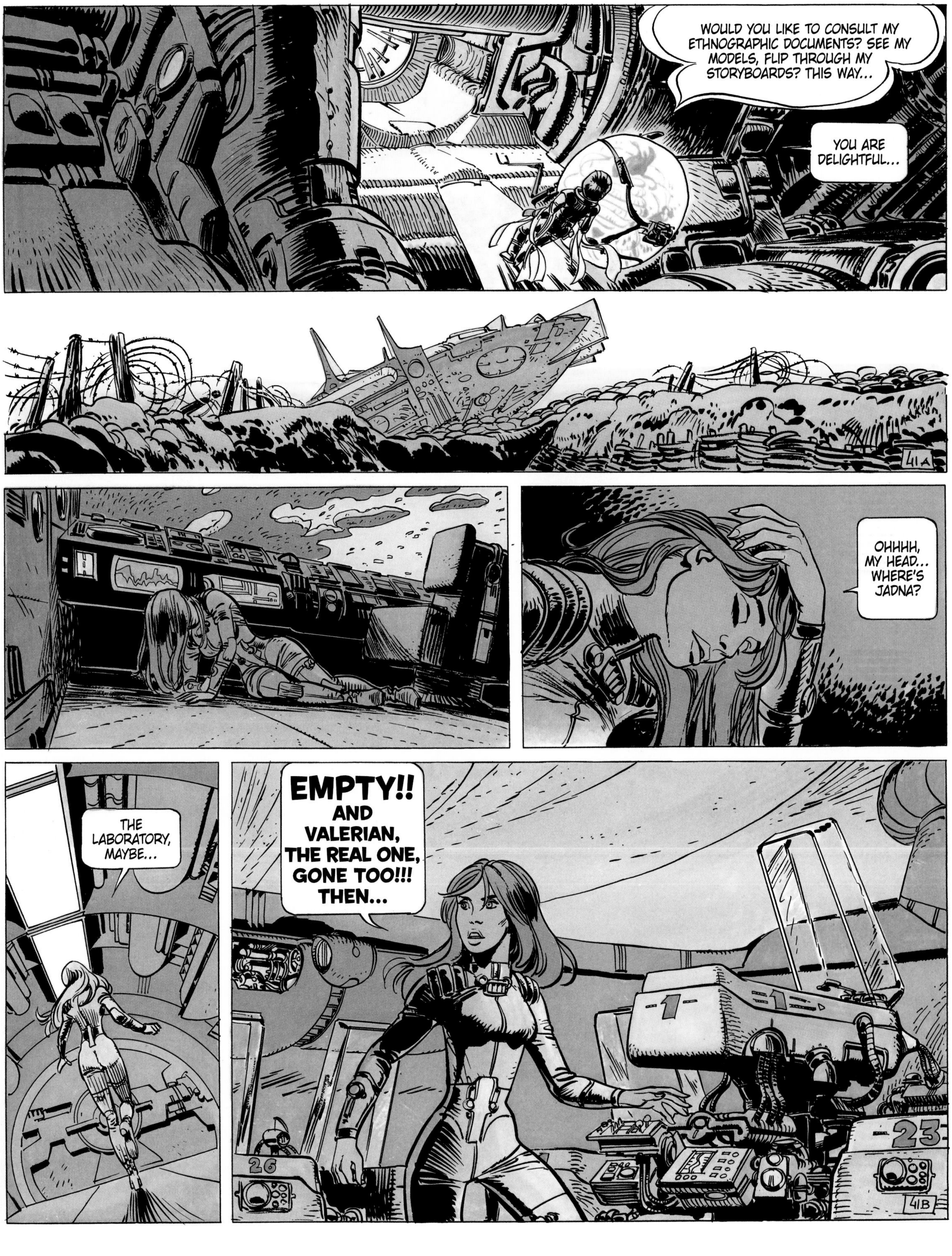
WOULD YOU LIKE TO CONSULT MY ETHNOGRAPHIC DOCUMENTS? SEE MY MODELS, FLIP THROUGH MY STORYBOARDS? THIS WAY...
YOU ARE DELIGHTFUL...
41A
OHHHH, MY HEAD... WHERE'S JADNA?
THE LABORATORY, MAYBE...
EMPTY!! AND VALERIAN, THE REAL ONE, GONE TOO!!! THEN...
1
1
26
23
41B

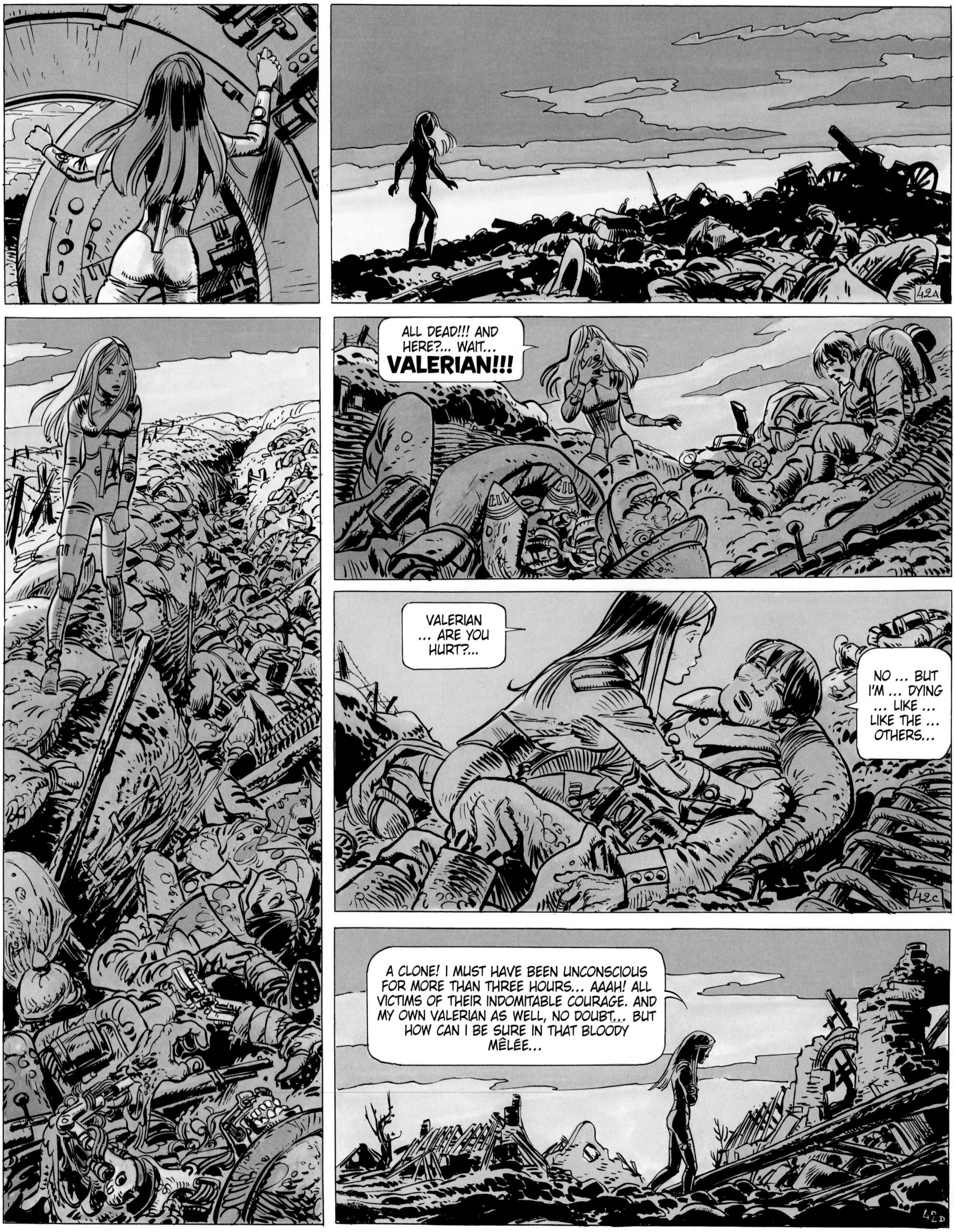
42A
ALL DEAD!!! AND HERE?... WAIT... VALERIAN!!!
VALERIAN ... ARE YOU HURT?...
NO ... BUT I'M ... DYING ... LIKE ... LIKE THE ... OTHERS...
42C
A CLONE! I MUST HAVE BEEN UNCONSCIOUS FOR MORE THAN THREE HOURS... AAAH! ALL VICTIMS OF THEIR INDOMITABLE COURAGE. AND MY OWN VALERIAN AS WELL, NO DOUBT... BUT HOW CAN I BE SURE IN THAT BLOODY MÊLÉE...
42D

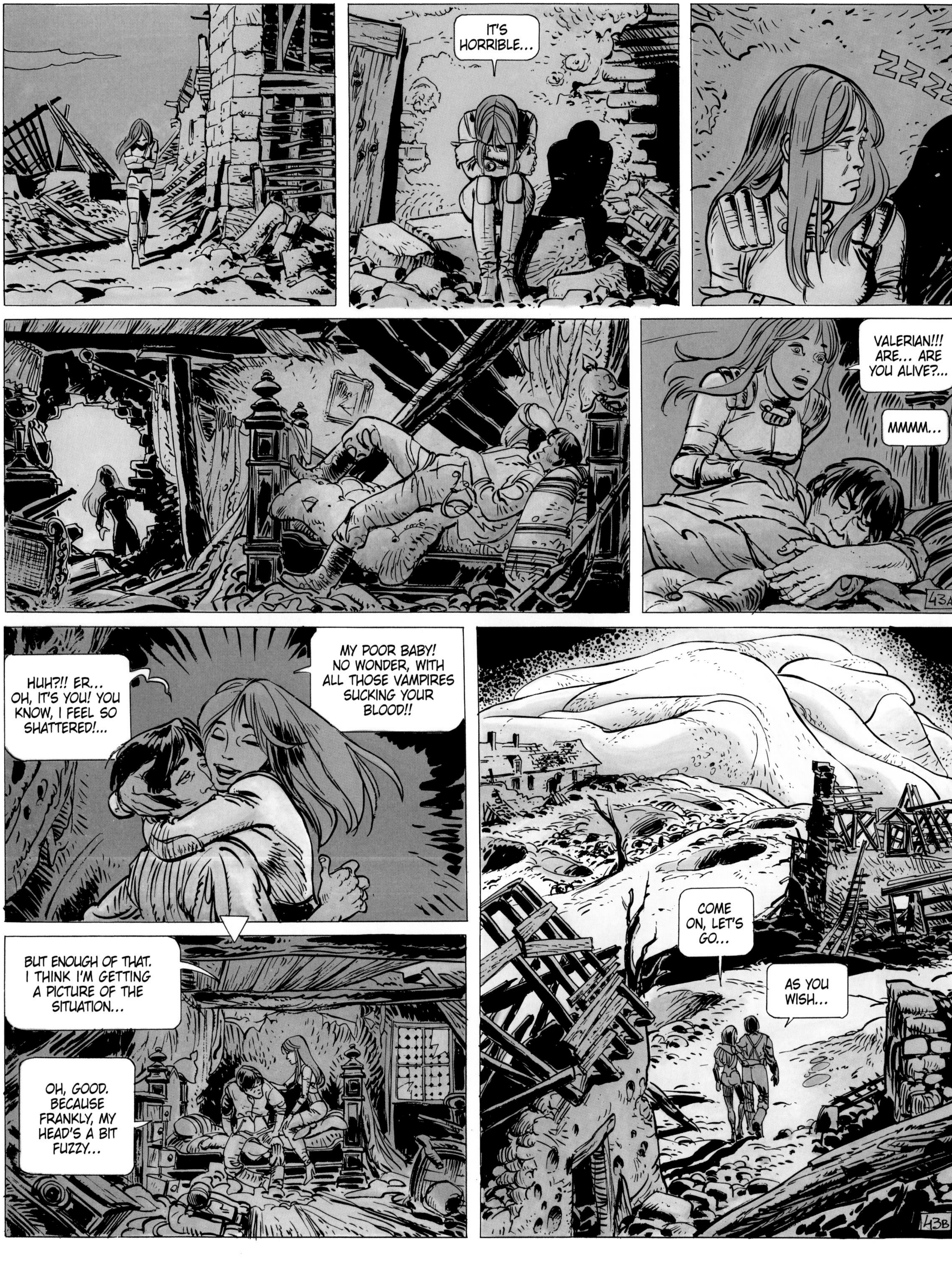
IT'S HORRIBLE...
ZZZZ
VALERIAN!!! ARE... ARE YOU ALIVE?...
MMMM...
43A
HUH?!! ER... OH, IT'S YOU! YOU KNOW, I FEEL SO SHATTERED!...
MY POOR BABY! NO WONDER, WITH ALL THOSE VAMPIRES SUCKING YOUR BLOOD!!
BUT ENOUGH OF THAT. I THINK I'M GETTING A PICTURE OF THE SITUATION...
OH, GOOD. BECAUSE FRANKLY, MY HEAD'S A BIT FUZZY...
COME ON, LET'S GO...
AS YOU WISH...
43B

THIS WAY...

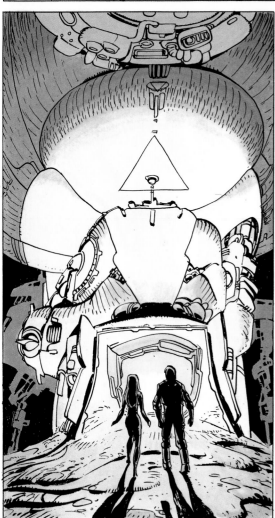

OH, YOU'RE HERE? I CONFESS, I FORGOT ALL ABOUT YOU – THE CONVERSATION IS SO FASCINATING.

A PLEASURE! DO JOIN US; WE'RE WORKING TOGETHER ON CONSTRUCTING NEW PROGRAMMED ACTIONS. AS SOON AS MY GENERATORS HAVE REBUILT MY RESERVES, WE...

AS SOON AS YOUR GENERATORS HAVE REBUILT YOUR RESERVES, I WILL BE TELLING YOU WHAT TO DO! IT'LL BE VERY SIMPLE!... DIG OUT **MY** SPACESHIP! IT'S TIME TO GO HOME!...

ISN'T IT ALSO ... ER ... A BIT MINE? I MEAN...

PAH...

YOU ARE SO CRASSLY COMMON, MY DEAR! DON'T YOU SEE IT? RECREATING THE PAST FROM SCRATCH! IT'S A POSITIVELY INCREDIBLE AESTHETIC GESTURE...

ON THE CONTRARY, I SEE IT PERFECTLY! YOUR NEW FRIEND POSES ABSOLUTELY NO DANGER TO GALAXITY! THAT'S GREAT, AND I'LL LET THEM KNOW. BUT BEYOND THAT, **WHY SHOULD I GIVE A FIG ABOUT THAT STUPID 19TH CENTURY OF YOURS?...**

LET'S TALK ABOUT YOUR SPLENDID RE-ENACTMENTS: THE CONQUEST OF INDIA, THAT'S COLONIALISM! GLADSTONE'S ENGLAND, OR WHOEVER IT WAS, THAT'S IMPERIALISM! THE UNITED STATES OF THE WESTWARD EXPANSION, THAT'S CAPITALISM! AS FOR THE FIRST WORLD WAR, TAKE A STROLL OUTSIDE AND SEE WHAT IT REALLY LOOKED LIKE!!...

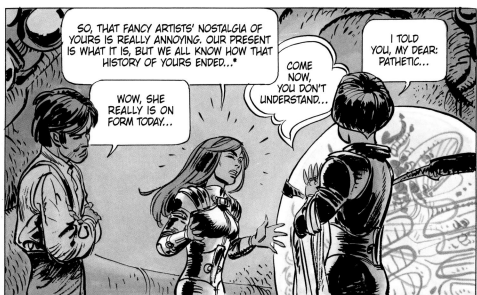

SO, THAT FANCY ARTISTS' NOSTALGIA OF YOURS IS REALLY ANNOYING. OUR PRESENT IS WHAT IT IS, BUT WE ALL KNOW HOW THAT HISTORY OF YOURS ENDED...*

WOW, SHE REALLY IS ON FORM TODAY...

COME NOW, YOU DON'T UNDERSTAND...

I TOLD YOU, MY DEAR: PATHETIC...

I'M GIVING YOU ONE EARTH HOUR TO FREE OUR SHIP, THEN VALERIAN AND I ARE LEAVING...

WHAT ABOUT ME...?

YOU, YOU'RE STAYING! ONCE YOU GET TIRED OF YOUR LITTLE GAMES, WE CAN ALWAYS SEND SOMEONE TO PICK YOU UP...

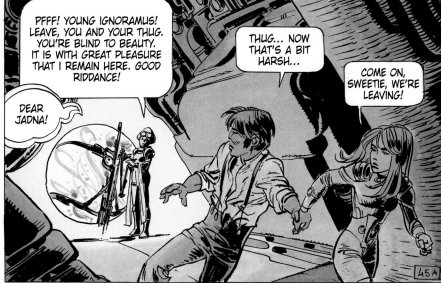

PFFF! YOUNG IGNORAMUS! LEAVE, YOU AND YOUR THUG. YOU'RE BLIND TO BEAUTY. IT IS WITH GREAT PLEASURE THAT I REMAIN HERE. GOOD RIDDANCE!

DEAR JADNA!

THUG... NOW THAT'S A BIT HARSH...

COME ON, SWEETIE, WE'RE LEAVING!

A LITTLE LATER...

THAT'S IT! WE'RE TAKING OFF!!!

VALERIAN, YOU KNOW WHAT WE'RE GOING TO DO?...

*THERE'S AN EXCELLENT BOOK ON THAT SUBJECT: *THE CITY OF SHIFTING WATERS*. SAME SERIES!

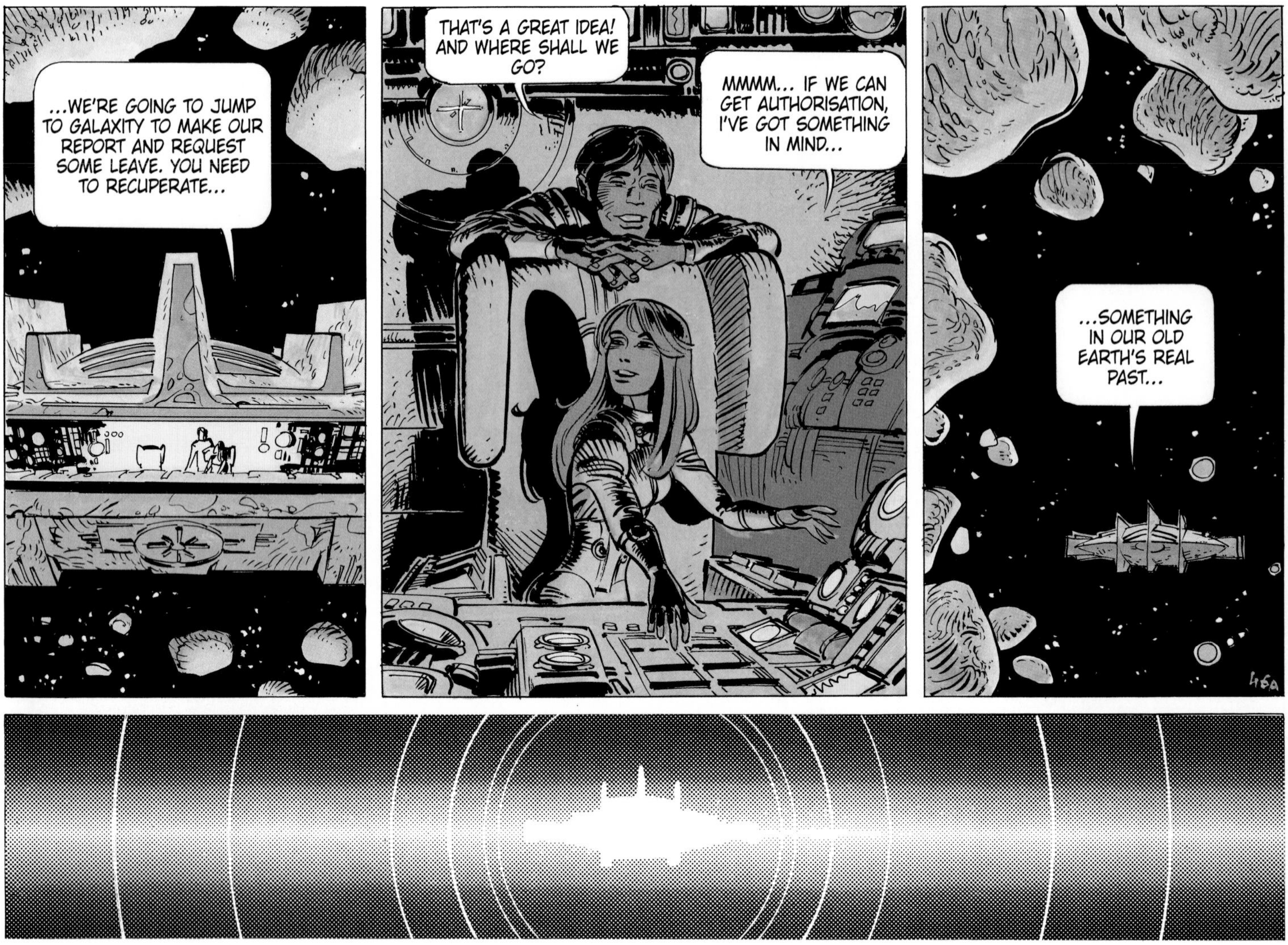
...WE'RE GOING TO JUMP TO GALAXITY TO MAKE OUR REPORT AND REQUEST SOME LEAVE. YOU NEED TO RECUPERATE...
THAT'S A GREAT IDEA! AND WHERE SHALL WE GO?
MMMM... IF WE CAN GET AUTHORISATION, I'VE GOT SOMETHING IN MIND...
...SOMETHING IN OUR OLD EARTH'S REAL PAST...

AND LATER STILL...

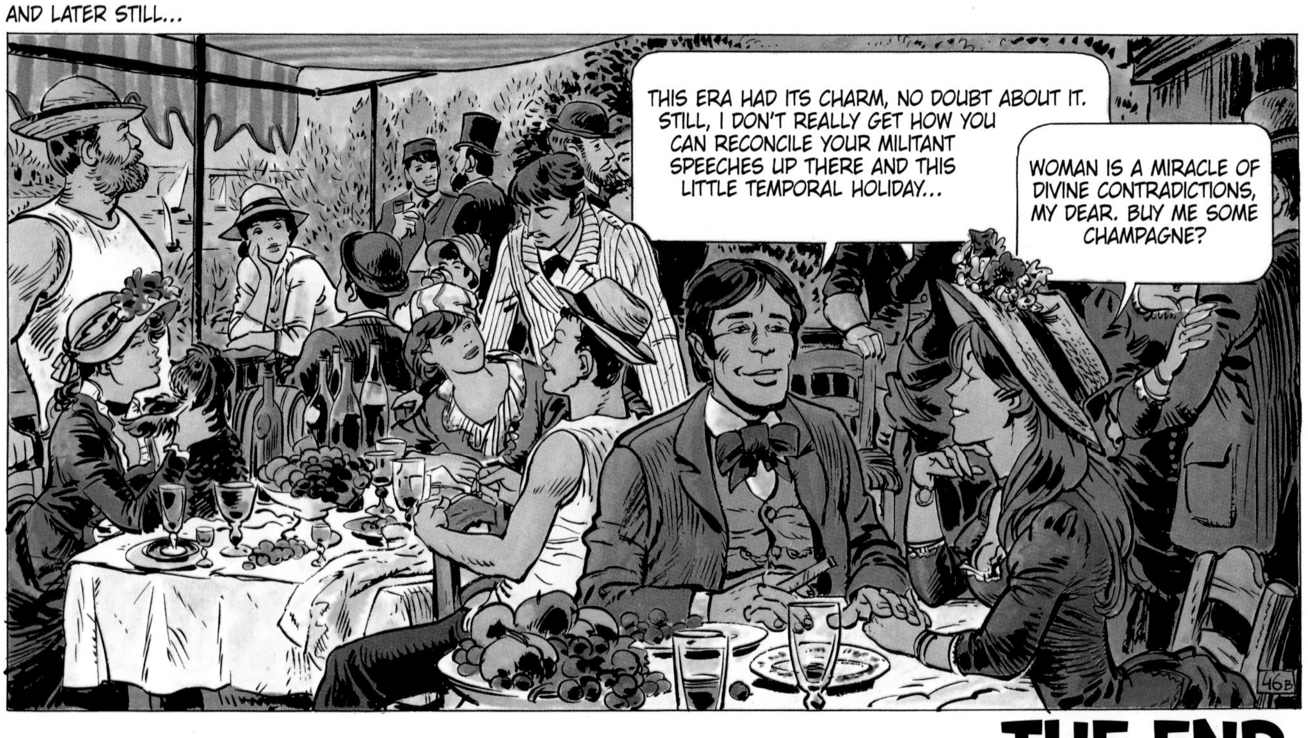
THIS ERA HAD ITS CHARM, NO DOUBT ABOUT IT. STILL, I DON'T REALLY GET HOW YOU CAN RECONCILE YOUR MILITANT SPEECHES UP THERE AND THIS LITTLE TEMPORAL HOLIDAY...
WOMAN IS A MIRACLE OF DIVINE CONTRADICTIONS, MY DEAR. BUY ME SOME CHAMPAGNE?

THE END

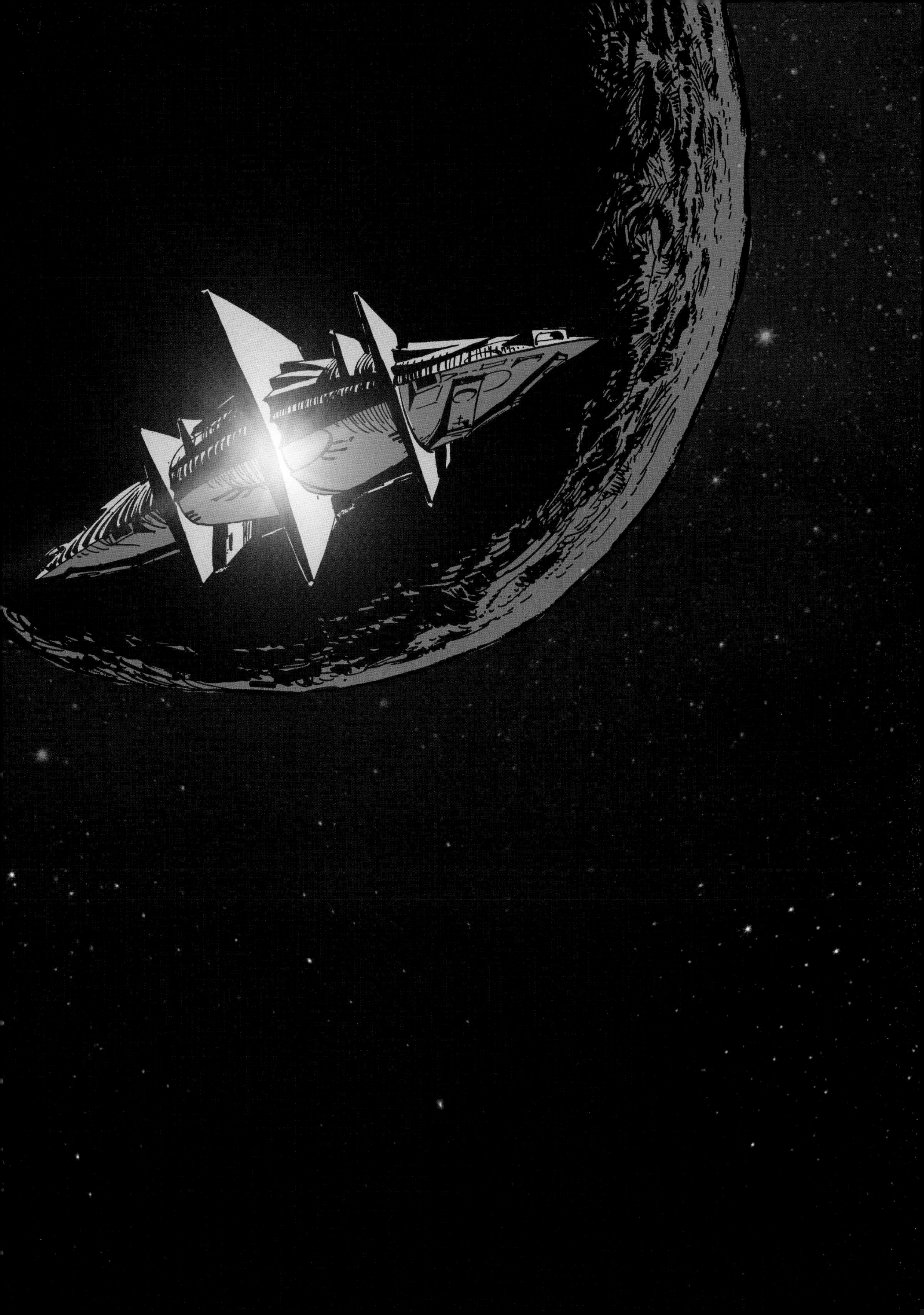

HEROES OF THE EQUINOX

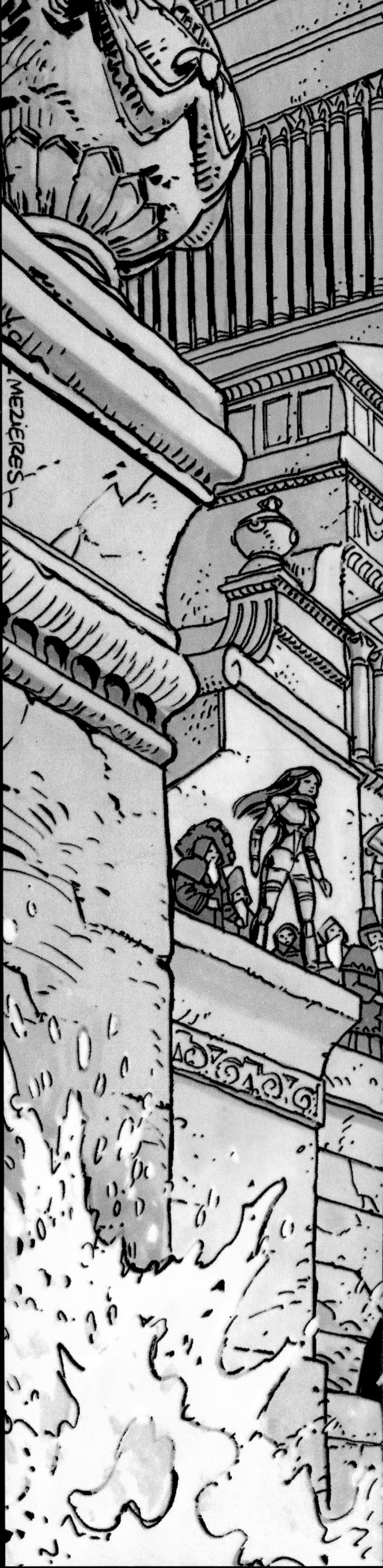
MEZIERES

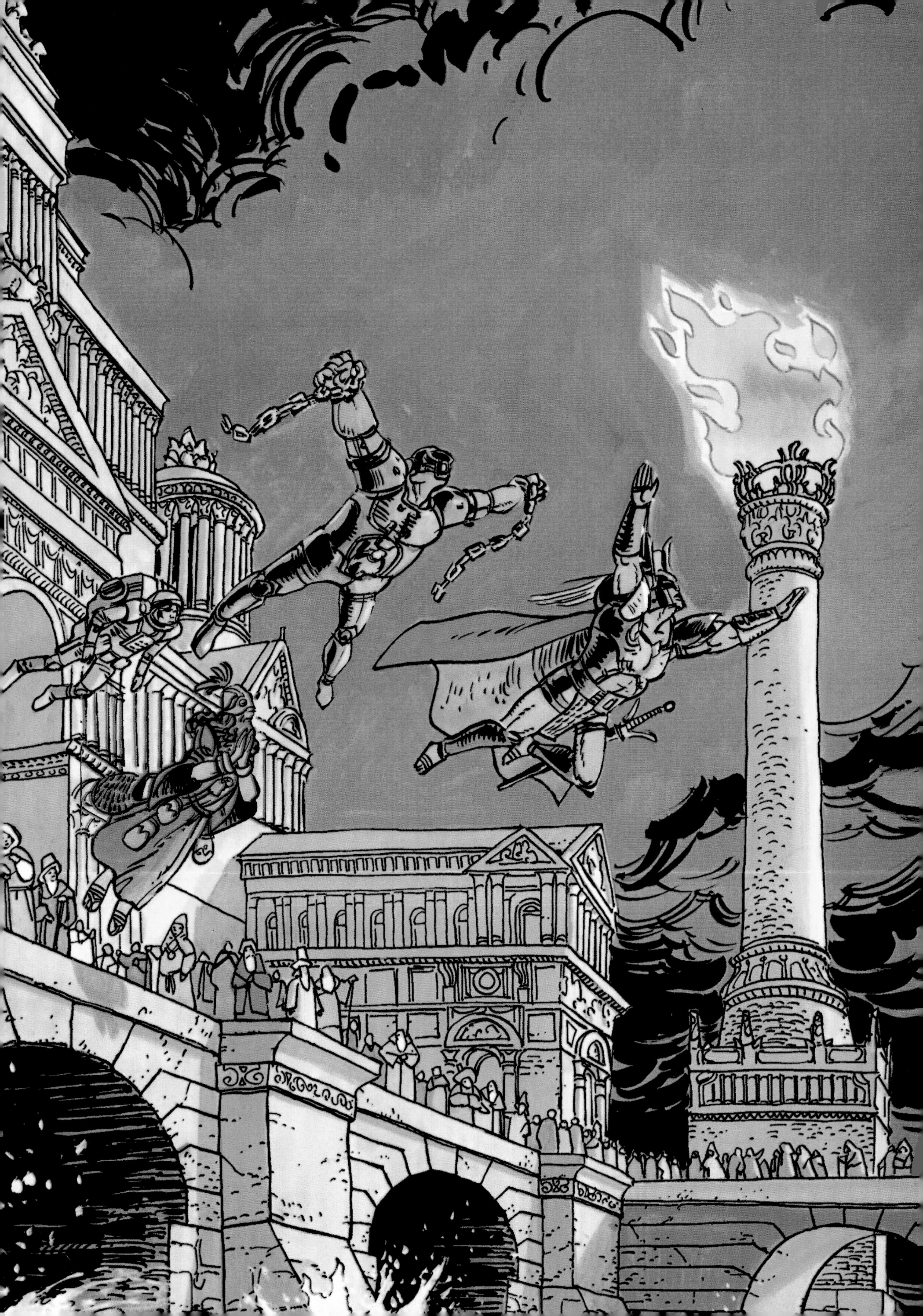

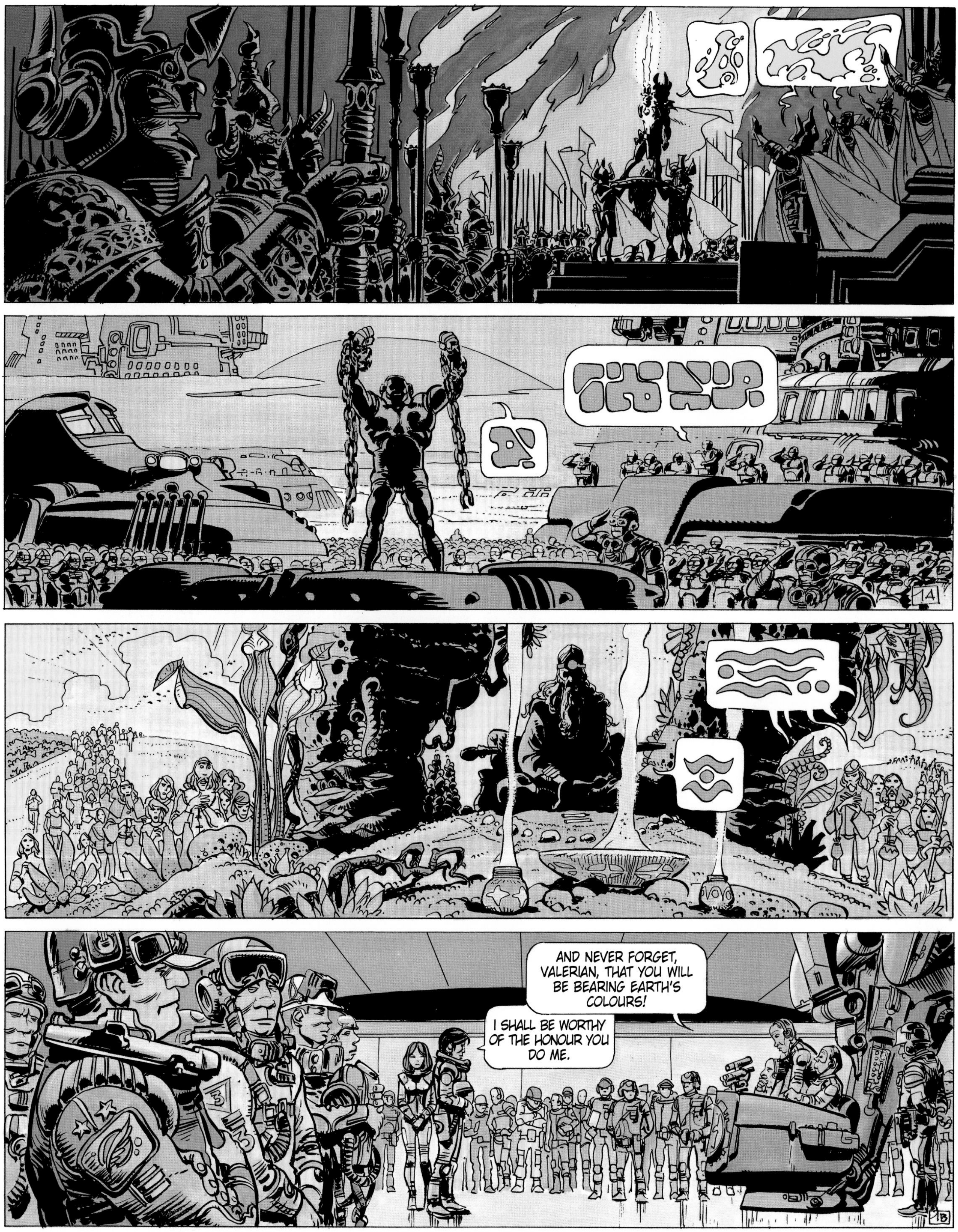
AND NEVER FORGET, VALERIAN, THAT YOU WILL BE BEARING EARTH'S COLOURS!
I SHALL BE WORTHY OF THE HONOUR YOU DO ME.

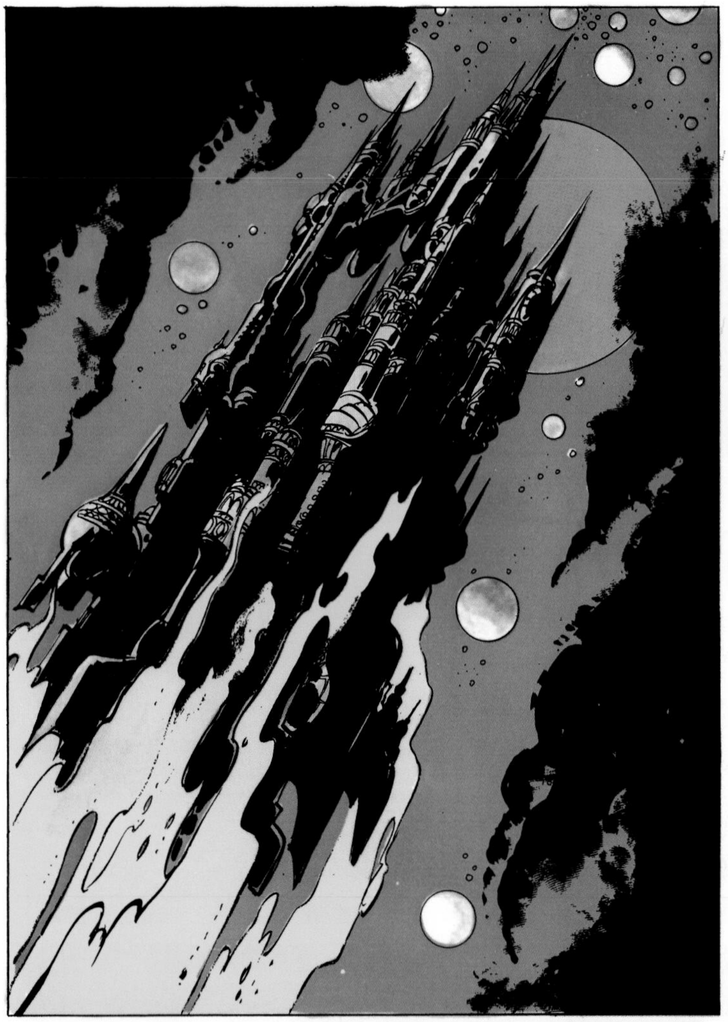
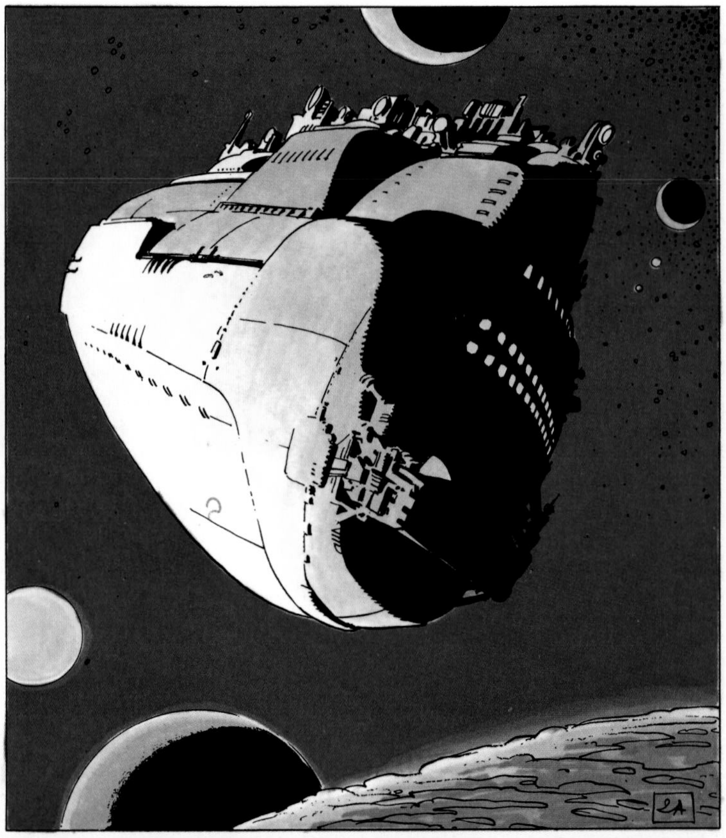
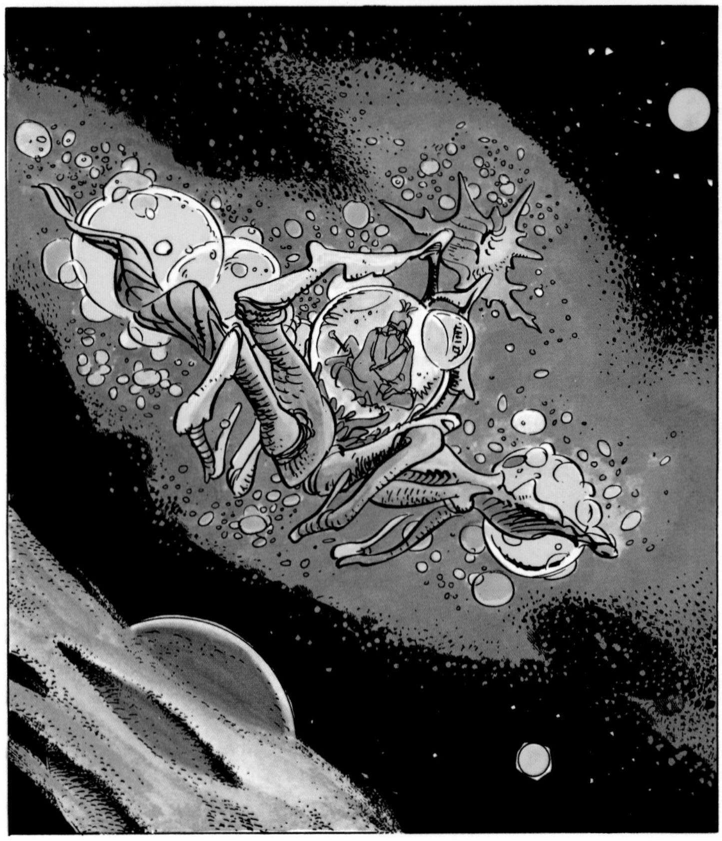
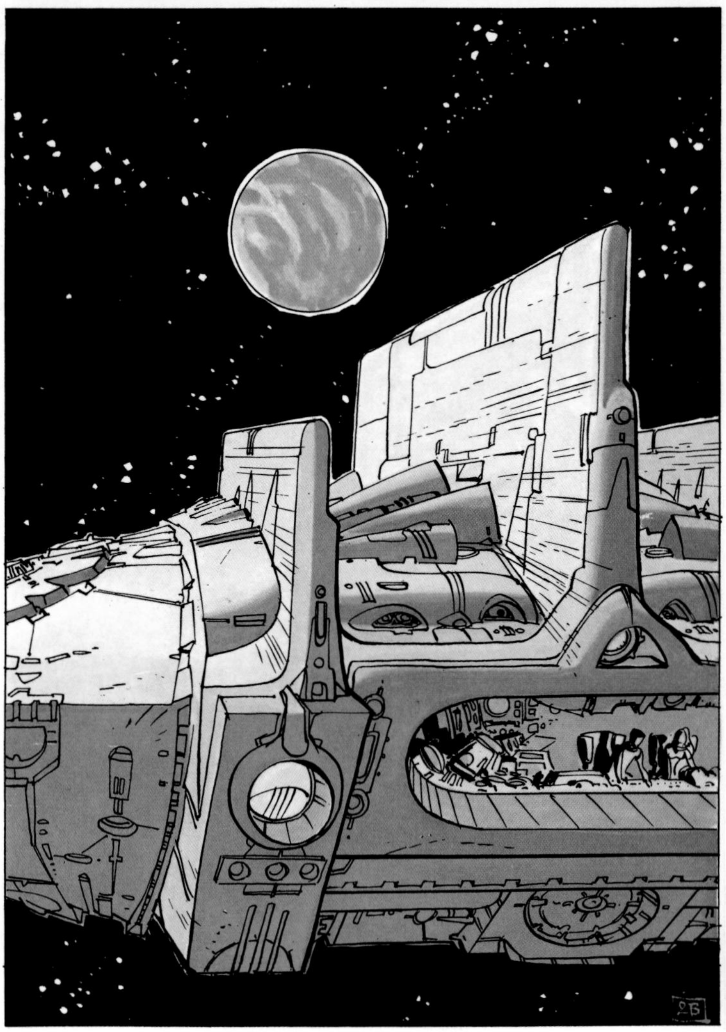

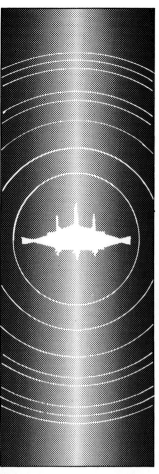

THE HONOUR OF EARTH, MY FOOT! THE TRUTH IS, YOU'RE OFF TO SELL GALAXITY'S BRAND IMAGE TO THE UNIVERSE...

BAH! NO NEED TO BE NASTY, LAURELINE. WHY DON'T YOU HELP ME MASTER SIMLANE'S BLASTED LANGUAGE INSTEAD?...

WELL, IF YOU ENJOY RISKING YOUR LIFE FOR THOSE OLD FOSSILS, GOOD FOR YOU...

AHEM... I HAVE DOUBTS ABOUT THE 'ENJOYING' BIT. FIRST OF ALL, I WAS... VOLUNTEERED. AND SECOND, THAT CONTEST IS NO PICNIC...

I CAN'T WAIT TO SEE WHAT THE OTHER COMPETITORS LOOK LIKE...

YOU SHOULD FIND OUT PRETTY SOON. HERE'S SIMLANE'S SPACEPORT...

...AND I HAVE A FEELING ALL THREE OF THEM ARE ALREADY HERE...

HMM... ASIDE FROM THEM AND US, IT'S PRETTY EMPTY...

YES. THE LOCALS DON'T TRAVEL OFF-PLANET, AND IT'S THE WRONG TIME OF YEAR FOR ALIEN TOURISM ...

131

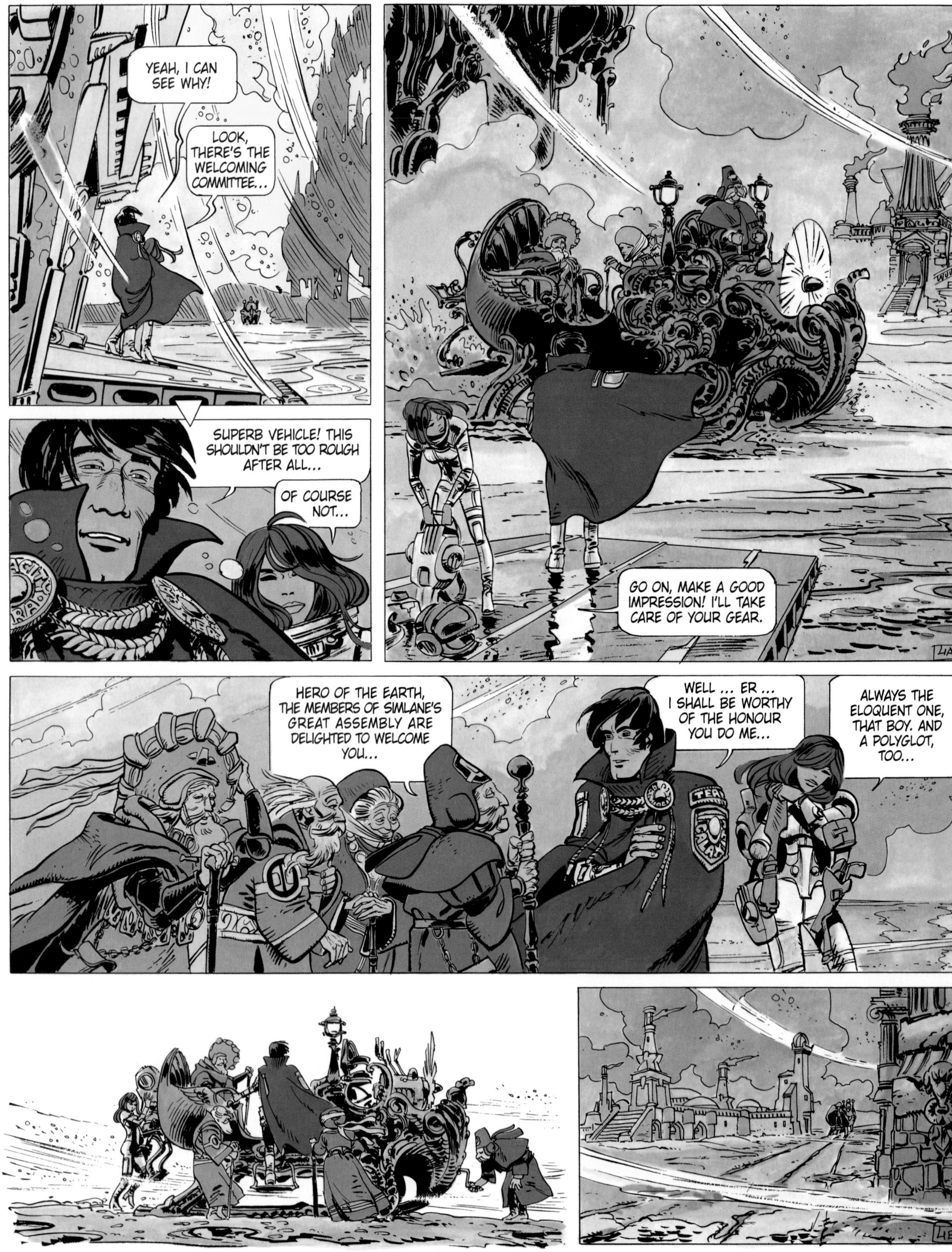
YEAH, I CAN SEE WHY!
LOOK, THERE'S THE WELCOMING COMMITTEE...
SUPERB VEHICLE! THIS SHOULDN'T BE TOO ROUGH AFTER ALL...
OF COURSE NOT...
GO ON, MAKE A GOOD IMPRESSION! I'LL TAKE CARE OF YOUR GEAR.
4A
HERO OF THE EARTH, THE MEMBERS OF SIMLANE'S GREAT ASSEMBLY ARE DELIGHTED TO WELCOME YOU...
WELL ... ER ... I SHALL BE WORTHY OF THE HONOUR YOU DO ME...
ALWAYS THE ELOQUENT ONE, THAT BOY. AND A POLYGLOT, TOO...
4B

THIS IS OUR CITY.

MAGNIFICENT!

ALAS, NOT REALLY. LOOK AT THE STATE OF THE PALACE OF TRUTH – WHERE JUSTICE IS METED OUT...

AND THE DOME OF EXCHANGE! IT USED TO BE OUR FINEST MARKETPLACE...

SOON, ALL WE'LL HAVE TO SHOW OUR VISITORS IS RUINS ...

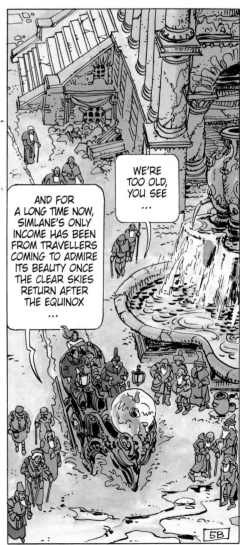

WE'RE TOO OLD, YOU SEE ...

AND FOR A LONG TIME NOW, SIMLANE'S ONLY INCOME HAS BEEN FROM TRAVELLERS COMING TO ADMIRE ITS BEAUTY ONCE THE CLEAR SKIES RETURN AFTER THE EQUINOX ...

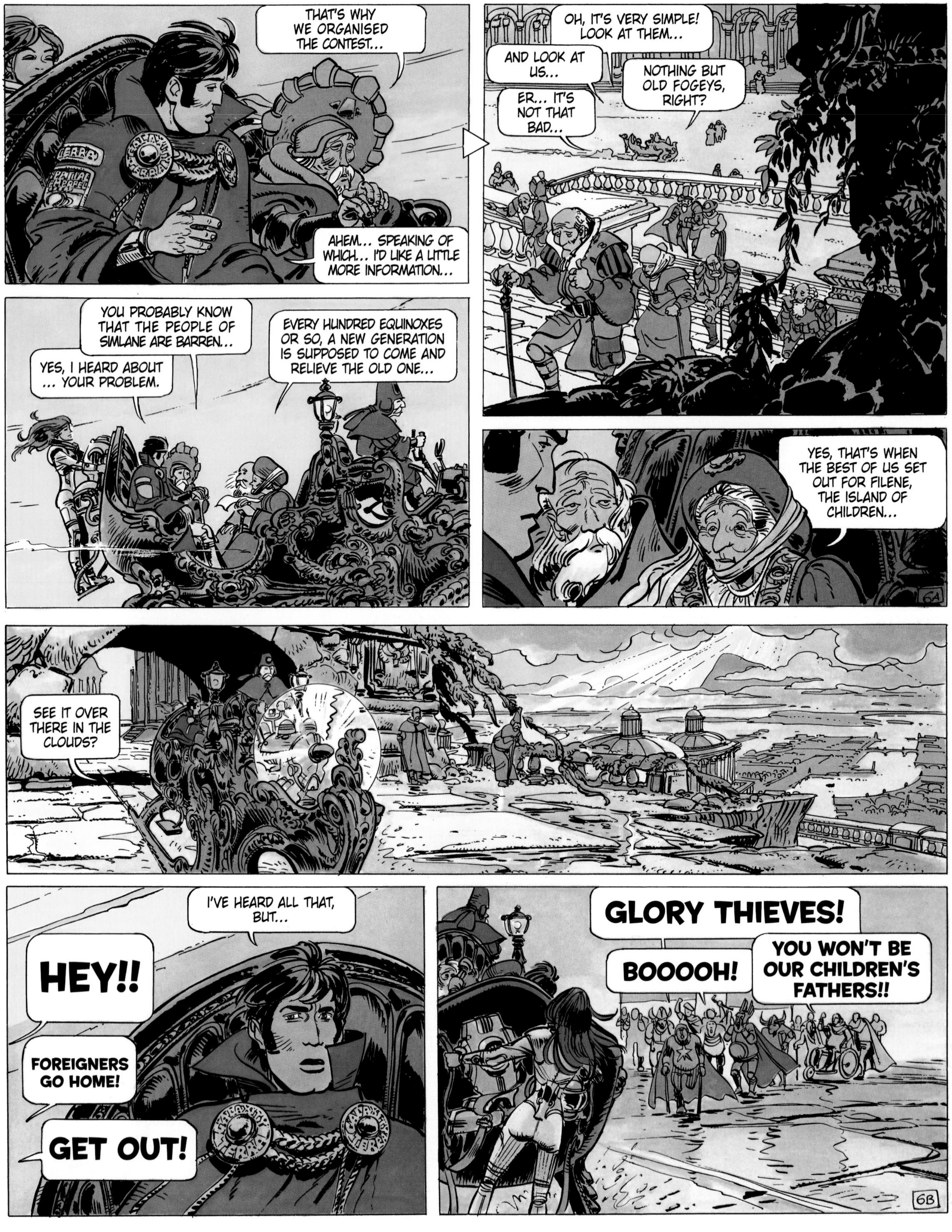
THAT'S WHY WE ORGANISED THE CONTEST...
AHEM... SPEAKING OF WHICH... I'D LIKE A LITTLE MORE INFORMATION...
OH, IT'S VERY SIMPLE! LOOK AT THEM...
AND LOOK AT US...
NOTHING BUT OLD FOGEYS, RIGHT?
ER... IT'S NOT THAT BAD...
YOU PROBABLY KNOW THAT THE PEOPLE OF SIMLANE ARE BARREN...
YES, I HEARD ABOUT ... YOUR PROBLEM.
EVERY HUNDRED EQUINOXES OR SO, A NEW GENERATION IS SUPPOSED TO COME AND RELIEVE THE OLD ONE...
YES, THAT'S WHEN THE BEST OF US SET OUT FOR FILENE, THE ISLAND OF CHILDREN...
6A
SEE IT OVER THERE IN THE CLOUDS?
I'VE HEARD ALL THAT, BUT...
HEY!!
FOREIGNERS GO HOME!
GET OUT!
GLORY THIEVES!
BOOOOH!
YOU WON'T BE OUR CHILDREN'S FATHERS!!
6B

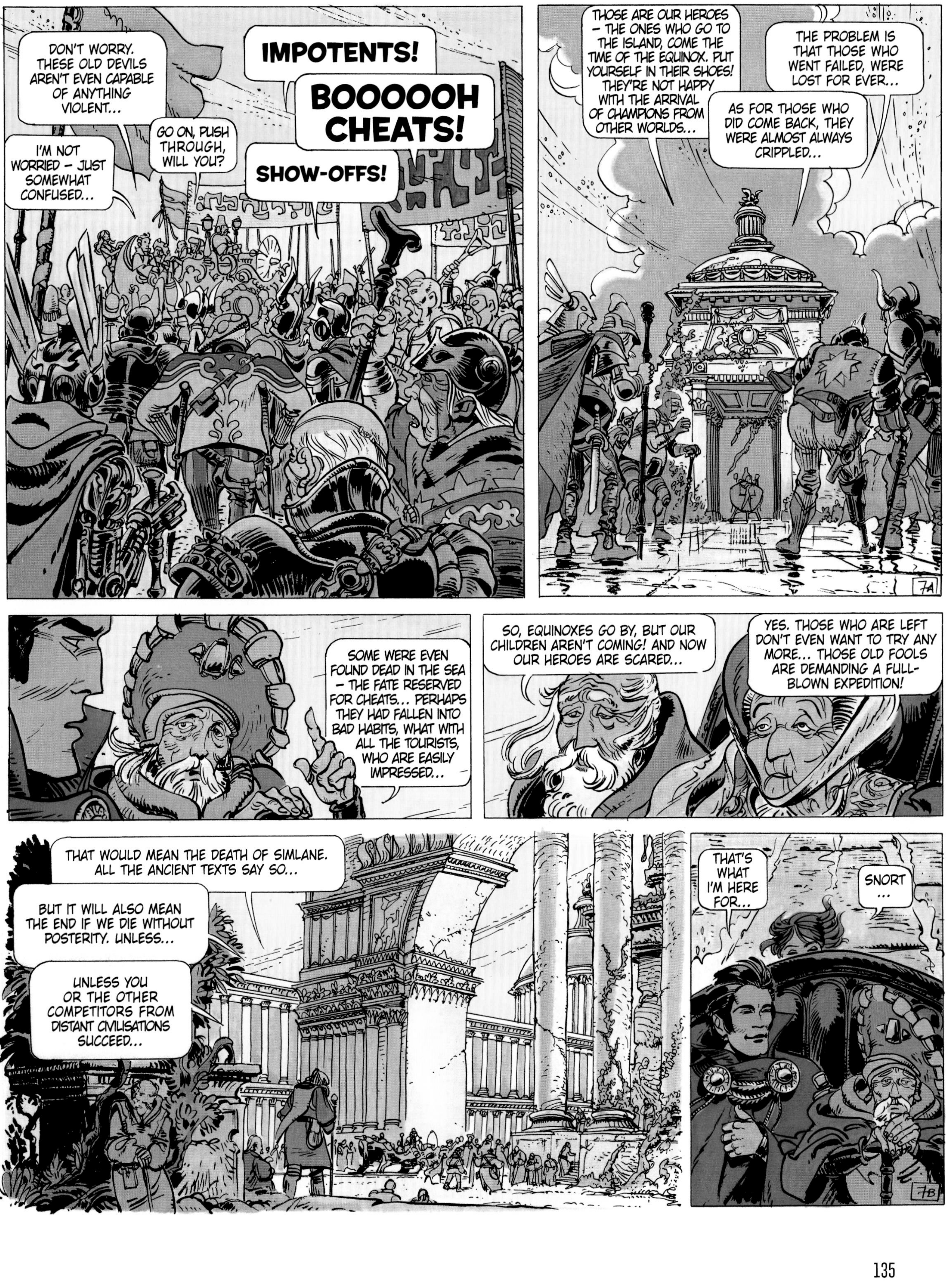
DON'T WORRY. THESE OLD DEVILS AREN'T EVEN CAPABLE OF ANYTHING VIOLENT...
I'M NOT WORRIED – JUST SOMEWHAT CONFUSED...
GO ON, PUSH THROUGH, WILL YOU?
IMPOTENTS!
BOOOOOH CHEATS!
SHOW-OFFS!
THOSE ARE OUR HEROES – THE ONES WHO GO TO THE ISLAND, COME THE TIME OF THE EQUINOX. PUT YOURSELF IN THEIR SHOES! THEY'RE NOT HAPPY WITH THE ARRIVAL OF CHAMPIONS FROM OTHER WORLDS...
THE PROBLEM IS THAT THOSE WHO WENT FAILED, WERE LOST FOR EVER...
AS FOR THOSE WHO DID COME BACK, THEY WERE ALMOST ALWAYS CRIPPLED...
7A
SOME WERE EVEN FOUND DEAD IN THE SEA – THE FATE RESERVED FOR CHEATS... PERHAPS THEY HAD FALLEN INTO BAD HABITS, WHAT WITH ALL THE TOURISTS, WHO ARE EASILY IMPRESSED...
SO, EQUINOXES GO BY, BUT OUR CHILDREN AREN'T COMING! AND NOW OUR HEROES ARE SCARED...
YES. THOSE WHO ARE LEFT DON'T EVEN WANT TO TRY ANY MORE... THOSE OLD FOOLS ARE DEMANDING A FULL-BLOWN EXPEDITION!
THAT WOULD MEAN THE DEATH OF SIMLANE. ALL THE ANCIENT TEXTS SAY SO...
BUT IT WILL ALSO MEAN THE END IF WE DIE WITHOUT POSTERITY. UNLESS...
UNLESS YOU OR THE OTHER COMPETITORS FROM DISTANT CIVILISATIONS SUCCEED...
THAT'S WHAT I'M HERE FOR...
SNORT ...
7B

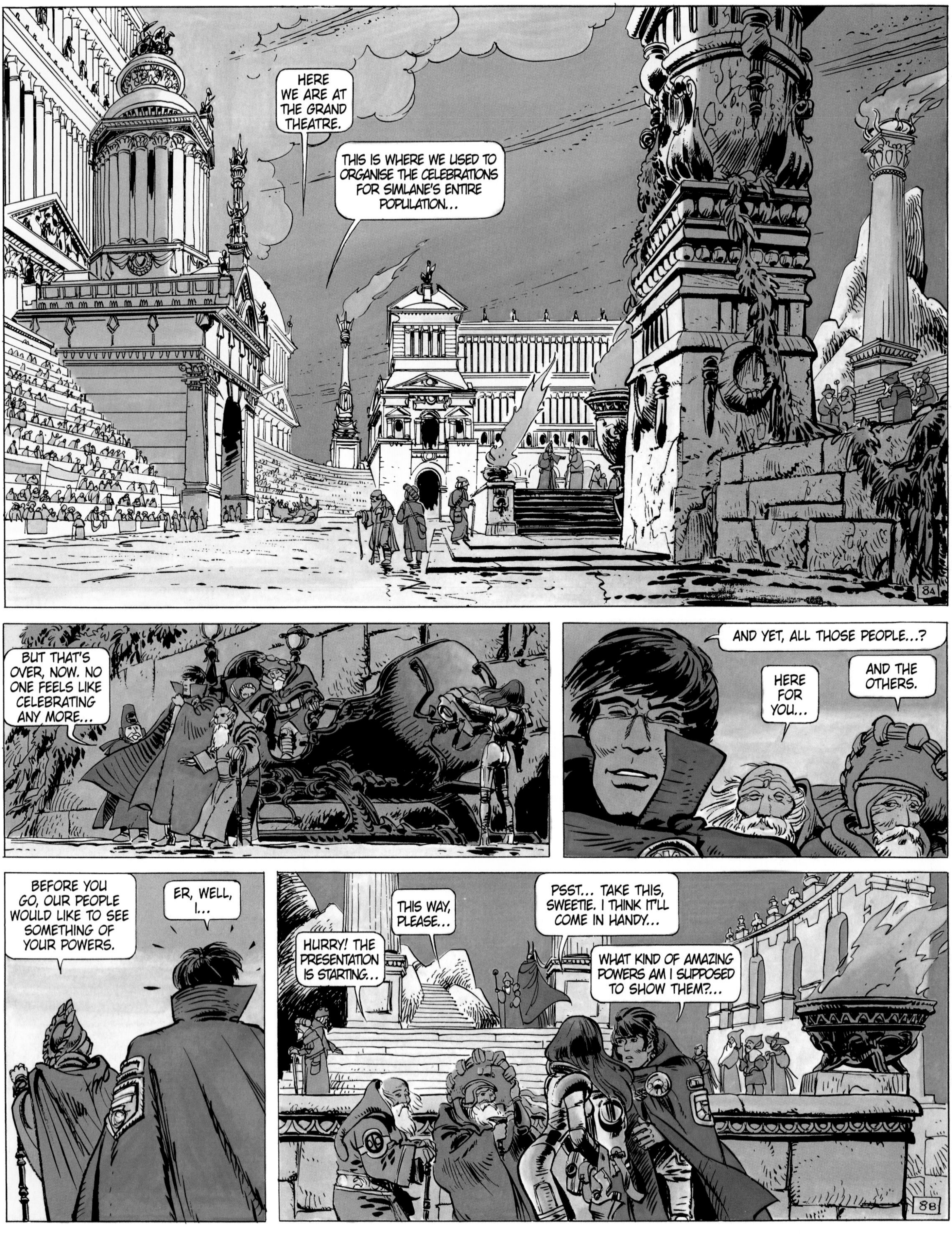
HERE WE ARE AT THE GRAND THEATRE.
THIS IS WHERE WE USED TO ORGANISE THE CELEBRATIONS FOR SIMLANE'S ENTIRE POPULATION...
84
BUT THAT'S OVER, NOW. NO ONE FEELS LIKE CELEBRATING ANY MORE...
AND YET, ALL THOSE PEOPLE...?
HERE FOR YOU...
AND THE OTHERS.
BEFORE YOU GO, OUR PEOPLE WOULD LIKE TO SEE SOMETHING OF YOUR POWERS.
ER, WELL, I...
HURRY! THE PRESENTATION IS STARTING...
THIS WAY, PLEASE...
PSST... TAKE THIS, SWEETIE. I THINK IT'LL COME IN HANDY...
WHAT KIND OF AMAZING POWERS AM I SUPPOSED TO SHOW THEM?...
88

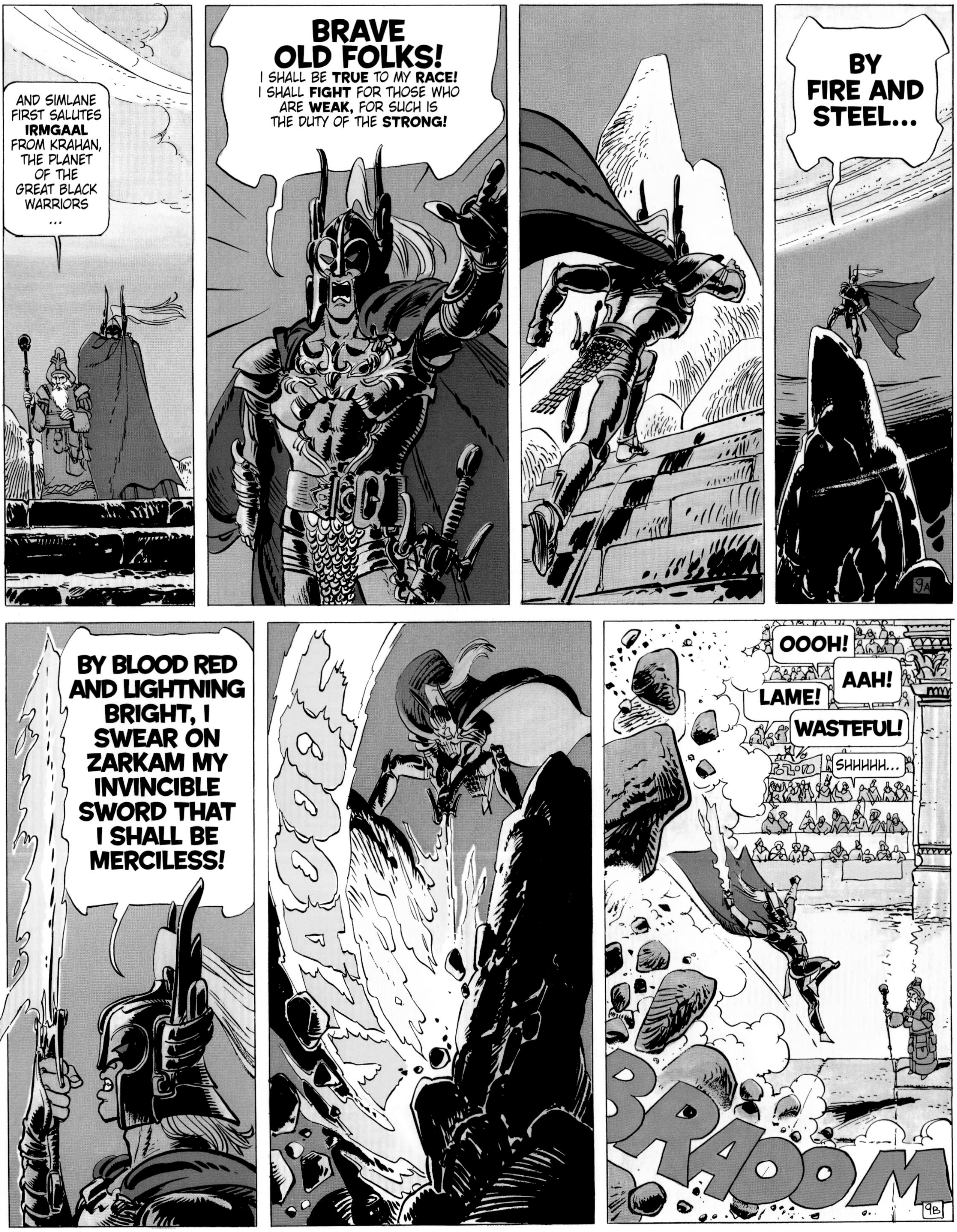
AND SIMLANE FIRST SALUTES IRMGAAL FROM KRAHAN, THE PLANET OF THE GREAT BLACK WARRIORS ...
BRAVE OLD FOLKS! I SHALL BE TRUE TO MY RACE! I SHALL FIGHT FOR THOSE WHO ARE WEAK, FOR SUCH IS THE DUTY OF THE STRONG!
BY FIRE AND STEEL...
9A
BY BLOOD RED AND LIGHTNING BRIGHT, I SWEAR ON ZARKAM MY INVINCIBLE SWORD THAT I SHALL BE MERCILESS!
OOOH!
AAH!
LAME!
WASTEFUL!
SHHHHH...
BRAOOM
9B

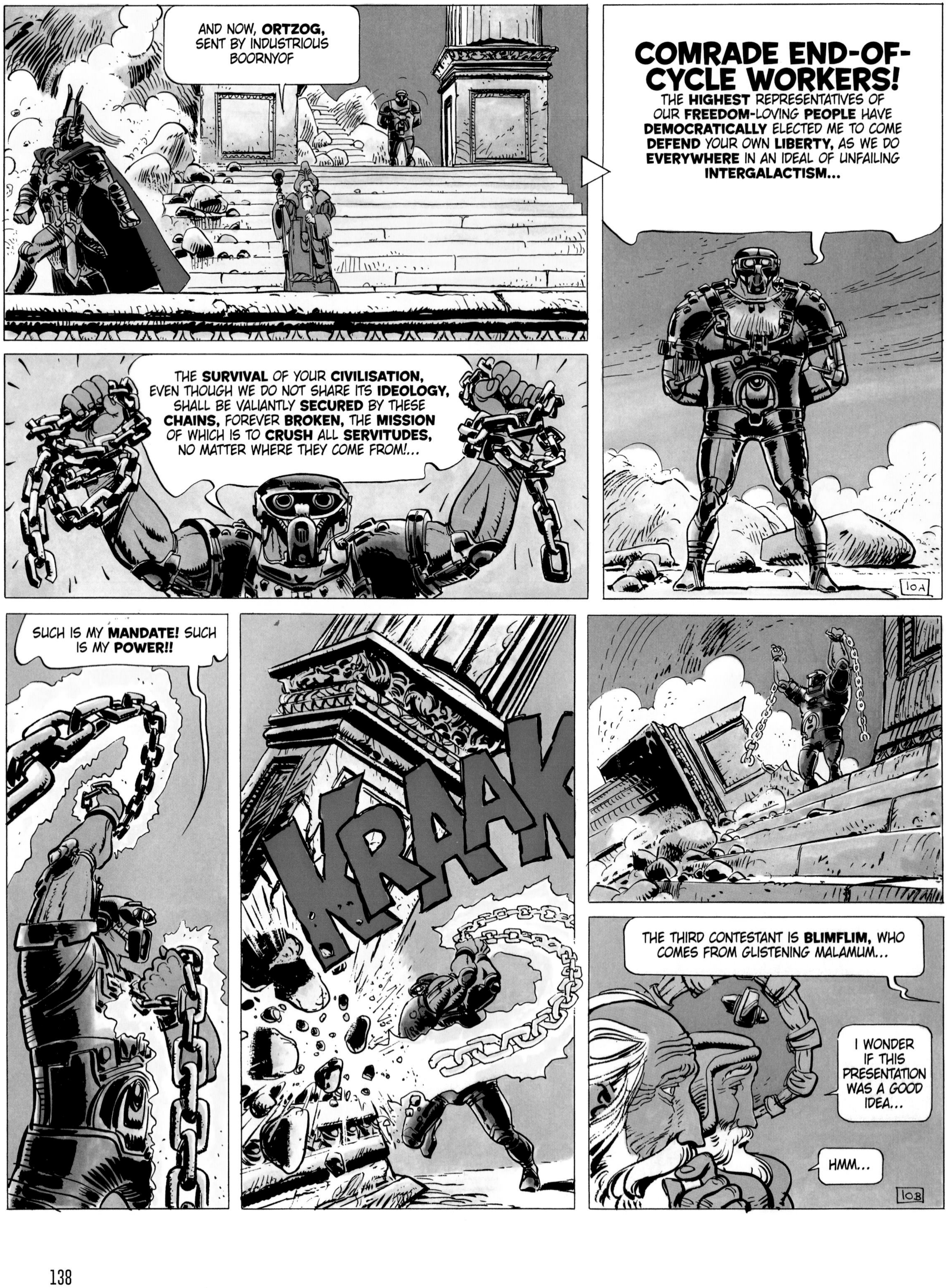
AND NOW, ORTZOG, SENT BY INDUSTRIOUS BOORNYOF
COMRADE END-OF-CYCLE WORKERS!
THE HIGHEST REPRESENTATIVES OF OUR FREEDOM-LOVING PEOPLE HAVE DEMOCRATICALLY ELECTED ME TO COME DEFEND YOUR OWN LIBERTY, AS WE DO EVERYWHERE IN AN IDEAL OF UNFAILING INTERGALACTISM...
THE SURVIVAL OF YOUR CIVILISATION, EVEN THOUGH WE DO NOT SHARE ITS IDEOLOGY, SHALL BE VALIANTLY SECURED BY THESE CHAINS, FOREVER BROKEN, THE MISSION OF WHICH IS TO CRUSH ALL SERVITUDES, NO MATTER WHERE THEY COME FROM!...
10A
SUCH IS MY MANDATE! SUCH IS MY POWER!!
KRAAK
THE THIRD CONTESTANT IS BLIMFLIM, WHO COMES FROM GLISTENING MALAMUM...
I WONDER IF THIS PRESENTATION WAS A GOOD IDEA...
HMM...
10B

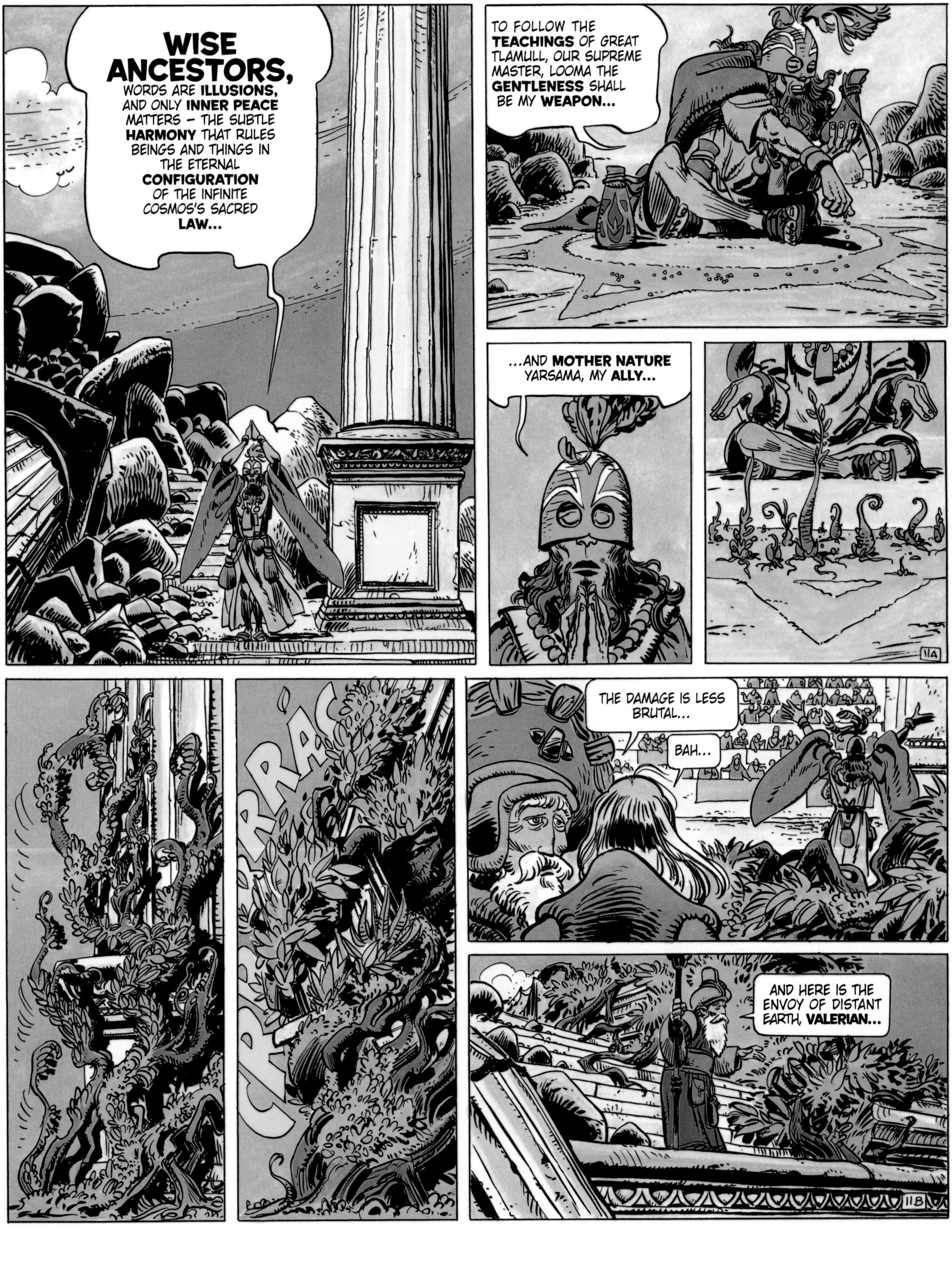
WISE ANCESTORS, WORDS ARE ILLUSIONS, AND ONLY INNER PEACE MATTERS – THE SUBTLE HARMONY THAT RULES BEINGS AND THINGS IN THE ETERNAL CONFIGURATION OF THE INFINITE COSMOS'S SACRED LAW...
TO FOLLOW THE TEACHINGS OF GREAT TLAMULL, OUR SUPREME MASTER, LOOMA THE GENTLENESS SHALL BE MY WEAPON...
...AND MOTHER NATURE YARSAMA, MY ALLY...
11A
CRRAC
THE DAMAGE IS LESS BRUTAL...
BAH...
AND HERE IS THE ENVOY OF DISTANT EARTH, VALERIAN...
11B

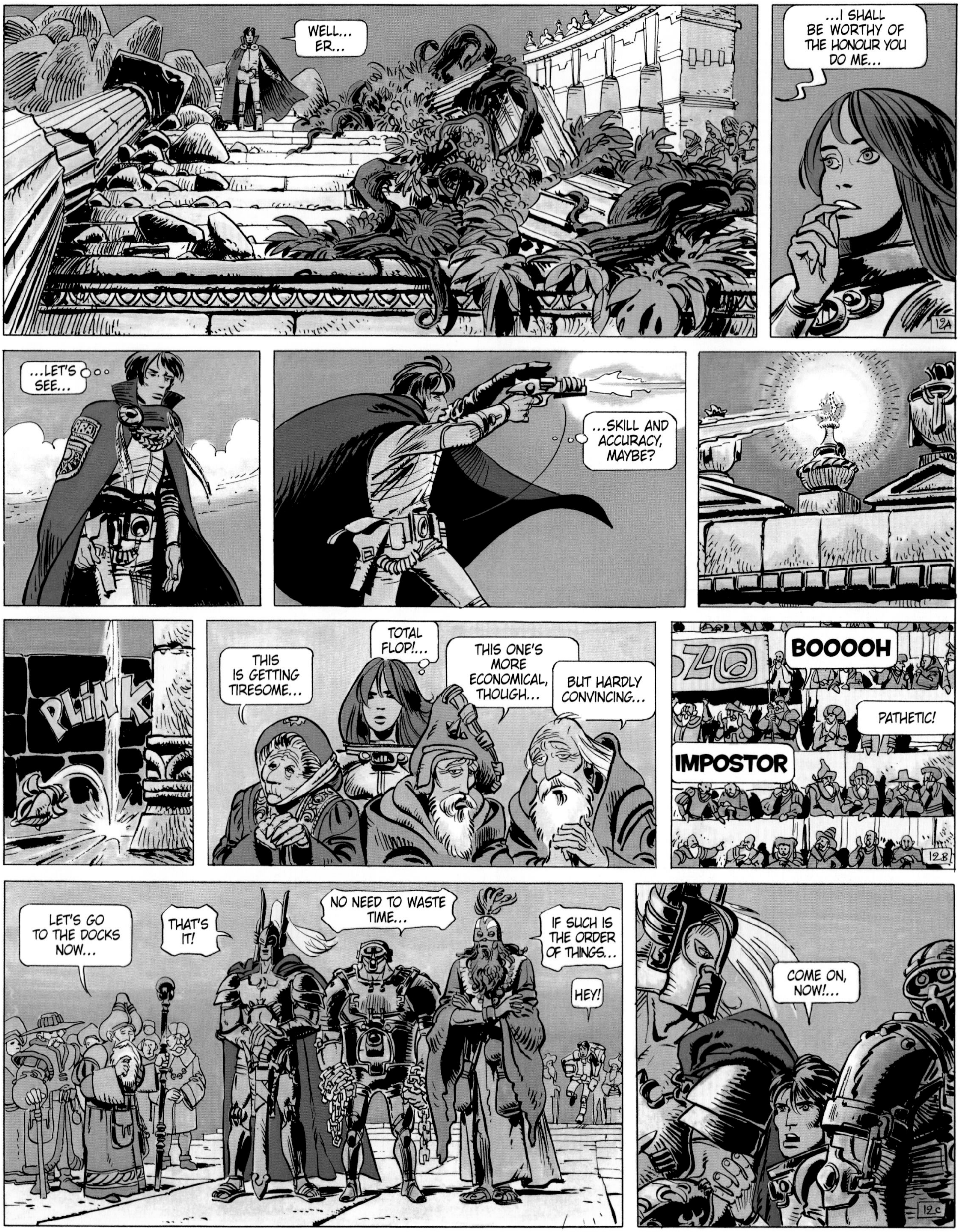
WELL... ER...
...I SHALL BE WORTHY OF THE HONOUR YOU DO ME...
12A
...LET'S SEE...
...SKILL AND ACCURACY, MAYBE?
PLINK
THIS IS GETTING TIRESOME...
TOTAL FLOP!...
THIS ONE'S MORE ECONOMICAL, THOUGH...
BUT HARDLY CONVINCING...
BOOOOH
PATHETIC!
IMPOSTOR
12B
LET'S GO TO THE DOCKS NOW...
THAT'S IT!
NO NEED TO WASTE TIME...
IF SUCH IS THE ORDER OF THINGS...
HEY!
COME ON, NOW!...
12C

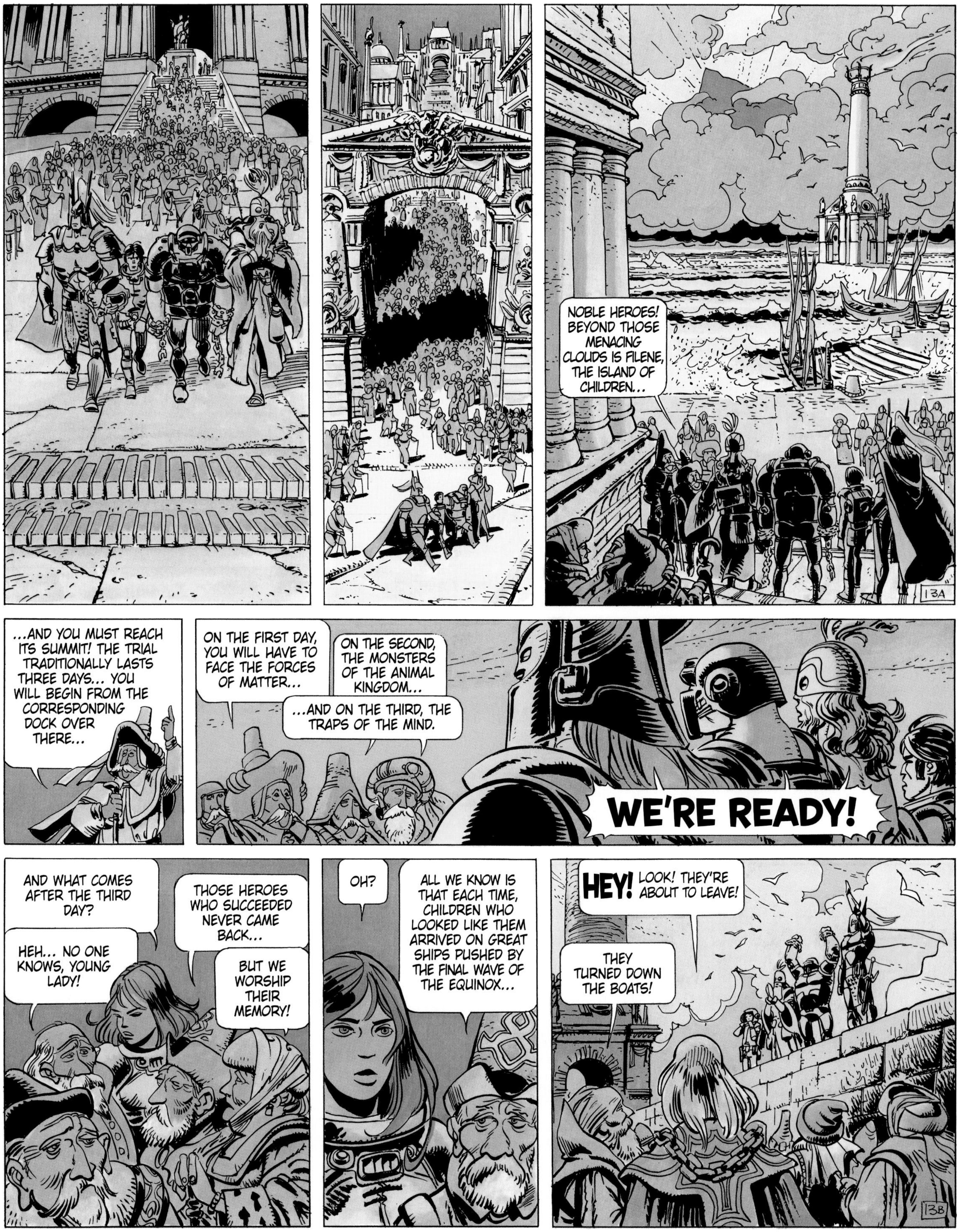
NOBLE HEROES! BEYOND THOSE MENACING CLOUDS IS FILENE, THE ISLAND OF CHILDREN...
13A
...AND YOU MUST REACH ITS SUMMIT! THE TRIAL TRADITIONALLY LASTS THREE DAYS... YOU WILL BEGIN FROM THE CORRESPONDING DOCK OVER THERE...
ON THE FIRST DAY, YOU WILL HAVE TO FACE THE FORCES OF MATTER...
ON THE SECOND, THE MONSTERS OF THE ANIMAL KINGDOM...
...AND ON THE THIRD, THE TRAPS OF THE MIND.
WE'RE READY!
AND WHAT COMES AFTER THE THIRD DAY?
HEH... NO ONE KNOWS, YOUNG LADY!
THOSE HEROES WHO SUCCEEDED NEVER CAME BACK...
BUT WE WORSHIP THEIR MEMORY!
OH?
ALL WE KNOW IS THAT EACH TIME, CHILDREN WHO LOOKED LIKE THEM ARRIVED ON GREAT SHIPS PUSHED BY THE FINAL WAVE OF THE EQUINOX...
HEY!
LOOK! THEY'RE ABOUT TO LEAVE!
THEY TURNED DOWN THE BOATS!
13B

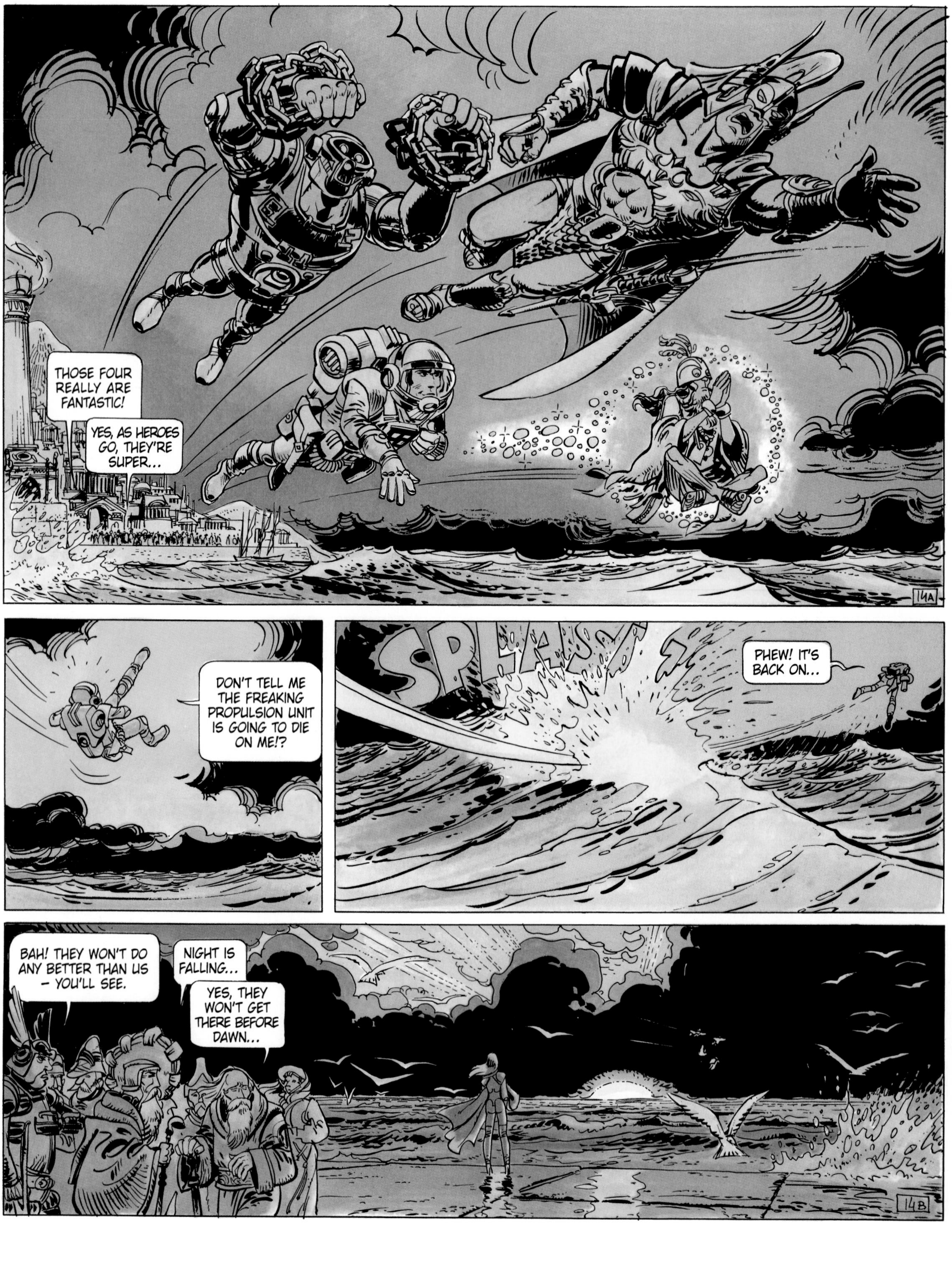

THOSE FOUR REALLY ARE FANTASTIC!
YES, AS HEROES GO, THEY'RE SUPER...
DON'T TELL ME THE FREAKING PROPULSION UNIT IS GOING TO DIE ON ME!?
PHEW! IT'S BACK ON...
BAH! THEY WON'T DO ANY BETTER THAN US – YOU'LL SEE.
NIGHT IS FALLING...
YES, THEY WON'T GET THERE BEFORE DAWN...

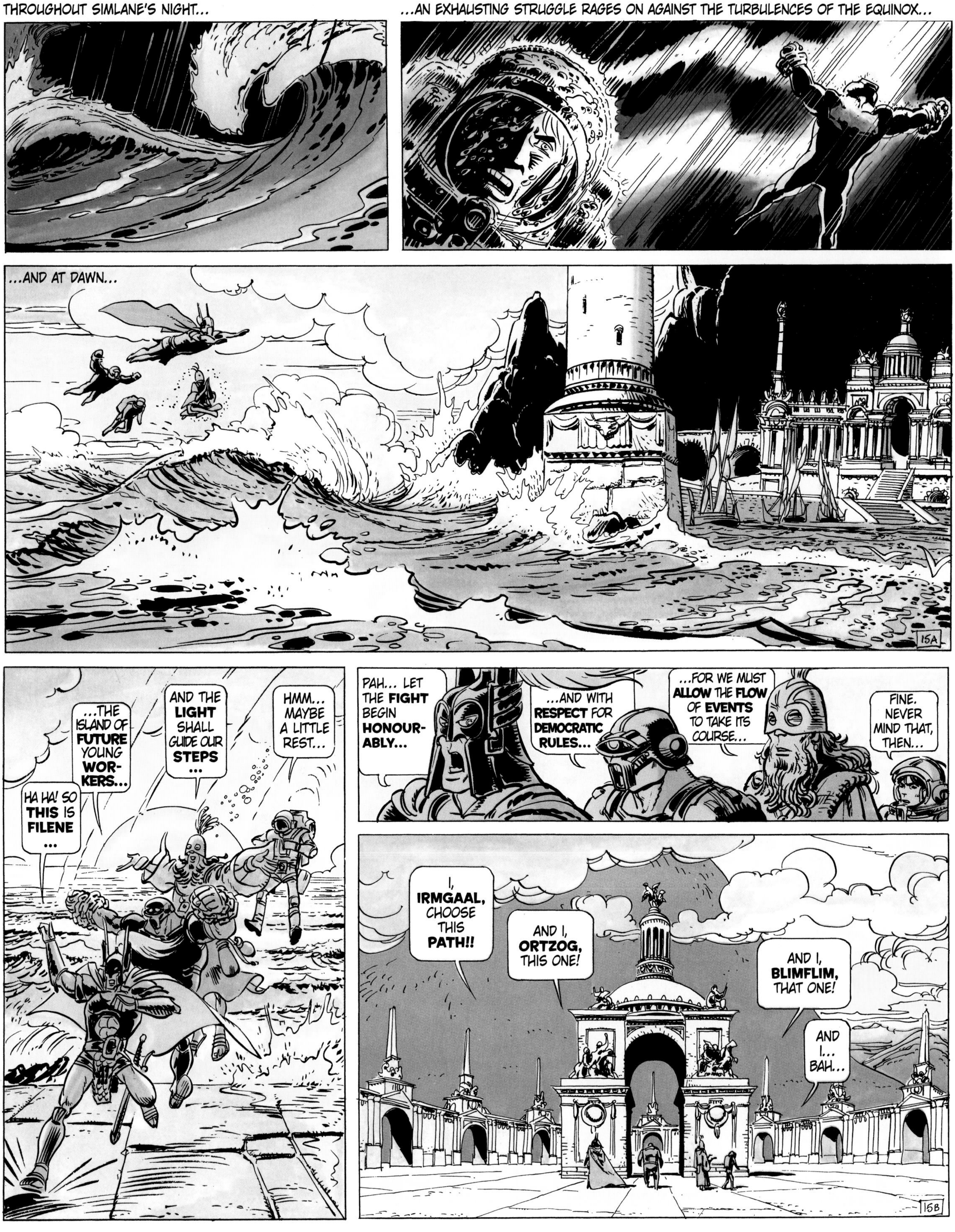

THROUGHOUT SIMLANE'S NIGHT...
...AN EXHAUSTING STRUGGLE RAGES ON AGAINST THE TURBULENCES OF THE EQUINOX...
...AND AT DAWN...
15A
...THE ISLAND OF FUTURE YOUNG WOR-KERS...
AND THE LIGHT SHALL GUIDE OUR STEPS ...
HMM... MAYBE A LITTLE REST...
HA HA! SO THIS IS FILENE ...
PAH... LET THE FIGHT BEGIN HONOUR-ABLY...
...AND WITH RESPECT FOR DEMOCRATIC RULES...
...FOR WE MUST ALLOW THE FLOW OF EVENTS TO TAKE ITS COURSE...
FINE. NEVER MIND THAT, THEN...
I, IRMGAAL, CHOOSE THIS PATH!!
AND I, ORTZOG, THIS ONE!
AND I, BLIMFLIM, THAT ONE!
AND I... BAH...
15B

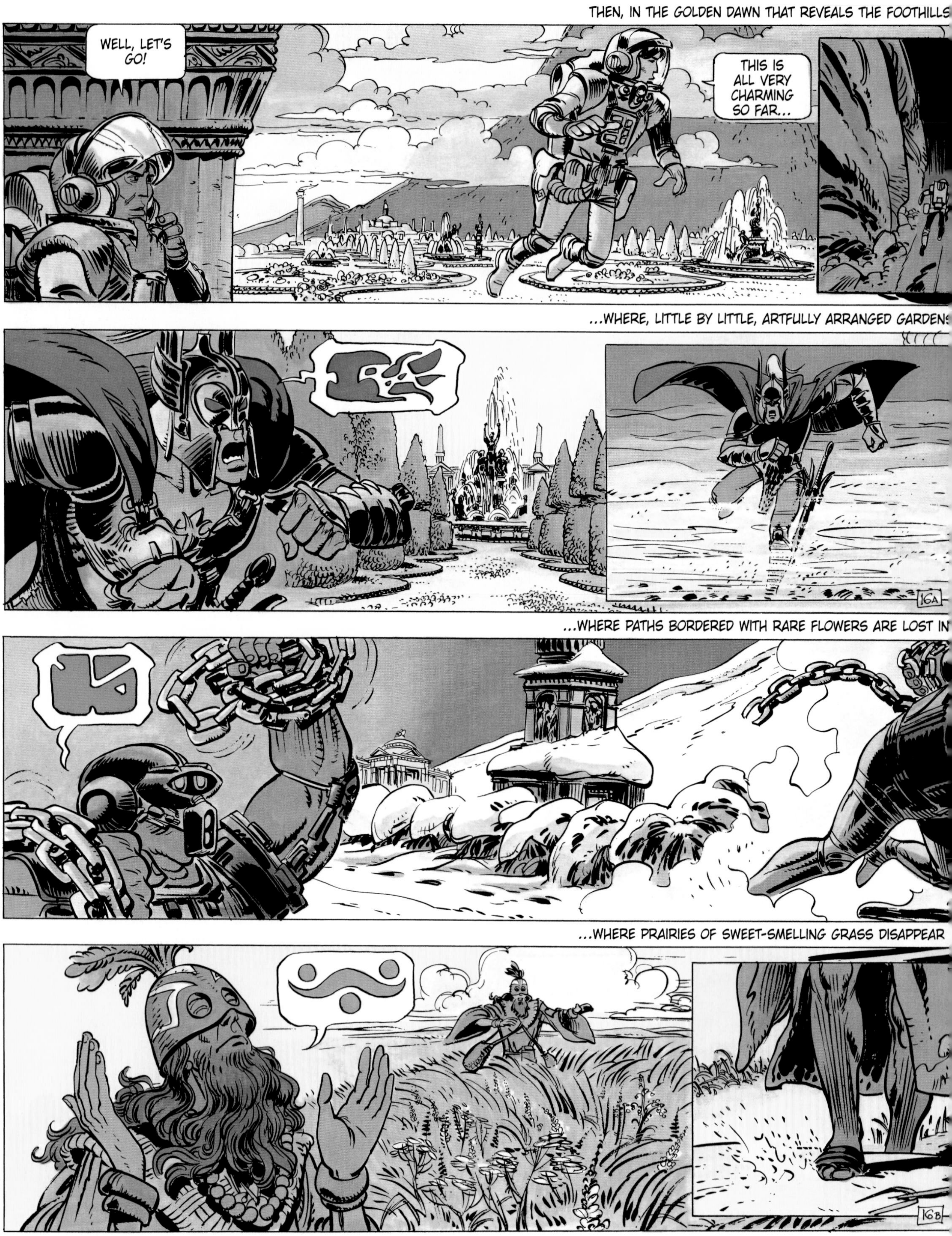
THEN, IN THE GOLDEN DAWN THAT REVEALS THE FOOTHILLS
WELL, LET'S GO!
THIS IS ALL VERY CHARMING SO FAR...
...WHERE, LITTLE BY LITTLE, ARTFULLY ARRANGED GARDENS
16A
...WHERE PATHS BORDERED WITH RARE FLOWERS ARE LOST IN
...WHERE PRAIRIES OF SWEET-SMELLING GRASS DISAPPEAR
16B

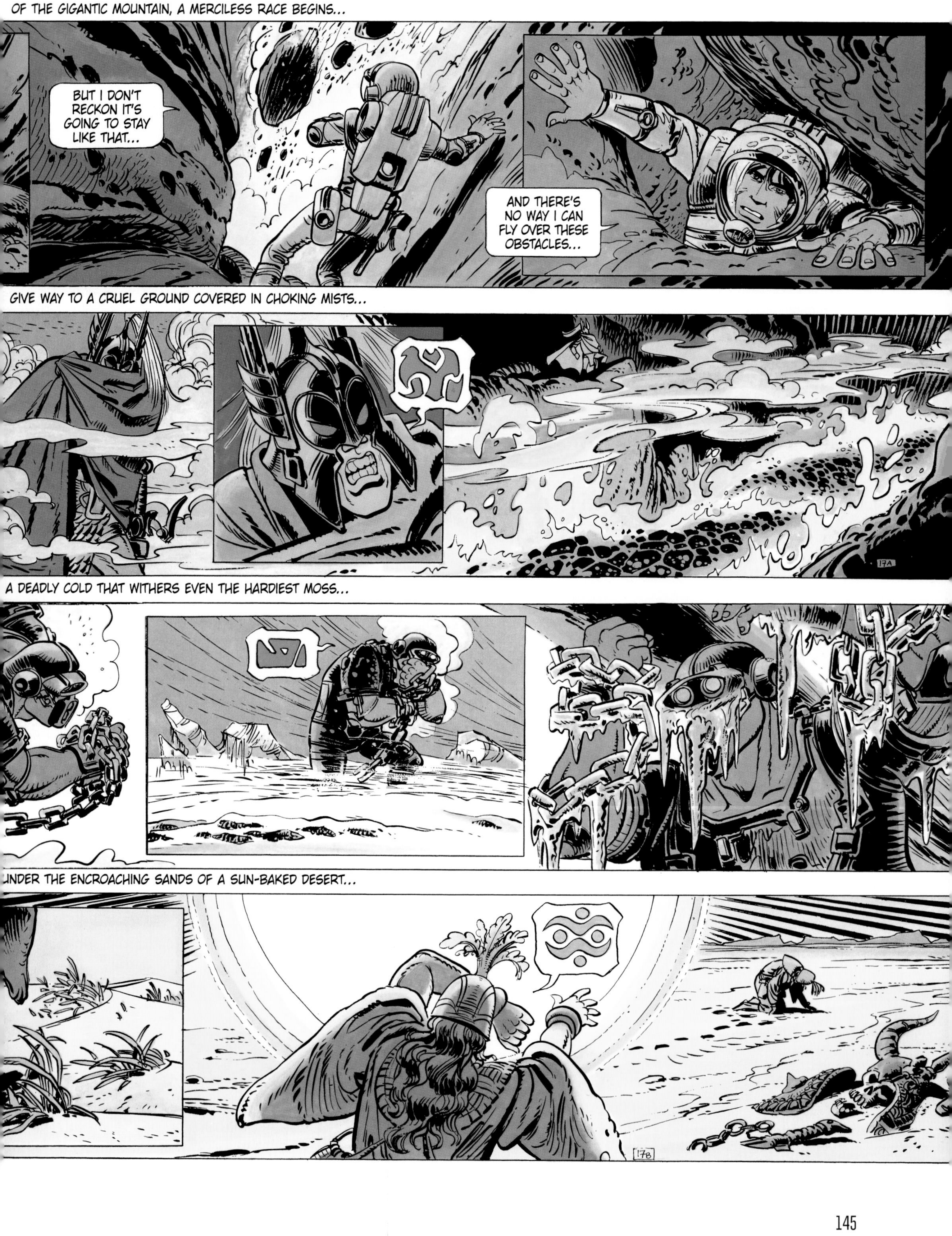
OF THE GIGANTIC MOUNTAIN, A MERCILESS RACE BEGINS...
BUT I DON'T RECKON IT'S GOING TO STAY LIKE THAT...
AND THERE'S NO WAY I CAN FLY OVER THESE OBSTACLES...
GIVE WAY TO A CRUEL GROUND COVERED IN CHOKING MISTS...
A DEADLY COLD THAT WITHERS EVEN THE HARDIEST MOSS...
UNDER THE ENCROACHING SANDS OF A SUN-BAKED DESERT...

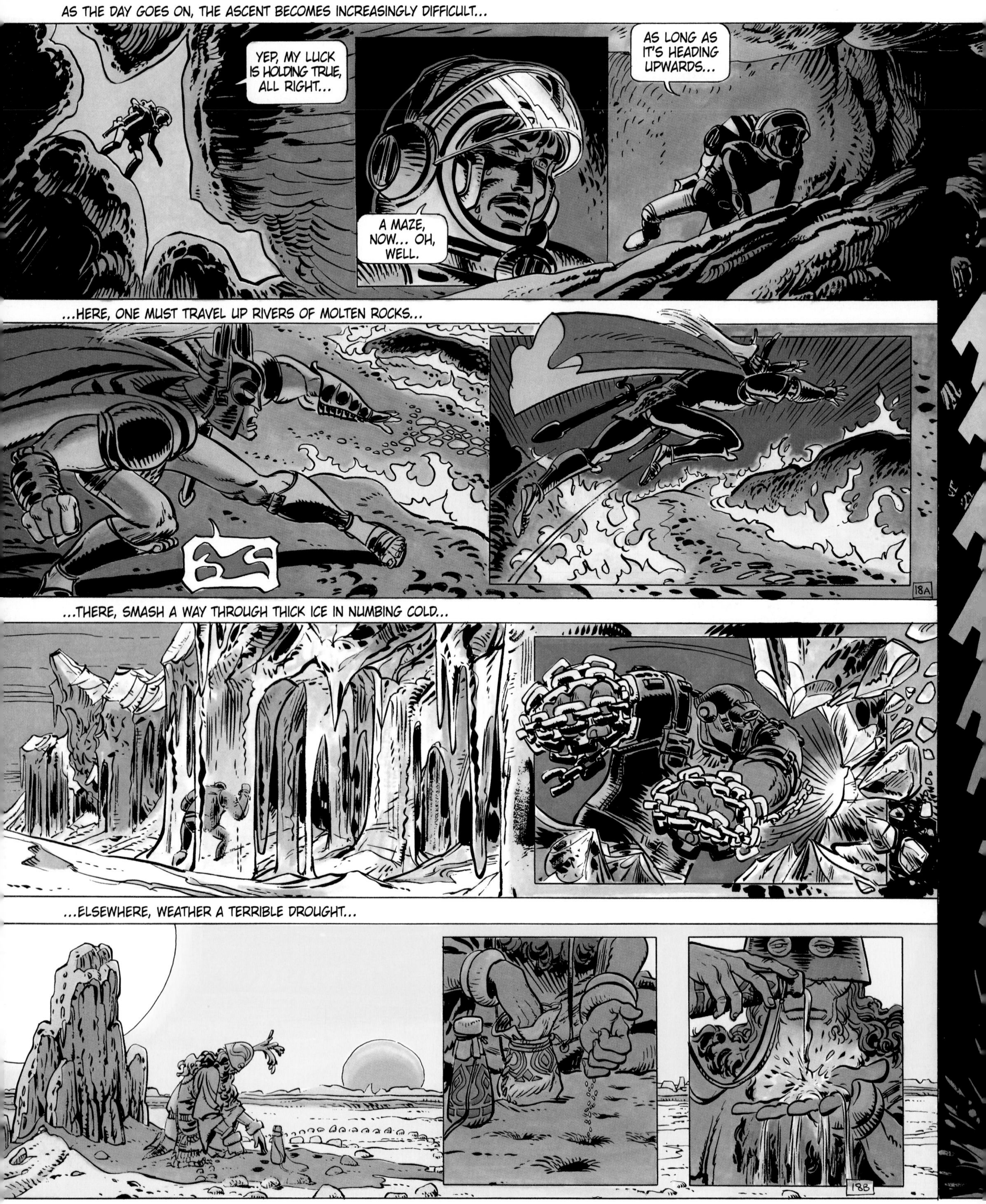
AS THE DAY GOES ON, THE ASCENT BECOMES INCREASINGLY DIFFICULT...
YEP, MY LUCK IS HOLDING TRUE, ALL RIGHT...
A MAZE, NOW... OH, WELL.
AS LONG AS IT'S HEADING UPWARDS...
...HERE, ONE MUST TRAVEL UP RIVERS OF MOLTEN ROCKS...
18A
...THERE, SMASH A WAY THROUGH THICK ICE IN NUMBING COLD...
...ELSEWHERE, WEATHER A TERRIBLE DROUGHT...
18B

AND AS THE SACRED — SWORD ZARKAM CARVES PERILOUS PATHS...

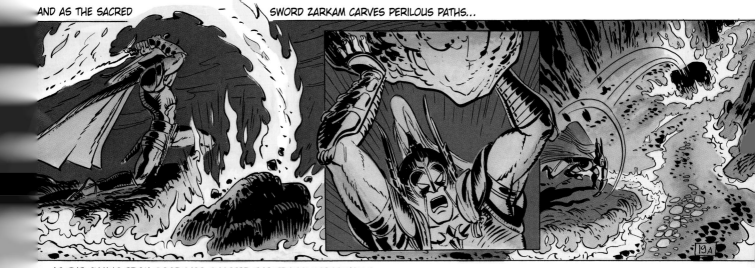

...AS THE CHAINS FROM BOORNYOF SHATTER THE TRANSLUCENT WALLS...

...AS THE SEEDS BROUGHT FROM MALAMUM CREATE FLEETING OASES...

...AND AS DARKNESS RULES OVER THE DEPTHS OF THE MOUNTAIN...

HAM

WHAT?!... WHERE AM I?...

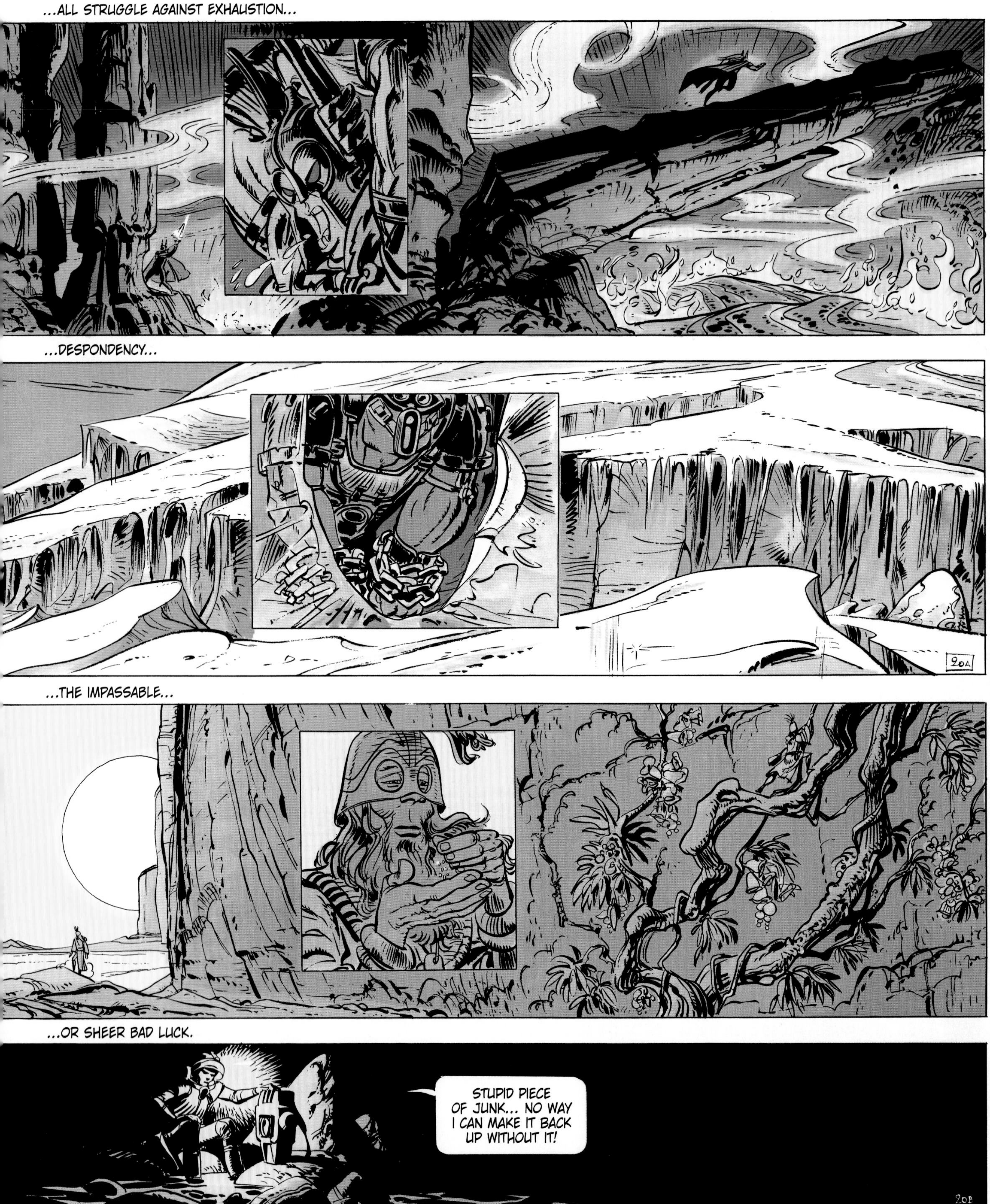
...ALL STRUGGLE AGAINST EXHAUSTION...
...DESPONDENCY...
...THE IMPASSABLE...
...OR SHEER BAD LUCK.
STUPID PIECE OF JUNK... NO WAY I CAN MAKE IT BACK UP WITHOUT IT!

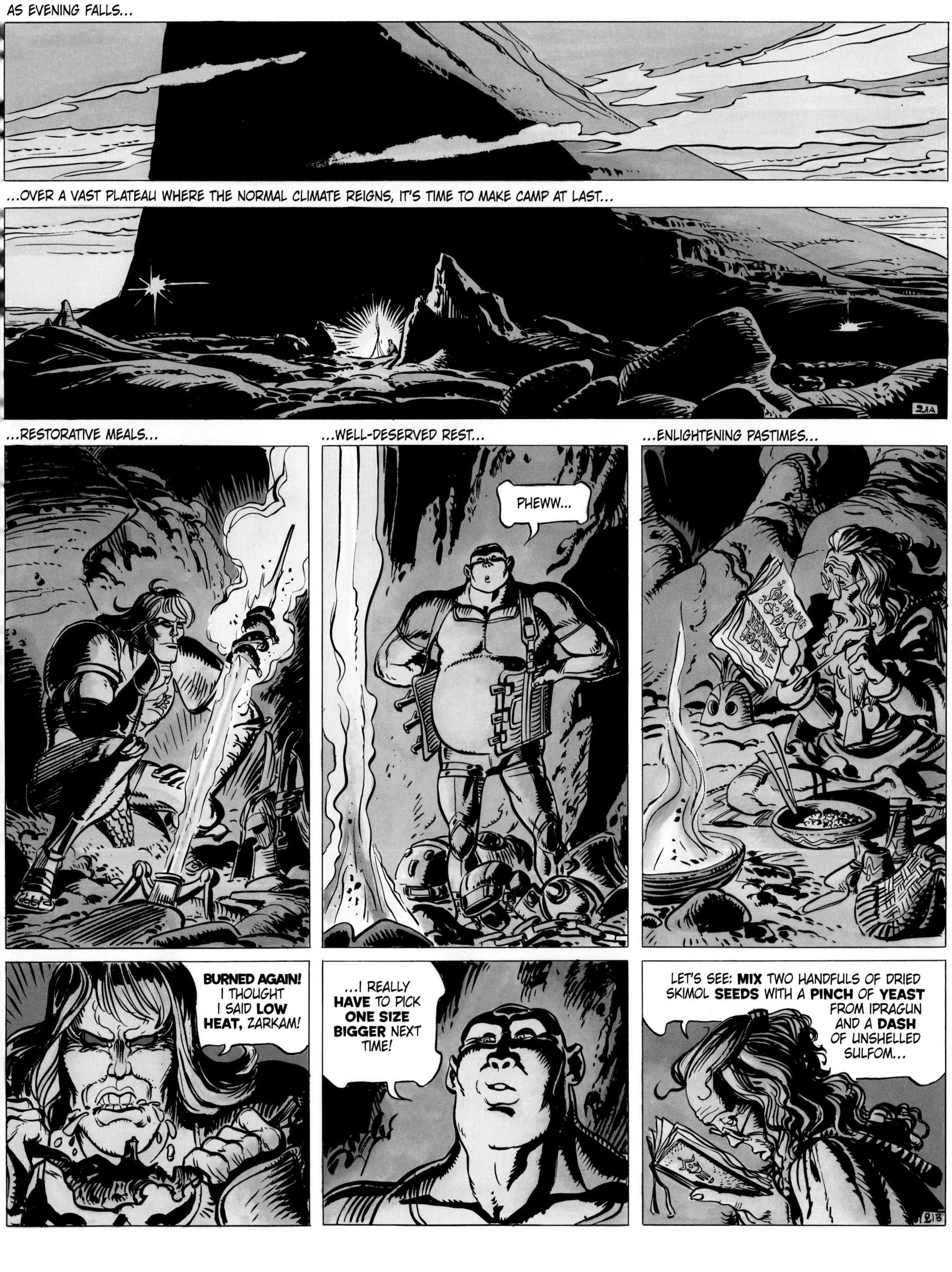
AS EVENING FALLS...
...OVER A VAST PLATEAU WHERE THE NORMAL CLIMATE REIGNS, IT'S TIME TO MAKE CAMP AT LAST...
...RESTORATIVE MEALS...
...WELL-DESERVED REST...
PHEWW...
...ENLIGHTENING PASTIMES...
BURNED AGAIN! I THOUGHT I SAID LOW HEAT, ZARKAM!
...I REALLY HAVE TO PICK ONE SIZE BIGGER NEXT TIME!
LET'S SEE: MIX TWO HANDFULS OF DRIED SKIMOL SEEDS WITH A PINCH OF YEAST FROM IPRAGUN AND A DASH OF UNSHELLED SULFOM...

...AND IN OTHER PLACES, SHORT BREAKS...

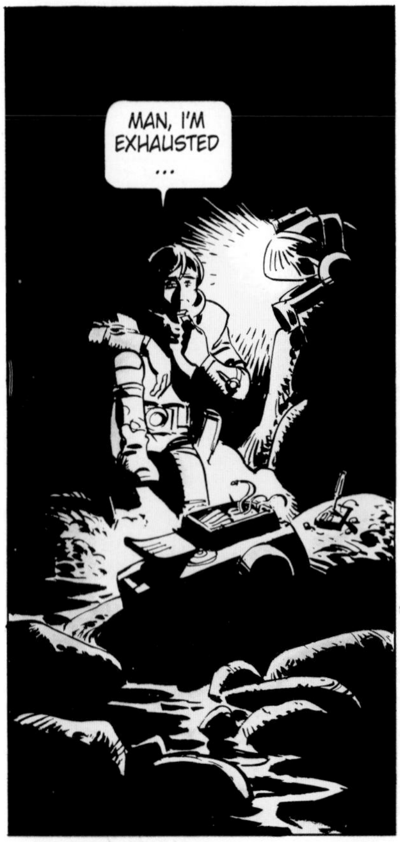
MAN, I'M EXHAUSTED ...

...AND TENSE CONCERN...

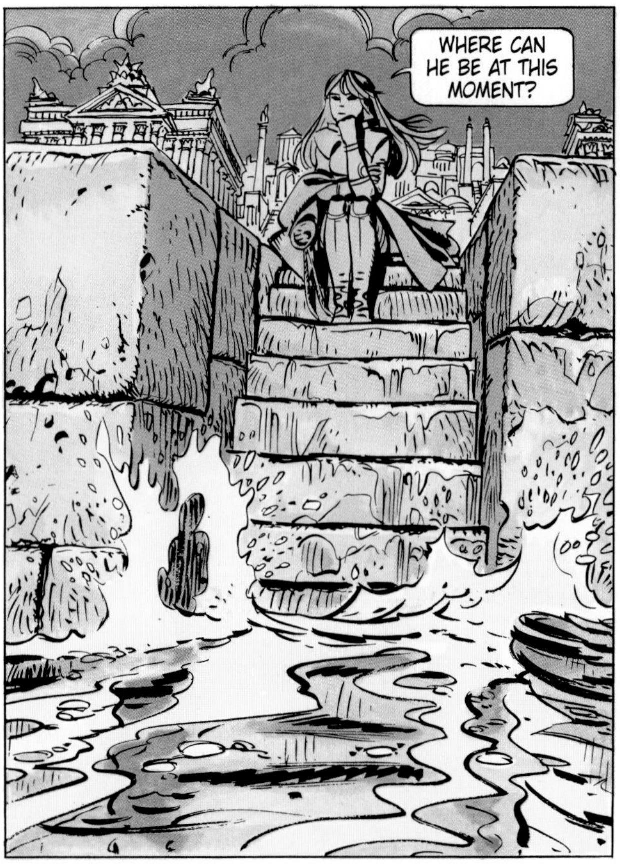
WHERE CAN HE BE AT THIS MOMENT?

...ALL LEAD TO A NIGHT FILLED WITH SUDDEN, VIOLENT STORMS.

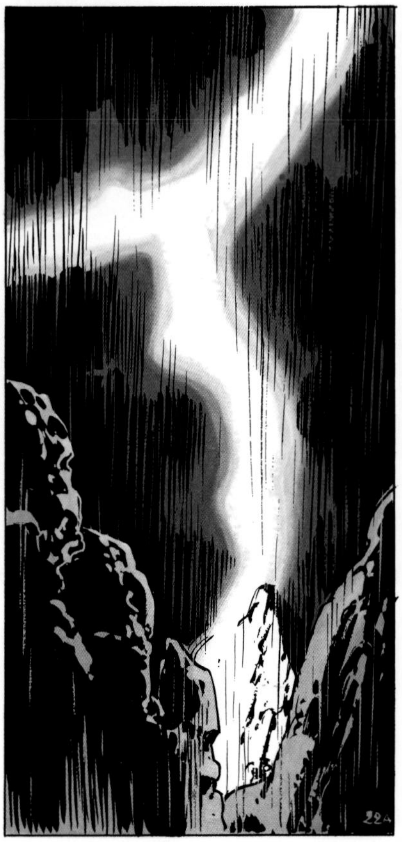

THE NEXT MORNING, AS THE SUNS RISE FOR THE SECOND DAY ON FILENE...

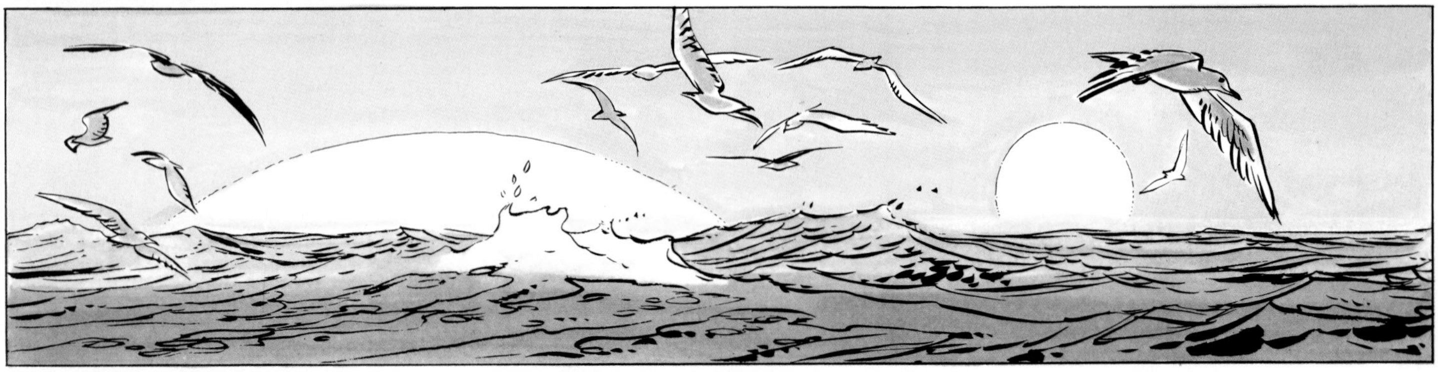

..THE TERRIBLE ASCENT BEGINS...

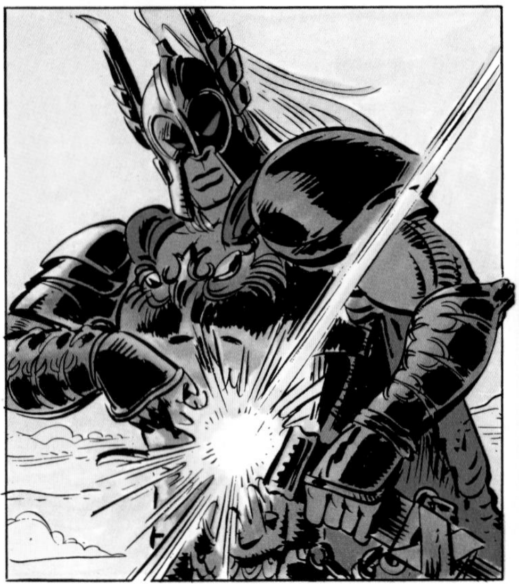

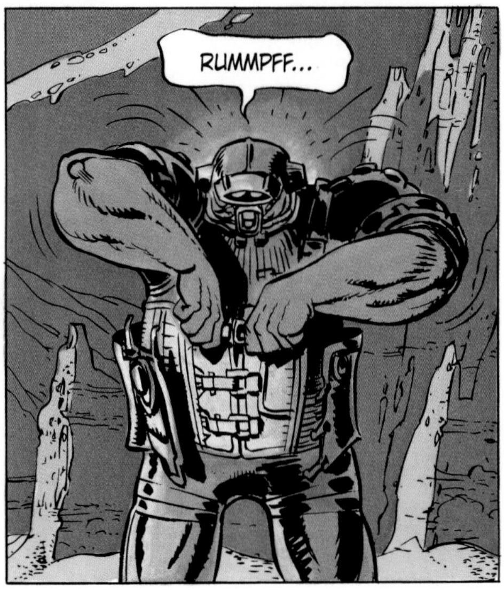
RUMMPFF...

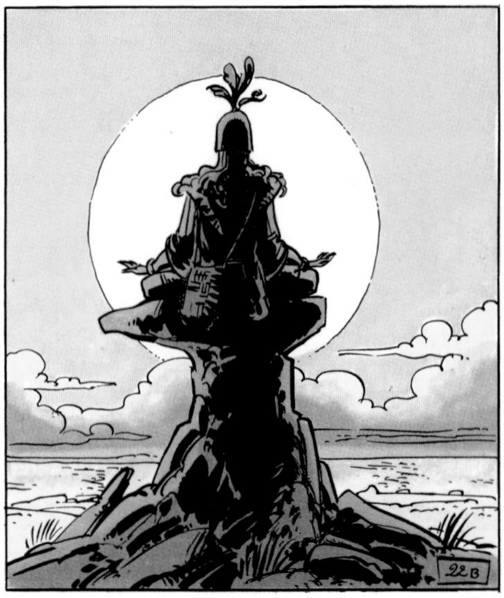

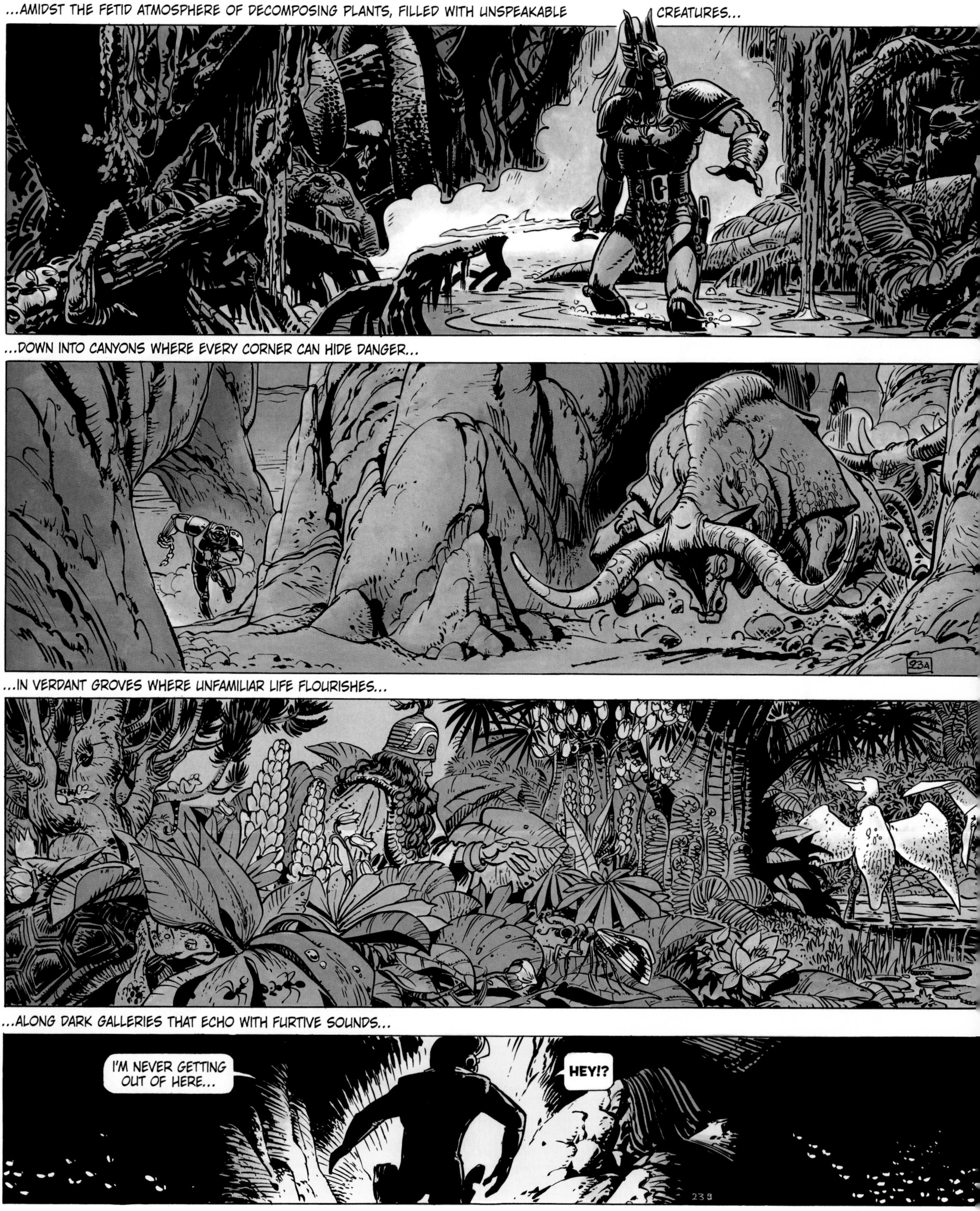
...AMIDST THE FETID ATMOSPHERE OF DECOMPOSING PLANTS, FILLED WITH UNSPEAKABLE
CREATURES...
...DOWN INTO CANYONS WHERE EVERY CORNER CAN HIDE DANGER...
...IN VERDANT GROVES WHERE UNFAMILIAR LIFE FLOURISHES...
...ALONG DARK GALLERIES THAT ECHO WITH FURTIVE SOUNDS...
I'M NEVER GETTING OUT OF HERE...
HEY!?

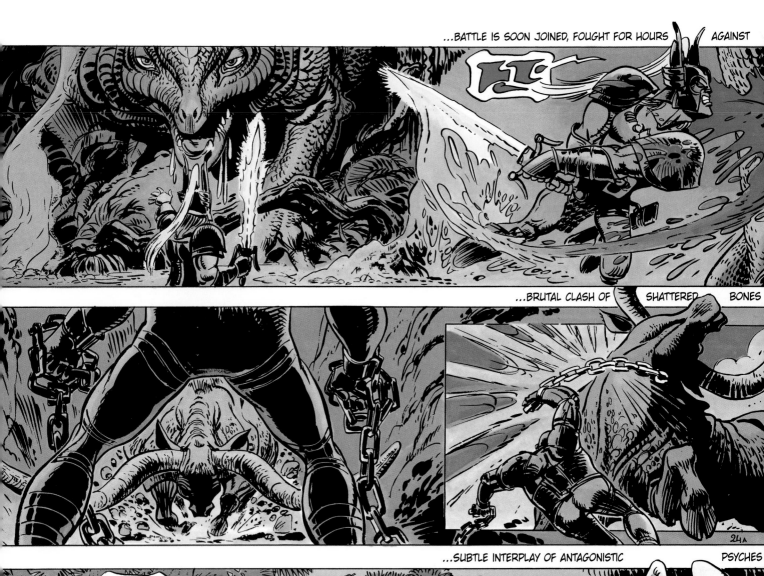

...BATTLE IS SOON JOINED, FOUGHT FOR HOURS
AGAINST
...BRUTAL CLASH OF
SHATTERED
BONES
24A
...SUBTLE INTERPLAY OF ANTAGONISTIC
PSYCHES
I AM THE ONE WHO CAN SPEAK TO BEASTS...
GA
I ASK THAT YOU BE MY TEMPORARY ALLY...
GLOOP?
...COMPLEX DIALECTIC OF TACTICAL
RATS!!
24B

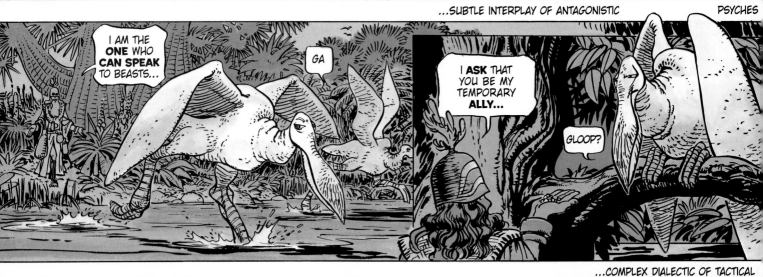

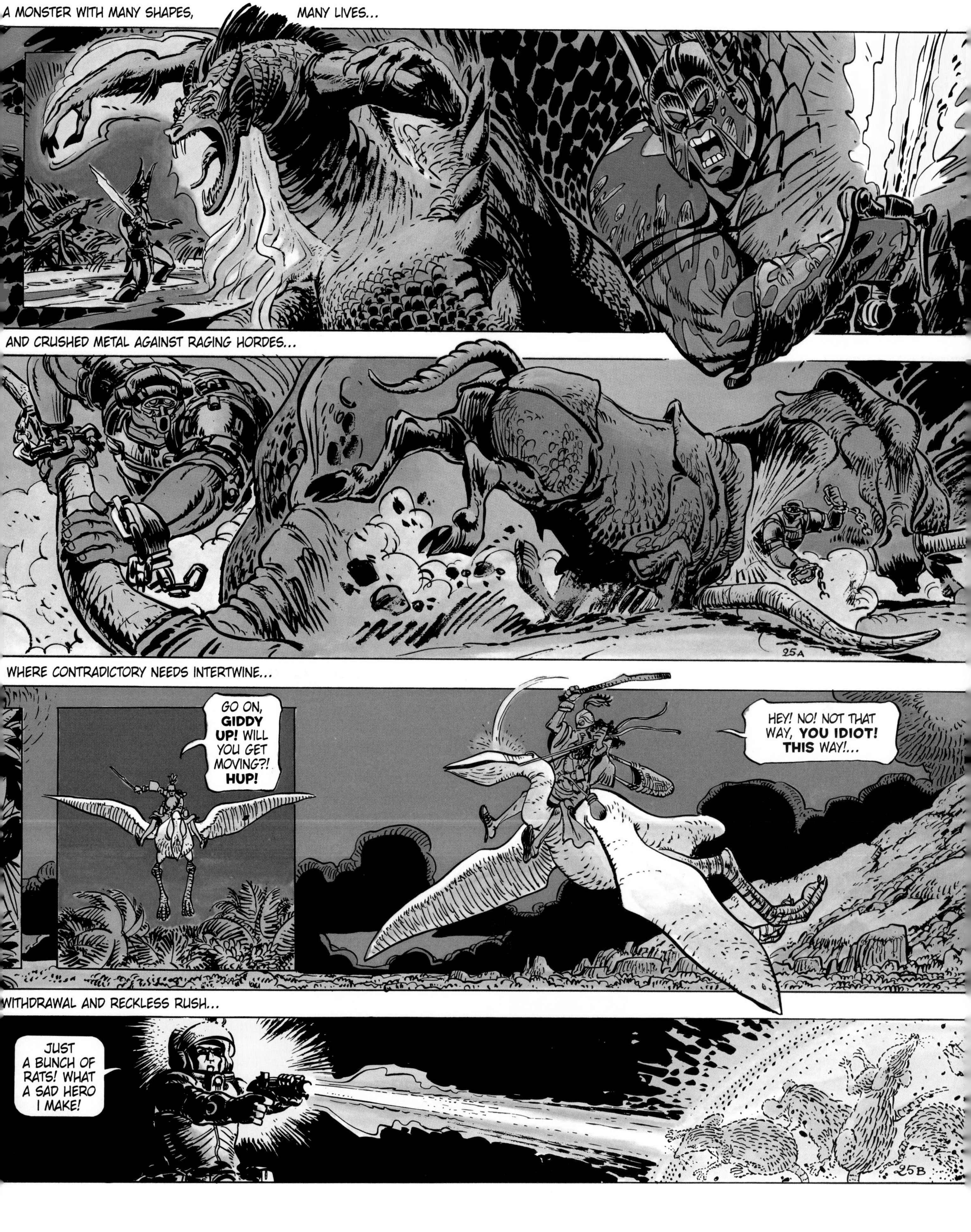
A MONSTER WITH MANY SHAPES,
MANY LIVES...
AND CRUSHED METAL AGAINST RAGING HORDES...
25A
WHERE CONTRADICTORY NEEDS INTERTWINE...
GO ON, **GIDDY UP!** WILL YOU GET MOVING?! **HUP!**
HEY! NO! NOT THAT WAY, **YOU IDIOT! THIS** WAY!...
WITHDRAWAL AND RECKLESS RUSH...
JUST A BUNCH OF RATS! WHAT A SAD HERO I MAKE!
25B

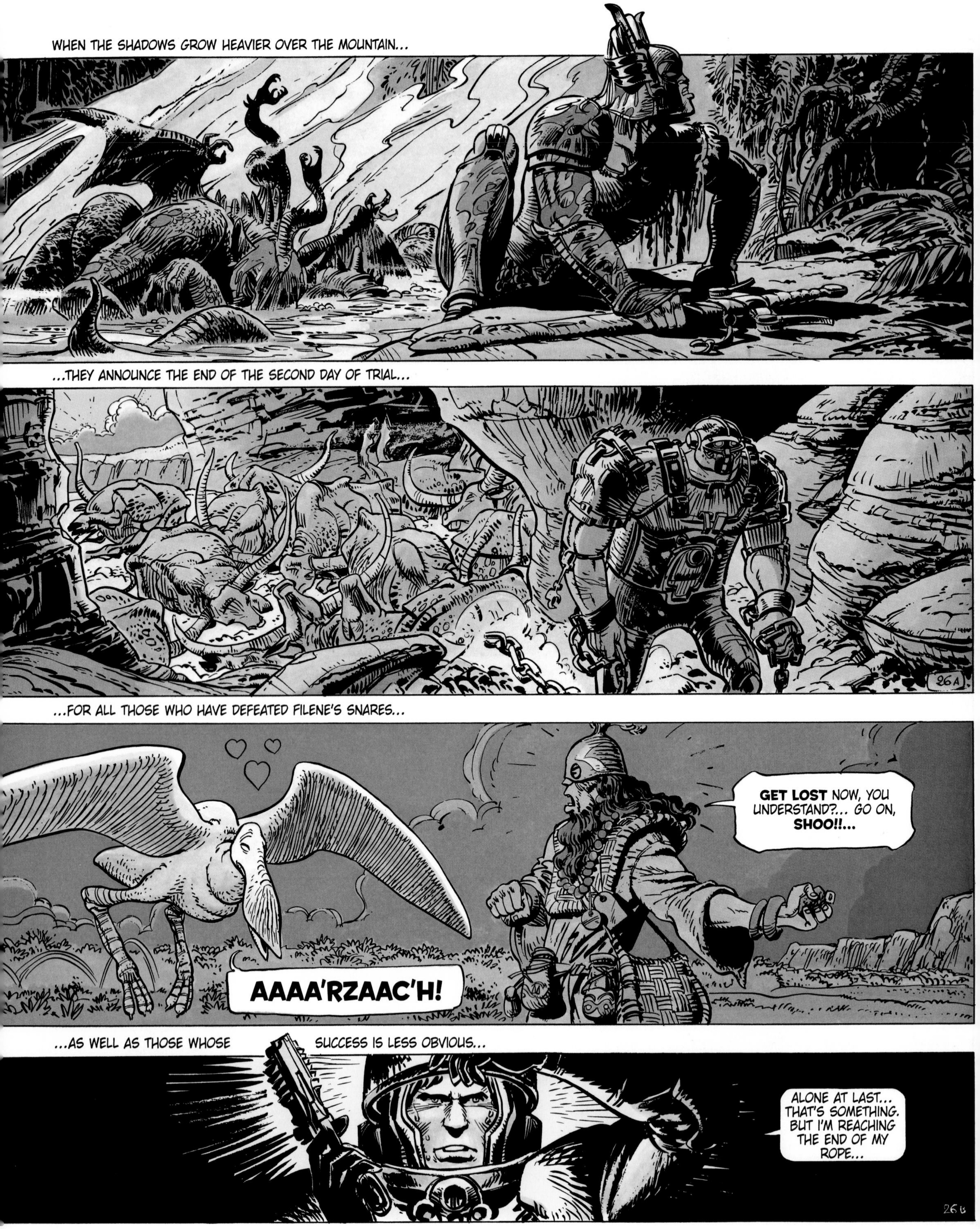
WHEN THE SHADOWS GROW HEAVIER OVER THE MOUNTAIN...
...THEY ANNOUNCE THE END OF THE SECOND DAY OF TRIAL...
...FOR ALL THOSE WHO HAVE DEFEATED FILENE'S SNARES...
GET LOST NOW, YOU UNDERSTAND?... GO ON, SHOO!!...
AAAA'RZAAC'H!
...AS WELL AS THOSE WHOSE
SUCCESS IS LESS OBVIOUS...
ALONE AT LAST... THAT'S SOMETHING. BUT I'M REACHING THE END OF MY ROPE...

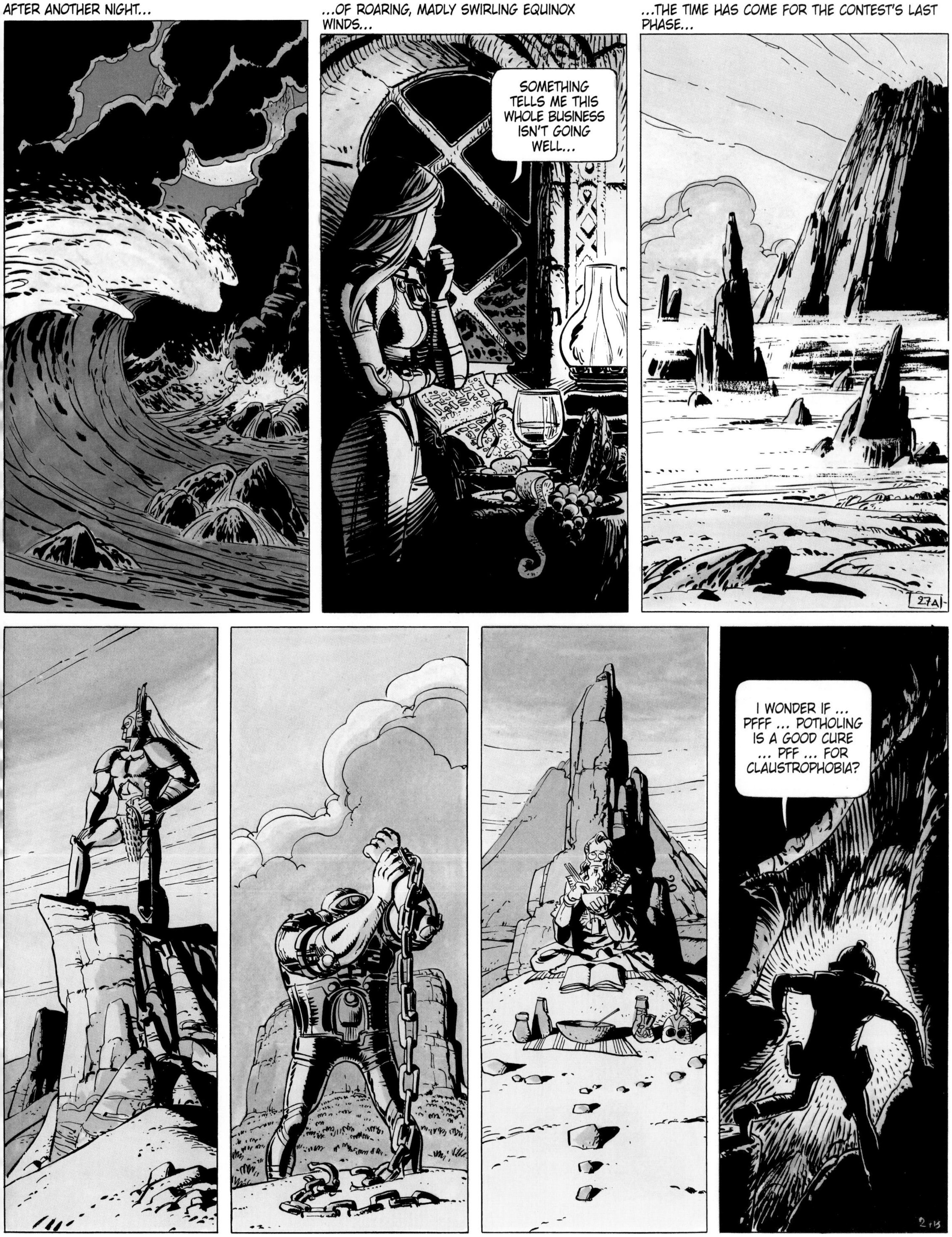
AFTER ANOTHER NIGHT...
...OF ROARING, MADLY SWIRLING EQUINOX WINDS...
SOMETHING TELLS ME THIS WHOLE BUSINESS ISN'T GOING WELL...
...THE TIME HAS COME FOR THE CONTEST'S LAST PHASE...
I WONDER IF ... PFFF ... POTHOLING IS A GOOD CURE ... PFF ... FOR CLAUSTROPHOBIA?

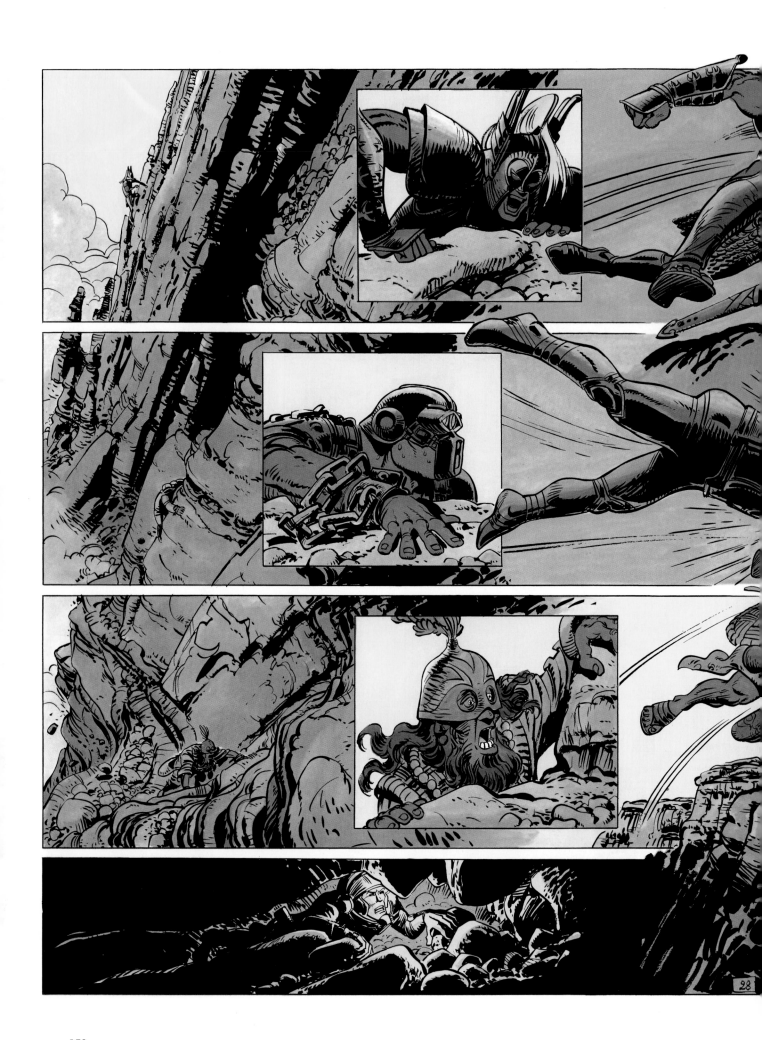

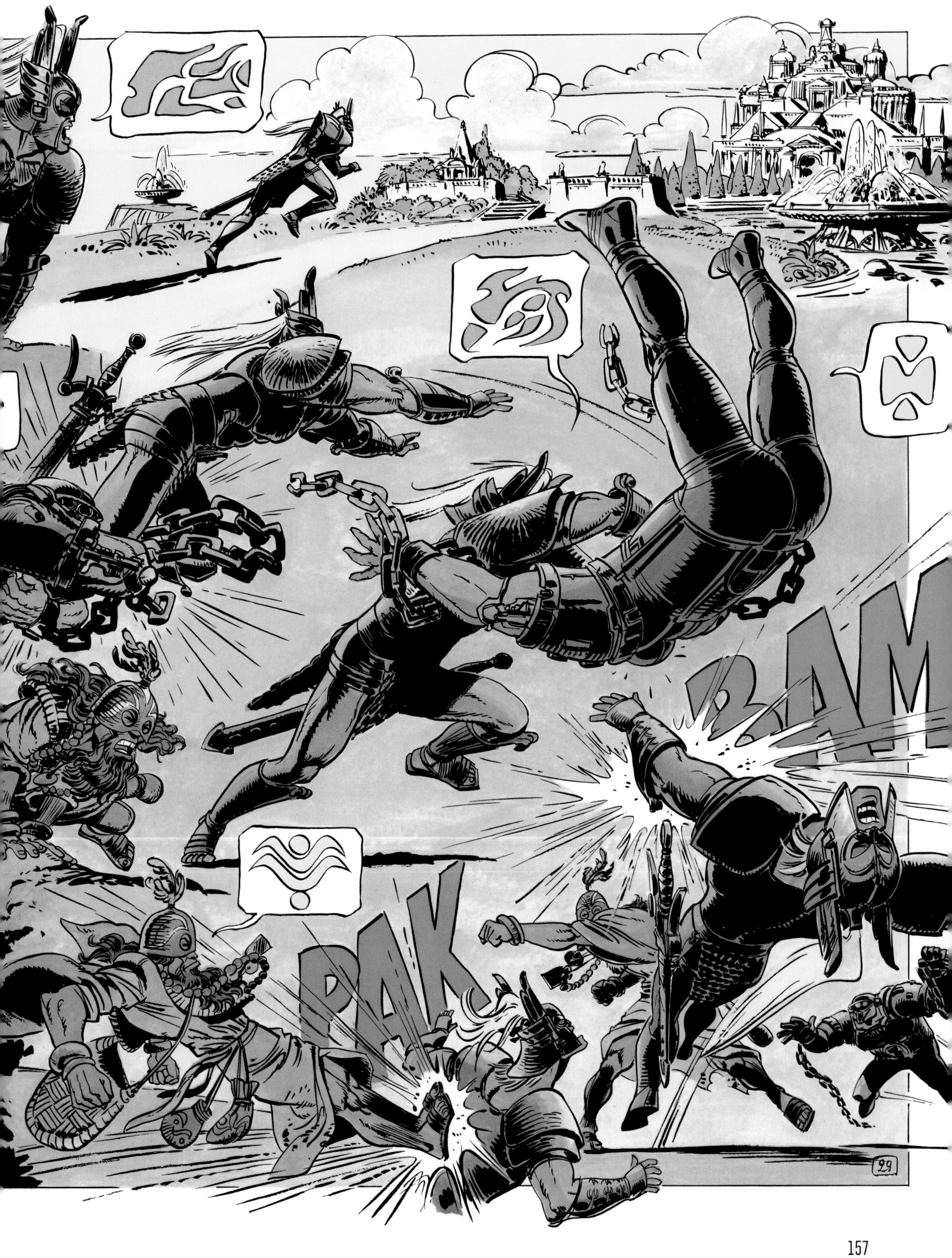
BAM
PAK

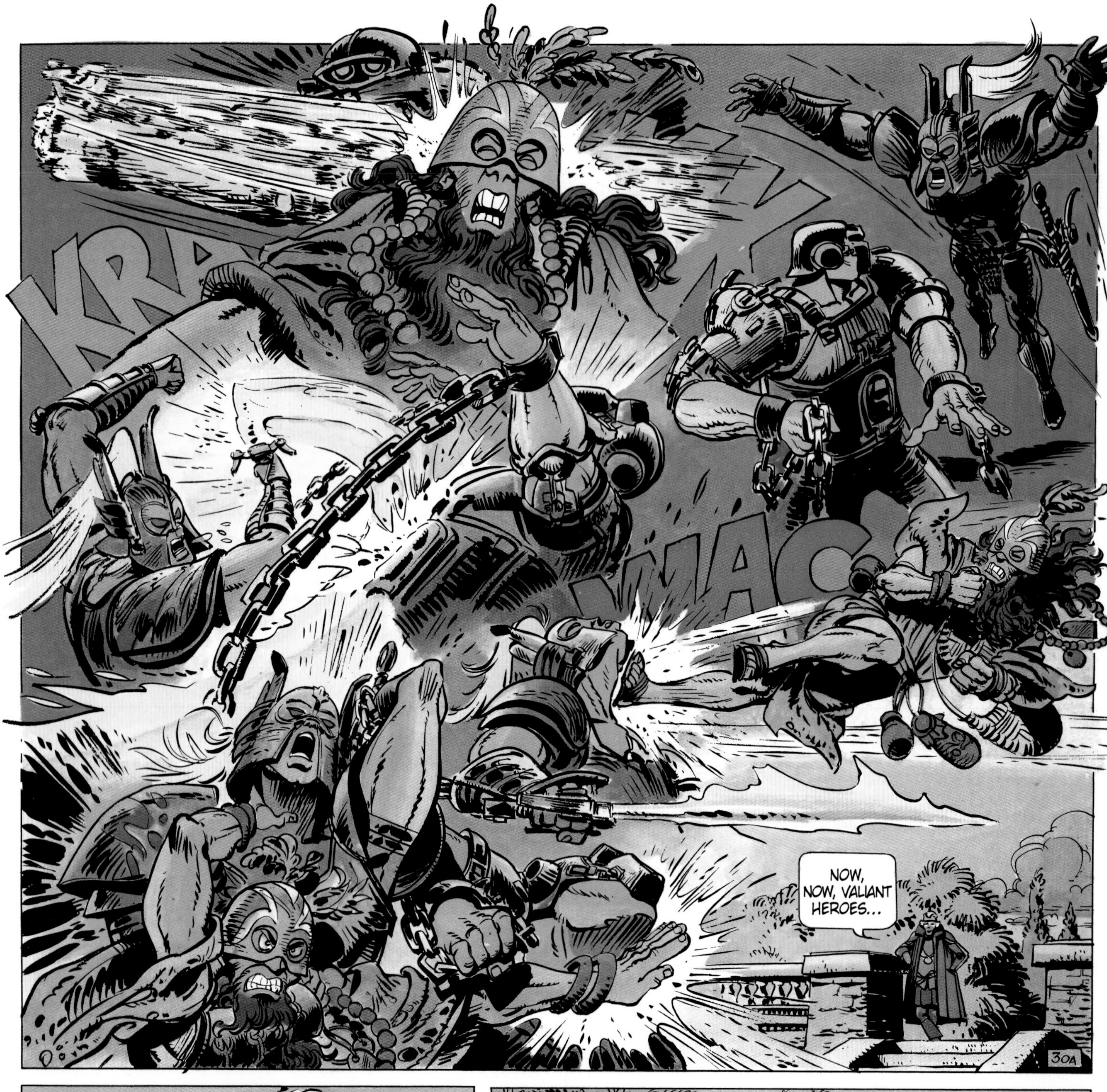
KRA
WHAC
NOW, NOW, VALIANT HEROES...
30A

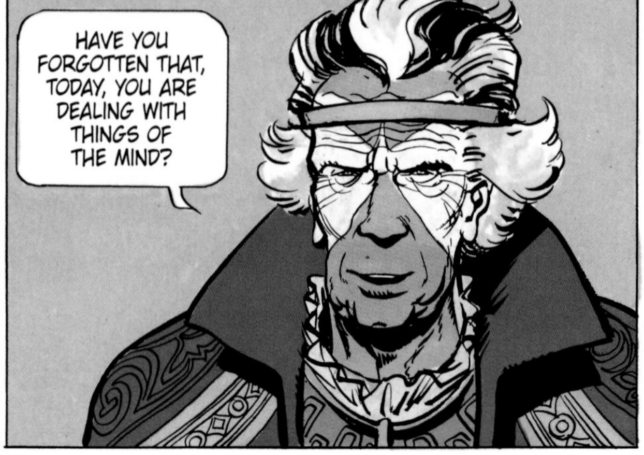
HAVE YOU FORGOTTEN THAT, TODAY, YOU ARE DEALING WITH THINGS OF THE MIND?

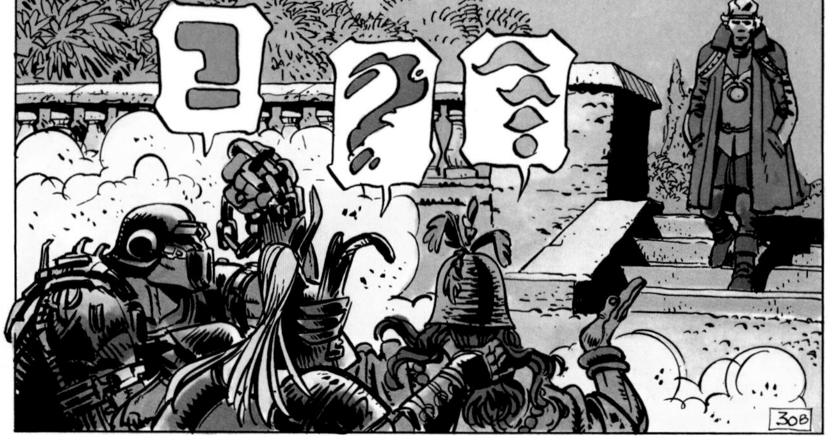
?
30B

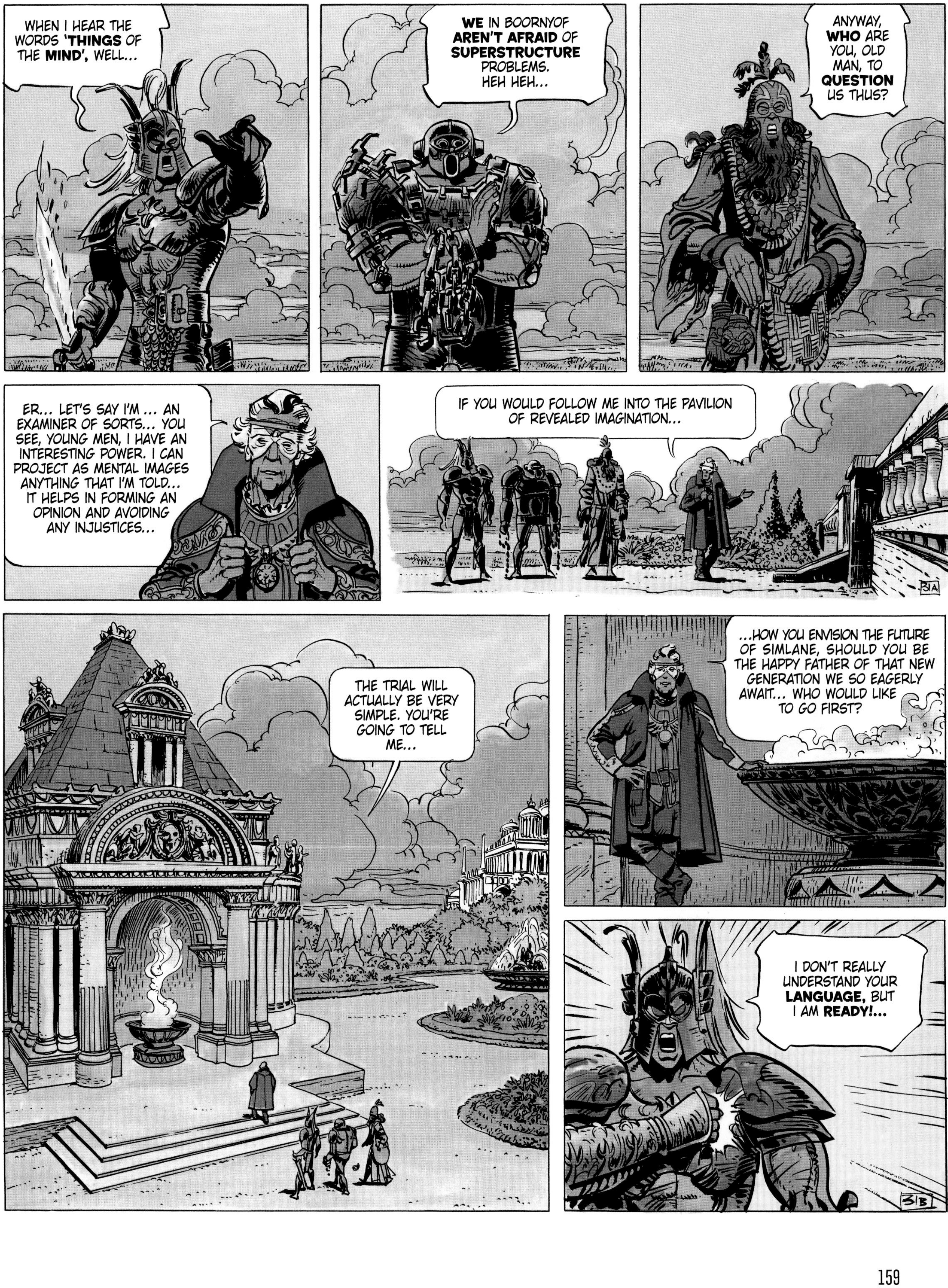
WHEN I HEAR THE WORDS 'THINGS OF THE MIND', WELL...
WE IN BOORNYOF AREN'T AFRAID OF SUPERSTRUCTURE PROBLEMS. HEH HEH...
ANYWAY, WHO ARE YOU, OLD MAN, TO QUESTION US THUS?
ER... LET'S SAY I'M ... AN EXAMINER OF SORTS... YOU SEE, YOUNG MEN, I HAVE AN INTERESTING POWER. I CAN PROJECT AS MENTAL IMAGES ANYTHING THAT I'M TOLD... IT HELPS IN FORMING AN OPINION AND AVOIDING ANY INJUSTICES...
IF YOU WOULD FOLLOW ME INTO THE PAVILION OF REVEALED IMAGINATION...
31A
THE TRIAL WILL ACTUALLY BE VERY SIMPLE. YOU'RE GOING TO TELL ME...
...HOW YOU ENVISION THE FUTURE OF SIMLANE, SHOULD YOU BE THE HAPPY FATHER OF THAT NEW GENERATION WE SO EAGERLY AWAIT... WHO WOULD LIKE TO GO FIRST?
I DON'T REALLY UNDERSTAND YOUR LANGUAGE, BUT I AM READY!...
31B

IF I WIN, THE **FLESH** OF MY **FLESH** WILL TURN THIS DECAYING, DECADENT PLANET...

...AND ITS ANCESTRAL **VALUES**, INTO A SHINING **BEACON** FOR THE UNIVERSE.

A **NEW RACE** WILL RISE, WHICH SHALL FIRST RAISE SIMLANE FROM ITS RUINS BEFORE **INSTILLING** IN ITS PEOPLE THE TASTE FOR **SPACE TRAVEL**...

...SO THAT THEY CAN CARRY THE **EXAMPLE** OF THE GREAT CIVILISATION THEY BUILT **WHEREVER** IT IS NEEDED...

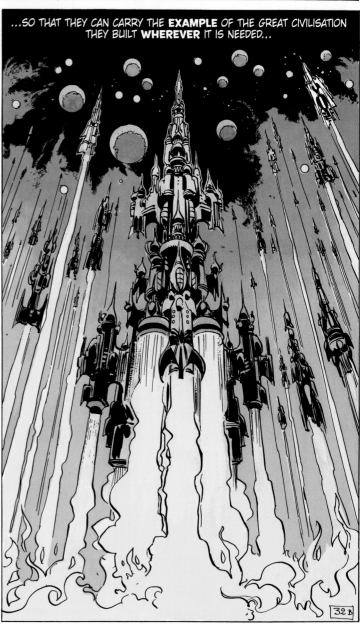

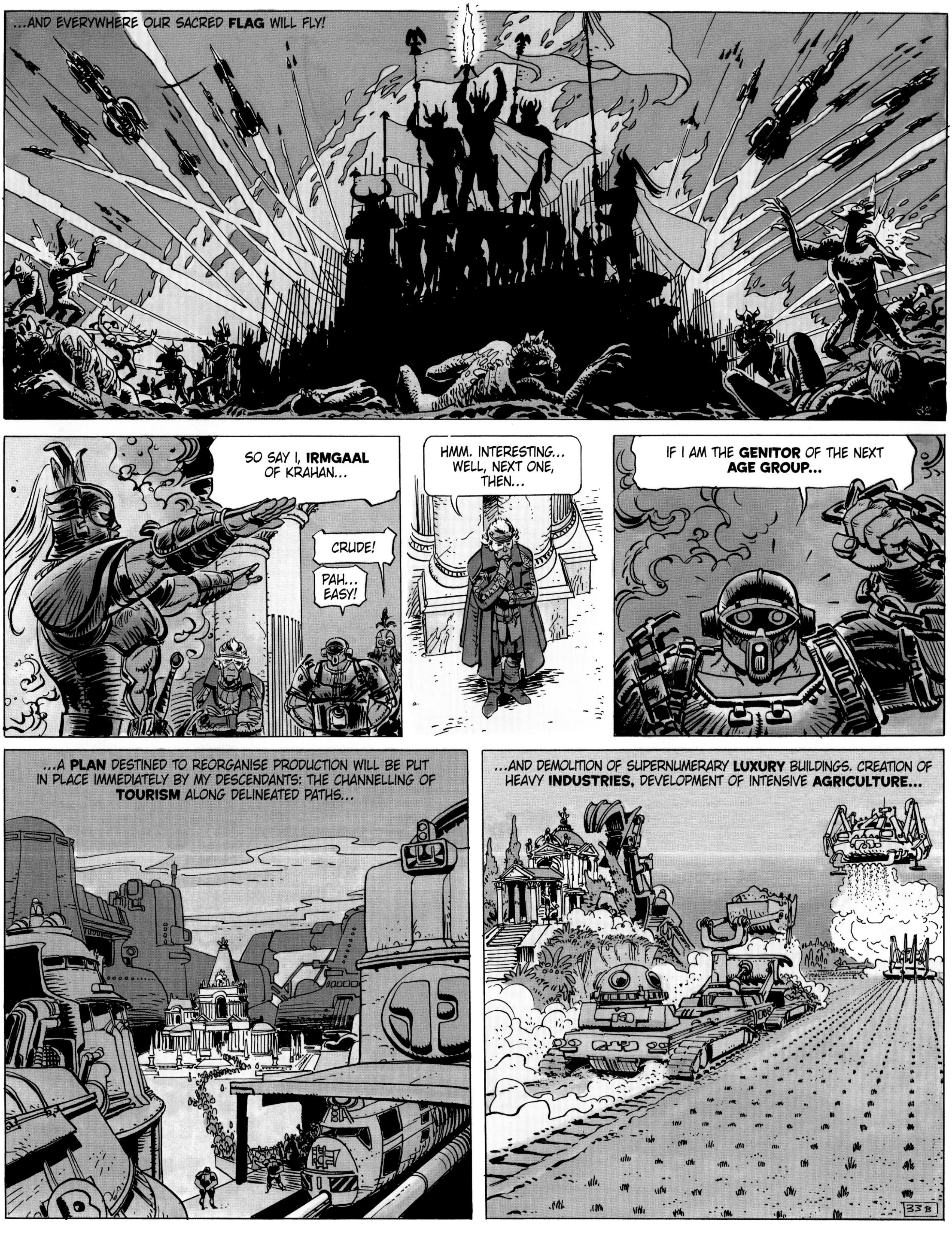
...AND EVERYWHERE OUR SACRED FLAG WILL FLY!
SO SAY I, IRMGAAL OF KRAHAN...
CRUDE!
PAH... EASY!
HMM. INTERESTING... WELL, NEXT ONE, THEN...
IF I AM THE GENITOR OF THE NEXT AGE GROUP...
...A PLAN DESTINED TO REORGANISE PRODUCTION WILL BE PUT IN PLACE IMMEDIATELY BY MY DESCENDANTS: THE CHANNELLING OF TOURISM ALONG DELINEATED PATHS...
...AND DEMOLITION OF SUPERNUMERARY LUXURY BUILDINGS. CREATION OF HEAVY INDUSTRIES, DEVELOPMENT OF INTENSIVE AGRICULTURE...
33B

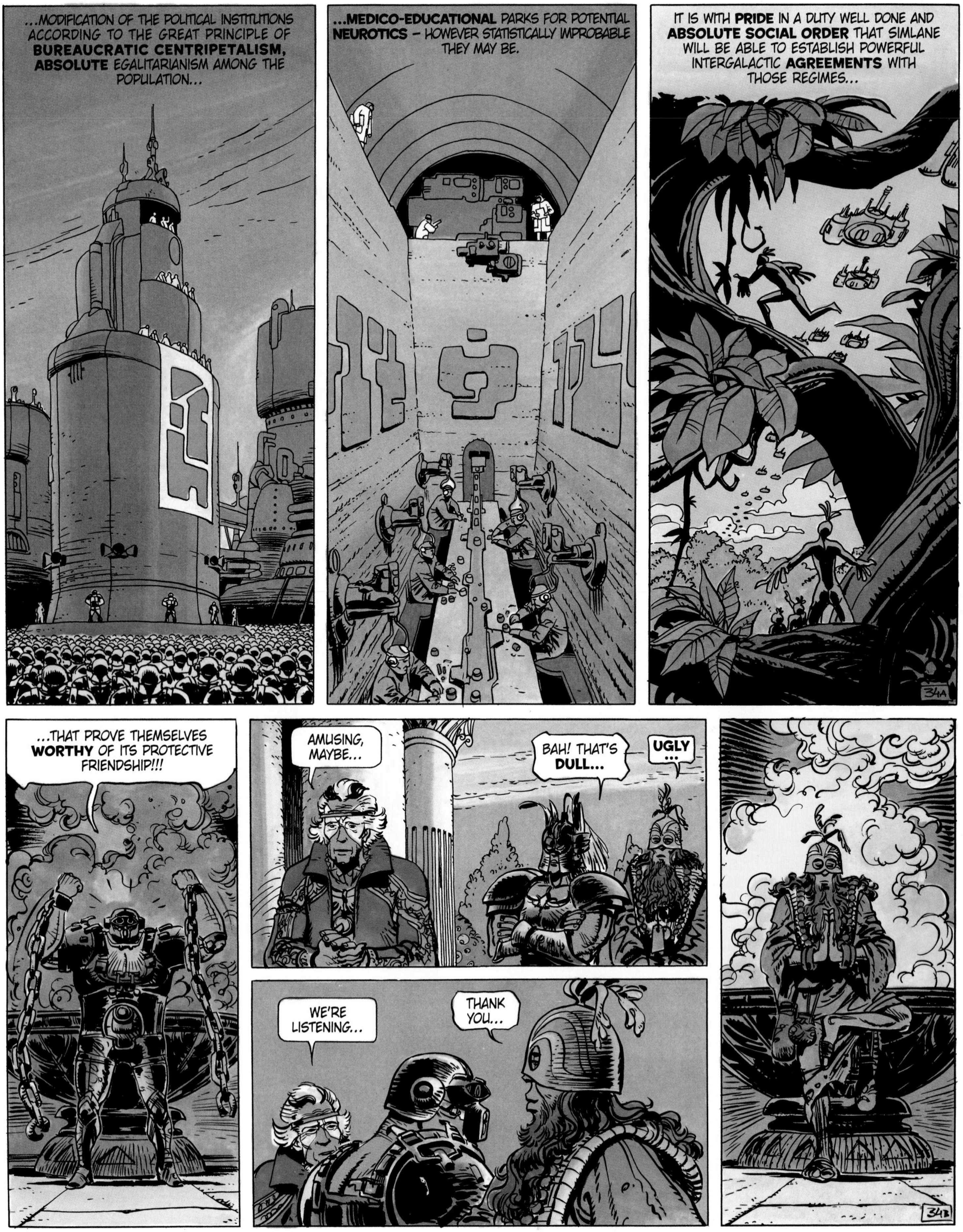
...MODIFICATION OF THE POLITICAL INSTITUTIONS ACCORDING TO THE GREAT PRINCIPLE OF **BUREAUCRATIC CENTRIPETALISM, ABSOLUTE** EGALITARIANISM AMONG THE POPULATION...
...MEDICO-EDUCATIONAL PARKS FOR POTENTIAL **NEUROTICS** – HOWEVER STATISTICALLY IMPROBABLE THEY MAY BE.
IT IS WITH **PRIDE** IN A DUTY WELL DONE AND **ABSOLUTE SOCIAL ORDER** THAT SIMLANE WILL BE ABLE TO ESTABLISH POWERFUL INTERGALACTIC **AGREEMENTS** WITH THOSE REGIMES...
...THAT PROVE THEMSELVES **WORTHY** OF ITS PROTECTIVE FRIENDSHIP!!!
AMUSING, MAYBE...
BAH! THAT'S **DULL...**
UGLY ...
WE'RE LISTENING...
THANK YOU...

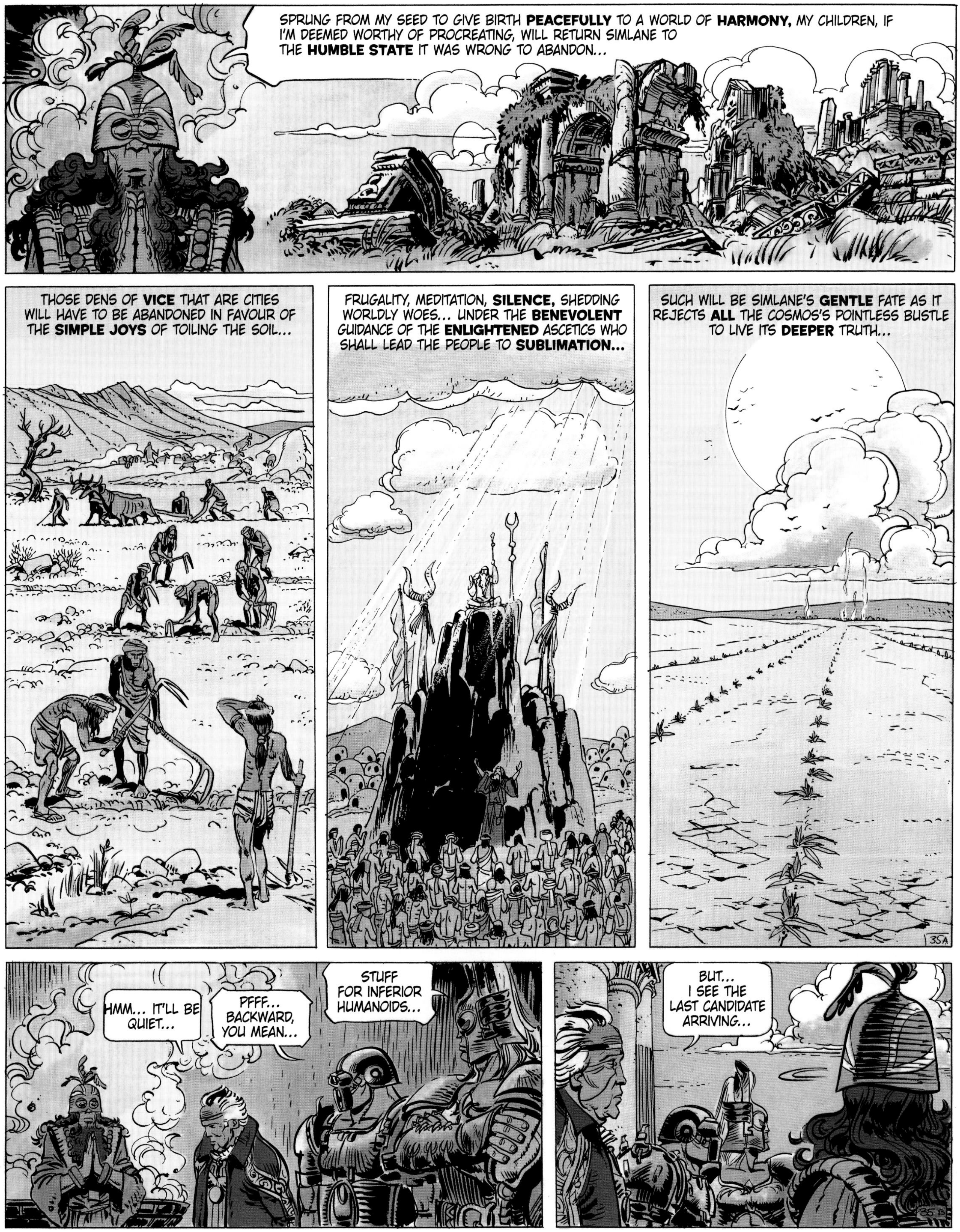
SPRUNG FROM MY SEED TO GIVE BIRTH PEACEFULLY TO A WORLD OF HARMONY, MY CHILDREN, IF I'M DEEMED WORTHY OF PROCREATING, WILL RETURN SIMLANE TO THE HUMBLE STATE IT WAS WRONG TO ABANDON...
THOSE DENS OF VICE THAT ARE CITIES WILL HAVE TO BE ABANDONED IN FAVOUR OF THE SIMPLE JOYS OF TOILING THE SOIL...
FRUGALITY, MEDITATION, SILENCE, SHEDDING WORLDLY WOES... UNDER THE BENEVOLENT GUIDANCE OF THE ENLIGHTENED ASCETICS WHO SHALL LEAD THE PEOPLE TO SUBLIMATION...
SUCH WILL BE SIMLANE'S GENTLE FATE AS IT REJECTS ALL THE COSMOS'S POINTLESS BUSTLE TO LIVE ITS DEEPER TRUTH...
35A
HMM... IT'LL BE QUIET...
PFFF... BACKWARD, YOU MEAN...
STUFF FOR INFERIOR HUMANOIDS...
BUT... I SEE THE LAST CANDIDATE ARRIVING...
35B

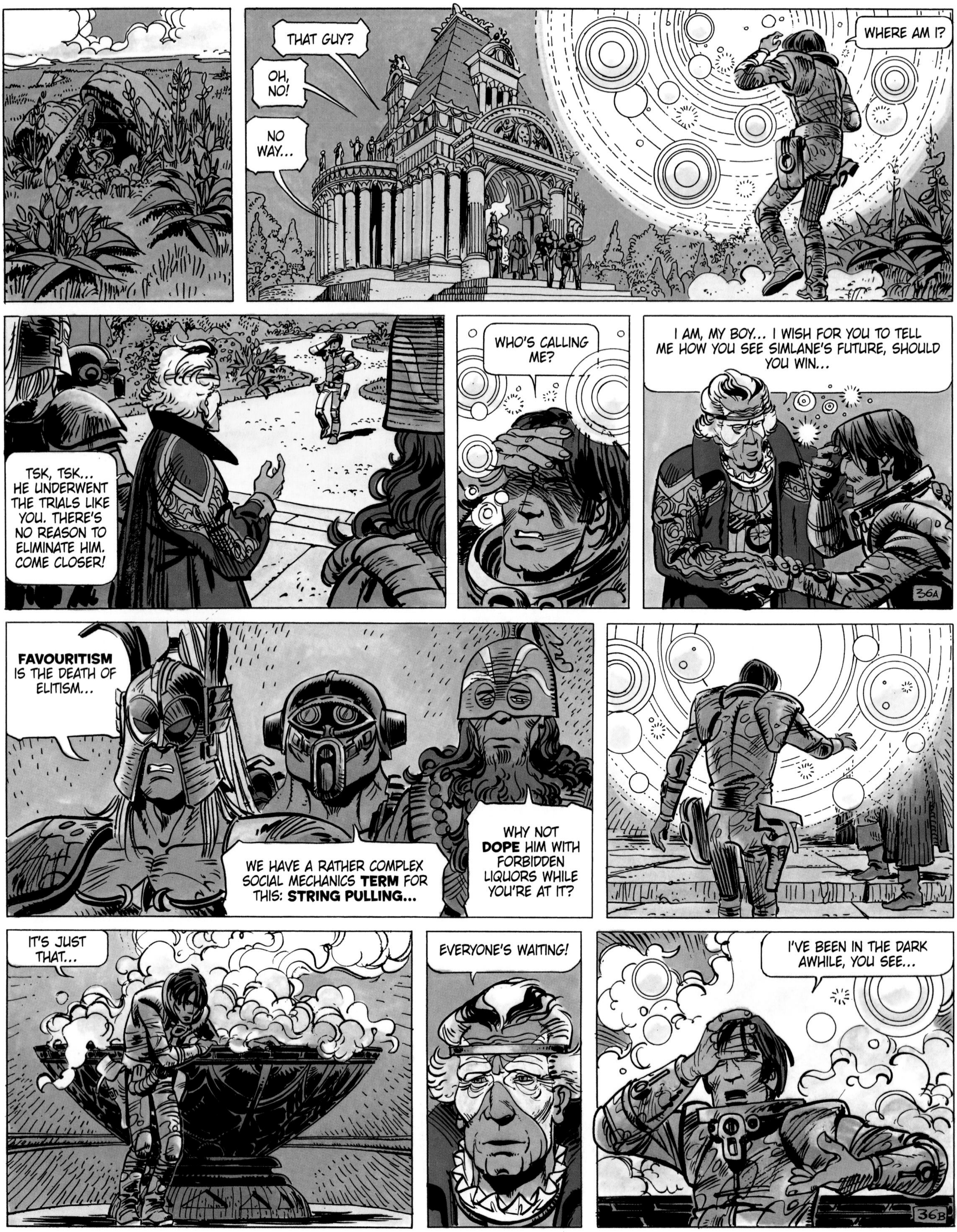
THAT GUY?
OH, NO!
NO WAY...
WHERE AM I?
TSK, TSK... HE UNDERWENT THE TRIALS LIKE YOU. THERE'S NO REASON TO ELIMINATE HIM. COME CLOSER!
WHO'S CALLING ME?
I AM, MY BOY... I WISH FOR YOU TO TELL ME HOW YOU SEE SIMLANE'S FUTURE, SHOULD YOU WIN...
36A
FAVOURITISM IS THE DEATH OF ELITISM...
WE HAVE A RATHER COMPLEX SOCIAL MECHANICS TERM FOR THIS: STRING PULLING...
WHY NOT DOPE HIM WITH FORBIDDEN LIQUORS WHILE YOU'RE AT IT?
IT'S JUST THAT...
EVERYONE'S WAITING!
I'VE BEEN IN THE DARK AWHILE, YOU SEE...
36B

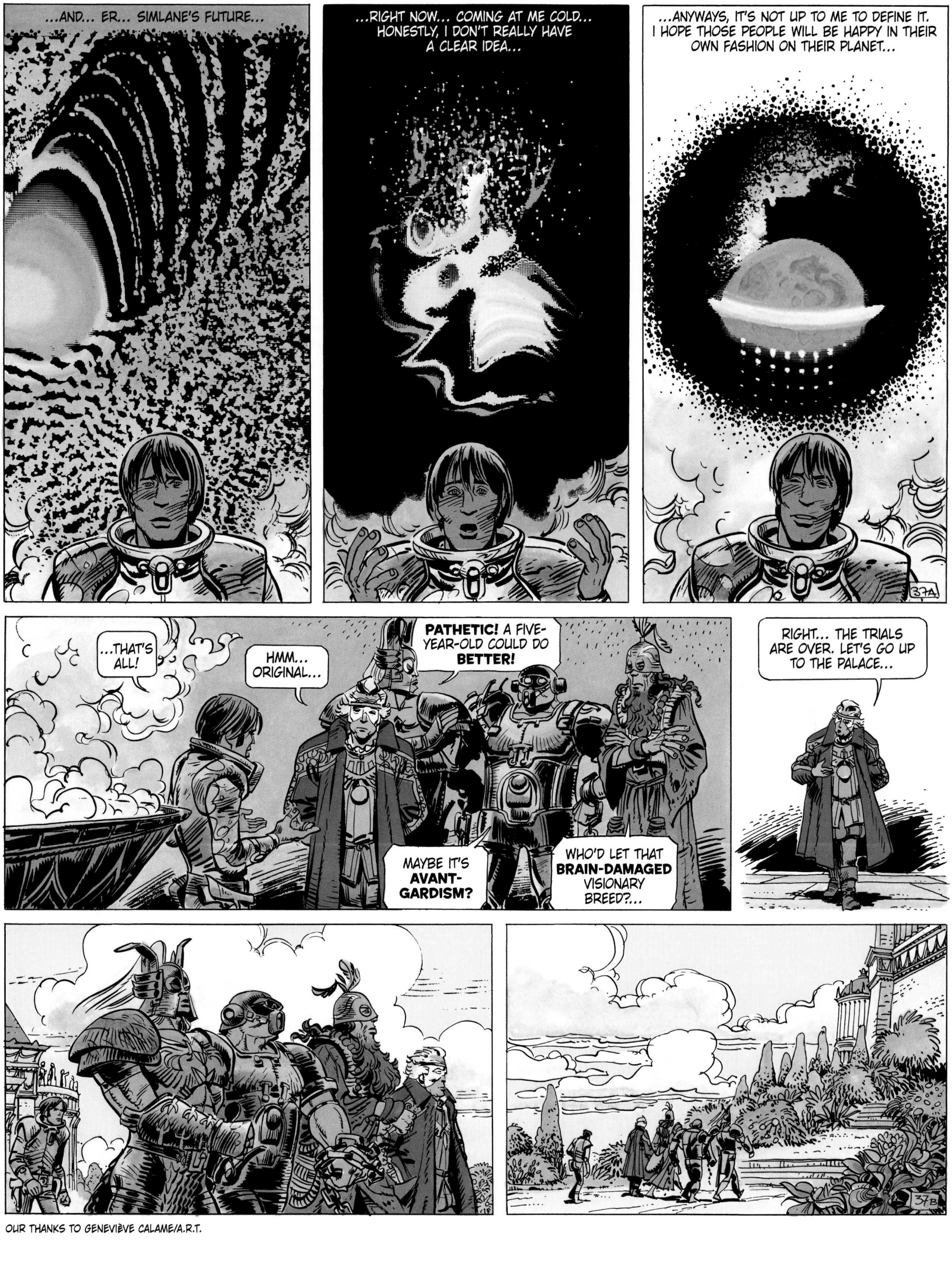
...AND... ER... SIMLANE'S FUTURE...
...RIGHT NOW... COMING AT ME COLD... HONESTLY, I DON'T REALLY HAVE A CLEAR IDEA...
...ANYWAYS, IT'S NOT UP TO ME TO DEFINE IT. I HOPE THOSE PEOPLE WILL BE HAPPY IN THEIR OWN FASHION ON THEIR PLANET...
37A
...THAT'S ALL!
HMM... ORIGINAL...
PATHETIC! A FIVE-YEAR-OLD COULD DO BETTER!
MAYBE IT'S AVANT-GARDISM?
WHO'D LET THAT BRAIN-DAMAGED VISIONARY BREED?...
RIGHT... THE TRIALS ARE OVER. LET'S GO UP TO THE PALACE...
37B

OUR THANKS TO GENEVIÈVE CALAME/A.R.T.

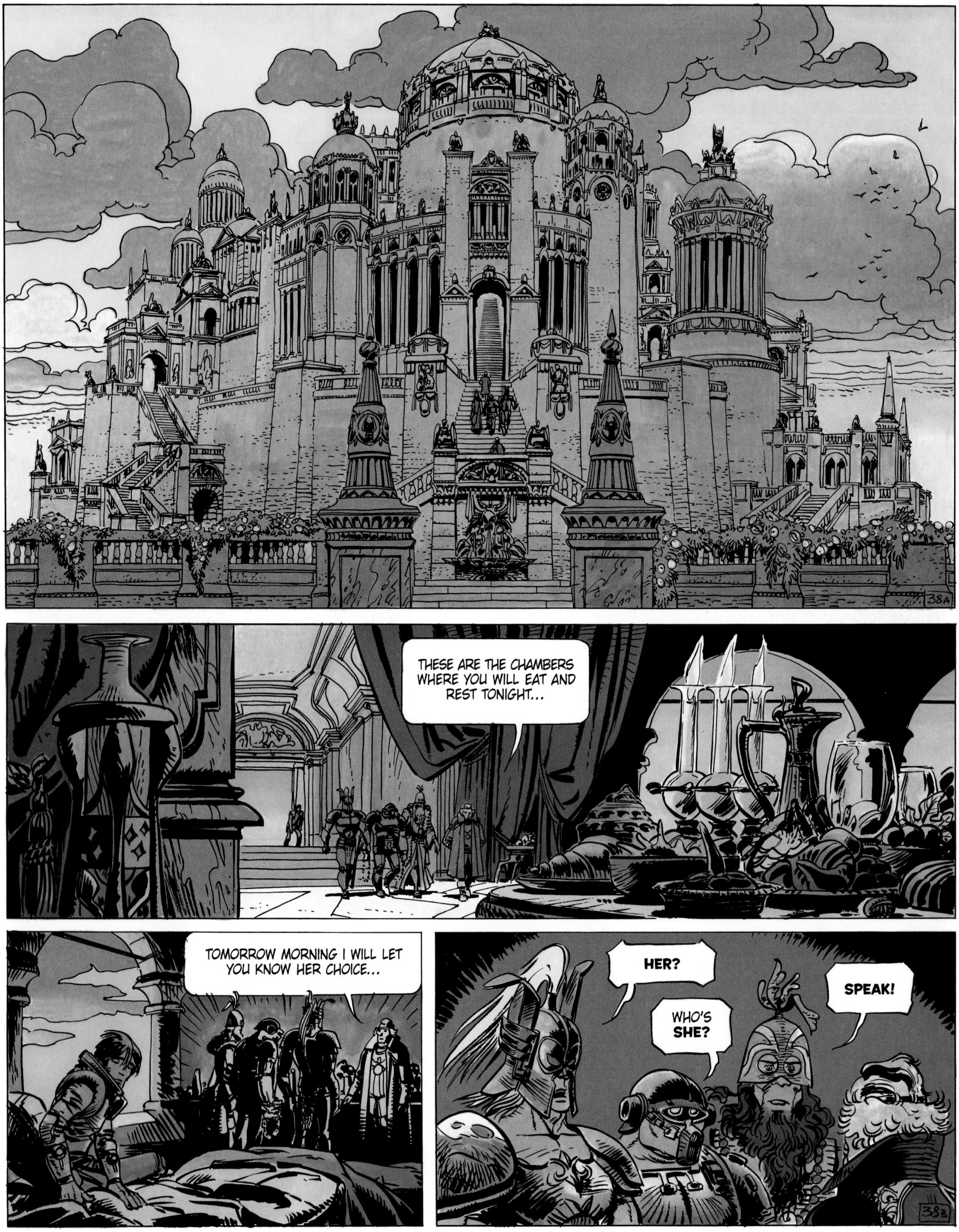
THESE ARE THE CHAMBERS WHERE YOU WILL EAT AND REST TONIGHT...
TOMORROW MORNING I WILL LET YOU KNOW HER CHOICE...
HER?
WHO'S SHE?
SPEAK!

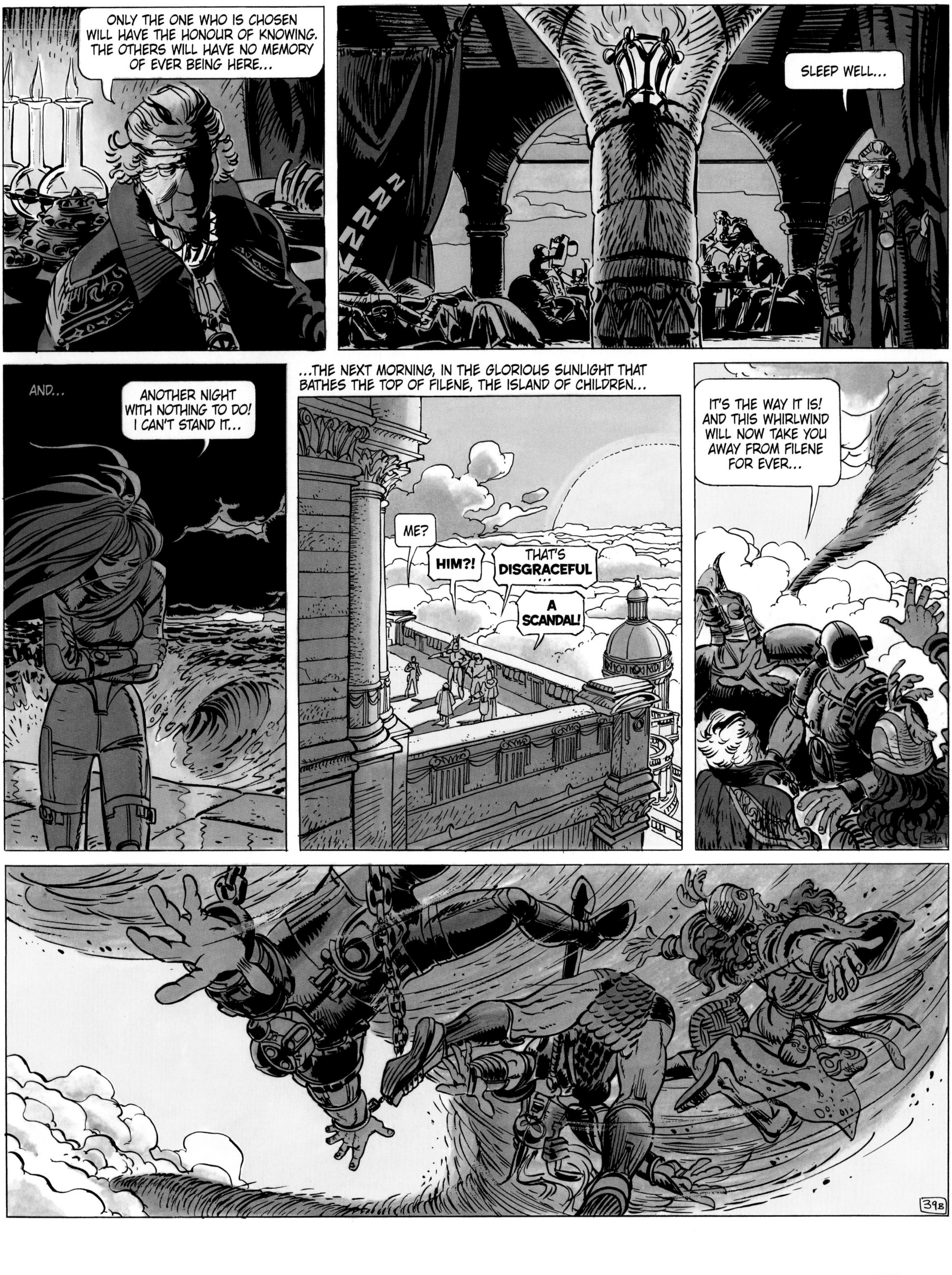
ONLY THE ONE WHO IS CHOSEN WILL HAVE THE HONOUR OF KNOWING. THE OTHERS WILL HAVE NO MEMORY OF EVER BEING HERE...
ZZZZZ
SLEEP WELL...
AND...
ANOTHER NIGHT WITH NOTHING TO DO! I CAN'T STAND IT...
...THE NEXT MORNING, IN THE GLORIOUS SUNLIGHT THAT BATHES THE TOP OF FILENE, THE ISLAND OF CHILDREN...
ME?
HIM?!
THAT'S DISGRACEFUL...
A SCANDAL!
IT'S THE WAY IT IS! AND THIS WHIRLWIND WILL NOW TAKE YOU AWAY FROM FILENE FOR EVER...

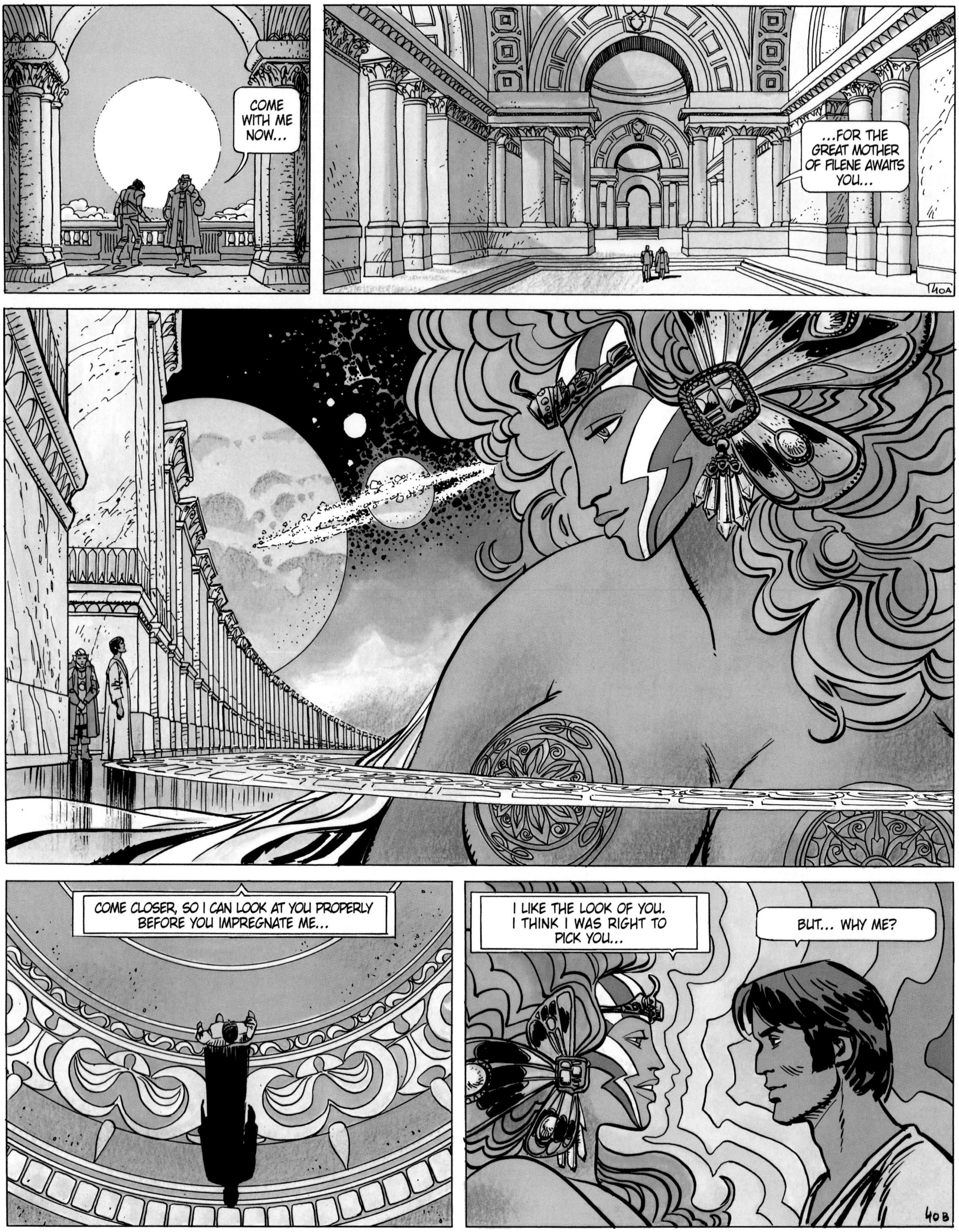
COME WITH ME NOW...
...FOR THE GREAT MOTHER OF FILENE AWAITS YOU...
40A
COME CLOSER, SO I CAN LOOK AT YOU PROPERLY BEFORE YOU IMPREGNATE ME...
I LIKE THE LOOK OF YOU. I THINK I WAS RIGHT TO PICK YOU...
BUT... WHY ME?
40B

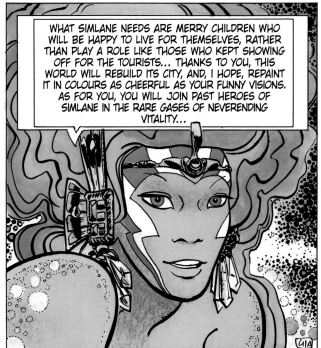

BECAUSE, IN YOUR OWN WAY, YOU WERE JUST AS BRAVE AS THE OTHERS. BUT, ABOVE ALL, BECAUSE YOU LEFT SIMLANE'S FUTURE OPEN... I DON'T LIKE THOSE PEOPLE WHO WOULD PUT THE FUTURE IN BOXES ONLY THEY WOULD HAVE THE KEYS TO...

WHAT SIMLANE NEEDS ARE MERRY CHILDREN WHO WILL BE HAPPY TO LIVE FOR THEMSELVES, RATHER THAN PLAY A ROLE LIKE THOSE WHO KEPT SHOWING OFF FOR THE TOURISTS... THANKS TO YOU, THIS WORLD WILL REBUILD ITS CITY, AND, I HOPE, REPAINT IT IN COLOURS AS CHEERFUL AS YOUR FUNNY VISIONS. AS FOR YOU, YOU WILL JOIN PAST HEROES OF SIMLANE IN THE RARE GASES OF NEVERENDING VITALITY...

LOOK AT THEM... IN ME, YOUR GENES WILL JOIN THEIRS, AND SOON FULLY FORMED YOUNG BEINGS WILL SPRING FROM MY WOMB...

AMONG THE FATHERS OF THIS PLANET'S INNUMERABLE GENERATIONS, THERE WERE GOOD ONES AND NOT-SO-GOOD ONES. YOU ARE THE FIRST TO COME FROM ANOTHER WORLD – AND IT'S ALL RIGHT, SINCE FOR YOU, TOO, IT'LL MEAN IMMORTALITY... COME NOW; IT'S TIME...

OH, WELL, IF IT'S FOR A GOOD CAUSE...

169

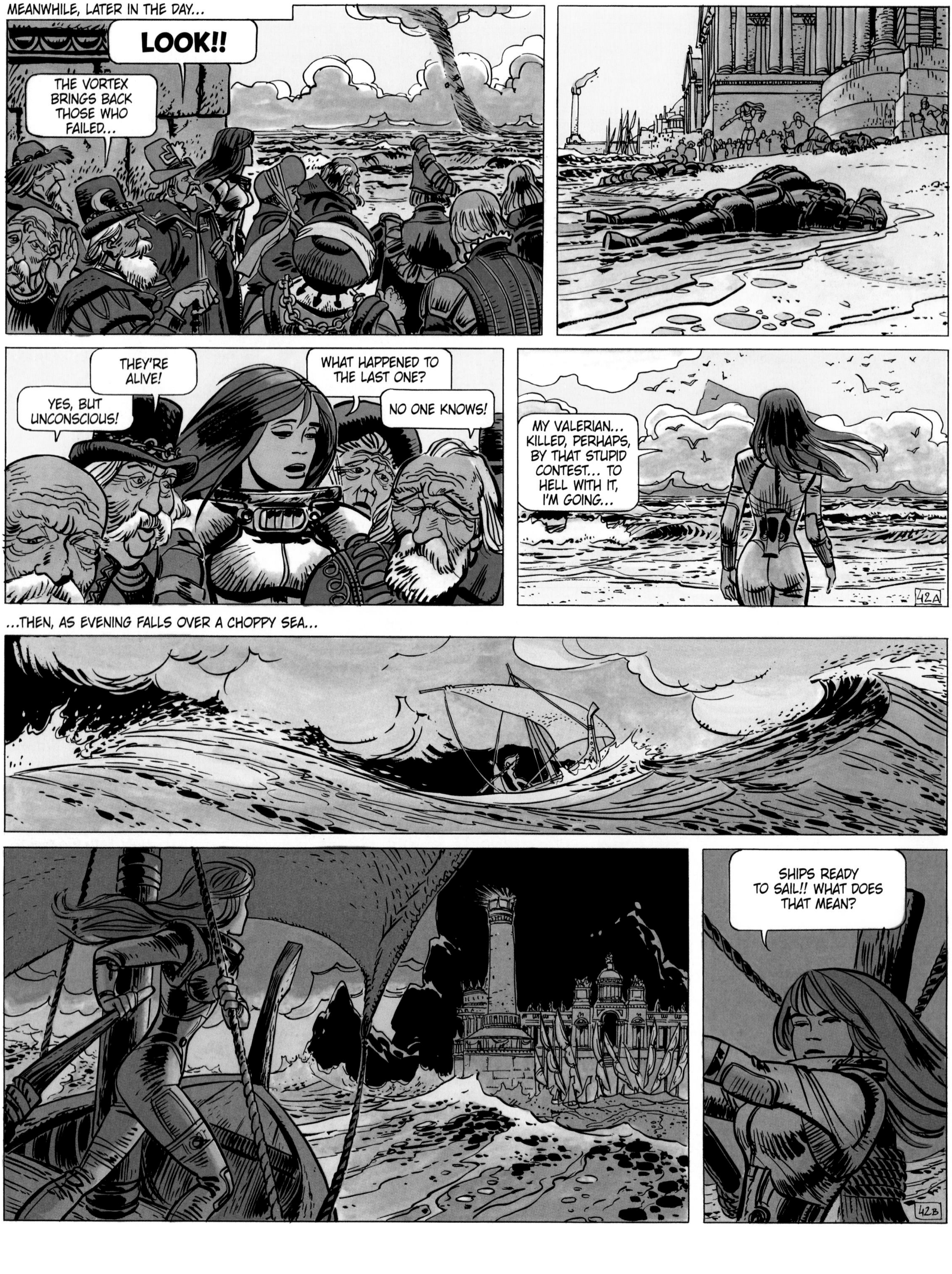
MEANWHILE, LATER IN THE DAY...
LOOK!!
THE VORTEX BRINGS BACK THOSE WHO FAILED...
THEY'RE ALIVE!
YES, BUT UNCONSCIOUS!
WHAT HAPPENED TO THE LAST ONE?
NO ONE KNOWS!
MY VALERIAN... KILLED, PERHAPS, BY THAT STUPID CONTEST... TO HELL WITH IT, I'M GOING...
42A
...THEN, AS EVENING FALLS OVER A CHOPPY SEA...
SHIPS READY TO SAIL!! WHAT DOES THAT MEAN?
42B

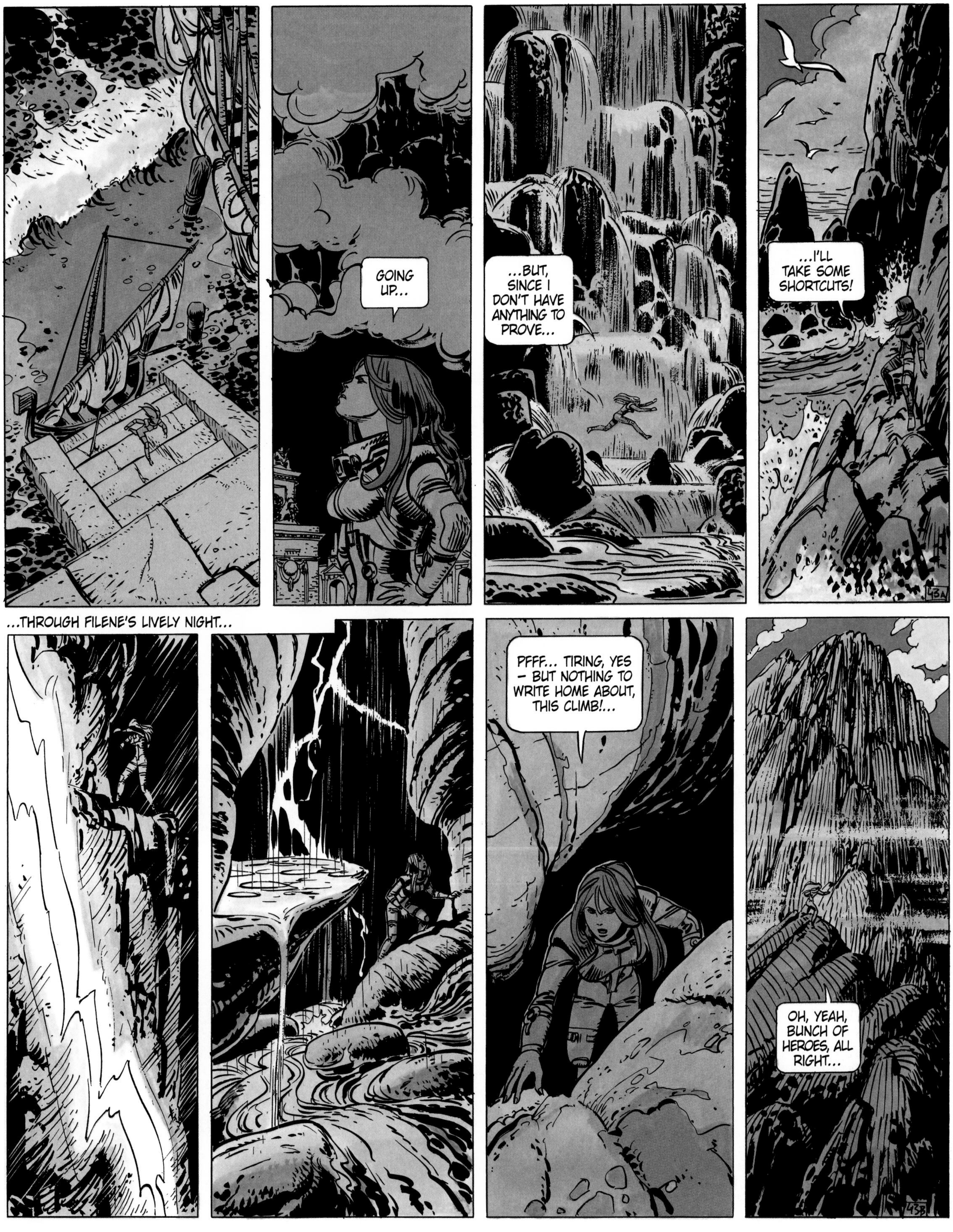
GOING UP...
...BUT, SINCE I DON'T HAVE ANYTHING TO PROVE...
...I'LL TAKE SOME SHORTCUTS!
...THROUGH FILENE'S LIVELY NIGHT...
PFFF... TIRING, YES – BUT NOTHING TO WRITE HOME ABOUT, THIS CLIMB!...
OH, YEAH, BUNCH OF HEROES, ALL RIGHT...

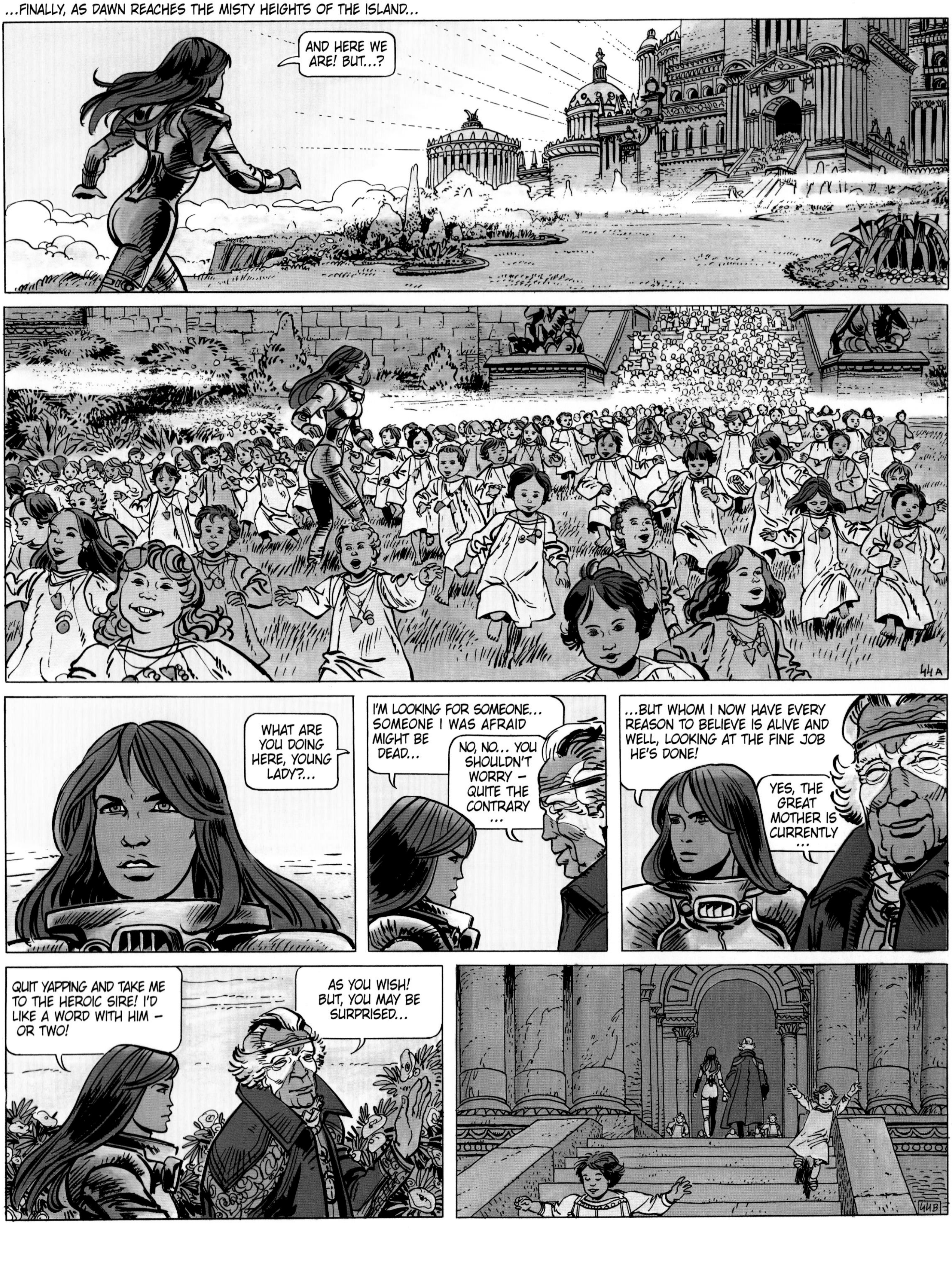
...FINALLY, AS DAWN REACHES THE MISTY HEIGHTS OF THE ISLAND...
AND HERE WE ARE! BUT...?
WHAT ARE YOU DOING HERE, YOUNG LADY?...
I'M LOOKING FOR SOMEONE... SOMEONE I WAS AFRAID MIGHT BE DEAD...
NO, NO... YOU SHOULDN'T WORRY – QUITE THE CONTRARY ...
...BUT WHOM I NOW HAVE EVERY REASON TO BELIEVE IS ALIVE AND WELL, LOOKING AT THE FINE JOB HE'S DONE!
YES, THE GREAT MOTHER IS CURRENTLY ...
QUIT YAPPING AND TAKE ME TO THE HEROIC SIRE! I'D LIKE A WORD WITH HIM – OR TWO!
AS YOU WISH! BUT, YOU MAY BE SURPRISED...

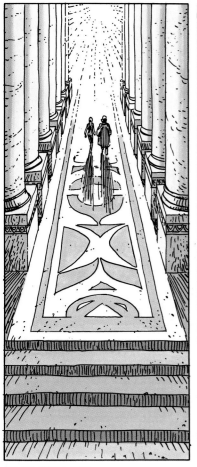

VALERIAN!!

INDEED... THIS IS WHERE THOSE WHO HAD THE HONOUR OF REPOPULATING SIMLANE ON THE GREAT EQUINOXES COME TO DWELL. IT'S AN EXHAUSTING TASK, WHICH EXPLAINS... ER...

...WHICH EXPLAINS WHAT, MISTER?...

LAURELINE, PLEASE, CALM DOWN!...

SOME TIME LATER...

...AFTER THE SHIPS CARRIED BY THE LAST WAVE OF THE EQUINOX HAVE DOCKED AT THE EUPHORIC CITY...

I HAVE NO IDEA WHAT YOU SAW IN THAT BIG LAYING HEN...

NOTHING, I ASSURE YOU! NOT TO MENTION THAT SHE WAS KIND ENOUGH TO LET ME GO...

...IGNORING THE FORMIDABLE ENTHUSIASM OF THE OLD PEOPLE AS THEY WELCOME THE PASSENGERS FROM THE ISLAND...

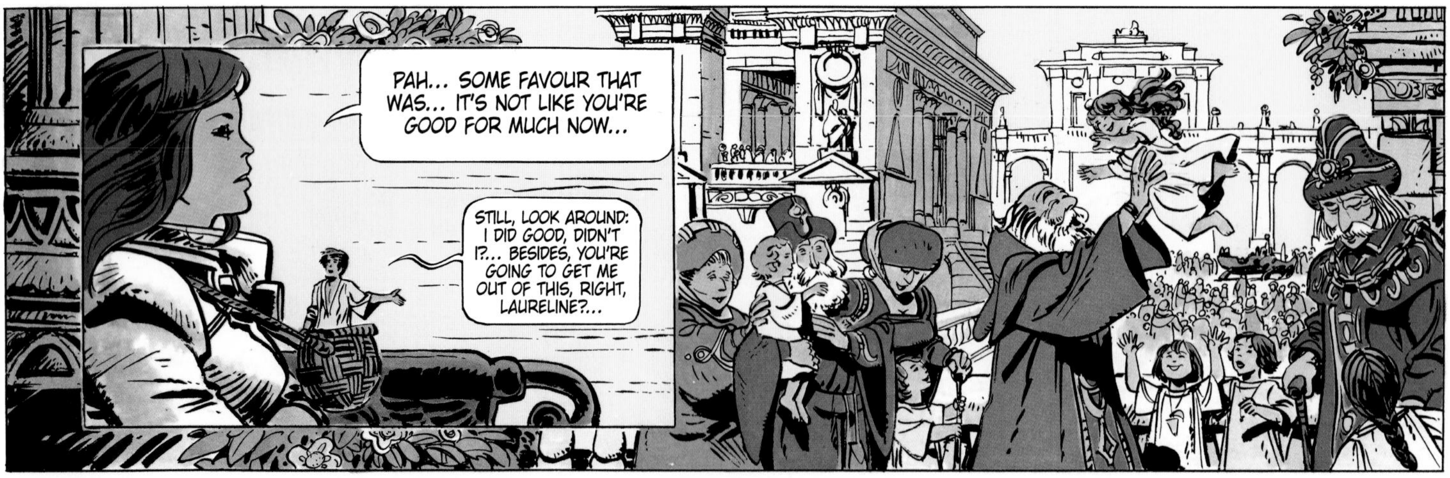
PAH... SOME FAVOUR THAT WAS... IT'S NOT LIKE YOU'RE GOOD FOR MUCH NOW...
STILL, LOOK AROUND: I DID GOOD, DIDN'T I?... BESIDES, YOU'RE GOING TO GET ME OUT OF THIS, RIGHT, LAURELINE?...

...A SUPERB VEHICLE RUSHES TO THE OLD CITY'S SPACEPORT THROUGH STREETS NOW FILLED WITH THE SWEET SCENTS OF SPRING...

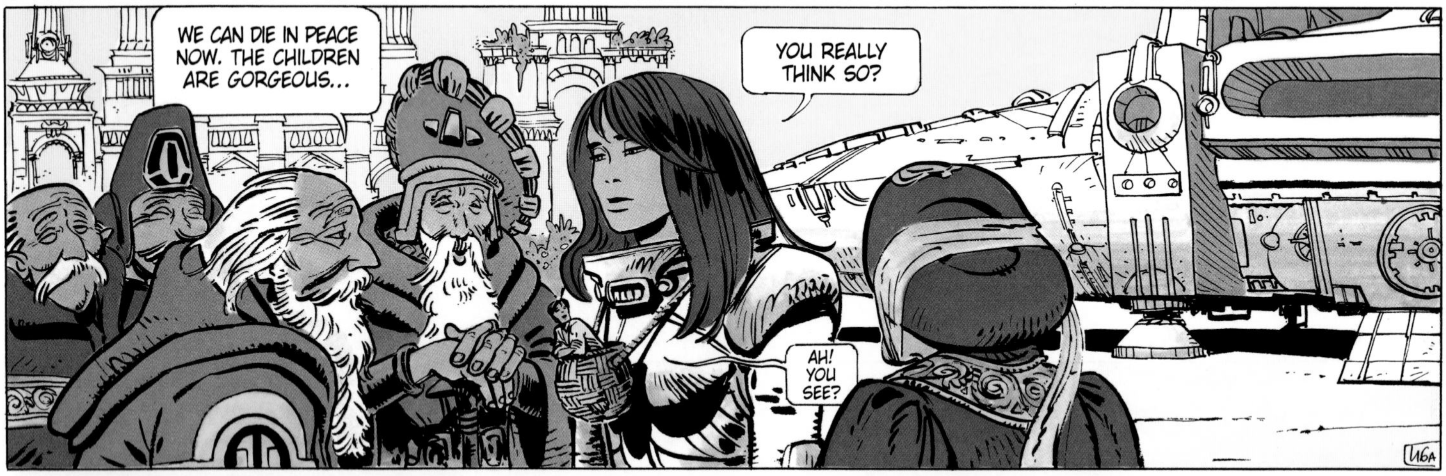
WE CAN DIE IN PEACE NOW. THE CHILDREN ARE GORGEOUS...
YOU REALLY THINK SO?
AH! YOU SEE?

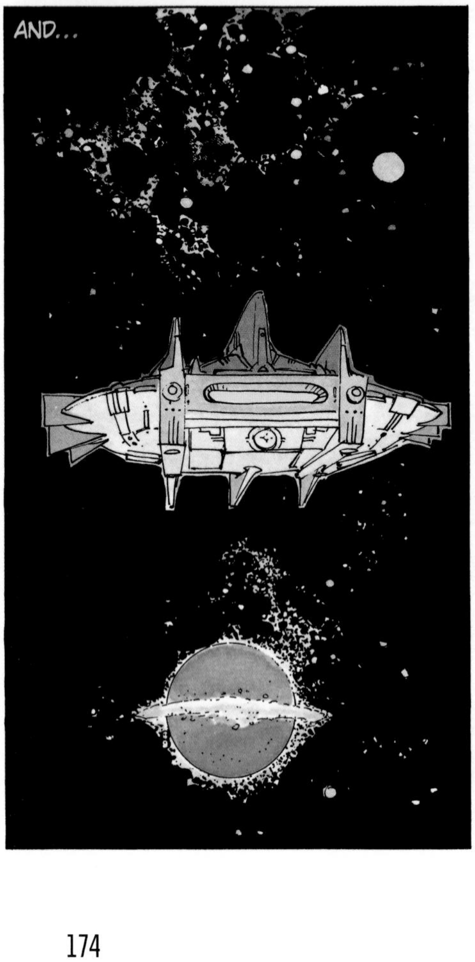
AND...

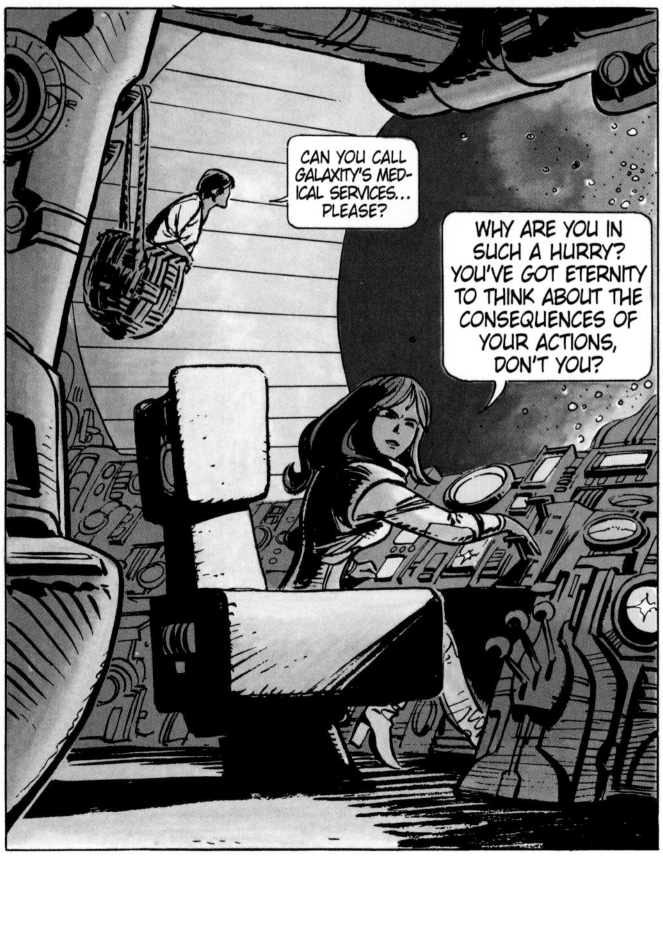
CAN YOU CALL GALAXITY'S MEDICAL SERVICES... PLEASE?
WHY ARE YOU IN SUCH A HURRY? YOU'VE GOT ETERNITY TO THINK ABOUT THE CONSEQUENCES OF YOUR ACTIONS, DON'T YOU?

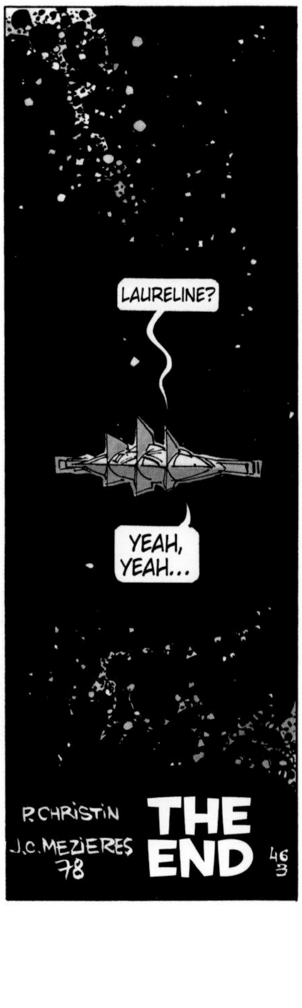
LAURELINE?
YEAH, YEAH...
P. CHRISTIN
J.C. MEZIERES 78
THE END

VALERIAN

CHRISTIN
MÉZIÈRES
VALERIAN
THE COMPLETE COLLECTION
VOLUME 1
CINEBOOK

CHRISTIN
MÉZIÈRES
VALERIAN
THE COMPLETE COLLECTION
VOLUME 2
CINEBOOK

CHRISTIN
MÉZIÈRES
VALERIAN
THE COMPLETE COLLECTION VOLUME 3
CINEBOOK

CHRISTIN
MÉZIÈRES
VALERIAN
THE COMPLETE COLLECTION VOLUME 4
CINEBOOK

CHRISTIN
MÉZIÈRES
VALERIAN
THE COMPLETE COLLECTION VOLUME 5
CINEBOOK

CHRISTIN
MÉZIÈRES
VALERIAN
THE COMPLETE COLLECTION
VOLUME 6
CINEBOOK

CHRISTIN
MÉZIÈRES
VALERIAN
THE COMPLETE COLLECTION VOLUME 7
CINEBOOK

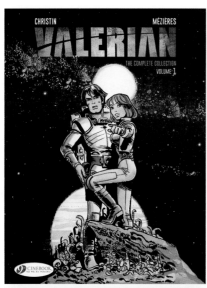

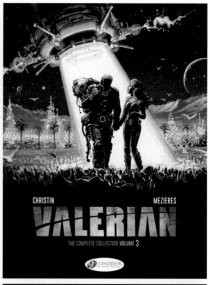

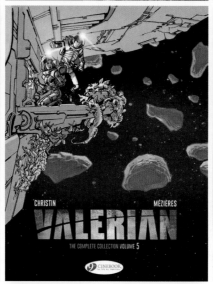

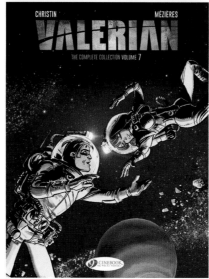

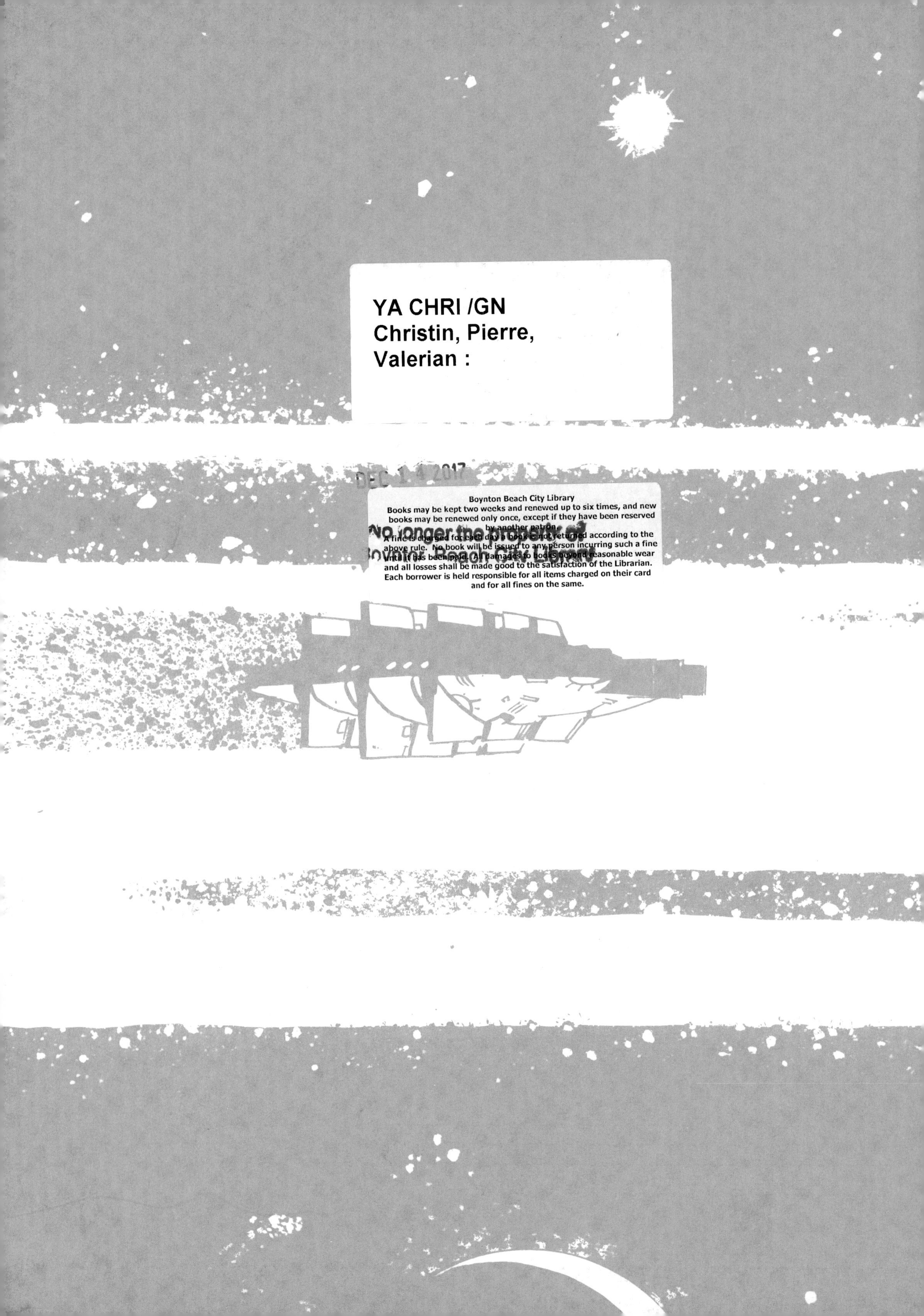